CAPTURED
HERITAGE

PTURED
RITAGE

The Scramble for Northwest Coast Artifacts

DOUGLAS COLE

UNIVERSITY OF OKLAHOMA PRESS
NORMAN

Library of Congress Cataloging-in-Publication Data

Cole, Douglas. 1938–
    Captured heritage : the scramble for Northwest Coast artifacts /
Douglas Cole.
        p.   cm.
    Originally published: Seattle : University of Washington Press.
1985. With new introd.
    Includes bibliographical references and index.
    ISBN 0-8061-2777-5 (alk. paper)
    1. Indians of North America—Antiquities—Collectors and
collecting—Northwest Coast of North America—History. 2. Indians
of North America—Northwest Coast of North America—Material
culture. 3. Collectors and collecting—Moral and ethical aspects.
4. Ethnological museums and collections—History. I. Title.
E78.N78C63   1995   95-35735
704'.03972—dc20   CIP

Zur Erinnerung an ein Märchen

Oklahoma Paperbacks edition published 1995 by the University of Oklahoma Press,
Norman, Publishing Division of the University, by special arrangement with the University of British Columbia Press, 6344 Memorial Road, Vancouver, British Columbia,
Canada V6T 1Z2. Originally published in 1985 by Douglas & McIntyre. First printing
of the University of Oklahoma Press edition, 1995.

The paper in this book meets the guidelines for permanence and durability of the
Committee on Production Guidelines for Book Longevity of the Council on Library
Resources, Inc. ∞

Cover design by George Vaitkunas
Text design by Barbara Hodgson
Typeset by Alphatext
Printed and bound in Canada by Friesens

Contents

Preface to the Reprint

ON 3 OCTOBER 1994, the four posts and interior screen of the Whale House — among the greatest treasures of Northwest Coast art and artifact — returned to Kluckwan, Alaska. Sold in 1984 by their family possessors to art dealer Michael Johnson and quietly removed while most residents were off playing bingo, their voyage to New York had been halted in Seattle by an injunction that disputed the right of the sellers to ownership. While the art remained locked away for a decade in a warehouse, the Kluckwan argued about ownership in American courts. The Whale House treasures were not family-owned but clan-owned, insisted Whale clan members. The legal dispute was decided only after the Anchorage federal district court shifted jurisdiction to a new village court that upheld clan ownership and had the five pieces returned.

This is merely the latest episode in the long saga of the Whale House, whose treasures have been sought by museum collectors for a century. The earlier episodes were touched on in *Captured Heritage,* published shortly after the Seattle internment (1985, pp. 259-64, 281, 311).[1]

Captured Heritage is about the Whale Houses that got away, about the flow of artifacts from Kluckwan and hundreds of other Northwest Coast villages to museums of the Western world during the great age of anthropological collecting. That current had lost its strength by the 1930s.

More recently a counter-current has begun, reversing the flow, if only weakly. Stockholm's museum transferred ownership of a pole to the Haisla in 1994, its repatriation awaiting a suitable venue in Kitimat. The Anglican diocese in Victoria returned five Nishga pieces after protests forced it to reverse its initial decision to sell the artifacts

vii

to help with cathedral maintenance. The Tsimshian are negotiating with the National Museum in Ottawa for return of a portion of their artifacts to a suitable home at Port Simpson.

American legislation, the Native American Graves Protection and Repatriation Act of 1990, requires the return of human remains and funerary and sacred objects to American Native groups who request them. The implications of this are still unfolding. The Smithsonian Institution, under its own legislative mandate, repatriated war gods to the Pueblo of Zuni, whose claim was clearer than that most Northwest Coast groups can make for their ceremonial objects. Most notably, the Museum of the American Indian (which figures prominently in the later part of this book), taken over now by the Smithsonian and directed by Native American professionals, intends to return significant parts of the collection to the communities from which they came. The returned items will include communally owned property, illegally acquired objects, and duplicate or abundant material. The museum has already agreed to return its identifiable portion of the potlatch-law surrenders to Kwakiutl museums at Cape Mudge and Alert Bay, where they will be reunited with those returned by the Canadian National Museum and the Royal Ontario Museum. These are a few examples of how current opinion, sometimes sanctioned by law, gives repatriation strong force.

At issue is an ownership that, until recently, went unquestioned. "The very right of old and established museums to the objects in their possession is now contested," wrote an anthropologist in the year that *Captured Heritage* appeared. "No longer is it possible for museum anthropologists to treat the objects of others without serious consideration of the matter of their rightful ownership or the circumstances of their acquisition."[2] Who "owns" a Kwakiutl dance mask? A Haida mortuary pole? A Chilkat dance screen? The museum that acquired it? Or the people who made it, invested it with its original purpose and meaning, whose name it still bears in the catalogue or label of the museum? These are not simple questions but part of the increasingly contested field of ownership. Possession is one thing; "ownership" now quite another.

The right to interpret has become an area as contested as the right of ownership. Who should control the exhibition and interpretation of museum artifacts? Is it the "colonizer" or the "colonized," the European curator or the Native people[3] represented? Whether at the American Museum in New York, the Rasmussan collection in

Portland, or the University of British Columbia in Vancouver, it is now a standard, even codified, principle that displays must be the result of collaboration between curators and the Natives whose past or present they depict.[4] "People have the right to the facts of their own lives."[5]

If the postcolonial age has affected museums, it has had at least an equal impact upon scholarship. Since the first appearance of *Captured Heritage*, a great deal has been written on museums and their collections. Some of it advances the history of Northwest Coast collecting.[6] Most, however, focuses on museums and collecting, often in the postmodern or cultural studies idiom. If postcolonial discourse and Native cultural concerns have eroded the self-confidence of museums, so too has the critical scholarship of postmodernism shaped the discourse about museums.

While different cultural critics read anthropological museums in different ways, the trend is to view them as part of a Western pattern, a discourse, that was constructed as part of the process of colonial dominance. The West invented its versions of "primitive" people while appropriating their objects. The nineteenth-century evolutionary discourse used these to demonstrate racial and cultural superiority. A twentieth-century liberal and relativist discourse tempered the racism but continued to see primitive culture as something that had ceased to exist, or would soon do so. In either case, the image of the "primitive" was an invention, alterable in its uses. The "traditional" and "authentic" American Indian was frozen in the past; postcontact alterations corrupted and destroyed that authenticity. The idea of a pristine, uncontaminated culture served romantic Western primitivists seeking an escape from their own industrial modernity. Even more, it served the interests of those who sought control over Native lands and resources. All was within the hegemonic framework of expanding Western capitalism, technology, and modernism. The display of Indian artifacts functioned in a context that communicated power relations — the power and authority of European elites not simply over Natives but also over workers and immigrants.

This invention of the primitive Other by Westerners and their museums served not merely to construct stereotypes of Indian cultures but, at least as much, to construct a Western identity opposite to all that was Native and primitive. A construction of the Other meant a simultaneous construction of the self. James Clifford describes how anthropological collection and display were crucial processes in the formation of a Western identity. This insightful theme has gained widespread currency. Jeremy MacClancy, discussing contemporary private tribal-art collecting, writes of how the collector makes objects "an aspect of himself. These appropriated items ... become the specimens and trophies of his personal mythology." Sally Price repeats the theme for primitive art: "We partake of an identification with African art; this allows *our* self-recognition and personal rediscovery and permits a renewed contact with *our* deeper instincts; the result is that *we* increase *our* understanding of *ourselves* and *our* relationship to art." Virginia R. Dominiguez, in the most trenchant comment on *Captured Heritage,* wrote that museums collected less because of the importance of the objects to Indians than because of what they told Europeans about themselves. Everything about these ethnological collections — the way they were collected, why they were collected, and how they were displayed — points to the process as part of a European effort at self-definition. To Lumilla Jordonova, museum objects are trophies of victory, mastery, ownership, control, and dominion.[7]

Although *Captured Heritage* deals with issues raised in the past about the authenticity of Northwest Coast artifacts and with shifting public and anthropological views of the Indian, the idea of culturally and ideologically constructed meanings is almost entirely missing. Such concerns, now so pervasive in museum literature, were not salient at the time of writing. The insights into the significance of collecting and exhibition and the motivations and world views that stood behind them are an important contribution to our understanding of the European, American, and Canadian societies that spent such effort to collect and display objects from the Northwest Coast and hundreds of other cultures.

On the other hand, postmodernist and cultural studies sometimes suffer from their own problems. They appear as part of post-Marxist, post-Marcuse discourse, which is itself the product of a particular ideological and historical condition. Words like "hierarchies," "elites," "trophies," and, especially, "capitalism," "colonialism," and "hegemony" characterize the writing. While intensely relativist, the concern remains Eurocentric. Offering valuable insights into the motivation of Western collectors and curators, they offer virtually none into the Native side of the collecting encounter.

That is seen only in reverse, largely through the ambiguous freight carried by the frequent use of the word "appropriation," itself an expression of the view from the European side. Significantly, it has no antonym. The Natives whose objects were "appropriated" remain anonymous, even disregarded. We learn much about Western constructions but little about any of those who were separated from the objects appropriated by Westerners.

This brings us back to the collecting process, to the question of ownership, of how museums came to possess the objects of Others. This is the theme of *Captured Heritage*. The book is, as professed, White history about Indians and their procurable culture; it deals with the process of altered possession, of the flow of material from Natives to Western museums, but it does seek to understand, however imperfectly, the other side.

One difficulty in achieving such understanding is that some of the material was simply stolen, and one curious fact about this book's reception was the eagerness of some readers to focus on the theme of theft. I had taken pains to point out that although theft was not uncommon, most objects were purchased. Yet the contemporary mind seems almost Proudhonian in its wish to see possession as theft. Press reviews were headed "They Plundered What They Could Not Buy," "Author Reveals Cultural Pillage," and "How Anthropologists Plundered a Culture."[8]

While most scholars were more restrained, Sally Price, in her widely noted *Primitive Art in Civilized Places*, made great play of Louis Shotridge's extraordinary purchase of the Kaguanton shark helmet and his attempt to take the Whale House treasures (pp. 259-65), along with African thefts by Michel Leiris and Marcel Griaule. Such selected examples allowed Price to conclude, "Such are the encounters that have supplied our museums, from the Musée de l'Homme to the Metropolitan Museum of Art, with the great bulk of their non-Western artistic treasures."[9] Emphasis upon theft creates its own deceptive fictions.

Northwest Coast museum artifacts were collected in a variety of ways. There were ambiguities in the process but they were not the simple travesties to which Price reduced them. Certainly, the museum collections can be seen as a product of a colonial encounter, an unequal trading relationship in which, in the long run, the terms of trade were stacked in favour of the dominating economic system (p. 311). Yet even that view lacks the whiff of field reality: that Natives entered the art and artifact market themselves, exploited it for their own uses, and often welcomed the opportunities it offered.

Indians were part of the process. They had their own interests, their own values, and their own needs. The most easily collected materials were household items that had become obsolete with the availability of new goods and materials. Horn spoons, stone tools, wooden bowls, cedar-bark mats, and bows and arrows were falling out of use by the time museum collectors arrived. They were willingly, probably eagerly, sold. Collectors gave them a value that, like last year's computer, they had lost. Even ceremonial objects were disposable. One Northwest Coast Indian view, even perhaps today, was that the objects were unimportant. What mattered was the idea behind them: "They represent the right to own that thing, and that right remains even if the object decays or is otherwise lost."[10]

To view museum collections as largely plunder risks making a travesty of the past. More seriously, it may verge on patronizing arrogance — a view of Natives as naïve victims of shrewd Westerners — itself a stereotype of some antiquity. While Native societies were not capitalist, they *were* commercial. Indians knew how to trade, how to swing a deal to their advantage, how to capitalize upon a field collector's haste, how to endow an article with a sacred function it may not have possessed, even how to fake old out of new. Collectors willingly volunteered their success stories but rarely recorded instances where they came out losers, where they had been bilked by Native traders. Some never realized that they had been had.

Some recent writing does give glimpses into the other side of the exchange. Ruth B. Phillips, examining why museums avoided collecting tourist art, also looked at Natives who had revealed their own ideas about what was valuable. The New Brunswick Malecite chief James Paul disputed instructions to collect old and obsolete paddles suitable to museum anthropologists' views of a pristine past culture. He complied, but asserted the value of new and replica paddles, giving them a much higher monetary worth and even urging "the proposition that a new paddle could be *more* beautiful than an old one."[11]

Analogous insights can be gained from Richard and Sally Price's contemporary collecting in French Guiana. *Equatoria,* the remarkable journal of their month-long collecting expedition among the country's Maroon peoples, tells us much about collecting, something of the "disappropriated" Other, and something about contemporary thought. The Prices agreed to "this strangely anachronistic enterprise," one they did not fully believe in, only because "if we don't someone else will" and the Maroons "would ultimately be the poorer for it." They deliberately avoided the "violence" of collecting, determined not to cajole objects from people who would rather not sell. As purchasers, they wished to offer prices that "reflect respect," but, like generations of collectors, were cautious about paying what might "influence the other transactions in the works." Many other attitudes and experiences duplicate those of collectors during the Northwest Coast scramble but, relevant here, the Prices discovered that the Aluka Maroons, like Chief James Paul, put a higher value on new things than on old. They found a striking discrepancy between Aluka criteria for price and those used in the art market or museum context. "People ask from 50 to 100F for old cloths, which are rare and especially valuable to a museum but obsolete items of Aluka fashion, and 200-300F for newly-sewn ones that, from a 'museological' perspective, are of relatively minor interest."[12]

What most surprised the 1990 collectors, though, was that their anticipated ethical dilemma, of having to deprive people of objects that had value to them, was overshadowed by its opposite, "of having to say no to people who offer us things we don't want, and who very much need the money it would bring them." Like Adrian Jacobson and George Dawson on the Northwest Coast, they were "surprised by people's behavior, as they literally rushed from their houses with things to sell." Selling, they learned, was "no big deal": a woman would "simply rather have the money than an extra paddle."[13]

Such experiences resonate with those of Northwest Coast collectors from a century before. At the same time, they contest the meaning of "appropriation," forcing us to ponder the differential and transient meanings of value and possession.

Objects become "artifacts" or "treasures" by a particular process. In themselves, they are merely artificially contrived bits of wood, stone, fur, or bone. Within their original setting, they possess whatever meaning that society may give them; they may even be valued as process rather than as products or possessions.[14] They may be commodities or they may be sacred. Even these values will change as Native society changes. When Western ethnologists and collectors enter, the objects move into another orbit of value, one determined by Europeans. In this orbit they have a different value, higher in monetary terms than the one they are given in their indigenous sphere. For a moment they are cross-cultural commodities, appropriated to science. But their biographies continue. They may become treasures of a European-conceived art, then also acquire a vicarious value as part of the heritage of Canadian and American societies, and then, in an evolution both remarkable and ironic, become transformed into a value to their former culture. The objects remain the same bits of wood or stone, but their meanings and their values are shifting, multiple, transitory, mutable, invented, even reinvented.

In the Kwakiutl museums and cultural centres of Alert Bay and Cape Mudge, redeemed and repatriated objects acquire values, as James Clifford notes, different and differing from those in European museums. At the U'mista Cultural Centre, they are community treasures that tell a history of colonization and continuing cultural struggle. At the Kwagiulth Museum, they are regarded as family possessions and community memorabilia tied to local meanings. In both settings, the old "master narratives" of anthropology are replaced by stories of revival, remembrance, and struggle and, perhaps, by local discourses of elites, power, and authority. The Kwakiutl have appropriated the museum context, investing it with meanings that contest values placed by others on objects as art or artifact.[15]

In the reconstruction of their cultures, North American Natives are also in a process of identity formation, partly by the construction of values — spiritual, environmental, communal, consensual, respect for elders — that stand in opposition to European ones, often by the appropriation of European ideas such as oppression and self-determination. The great age of ethnological collecting is long over, but the objects collected continue to have lives of variable value, meaning, possession, and even ownership.

NOTES

1 For this reprint, *Captured Heritage* is reproduced with minor correction of factual and typographical errors. The page numbers remain the same.

2 Richard Handler, "On Having a Culture: Nationalism and the Preservation of Quebec's *Patrimoine*," in George W. Stocking, Jr., *Objects and Others: Essays on Museums and Material Culture,* vol. 3 of *History of Anthropology* (Madison: University of Wisconsin Press, 1985), 193; Stocking, "Introduction," in *ibid.,* 11.

3 Names are a problem. *Native American*, the now common U.S. usage, is inappropriate to Canada's Indians. *First Nations* or *First Nations people,* the now common Canadian usage, is unknown in the U.S. For lack of a better or common term, I use *Native* or *Indian*, both of which, in the context, are unambiguous.

4 Michael M. Ames, *Cannibal Tours and Glass Boxes: The Anthropology of*

Museums (Vancouver: UBC Press, 1992), esp. 49–58, 77–88; Assembly of First Nations and Canadian Museums Association, *Turning the Page: Forging New Partnerships between Museums and First Peoples* (Ottawa, 1992).

5 Ames, *Cannibal Tours,* 140.

6 See Susan A. Kaplan and Kristin J. Barness, *Raven's Journey: The World of Alaska's Native People* (Philadelphia: University Museum, 1986), about G.B. Gordon, Louis Shotridge and the University Museum; Peter L. Corey, ed., *Faces, Voices and Dreams: A Celebration of the Centennial of the Sheldon Jackson Museum* (Sitka: Alaska State Museum and Friends of the Alaska State Museum; Seattle: University of Washington Press, 1987); Aldona Jonaitis, *From the Land of the Totem Poles: The Northwest Coast Indian Art Collection at the American Museum of Natural History* (New York and Seattle: American Museum of Natural History and University of Washington Press, 1988); Aldona Jonaitis, ed., *Chiefly Feasts: The Enduring Kwakiutl Potlatch* (New York and Seattle: American Museum of Natural History and University of Washington Press, 1991), especially contributor Ira Jacknis writing on George Hunt; and Diane Fane, Ira Jacknis, and Lise M. Breen, *Objects of Myth and Memory: American Art at the Brooklyn Museum* (Brooklyn and Seattle: Brooklyn Museum and University of Washington Press; Vancouver: UBC Press, 1991), especially Ira Jacknis writing about Stewart Culin's collections.

   Articles include Aldona Jonaitis on the implications of the Edenshaw model poles, "Franz Boas, John Swanton, and the New Haida Sculpture at the American Museum of Natural History" in Janet Catherine Berlo, *The Early Years of Native American Art History: The Politics of Scholarship and Collecting* (Seattle: University of Washington Press; Vancouver: UBC Press, 1992), 22–61, and Aldona Jonaitis and Richard Inglis, "Power, History, and Authenticity: The Mowachaht Whalers' Washing Shrine," *South Atlantic Quarterly* 91 (Winter 1992), 193–213.

7 James Clifford, *The Predicament of Culture: Twentieth-Century Ethnography, Literature and Art* (Cambridge: Harvard University Press, 1988), 220–21; Jeremy MacClancy, "A Natural Curiosity: The British Market in Primitive Art," *Res* 15 (1988), 176; Sally Price, *Primitive Art in Civilized Places* (Chicago: University of Chicago Press, 1989), 34; Virginia R. Dominiguez, "The Marketing of Heritage," *American Ethnologist* 3 (1986), 554; Lumilla Jordonova, "Objects of Knowledge: A Historical Perspective on Museums," in Peter Vergo, ed., *The New Museology* (London: Reaktion Books, 1989), 34.

8 *Vancouver Sun,* 13 July 1985; *Calgary Herald,* 22 September 1985; *Winnipeg Free Press,* 31 August 1985.

9 Price, *Primitive Art in Civilized Places,* 69–74.

10 Gloria Cranmer Webster, "Conservation and Cultural Centres: U'Mista Cultural Centre, Alert Bay, Canada," in R. Barclay *et al.,* eds., *Symposium*

86 (Ottawa: Canadian Cultural Institute, 1986), 77–78.

11 Ruth B. Phillips, "Why Not Tourist Art? Significant Silences in Native American Museum Representations," in Gyan Prakash, ed., *After Colonialism: Imperial Histories and Postcolonial Displacements* (Princeton: Princeton University Press, 1995), 108–9.

12 Richard Price and Sally Price, *Equatoria* (New York and London: Routledge, 1992), 17, 57, 85, 189.

13 *Ibid.,* 91, 155. Collecting ethics were all askew. Sally Price's negative feeling about the expedition seemed to come from a preference for being back home doing something else rather than from "her nobler ideological concerns about imperialism, oppression, cultural integrity." Issues were absent: "nothing matters much one way or another" (183).

14 As among the African Igbo. See Chinua Achebe, "Foreword" to H.M. Cole and C.C. Aniakor, eds., *Igbo Arts: Community and Cosmos* (Los Angeles: Museum of Cultural History, UCLA, 1984), ix, cited in Clifford, *The Predicament of Culture*, 207.

15 James Clifford, "Four Northwest Coast Museums: Travel Reflections," in Ivan Karp and Steven D. Lavine, eds., *Exhibiting Cultures: The Poetics and Politics of Museum Display* (Washington: Smithsonian Institution, 1991), 212–54.

Introduction

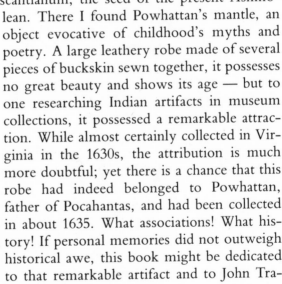

WHILE RESEARCHING in the Balfour Library at Oxford, I spent a noon hour in the Ashmolean. I wandered, quite fortuitously, into a little room set aside as a reconstruction of what remained of the old Museum Tradescantianum, the seed of the present Ashmolean. There I found Powhattan's mantle, an object evocative of childhood's myths and poetry. A large leathery robe made of several pieces of buckskin sewn together, it possesses no great beauty and shows its age — but to one researching Indian artifacts in museum collections, it possessed a remarkable attraction. While almost certainly collected in Virginia in the 1630s, the attribution is much more doubtful; yet there is a chance that this robe had indeed belonged to Powhattan, father of Pocahantas, and had been collected in about 1635. What associations! What history! If personal memories did not outweigh historical awe, this book might be dedicated to that remarkable artifact and to John Tradescant, whose museum preserved it.

Captured Heritage is an extension of the Powhattan mantle story. It deals with the collecting of Amerindian pieces by Europeans, by Americans, by Canadians — and even by native Indians — for museums like the Tradescantianum-cum-Ashmolean. It is only a small part of the story. It is concerned only with items bought and stolen from Indians who live almost diagonally across the continent

xvii

from Powhattan's Virginia, with those Northwest Coast Indians who form a cultural area extending from Puget Sound and the Olympic Peninsula northward through coastal British Columbia and into Alaska where they merged into the Eyak and the Chugach.

A hundred such geographically circumscribed books could be written and the story of ethnological collecting would not be complete, but there are few precedents and no models upon which I could lean in the writing of such a book. Polly and Leon Gordon Miller have a good chapter in their *Lost Heritage of Alaska* and Edmund Carpenter contributed a provocative introduction to *Form and Freedom,* both of which deal with the area, but *The Heyday of Natural History* and *Foreign Devils on the Silk Road* provided equal inspiration. I only wish that I could have written it with a fluency and excitement equal to Lynn Barber and Peter Hopkirk.

When I stumbled upon this subject and became fascinated by the question of how all the artifices of the natives of the area in which I live got from here to there, from coastal British Columbia, northwest Washington, and southeast Alaska to a score and more museums as far distant as New York, Berlin, and Leningrad, my initial immersion was into the C. F. Newcombe papers at Victoria. In their comfortably unsorted way, they told me that I had to look not just at Newcombe, major collector though he was, but at as many collectors and at as many museums as I could.

I persevered, assisted by a generous grant from the Social Sciences and Humanities Research Council of Canada (SSHRCC), and looked at the records of some twenty-five museums as well as a dozen sets of collectors' papers. I have been helped by individual studies on Emmons, Newcombe, Brady, Hunt, and others, and by monographs on several museums. In the end, of course, I had to sit down and try to weave my own book, a process that excited and then repelled me. The material was not very malleable and if the reader finds himself shoved from collector to museum and then back to collector, he will dimly perceive the difficulties I confess to have experienced and not entirely solved. This is, except for the last chapter, narrative history, the only way I felt would do justice to the historical process with which I am dealing, though even that vehicle imposes a certain coherence upon an often inchoate process that was directed and felt from a dozen different sources.

It is white history about Indians and about their procurable culture. It is contact history, not ethnohistory; it is partly cultural history, partly museum history, partly the history of anthropology, and even a little the history of taste. It is written by a professional historian aiming at the (quite impossible) task of satisfying his peers, but with a realization that if it interests anyone, it will likely be anthropologists and ethnohistorians and that it is they, rather than my historical colleagues, who will make the most judgments upon it.

The book deals with but one small thread of the interaction of Indians and Euro-Americans on the Northwest Coast. No doubt other themes are more important to both groups: land tenure, fishing rights, labor relations, government policy, even the suppression of the potlatch. There is no claim here that the trade in artifacts occupied a central place in the Indian economy or that their display in museums and expositions greatly affected Indian-white relations. It is a sub-theme, though now important to a new generation of heritage-conscious Indians. Its story lacks a broad museum context for it is written in ignorance of what similar processes were going on among the Arapahoe, the Ife, or the Bororo.

Furthermore, I could not bring myself to write yet another introductory ethnology of the peoples of the Northwest Coast. Many, perhaps too many, already exist. The book thus assumes some reader's knowledge, but not too much, of Northwest Coast cultures. Nor do I supply a very complete Euro-American context. Other authors have done this, notably Wilson Duff, Robin Fisher, and Rolf Knight, and I defer to their work while granting to the reader a presumption of awareness of the general process of white exploration and settlement of the region.

An author is always indebted to so many that it is difficult to do justice to them. Maria Tippett, then finishing her landmark study of Emily Carr, made me aware of the rich potential of the Newcombe papers. The President's Research Grants Committee of Simon Fraser University gave initial assistance, then the SSHRCC. Peter Gathercole and the Master and other Fellows of Darwin College, Cambridge, allowed pleasant surrounding for some of the writing, as did the staff and facilities of the University Library, Cambridge. Particularly helpful were members of the staff of the Provincial Archives of British Columbia and those of the Smithsonian Institution Archives. Wolfgang Haberland at the Hamburg museum, Horst Hartmann at Berlin, and Stanley A. Freed of the American Museum in New York were very helpful, as were Stephen Catlett of the American Philosophical Society, Philadelphia, and Jonathan King of the Museum of Mankind, London. Individuals whose kindly assistance deserve special acknowledgment were Adrienne Kaeppler, Vicky Wyatt, Jean Low, Ronald Weber, and especially Ira Jacknis.

Much of the research was done while I was chairman of the history department at Simon Fraser and the university was kind enough to allow some research assistance. David Adams, Jeanne Cannizzo, Stephen Turnbull, David W. Penny, and David Darling had a hand in the research. Jean Low, Aldona Jonaitis, Christine Mullins, Robin Fisher and Bill Holm made invaluable comments and corrections to all or parts of the completed manuscript.

In earlier forms, parts of chapter 11 were presented at Darwin College and the B. C. Studies Conference and then published in volume 63 of the *Canadian Historical Review* (December 1982), whose editors I thank for allowing me to reuse it.

Lest I seem ungrateful, the typing was my own, although the history department at Simon Fraser University paid the computer account.

IN DECEMBER 1930, Franz Boas watched a potlatch feast at Fort Rupert, British Columbia. He had seen his first Northwest Coast feast forty-five years earlier and he now noted some of the changes that had occurred. The host chief, Boas wrote, made a speech while the meat was distributed, saying " 'This bowl in the shape of a bear is for you,' and you, and so on; for each group a bowl." The speech was the same one that he had heard often before, "But the bowls are no longer there. They are in the museums in New York and Berlin!"★

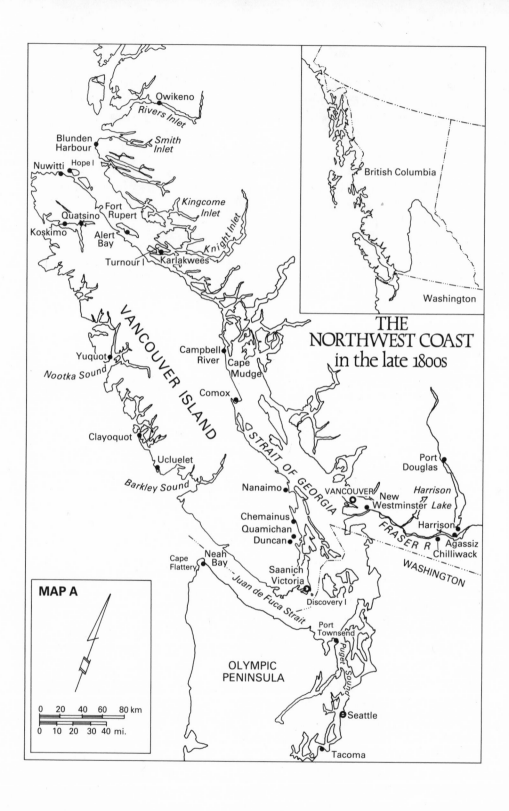

Owikeno

Rivers Inlet

Blunden
Harbour

*Smith
Inlet*

Nuwitti   Hope I

Quatsino   Fort
Rupert

Koskimo

Alert
Bay

Turnour I   Karlakwees

*Kingcome
Inlet*

Knight Inlet

VANCOUVER ISLAND

Yuquot

Nootka Sound

Clayoquot

Ucluelet

Barkley Sound

Campbell
River   Cape
Mudge

Comox

Nanaimo

Chemainus
Quamichan
Duncan

Cape
Flattery   Neah
Bay

Saanich
Victoria

Juan de Fuca Strait

Discovery I

STRAIT OF GEORGIA

VANCOUVER   New
Westminster

Port
Douglas

*Harrison
Lake*

Harrison

FRASER R   Agassiz
Chilliwack

WASHINGTON

Port
Townsend

Puget Sound

OLYMPIC
PENINSULA

Seattle

Tacoma

British Columbia

Washington

THE
NORTHWEST COAST
in the late 1800s

MAP A

0   20   40   60   80 km

0   10   20   30   40 mi.

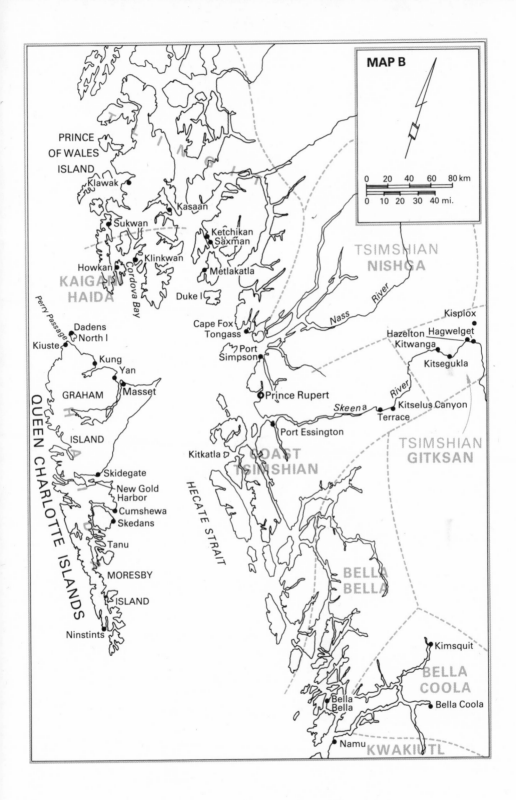

MAP B

0 20 40 60 80 km
0 10 20 30 40 mi.

PRINCE
OF WALES
ISLAND

Klawak

Kasaan

Sukwan

Ketchikan
Saxman

Klinkwan

Howkan

Metlakatla

KAIGANI
HAIDA

Cordova Bay

Duke I

TSIMSHIAN
NISHGA

Nass
River

Kisplox

Cape Fox
Tongass

Hazelton Hagwelget
Kitwanga

Perry passage

Dadens
North I

Kiuste

Kung

Yan

Port
Simpson

Kitsegukla

Masset

GRAHAM

ISLAND

Prince Rupert

River

Kitselus Canyon

Skeena

Terrace

QUEEN CHARLOTTE ISLANDS

Port Essington

Kitkatla

COAST
TSIMSHIAN

TSIMSHIAN
GITKSAN

Skidegate

New Gold
Harbor

Cumshewa

Skedans

HECATE STRAIT

Tanu

MORESBY

ISLAND

Ninstints

BELLA
BELLA

Kimsquit

BELLA
COOLA

Bella
Bella

Bella Coola

Namu

KWAKIUTL

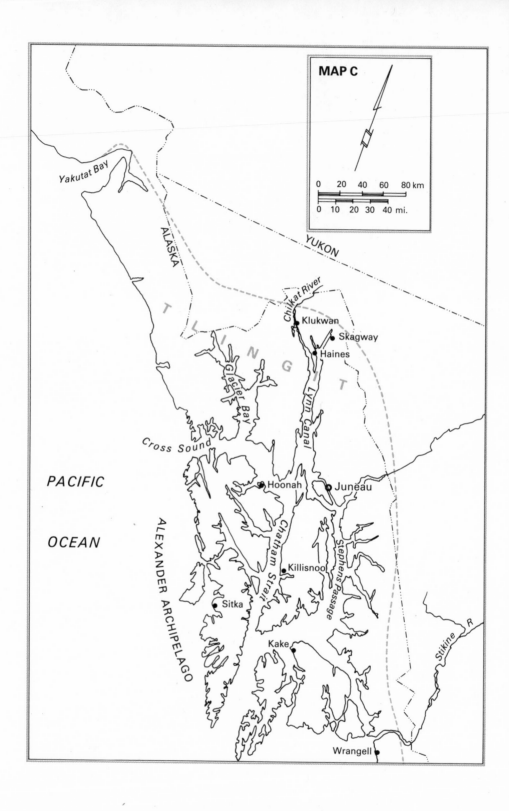

MAP C

Yakutat Bay

ALASKA

YUKON

0 20 40 60 80 km
0 10 20 30 40 mi.

T L I N G

Chilkat River

Klukwan

Skagway

Haines

Glacier Bay

G   T

Lynn Canal

Cross Sound

PACIFIC

OCEAN

Hoonah

Juneau

ALEXANDER ARCHIPELAGO

Chatham Strait

Stephens Passage

Killisnoo

Sitka

Kake

Stikine R

Wrangell

Chapter One

Prelude

ON JULY 19, 1774, three Haida canoes ceremonially welcomed a Spanish vessel, the *Santiago,* to the waters off the northernmost island of the Queen Charlottes. One of the ship's officers threw a gift into a canoe — it was merely a cracker wrapped in a kerchief — which drew the natives alongside. Trade between the Haida and Commander Juan Pérez commenced and then was taken up again the next day when the ship found itself surrounded by about two hundred Indians in twenty-one canoes. In exchange for clothing, shells, beads, and especially iron, the Haida offered sea otter and other skins, fur clothing, woven and ornamented blankets, cedar bark mats, basketry hats, and a variety of carved dishes, boxes, and spoons. Thus, on the occasion of the first contact of Europeans with the Northwest Coast Indians, the trade in artifacts had begun.[1]

Over the next fifty years more than four hundred and fifty vessels are thought to have visited the coast. These maritime explorers and fur traders did not come for native artifacts; such collections were incidental to more serious purposes. Most came for fur, for the sleek black coat of the sea otter whose pelts fetched a high price in China. Others, Pérez, Cook, and then Vancouver, Malaspina, and Lisianskii, were on government-sponsored expeditions, impelled by exploratory, scientific, and diplomatic purposes.

The collection of curiosities was secondary to the fur trade and to exploration, but many of the visitors took the opportunity to

1

buy exotic souvenirs to take home. Some among these visitors were avid collectors, either from personal whim or with an eye to sale or donation when they returned to their native ports. The largest collections were usually made by the government vessels, not only because they tended to stay longer in a single harbor, but because their officers were more interested in such "artificial curiosities" and appreciated the interest they would arouse among friends and patrons at home. Two of the voyages, Alejandro Malaspina's for Spain and George Vancouver's for England, carried explicit instructions to gather such articles. Malaspina, who spent nine days at Yakutat and fifteen at Nootka Sound, went out of his way to collect ethnological objects for the Royal Museum in Madrid.

The lively market in curiosities that sprang up in the coves and on the beaches of the north Pacific coast in the eighteenth century showed some features which would mark the entire history of the collecting process. One of the most striking was the keen trading abilities of the natives. Pérez was the first but not the last to note that the Indians were accomplished traders.[2] The Nootkan who greeted Cook's *Discovery* as she came into the Sound offered his hat and other things for sale when he had finished his welcoming speech. Midshipman Edward Rioux and his mates were at once convinced that these people "were no novices at that business." The stratagems of the practiced trader were immediately recognizable, even where they differed slightly from European custom. Malaspina, echoing George Dixon, wrote that "they not only keep hidden the goods which they intend to trade, but also never act with greater indifference than at these times." The Tlingit would delay, often over an hour, before even uncovering the pelt, doll, or spoon which they then offered for everything within view.[3]

Cook's remark that his trade was conducted "with the Strictest honisty on boath sides" was not everywhere true; Samwell noted that the Nootka possessed "sufficient confidence in their own abilities as to suppose themselves capable of deceiving us by some legerdemain Tricks with which they were acquainted." They tried to sell Cook bladders filled with water instead of oil and later added charcoal to furs to give them a more valuable gloss. One clever Nootkan put on a bird's mask and offered it for sale, while another sitting next to him stealthily used a whistle to imitate a bird call so effectively that the sound seemed to come from the mask itself. One collector of curiosities, Cook noted, was tricked into paying ten times the mask's value. Ensign Alexander Walker suspected that the respect paid to some carved figures "was pretended in order to raise their price."[4]

In their avidity for European metal, the natives seemed willing to part with almost everything, from lances, whistles, and masks to the skins off their backs. "These people offered every thing for Sale, apparel, paddles, Canoes, and spears would have been indiscriminately parted with," wrote an early trader to Nootka Sound.[5] When Cook saw some carved posts in a Yuquat house, some of his party speculated on their divinity. Cook was doubtful. If so, the natives "hild them very cheap, for with a little matter of iron or brass, I could have purchased all the gods in the place, for I did not see one that was not offered me." James Strange, "notwithstanding all this Parade of Devotion" paid to such a "god," bought one from Maquinna.[6]

While much evidence suggests that everything — at least everything seen — was subject to sale, there were distinctions. The valued position of metal insured that the copper earrings already owned by the Moachat Nootka were not parted with "for a trifle." Walker found it difficult to buy "Instruments of War," which, he observed, the Nootka kept carefully concealed and "showed great unwillingness to part with."[7]

One of Cook's officers noted that the Nootka had a great variety of animal masks, which they parted with willingly, but that those with a human face were treated quite differently. "If they sold any of these, it seemed to be with repugnance, as if they were parting with the image of a friend or relative, and were ashamed to be so doing." James King noted similar behavior. "We also observ'd that frequently in their selling us their masks, which would be covered carefully up, they would use a mysteriousness & often a secrecy, bringing them slily to us, which shewd that they were conscious of committing perhaps an impious crime in selling us their Gods."[8]

The best eighteenth-century record of a reluctant transaction is Ensign Walker's description of a mask he purchased from Maquinna in 1786. It took a great deal of persuasion for the Moachat chief to show the mask and then only "with much privacy and ceremony." Only after the chief's apartment had been carefully closed off and Maquinna had donned an ermine and otter cloak, did his wife "take from one of their finest decorated chests something wrapt up in Mats, and gave it to him." The wrapping was opened carefully, the mask brought out before the respectful gaze of all the family, and Maquinna, after fastening it to his face, crept around on hands and feet blowing into a whistle as if in imitation of a wild animal. Walker twice saw the ceremony performed and each time tried to purchase the mask. "At first they appeared unwilling to part with it, but after deliberating together; this God was sold for a pair of Copper Bracelets; which indeed were of considerable value."[9] One of Cook's officers noted that the Nootka, on the other hand, would bring "strange carv'd heads, & place them in a conspicuous part of the Ship, & desire us to let them remain there, & for these they would receive no return." He mentions another occasion when a carved screen and four "wooden busts" were ceremoniously placed in the Captain's cabin.[10]

Thus, it appears that animal masks were readily sold, human masks less readily, and that carved heads not used as masks might even be given away. The ethnological basis for these distinctions is not entirely clear, but it seems likely that much of the secrecy and embarrassment involved in selling some kinds of masks arose from their being secret society items which were not supposed to be seen by the uninitiated or to which the vendors did not have an undivided and indisputable right. This resort to privacy in the sale of certain items would enjoy a long history. The gifts remain a mystery.

While the natives, especially at Nootka Sound, had a reputation as incorrigible thieves of anything left unguarded, and at least one European fur trader resorted to stealing fur off the backs of Indians caught defenseless, the curio seekers kept their collecting largely within commercial avenues. There are few recorded examples of robbery.

One theft was a by-product of Alexander Baranov's devastation of the Tlingit villages in Cross Sound, Stephens Passage, and Chatham Strait in retaliation for the Indians' destruction of his Sitka fort five years earlier. The Tlingit fled on his approach and he had "therefore to content himself with demolishing their habitations," including some hundred mortuary poles. He kept some of the artifacts as trophies of war and when he visited Captain

Iurii Lisianskii aboard the *Neva* he gave him a number of the masks, "very ingeniously cut in wood, and painted with different colours," a "very well finished" raven rattle, and a large decorated copper.[11]

Malaspina was less brutal. His geographer had spotted a site with various monuments a little distance from Yakutat village and he and several officers rowed off to see it. They found two boxes, each raised about eight feet above ground on four square posts. Only one was decorated. On the ground there were other boxes, one of which they opened to find skeletons wrapped in mats. Some Indians were present, but they were from another village and, "satisfied by some gifts," it was they who carried one of the ornamented boxes to the boat. The removal of the Yakutat burial box was a harbinger of future practices; so too was the rapid adaptation by the Tlingit to the new demand for their goods. As soon as Malaspina's officers had "found much that was worth obtaining for the Royal Museum" from among the domestic utensils and weapons of the Yakutat, "the women were observed much occupied making [baskets] and the men in making dolls, spoons and other articles of wood which the men and even the officers purchased eagerly."[12] The production of artifacts for the European market commenced very early.

The collections of curiosities made by the maritime visitors to the coast were quickly scattered. Some never made it to home ports. The Russian governor of Kamchatka was presented "a complete assortment" of the curiosities from Cook's third voyage in recognition of his generous assistance, and more items were given to another hospitable Russian. Some were left at Cape Town. When the *Resolution* and *Discovery* returned to London the crew discovered that British collectors were more interested in natural history specimens than in native curiosities and that there was little demand for their ethnological pieces. One naturalist was very disappointed: "Instruments of warr & dresses of the Natives seem'd the only Cargo they had brought[.]not an Insect, or Animal could I find Except one Starved Monkey."[13]

Many of the Cook pieces and also George Dixon's later Haida collection were given to Sir Joseph Banks, who in turn passed most on to the British Museum. Lt. James King divided his holdings between Trinity College, Dublin, the British Museum, and

Sir Ashton Lever's London museum. At least twelve others of Cook's crew made presentations to the British Museum, as did Archibald Menzies, the naturalist with the Vancouver expedition. Cook's artist, John Webber, presented his material to the library in his native city of Bern. Cook's own collection was given to the Leverian Museum; while David Samwell, after offering his large one to a lady for £100, sold it, about four hundred ethnological pieces, at public auction.

The collections in Sir Ashton Lever's museum were sold at auction in 1806, following the demise of that famous early museum. A large number of lots, including thirty-five Nootka pieces, were bought by a representative of the Austrian royal museum. Florence, too, bought a number of Cook voyage objects, and others from the sale ended up in the British Museum and the museums at Cambridge and Exeter; others drifted eventually to the American de Menil, John Hauberg, Susanne Bennet, and University of Michigan collections. The gift to Governor Behm at Kamchatka remains in Leningrad. The Spanish material from the Malaspina expedition was retained by the Royal Cabinet in Madrid and what remains is now at the Museo de América.[14] The collections by New England fur traders were all private, though a number of pieces were given by the maritimers or their relatives to various scientific societies and some, poorly documented, are now at the Peabody museums of Yale and Harvard and in the Maritime Museum of Salem, Massachusetts.

Curiosity collecting continued after the decline of the maritime fur trade, but it was, if anything, more haphazard and the pieces were often scattered and lost. The Hudson's Bay Company, which reached the coast early in the nineteenth century, did little collecting and little of that can be traced. Sir George Simpson made a small collection and Hudson's Bay House, the London headquarters of the company, had a museum of Indian objects. In the late 1830s, William Fraser Tolmie, a surgeon and factor with the HBC, shipped several lots home to the Inverness museum and a collection of natural history pieces and artifacts, including several argillite pipes and dishes, to savant Dr. John Scouler. The latter probably became part of Scouler's 1870s gift to Paris's Musée du Trocadéro.[15]

The Russian-American Company officials seem to have been more conscientious. Baron F. P. Wrangell, K. T. Khlebnikov, and

A. A. Baranov, among others, sent material to the Imperial Academy's Cabinet of Curiosities, and naval visitors gathered more.[16] Adolph Etolin, a Finn in charge of the company in the early 1840s, sent a collection to Helsinki, at that time a Russian grand duchy. By then there was also a museum at New Archangel (Sitka), in the governor's mansion. It comprised nautical material, a zoological collection from Russian America, and "the costumes of all the savage peoples of the northwest coast of America."[17]

After the establishment of the small settlements in Puget Sound and Fort Victoria and especially during the gold rush period of the 1850s and 1860s, many more people came to the coast. They often picked up Indian souvenirs or made small collections which drifted into museums on their return to their home countries. The names of some of these collectors are well known: Paul Kane, the artist, a few of whose artifacts are now in the Royal Ontario Museum; Edward Belcher, the Arctic explorer for the Royal Navy, whose 1830s collections now reside in the British Museum; and Robert Brown, the Edinburgh naturalist, who gave his collections to Bloomsbury. Others, like Frederick Dally, a Victoria photographer of the 1860s, donated his collection to General Pitt Rivers's collection after showing it at the Archaeological Institute, and Bishop George Hills donated his Indian pieces to the Great Yarmouth Seaman's Museum. A large number of naval officers gave to a variety of local or national museums in the United Kingdom.

There were a few official or semi-official expeditions during the period, the Russians being particularly active. The most significant was that of I. G. Voznesenskii, a preparator at the Zoological Museum of the Imperial Academy of Sciences. He arrived at New Archangel in May 1840 and spent much of the next five years in Russian America collecting zoological, geological, and ethnological material, as well as making a remarkable set of drawings.[18] His ethnological collections were the most extensive of any made by the Russians, perhaps larger than those of any other single collection to that time, and form more than two-thirds of Leningrad's Northwest Coast holdings.

In 1841, while Voznesenskii was making his rich scientific harvests in Alaska, the United States Exploring Expedition under Captain Charles Wilkes explored Juan de Fuca Strait and Puget Sound as part of its three year round-the-world voyage. A large number of paddles, masks, model canoes, crania, and other curiosities were gathered by the expedition's officers and crew, much of the collection acquired from the *Columbia,* an HBC ship encountered at the mouth of the Columbia River. Wilkes ordered that all collections be surrendered at the end of the voyage. These were placed with the recently founded National Institution for the Promotion of Science and displayed at the Patent Office's glittering new building in Washington, D. C., though not before one of the expedition members, Titian Peale, had purloined a number for the Philadelphia museum of his father, Charles Willson Peale. Peale's Independence Hall museum already contained some items collected by Meriwether Lewis and William Clark, the more famous American expedition to the Northwest.[19] In 1857 the Wilkes collection was transferred to the Smithsonian Institution.

Chapter Two

Secretary Baird and
Judge Swan Build
a Collection

IN 1846 AN ACT OF CONGRESS created the Smithsonian Institution to fulfill the terms of the will and utilize the bequest of James Smithson, an Englishman whose estate was left for the founding in Washington of an institution for "the increase and diffusion of 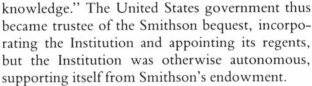 knowledge." The United States government thus became trustee of the Smithson bequest, incorporating the Institution and appointing its regents, but the Institution was otherwise autonomous, supporting itself from Smithson's endowment.

Joseph Henry, a distinguished Princeton physicist whose appointment as secretary made him the executive officer of the fledgling Institution, had definite ideas on the direction that the Smithsonian should take. The new body must dedicate itself primarily to encouraging research and publication in all areas of knowledge, including "ethnological researches." While Congress had entrusted to it custodial rights over all federal government collections, Secretary Henry had no interest in squandering the small income from the bequest in the accumulation and maintenance of museum collections. Collecting would steal money from the promotion of science through research and publication. A national museum would have to be funded by other means, most appropriately by specific Congressional appropriations.

The appointment in 1850 of Spencer F. Baird, a young zoology professor from Dickinson College, as assistant secretary in charge

9

of publications and collections inevitably altered Henry's resolve. Baird was a born collector, beginning as a boy to accumulate a complete series of Pennsylvania's Cumberland County birds. Primarily interested in ornithology (he was a youthful collaborator of Audubon), his natural history collecting expanded to include mammals and fossils. In moving to Washington he brought with him his own large natural history collection and, though acquiescing in Henry's aversion to indiscriminate collections, was soon expressing his desire that the Smithsonian acquire at least "a complete North American" collection. Henry seems to have been brought around to agreement; the Institution ought to possess a collection which would fully illustrate the natural history of North America.

Within three years of his appointment, Baird had succeeded in raising the Smithsonian's collection "from nothing to front rank among American cabinets." Indeed, his efforts were extended not merely toward acquisition of speciments, "but to their concentration in mass so as to supply all working naturalists with the materials of research." Baird's enthusiasm overcame any resistance from Henry. With the completion in 1854 of the Institution's towered and turreted "Lombardy revival" building on the South Mall, Baird's collecting instincts were no longer to be restrained. He adopted a strategy to secure government funding for a national museum by encouraging government expeditions and surveys to collect such "a mass of matter" that it would force the Congress into establishing a national museum under the Smithsonian's direction.[1]

Henry held off accepting custodianship of the "National Cabinet of Curiosities" — that farrago of specimens and relics in the Patent Office — until Congress appropriated money to the Smithsonian for its care. When this occurred in 1857, the collection, comprising the Wilkes expedition material, Indian curiosities and portraits from the War Department, the moribund National Institute's collections, and James Smithson's mineral cabinet and personal effects, was moved to new cases in the Institution's picturesque brownstone building. Baird's acquisitiveness in the previous eight years could be measured by the fact that the Patent Office material increased the total collection by only 20 percent.

Although an 1859 *Guide to the Smithsonian Institution and National Museums* claimed possession of "one of the most extensive and curious ethnological collections in the world," Baird's collecting enthusiasm had not yet been extended to ethnological material.[2] Most of the Museum's holdings in the field were pieces from the Wilkes expedition, and of fifteen cases on display only one was devoted to North American Indians. Not until 1860 did Baird's annual tabulation of accessions include an ethnology category, initially totalling a mere 550 entries, of which Wilkes material alone might account for at least 440 pieces.

Secretary Henry, on the other hand, had long sought to promote ethnology, though not necessarily ethnological collecting. He had launched the "Smithsonian Contributions to Knowledge" publications series with a study of the prehistoric mounds of the Mississippi Valley by Ephriam G. Squire and Edwin H. Davis. By 1861 he was reporting that no part of the Institution's operations "has been more generally popular" than ethnology. At the same time, he announced the Smithsonian's desire "to collect all the reliable information on this subject which it can possibly obtain." To this end he had a circular prepared by George Gibbs for distribution to correspondents and institutions in the West, including Vancouver Island and British Columbia. While the emphasis of the circular was philological, upon the collection of vocabularies, a revision in 1863 put added emphasis on ethnological material and carried a covering remark by Henry that the Smithsonian was "desirous of extending and completing its collections of facts and materials" on the races of mankind inhabiting the continent of America. Henry solicited the cooperation of all government officers, travellers, and residents for this purpose.

The circular's instructions were broad, emphasizing the desire for a full series of American skulls (to be procured "without offence to the living") and for implements and arts. Aside from skulls, Gibbs refused to single out types of objects or material: "almost every thing has its value in giving completeness to a collection." Immediacy was emphasized, however, for "many articles are of a perishable nature, and the tribes themselves are passing away or exchanging their own manufactures for those of the white race."[3]

Collections now began to come in from correspondents as well as from government explorers and surveyors, increasing the museum's collections in ethnology with greater rapidity than any other division. From a mere 825 catalogued specimens, the ethnology collection increased to 13,084 items in 1873. Henry encouraged the accumulation by reissuing the circular in 1867 with the remark that the Institution intended to give archaeology and ethnology "especial prominence" and hoped to gather "as full a series of the objects in question as it may be possible to collect at the present day."[4]

From the American Southwest came collections by Edward Palmer and Major J. W. Powell of the Rocky Mountain Survey; from the Mackenzie Basin, collections made by Robert Kenicott; from northern Alaska, by W. H. Dall and E. W. Nelson. These relatively systematic collections gave depth to the scattered donations received from virtually every state and territory of the country. Henry emphasized the scientific value of these growing collections. They were not to be viewed as "mere curiosities collected to excite the wonder of the illiterate, but as contributions to the materials from which it will be practicable to reconstruct by analogy and strict deduction the history of the past in its relation to the present." Admittedly, ethnology was as yet in the elementary stage of collecting materials, but through such a period "all science must necessarily pass."[5]

The notable increase in the collection was almost entirely by donation or government deposit. With congressional appropriations providing little more than bare maintenance, neither the Institution nor the museum had money for large purchases. Henry and Baird were particularly reliant upon government agents — customs, military, and naval officers and survey officials — for ethnological specimens. Gibbs, a member of the 49th-parallel boundary survey, contributed small collections of Northwest Coast objects in 1862–63 and again in 1871.

The purchase of Alaska by the United States in 1867 meant the despatch of a number of civil and military officials to the new territory. The museum was quickly able to acquire Tlingit material via members of the army, navy, and revenue service. Dr. Thomas T. Minor, surgeon aboard the revenue steamer *Wayanda* on its 1868 cruise from the Bering Sea to the southern tip of Alaska, sent a carved Tlingit head ornament along with much Eskimo material. Henry, informed by Minor that artillery officer Lt. F. M. Ring would be willing to collect, quickly wrote of his desires to obtain full native collections, "ancient or modern";

doubtless there were old graves "which only await excavation to furnish materials of importance." Objects of every variety would be welcome, "nothing being considered trivial or commonplace that serves to elucidate the manners and customs of the people." Ring promptly replied with a collection of dishes, spoons, labrets, masks, and rattles.[6] Dr. Alexander H. Hoff, chief army medical officer in Alaska, also contributed a collection.

Before Vincent Colyer, secretary to the Board of Indian Commissioners, departed for an Alaskan visit, he received a letter from Henry that commented upon "the duty of this country to collect and preserve all the relics possible of the races-of-men who have inhabited the American Continent." No time should be lost; the tribes "are rapidly disappearing and their original modes of life continually undergoing changes."[7] Colyer complied with the call to patriotic duty, bringing back from his official tour a nice collection from southern Alaska and elsewhere.

The Smithsonian continued to make modest catches among officers and officials posted in Alaska. Some slipped through the net, realizing that there might be more value to their exertions than the honor of a contribution to science and an acknowledgment in Henry's annual report. Army lieutenant Edward G. Fast used his time in Sitka to gather a rich and enormous collection, which he exhibited commercially in San Francisco and New York, then placed on sale for $10,000. Harvard University's Peabody Museum of Archaeology and Ethnology, acting on the advice of two Smithsonian collaborators, old Northwest Coast hands W. H. Dall and George Gibbs, purchased the collection for $2,500. Gibbs had little sympathy for Fast, now ill and impoverished. The man, he wrote, "has simply traded on his position as an accidental officer of the army," but the collection was valuable and it would cost considerably more than $2,500 to duplicate it.[8]

Fast's sale to the Peabody was an exception. Most personnel in Alaska picked up a few curios as souvenirs of their experience, but none capitalized upon their tours of duty with such thoroughness as Fast. For the most part the Smithsonian was fortunate in obtaining the voluntary services of government people and of its own correspondents and friends. One such correspondent, who worked in varying capacities for two decades and more, was a pioneer resident of Washington Territory, James G. Swan.

The Smithsonian's 1863 circular was read with special interest by James Swan, then teaching at an Indian school in Neah Bay, W. T. He had met Henry and Baird in 1857 while in the nation's capital as secretary to the territorial delegate, Isaac Stevens. Settling in Neah Bay near Cape Flattery, among the Makah, a group affiliated with the Nootka of Vancouver Island, he nursed intentions of making contributions to the Smithsonian and the National Museum. He was spurred into action by the urging of Dr. George Suckley, a member of the Pacific Railroad Survey who was himself sending natural history specimens to Washington.

Swan entered into a correspondence with Baird and Henry, keeping meteorological records for them and, early in 1860, sending his first package, specimens of shellfish, to the Institution. For the rest of his life he occupied himself by adding to "the treasury of universal knowledge."[9] Initially he collected natural history material; his pickled clams and fishes were welcomed contributions from a region as yet little represented in the Museum's conchological and ichthyological series. The circular, "Instructions for Research Relative to the Ethnology and Philology of America," opened a large and much more congenial area to Swan, who had developed a sympathetic interest in the territory's native inhabitants.

Born in Massachusetts in 1818, Swan had left a business and a family to sail in January 1850 for the golden land of California. A few years later he turned up in Shoalwater Bay, just north of the Columbia estuary, where he survived on a land claim by working as an oysterman. In 1857 Harpers published his account of his life in Washington Territory.[10]

Swan helped Governor Isaac Stevens negotiate with Indian bands at Chehalis and this assistance was converted into a secretaryship to Stevens in Washington, D. C. He remained East only a short while, moving back to the territory in 1858 with hopes for a whaling operation in Port Townsend, a town whose future seemed promising as the prospective terminus for a northern Pacific railroad. When whaling soured, Swan tried to get a job with the Indian Bureau, but he was now without the necessary political influence. He did some legal and commercial work, made a little money writing for local newspapers, and finally in 1862, secured a teaching position at Neah Bay, which he held for nearly four years.

James G. Swan in his Port Townsend office, 1891. From the Photo Collection of the Washington State Historical Society, Tacoma, Washington.

By this time he was in his mid-forties, willfully separated from his Boston roots and from his wife (she would die in 1864) and two children, and with an accumulation of collapsed career projects that only intensified his desire for recognition and success. Perpetually dissatisfied, always seeking any small honor that would help elevate his position to where his self-esteem placed it, Swan is an example of the shiftless, unsuccessful man of the territories. He pieced together a hand-to-mouth living as journalist, ticket agent, notary, probate judge, and occasional counselor in admiralty law, "performing odd jobs of simple literacy in a society where simple literacy was in demand."[11]

Not without talent, he lacked judgment and, in later years, sobriety. He possessed a sensitivity, rare for the time and place, toward his Indian contemporaries. His sincere and only occasionally supercilious interest in them was reciprocated by an unusual trust and openness. The Makah even named a sealing ship after him. On the other side, he found, as correspondent with the great scientists of Washington, especially Henry, Baird, and Gibbs, and as a collector for the Smithsonian, a measure of flattering prestige. He could contribute to the universal world of science, be recognized by the best minds of his country, and be honored for his long and intimate knowledge of the Pacific Coast and its native inhabitants.

The Smithsonian's interest in ethnology gave him another opportunity to make a mark in life. Neah Bay seemed a perfect place to collect curiosities — "there are few Indians that have come under my observation who have more of such articles than the Makahs." A collection of their fisheries, including whaling, their canoes, baskets, blankets, wooden wares, and tools, he wrote Henry after reading the 1863 circular, "could not fail of being attractive objects in your collections." He would try to make such a collection, doing it with "a hearty good will, for I need not assure you of the deep interest I feel and have long felt in anything connected with the Indians of the Northwest coast." There were problems to be faced. Ethnology was not like natural history where specimens belonged to no one and might be picked from land or sea without charge. To make a full ethnological collection required time but also money, "for these people are great traders and will not part with the merest trifle without compensation."[12]

Henry was prepared to offer a small amount toward purchases, wondering if $50 would go any distance toward a collection. Swan found it difficult to estimate costs but he would begin a collection, keeping an account, and hoping "somehow or other for remuneration." So Swan's first curiosities went off to Washington. They included two skulls and some bark capes, followed shortly by blankets, more bark capes, two cradles, rattles, and basketry. The blankets and capes had cost him $8.50, but the rest had been procured by barter, mostly for potatoes raised on the reservation, for which he made no charge. Natural history specimens — bird skins, eggs, shells, and fish — accompanied each shipment of curiosities. Baird was delighted and asked for more.[13] Swan had found a role in which his service and expertise were useful and appreciated. Encouraged by Baird, he turned his hand to a paper on the Makahs, the first of a series of memoirs and papers he produced for the Institution.[14]

That next year he quit his frustrating teaching job and went East. It was merely a visit, he assured Baird; "as we say in Chinook, my 'tumtum' is with the productions of the west coast." He hoped to return as an Indian agent, but that was not his luck. He settled again in Port Townsend, living from his variety of minor occupations. But Port Townsend was not as favorable a location for ethnology as Neah Bay. The surrounding Klallam, he told Baird, were too close to the white community and had nothing but coarse baskets and mats.[15] His contributions dropped off to virtually nothing. It was frustrating for him to watch the departure and arrival in the harbor of Alaskan ships, especially the revenue cutters with their government officials on board. Why was not the government utilizing such opportunities to collect from the north coast tribes?

Swan grew increasingly disturbed by the casual, unsystematic methods of the Smithsonian. Its continued dependence upon flying visits by officials unfamiliar with the coastal Indians could only produce unsatisfactory results. Items were wrongly or inadequately labeled, totem poles were called idols, and other errors were committed or perpetuated by such erratic methods. Letter after letter told Baird of great collecting opportunities, some already lost, some tantalizingly near. Had he been sent on the *Wayanda* to Sitka in 1869 he could have sent "a collection that would have been the admiration of the visitors of the Smithsonian." The *Reliance* under his old friend Captain Selten was fitting out for an 1870 cruise to Alaska, "a splendid chance for collections and yet, no one has been detailed to go." "Carefully and correctly made" collections could only be done by someone long resident on the coast with a familiarity with the language and customs, adequately provided with time and money for travel and purchases. Swan was not so humble as to hide his own qualifications: "I can do this work as well, and probably better than anyone on the Pacific Coast."[16]

His frustration at the Smithsonian's impoverished ineptness and his confidence in his own ability were only further increased by a chance meeting with a party of Haida who stopped in Port Townsend for a few weeks in 1873. He spent hours with Chief Kitkune of Klue and three others, making copies of Haida designs and securing explanations of tatoos and carvings. If only the government would allow him a salary and sufficient funds, he could produce results. He could cover every part of the country from the Columbia River to the Bering Strait and organize a network so that collections would come from Sitka to Port Townsend every month. He knew the country, was on the spot, and had the goodwill of all the coastal tribes. His "whole heart and soul" was in this work, but he was past the point where he could gratuitously exert himself for the government. It was hardly adequate to be told that the museum was fitting up the finest room in

America for an ethnological museum, that no specimens would have "a more prominent place" in it than his own. He would do no more unless compensated for his efforts: "the time has gone by for me to work for fame or honor," he wrote, "I must work for pay." The declaration was more a measure of his frustration than of his intention. He could abandon neither the Institution nor his own interest in ethnology. The fact was that the Smithsonian had become an important part of his life and he secured from correspondence with Henry and Baird a sympathetic friendship as well as a feeling of importance and purpose. He was a lonely and unappreciated man in his community, something of a character to be sure, but also a periodic drunk and an ageing ne'er-do-well. There "is not one solitary individual on Puget Sound that I know who takes any interest or sympathises with me in this work." At least Baird paid attention, if not salary.[17]

Baird continued to encourage Swan, nursing the man's ineradicable enthusiasm as best he could. He recommended him to the Indian Bureau for an agent's position and was willing to reimburse him for "any moderate expense," but the Smithsonian simply did not have the resources either to put its correspondent on salary or to make large-scale purchases. Baird shared Swan's regret over the Smithsonian's inability to employ a systematic and salaried collector. Regret turned to alarm when he received reports of an 1873 French expedition to Alaska, amply provided (so it was reported) with means for securing everything of anthropological interest. It was now Baird's turn to deplore the astonishing inability of the United States to secure material belonging to the tribes within its own borders before foreigners came "carrying off all that is especially worth having." Swan welcomed the French expedition "if it will only awaken our Government" and Baird hoped that exactly this would happen.[18] He intended to seek an appropriation and, should he succeed, then to obtain as much as possible of Swan's time and help.

The French expedition that so alarmed Baird was Alphonse Pinart's visit to the Aleutian and Kodiak islands, which resulted in a large collection, though none from the Northwest Coast area. The assistant secretary's fear of foreign incursions was hardly allayed when, scarcely seven months later, he heard of yet another foreign collector, this time securing specimens through Swan himself.

In late November 1873, Franz Steindachner, director of the Imperial Museum of Natural History in Vienna, called on Swan at Port Townsend. Swan, in his isolation, found the visit delightful and reported it with obvious relish (and, no doubt, exaggeration) to Washington. Not only had the Austrian scientist proposed an enlarged translation of Swan's Makah memoir, but he had bought everything ethnological that Swan had on hand and placed an unlimited order for further collections of any kind. Indeed, Swan had also been solicited to collect for "parties at Amsterdam" but as that request was unaccompanied by arrangements to pay, he would confine his services to Dr. Steindachner. He preferred working for his own country, but only "if they will be as liberal as the foreigners." Baird did not like the tenor of this and countered with a weapon of his own. It was likely, he told Swan, that the Congress would appropriate money for a collection for the 1876 Centennial Exhibition in Philadelphia. He dangled this opportunity before Swan while warning that an Austrian commitment would hinder an appointment.[19]

Swan kept up his posture: he would confine his contributions to the Smithsonian "to the work of my own hands" (presumably the Haida paper he was finishing), for which he asked no compensation, but in Indian collecting, "I am willing to work for those who will pay me the best." On the other hand, he wanted Baird clearly to know that he had no engagement with Steindachner which precluded him from giving preference to his own government.[20]

Swan was bluffing. Steindachner did acquire a small Northwest Coast collection for his museum, about half of it bought for cash from Swan. This amounted to about twenty pieces for no more than $75. There were no more purchases by Vienna and we have only Swan's self-interested testimony of Steindachner's unlimited order or enquiries from Amsterdam. Only weeks later, Swan was offering Baird new material from Sitka without making reference to competing buyers.[21] He had been gratified, however, to be able to tell Baird that his services were elsewhere appreciated, that he was not totally reliant upon the Smithsonian. Having thus demonstrated that he was not a captive correspondent, he went back to his collecting for Baird.

He was passionately involved and, with the Centennial Exhibition proposal, never had the possibilities been so promising. Fortunately, personal business called him to Boston and he stopped in Washington where he and Baird discussed prospective arrangements for a Centennial collection. Although no congressional decision on appropriations would be made until the winter, Baird was confident of favorable action and assured Swan that he would have "entire direction" of the collection from the Northwest Coast. Swan was anxious to begin and bridled at the congressional delay — a winter's authorization would allow insufficient time for a proper collection — but he had to be satisfied with Henry's circular soliciting donations of ethnological material.[22]

Swan returned to Port Townsend to wait impatiently for word from Washington. In the meantime he began to hatch plans that would "make this Indianology a great feature" of the celebration. He bouyantly ordered "Centennial Commissioner" stationery, had his office freshly whitewashed, and set his imagination soaring. He would ask agents at all coastal locations to collect and would himself visit the north coast in the spring to make a complete collection of ethnological specimens, explore shell heaps, and gather material for a full, publishable account. He consulted with Israel W. Powell, the Indian Commissioner for British Columbia, who had cruised the coast in the summer on H. M. S. *Boxer* and who now promised, if officially asked, to take Swan with him in the coming spring on a similar voyage along the entire B. C. coast.

According to Swan's plan, collections from every coastal tribe would be exhibited at Philadelphia within a full-sized Tlingit house complete with inside carvings and outside poles. The separately installed productions of each tribe would allow comparisons. Equally striking would be a display of the distinctive canoe types, Makah, Salish, and Haida (as well as an Aleut baidarka), each of which could be manned by native crews. The whole would require $100,000.[23]

While Swan made his plans in Port Townsend, Baird was busy in Washington. Hitherto his National Museum had been dependent upon random donations and the cooperation of sympathetic government officials, with only a portion of the Smithson endowment available for purchases. The Centennial Exhibition, commemorating at Philadelphia the 100th anniversary of American independence, offered the possibility of direct congressional funding for a United States government exhibition. Baird intended to make the most of this unprecedented opportunity.

As the Smithsonian Institution's member on the Board of Managers established by President U. S. Grant in January 1874 to supervise the federal government's effort, Baird discovered that the Interior Department's Indian Bureau foresaw an exhibition of Indian life. Making the quite sensible point that all collections gathered by the Bureau would, under law, revert to the National Museum at the exhibition's close, Baird adroitly secured the agreement of the Bureau to unite its efforts with those of the Smithsonian to secure an "exhaustive and complete" display that would satisfy the public's "very great interest in subjects of this character."[24] Though Baird exercised almost complete direction of the collecting, the Bureau bore virtually the entire cost. In this way the Smithsonian's share of the eventual appropriation, about $52,000, was considerably increased by control over a portion of the Interior Department's larger sum.

Initial strategy for the Indian exhibition ("Indianology" Baird and Swan sometimes called it) included plans to secure collections from Indian agents throughout the West. Returns from the agents proved few and unsatisfactory: these potential collectors were unenthusiastic and inexperienced.[25] Baird was not really disappointed. He considered it more important "to have a perfectly exhaustive representation of a few interesting tribes than to have a skimming of material from a large number." Only complete series could give "a satisfactory idea of the character, disposition and peculiarities of the American aborigines."[26] For these he preferred to rely upon known, experienced, and trusted collectors: on Major J. W. Powell and Edward Palmer for the Southwest, on Paul Schumacher for California and Oregon, on Emil Bessels for northern Alaska, and on Swan for the Northwest Coast. Funding was not clarified until March 1875, allowing only thirteen months before the exhibition's scheduled opening in April 1876.

When the appropriation was firm, Baird despatched a telegram to Port Townsend, informing Swan that the Indian Bureau proposed to make him their special agent under Baird's direction at two hundred dollars per month salary, with travel expenses, and an allocation of three to four thousand dollars for purchases.[27] Swan could at last try his hand at the full-scale systematic collecting he had so long urged upon Washington. Conditions were not ideal — he wished he had more time — but now he was a salaried, commissioned collector with a sizable purchasing account. In fact, he was the first such collector to operate on the Northwest Coast and among the first group ever commissioned by the U. S. government specifically for ethnological collecting. It was as much a precedent for Baird as it was for Swan.

Swan was more than ready. He had been preparing his plans for nine months, had talked with the commanders of coastal vessels and several times with Commissioner Powell. Within days he was negotiating for his most sensational purchase — a sixty-foot canoe. Built for Maquinna of Nootka Sound, who sold her to Kla-ko-tlas, a Nimkish chief who lost her for debts, she now belonged to R. H. Hall, the Hudson's Bay Company factor at Alert Bay. Swan was told he could secure the huge canoe, delivered to Victoria, for 100 blankets or $250.[28] Swan saw the purchase as the coup it was and the monster canoe would remain his pride throughout the vicissitudes he encountered in getting it safely to Philadelphia.

Almost immediately, however, Swan received a setback. Powell was forced to cancel his spring cruise. Recovering quickly, Swan busily collected whatever was locally available, and secured the cooperation of William Charles, the HBC's chief factor in Victoria, for collections to be made by the company's factors along the coast. With Baird's assistance in Washington he made arrangements with Capt. Charles M. Scammon for a journey north on the U. S. revenue cutter *Oliver Wolcott*.

The *Wolcott* departed Port Townsend early in June with Swan on board. The northern tribes had always occupied a higher place in his estimation than his Klallam and Makah neighbors. He regarded the northern groups as expert carvers while the southern "seem to have little skill in this particular, and the Makahs do little more than carve rude faces and images of animals."[29] Now he would have an opportunity personally to visit some of these northern groups that he hitherto had known only by report, by his one brief visit to Sitka, and by their occasional visits to Port Townsend or Victoria.

At Fort Simpson Swan was the guest of Rev. Thomas Crosby who impressed him with the advances made by the Tsimshian under his pastorate. Inducing the Indians to give up their heathen ways, Crosby had persuaded many to remove poles from outside their houses, and, though some of these had been burned, others were collected "in a sort of museum." Swan bought one, a finely-carved forty-foot specimen, and he hoped for more. Both Crosby and C. E. Morrison, the HBC trader, agreed to gather a collection for Swan which they would send to Victoria.[30]

Despite these successes, Swan was disappointed at the results of the first ten days of his cruise. The material hardly matched his expectations. He consoled himself that he had been unable to give advance notice to traders, that he had not yet reached "the country where Indian manufactures are plenty." He hoped to do better at Sitka, Taku, and the Chilkat, but "unless I find better places than I have yet seen," he would have to "rely more upon Dr Powell & the Chief Factor of the H. B co. at Victoria to make collections than any thing I could do." A fall cruise with Powell to the Queen Charlotte Islands would be very productive: "I can do more with his assistance in one month than I can do in a Revenue Cutter in a year."[31] Certainly the cutter was not a perfect instrument. Captain Scammon was sick and confined to his cabin and the ship had its own customs-enforcement business which ill-matched Swan's purposes. Moreover, it was too small to carry much baggage. Nevertheless, Swan did better in Alaskan waters than he had been able to do at Alert Bay or Fort Simpson.

At Fort Wrangell he bought boxes, dishes, and three Chilkat shawls, highly priced at $25 to $37.50, but valuable prizes. At Sitka he secured, for $124, "a good assortment of Indian manufactures" from A. T. Whitford, "a trader who deals largely in Indian curiosities" (the dealer had already come to the coast). Most of the Kootsenoo were away during the fishing season, but enough remained for him to buy a number of pieces, "most of them of an ancient date." More items came his way at Kake and Shigan. At Klawak, a Kaigani Haida village, he saw a very fine stand of poles and posts but was unable to buy any. A chief's wife, "the most intelligent woman I have met," told him that most were in memory of the dead and " 'we will not sell them any more than you white people will sell grave-stones or monuments in your cemeteries, but you can have one made.' " At Cordova Bay he saw the largest village, Klommakowan (probably Klinkwan), with the greatest number of poles that he had yet seen, but, again, the Indians were unwilling to part with any. He settled for two wooden helmets, several masks, a headdress, and other items, such as some silver jewelry by Chief Kinowen, the "celebrated silversmith."[32]

Swan arrived back in Port Townsend on July 22 with what he called "an interesting collection," but which numbered only about 240 pieces. He admitted that he had not succeeded as well as he had expected. Captain Scammon's illness had been a continual handicap and the Indians were mostly absent from their winter quarters where they kept their most valuable things. He had, however, been able to arrange for collections to be made and sent down in the fall.[33] This, rather than the 240 pieces for six weeks' time and $360 cash, was the most significant result of the voyage. While he did use the *Wolcott* for a trip to Neah Bay where, with the assistance of Rev. C. A. Huntington, he secured a good collection (including a striking eleven-foot Makah figure for $35), and to Puget Sound, most of the remainder of his collecting was by means of the network of missionaries, traders, and officials he had begun to cultivate before the *Wolcott* cruise, a network he continued to enlarge and develop.

Commissioner Powell was helpful throughout, arranging for the storage and painting of the big canoe at the Songhees Reserve near Victoria, selling Swan a Fort Rupert canoe, and providing other pieces, including some gold work from a Haida working at the Cassiar mines. Morrison and Crosby fulfilled their promises and shipped collections which arrived in September, as did a consignment from the HBC factor at Bella Bella. Other shipments came from Barclay Sound and from Alaska. At Kasaan on Prince of Wales Island, Charles Baronovich not only gathered a collection for Swan, but oversaw the carving of a new, thirty-foot pole which Swan had commissioned when he could buy none.

Swan would doubtless have done more collecting himself (though still relying upon his agents) had his accounts been better arranged by Washington. He was victim of disbursing procedures that severely hampered his collecting. The Indian Bureau had allocated $3,000 to him, but despite his deposition of a $5,000 performance bond pledging faithfully to dispense and account for all money, the Bureau was unable to advance him funds. Payment came only as reimbursement for signed vouchers and then as paper currency (the famous "greenbacks"), a form which in the Northwest was discounted at 10 to 16 percent against gold. In British Columbia, indeed almost everywhere, Swan had to pay in coin and on the spot. Indians would not accept U. S. government vouchers, which were, in effect, promissory notes for eventual payment in currency.

Local conditions simply did not permit the "practice of sending receipted vouchers to Washington and awaiting the tardy action of the Department clerks before funds can be obtained." People, especially natives, would sign vouchers and surrender goods only when "they first receive the money." How could he make out vouchers for purchases among Indians? The articles had been bought with his own money and were collected among hundreds of Indians; "sometimes there would be 20 or 30 natives with articles for sale, from a bit to 10 dollars." Swan asked in vain that his allocated money, or at least $1,000 of it, be placed on account in a Portland or San Francisco bank. He had used his own money for the *Wolcott* purchases and Powell had advanced money for the big canoe (and Swan "felt considerably mortified" to tell Powell that he had no funds to repay the advances). In August he had still received no funds from Washington. He refused to do more until payment arrived. Donations he would continue to accept, "but [I] shall make no purchase, nor shall I ship what I have purchased until the money is sent me."[34]

At last Baird stepped in with advice on the voucher problem, but slowness of payment caused Swan virtually to halt his efforts for almost two months, thus cancelling any possible voyage to the Queen Charlotte Islands or the west coast of Vancouver Island. He had to borrow money at the very high rate of 2.5 percent per month when he resumed work late in September. By that time he had spent, he claimed, over $2,000 of his own and borrowed money and had yet to receive a single cent of the appropriation. Only in November did he receive salary and reimbursement of $2,460.66, most of which had long been spent, and he still had to manage with a cash shortage. When in March he received notice (but no explanation) that $900 of his expenditures had been disallowed, he was brought almost to apoplexy. "I have worked earnestly, diligently and faithfully and have collected the finest specimens and largest amount that ever has been collected on the Northwest Coast," he wrote, but he was now "so thoroughly disgusted with the treatment I have received that I do not care whether I have any more to do with the matter or not."[35] He had lost all confidence in the management of the Centennial and he decided to wash his hands of the affair by shipping everything off. The matter was eventually resolved (it was a confusion over currency versus gold drafts) with Swan receiving payment, but it had been frustrating and disheartening.

There were other reasons for discontent. His very earliest plans for the exhibition had included not only Indian manufactures, but actual Indians on the site in Philadelphia. He had collected his canoes with this very much in mind, having visions of at least three sets of natives paddling on the Schuykill River which bordered Fairmount Park. Baird fully entered into the project, foreseeing "an exhibition of living representatives of the principal Indian tribes" from Eskimos to Seminoles, some twenty groups in all. Each "series" would be made up of four to eight individuals, "picked specimens of their humanity" — the language is curiously from the laboratory. Equipped with native clothing, implements, and dwellings, they would be grouped on a reservation at the Centennial grounds where they could "carry on their various occupations." Swan planned to bring his canoesmen, especially Makah whalers, and he thought some Haida and Tsimshian silversmiths ought also to be at Philadelphia. They could not only demonstrate their skills, but be living examples of the civilization of these northern tribes, products of their superior native intelligence and of the beneficent work of Canadian missionary teachers as contrasted to baneful American Indian agents.[36]

The whole scheme collapsed when money ran short and Congress refused a supplementary appropriation. Baird pleaded personally before a House committee and President Grant seconded him with a message to Congress, but an appropriation was denied. Swan was extremely disappointed. To exhibit his fine canoes without the Indians was "like the play of Hamlet with the prince left out." He blamed the currently scandalous "Indian Ring" for Congress's failure. "Whoever lives at the next Centennial will find but few Indians to display."[37]

By this time, May 1876, Swan had also been trying his hardest to get himself to Philadelphia, but his own appropriation was exhausted. He had already tried to ensure the trip by taking masks and other objects apart for "good packing," telling Baird that he could easily put them back together when in Washington or Philadelphia. He continued to insist that his expertise was required. No one in Washington could do his collection properly: "the fact is, my dear Professor, that I should be with my collection and direct and assist in properly arranging it." Baird refused to offer more than expenses; Swan insisted upon payment for his services. Baird was annoyed that much of the British Columbia material, shipped from Victoria in April, was inadequately labeled and catalogued. Swan's response, that he had done his best while in the B. C. city, but that he fully expected to go to Philadelphia to do it properly, must only have been further annoying.[38] In any event, Baird did not find Swan so indispensable as he had tried to make himself. Swan sat out the Centennial in Port Townsend.

The Centennial Exhibition, without Swan or his Indian canoesmen, opened on May 10 at its 231-acre Philadelphia site. Swan's collection filled a large part of the United States Government Building, a huge cross-shaped wooden structure designed by James H. Windrim of Philadelphia. Built at low cost so as not to subtract unduly from the total government budget for the exhibition, the building, lacking much of the ornate embellishments of the age, seemed both cheap and commonplace. Into it went displays by War, Navy, Argriculture and other executive departments, as well as those of the Interior and the Smithsonian. The Indian exhibition was installed by Smithsonian ethnologists Edward Freeman and Frank H. Cushing and by Charles Rau, specialist in archaeology.

A vast number of specimens competed for attention in the 8,000 square feet of the Indian section. Most were set in orderly rows of walnut cases, but many objects were placed on top of the cases, on the floor, or hung on lines across the ceiling. The curators' inexperience in exhibition technique was obvious in the endless, jumbled installation. More effective, perhaps, were the dozens of life-size papier-mâché manikins created by the National Museum to display native costume and ornament.[39] Swan's collection of masks, bowls, clubs, and knives was stuffed into display cases, his canoes lay in the aisles, and the poles stood freely nearby. A photograph shows one of his Chilkat blankets hanging high in the air, with a model house and a large carving sitting atop some cases.

Swan's contribution to the exhibition was significant. He was entitled to "safely say that I have the most extensive and valuable collection of Indian curiosities that were ever collected on the Northwest coast." His collection for 1875–76 totalled about five

Ethnological exhibit, U. S. Government Building, Centennial Exhibition, Philadelphia, 1876. Smithsonian Institution photo #74–4541.

hundred objects, among which the big canoe took pride of place. "I think more of the canoe," he wrote, "than of any other thing I have collected." Although virtually the first and easiest thing for him to buy, that canoe cost a great deal in anguish before reaching Philadelphia. She was towed by steamer to the Songhees Reserve at Victoria without difficulty and there Powell had two coats of paint applied and a temporary shed erected to prevent the summer sun from cracking her hull. Further work was interrupted by Swan's cash shortage until September when he had a third coat of paint applied and hired Geneskelos, an aged Haida, to decorate her. That completed, the canoe excited, Swan claimed, strong interest among Victorians, a great many ladies and gentlemen taking the ferry across to see her on the reserve. She was "something unusual to attract so much attention among people who see hundreds of canoes every day in the year."[40]

Transportation from Victoria now became a major problem. He had been initially and characteristically optimistic. By removing the separately attached bow and stern pieces, he could shorten her so there would be no difficulty in shipping. Now he hesitated to move her in the summer for fear of the hot desert sun; then he feared a winter's rough sailing would be too dangerous for the fragile frame. The *Pacific* refused to take her to San Francisco because of her size, and the *City of Panama* would charge $200. He could get no response from the Alaska Commercial Company, San Francisco agents of the Smithsonian, and he hesitated to move the canoe until arrangements had been perfected there for railcars — it would require two, the rear one with a swiveled base. He decided to keep her over the winter. "To tell the truth," he wrote Baird, "I feel a little doubtful of sending these fine canoes and trusting them to the tender mercies of baggage smashers." The best arrangements would be for a party of Indians to go with both canoes: they would "take better care of them than any other person." A winter's gale wrecked the temporary shed and he rebuilt a better one — it took 1,000 board feet — to keep out the snow. Finally, in April 1876, the canoe was put aboard the *Dakota* using special chocks and slings that Swan had had made. She was too heavy for the donkey engine, and one hundred passengers and crew helped the steam crane lift her from the water to the deck. "She has caused me a deal of anxiety," wrote Swan, "and I am glad she has gone."[41] In San Francisco, the Alaska Commercial Company advised that $1,000 in railway costs could be avoided by cutting the canoe in half. With his appropriation nearly exhausted and Congress unwilling to supplement it, Baird consented. The Fort Rupert canoe, at only half the length of the larger model, survived in one piece.

Next in Swan's esteem to the big canoe were the carved poles. These were certainly the most impressive objects at the Centennial. One came from Fort Simpson, a thirty-foot pole depicting the Bear Mother, Thunderbird, "Cutting Nose," and Grizzly Bear motifs, with two impressively extended beaks. Swan had secured it on his *Wolcott* voyage with the help of Crosby and Morrison. They arranged for some Tsimshian to clean and repaint it, though the back was left with "some of the moss, which indicates its age." Crosby bought another pole, a Kwakiutl column at Alert Bay. But Swan thought more of his Haida pole than either the Tsimshian or the Kwakiutl pole. He ·had himself initiated the arrangements in Kasaan for it to be specially carved after finding he could purchase no existing pole there.[42] Charles Baronovich, the resident trader, had overseen the project and arranged transportation to Port Townsend without charge. For shipping to Philadelphia, Swan cut the Tsimshian pole in two and the Alert Bay pole into four, but he insisted on sending the new Kasaan pole whole. The eventual freight charges on it were enormous.

At least as important as these poles was a complete house front, procured by Crosby and the work of the oldest man in Fort Simpson. Consisting of ten planks, each four to five feet wide and eight to ten feet high, it showed a "salt-water bear" in the center doorway and killerwhales to each side. Crosby had it repainted with native pigments. Swan judged such a specimen as "very difficult to obtain" and this the only front he could procure at any price.[43]

These objects, reassembled as wholes where necessary, stood prominently in the U. S. Government Building; the house planks and one pole were placed outside the building. They evoked the wonder if not the admiration of visitors. Published impressions speak of "rude carvings," of idols "made into the most outlandish and grotesque shapes," and posts that resembled Chinese or Hindu workmanship.[44]

A writer for *Atlantic Monthly* wrote of house fronts "daubed with the most grotesque and barbarous devices, among which a lidless, browless eye recurs with disquieting frequency," and of poles "rudely carved into a series of hideous monsters one on top of the other, painted in crude colors." Some figures, the writer continued, have a distinct but deformed resemblance to man, some to lower animals, "the mankind having huge noses projecting like pump-handles." This curious but uncomprehending reception of the Northwest Coast objects seems characteristic of the general response to the Indian display. William Dean Howells was only slightly exaggerating in his description of the Indian as perceived by the exhibition viewer as 'a hideous demon, whose malign traits can hardly inspire any emotion softer than abhorrence.'[45] As an educational display, Baird's Indian exhibit was not a success. The ethnological materials were merely repellent curiosities.

Swan's 1875–76 work for the United States government was the first major commissioned collecting on the Northwest Coast. On an officially paid salary for months, given a budget of $3,000, later raised to $10,000, the precedent was an impressive one, even if flawed by inappropriate execution. Baird, accustomed to receiving collections from government surveys, had little idea of how to direct his own expedition to the remote areas in which Swan labored. It was at best naive to have expected Swan to operate efficiently with no cash advances and payment in currency drafts. There was no bank to honor drafts in Port Townsend; the closest American ones were in Portland and San Francisco. Swan was slow in realizing the constraints of government procedures, but he was not responsible for their inappropriateness. Baird seemed unsympathetic, even obtuse, in comprehending Swan's problem and slow in alleviating it. As a result, time was lost, trips were not taken, and specimens not collected.

Swan, despite his long residence on the coast, proved somewhat less expert than he had intimated. He did not really know the country north of Victoria and his acquaintance with the north coast Indians was limited to the groups he casually met at Port Townsend, Neah Bay, or Victoria. He seemed surprised to find the Tlingit and Kaigani Haida villages virtually deserted in June and July, their occupants having left for their customary fishing areas. Yet he proved reasonably adept in securing assistance, relying quite wisely and appropriately on deputized agents — on commercial traders at Fort Simpson, Kasaan, Barclay Sound, Sitka, and Bella Bella, on missionaries at Neah Bay and Fort Simpson, and on Commissioner Powell. These agents proved effective in gathering material, but tended to be even more casual than Swan in describing and cataloguing their objects.

The collection itself was comprehensive, both in ethnic distribution and in range of specimens. It included materials from the Makah and Nootka, from the Coast Tsimshian, Bella Bella, Kaigani Haida, and Tlingit. The Salish, the major group closest to Swan's home, were under-represented. He did not consider the work of the natives of nearby Victoria and southern Vancouver Island or of the Fraser Valley sufficiently interesting. The Kwakiutl, too, were under-represented. He had secured little himself at Alert Bay and his contact there, R. H. Hall of the HBC and independent trader Westly Huson, seem not to have fulfilled Swan's expectations of a collection.

His own collection consisted of bowls, baskets (some unfinished), spoons, daggers, hats, clubs, gambling sticks, rattles, and masks. He included tools, such as a stone hammer, curved wood-carving knives, bark-scraping knives, and paint brushes. His acquisition of dried berry cakes and a "string of Indian glue made of dried fish tongues" was certainly not made on aesthetic but on ethnological grounds. He bought newly made, non-traditional material, especially jewelry, without compunction. In addition to the bracelets from the Cassiar procured through Powell, he bought seventeen silver bracelets (at $2–$3 each), earrings and finger rings, two of which were embellished with gold and cost $3.75 each. A lady's silver belt-buckle cost him $7.50, considerably more than the price of masks, rattles, or, indeed, anything except Chilkat shawls, a copper, and a fine, richly carved and inlaid horn dish.

Swan had a high appreciation for new items of artistry, whether in argillite or silver. He did stop short at "fancy articles" carved for the Sitka trade and differentiated between these, with no scientific interest, and Haida argillite, which had "an ethnological value in being the totems of the tribe and as indicating tribal customs." His willingness to accept modern productions seems part of his almost complete lack of bias toward "ancient" artifacts, and it raised some critical comment about his collecting. His almost perverse preference for current products was certainly reflected in his decision to ship the new Kaigani pole entire while cutting up the two older posts, as well as in a revealing statement he made to Baird in January 1876: "My experience of the past year shews me just how I could work to get up a magnificent collection and have every article made new."[46] In the meantime, he was hardly able to collect at all.

His deep disappointment at not being sent to the great Philadelphia exhibition, at not being permitted to install and arrange his own collection, brought a personal crisis that may have been abetted by a bout of drinking. For a time he was quite ill, claiming that his doctor attributed it to "a state of great mental depression, caused by the terrible disappointment of not being able to be in Washington to arrange my collection." Flu, a chill, then a violent attack of erysipelas developed in his head. He lay feverish and unconscious for three days.[47] When he recovered he was forced to realize that the great collecting days of the Centennial were past. Baird was again without special appropriations; the Smithsonian was back to a shoestring budget.

As the Centennial Exhibition closed its doors in November 1876, Spencer Baird busied himself with persuading foreign exhibitors to leave the contents of their displays with the National Museum. This material, together with that from the U. S. Government Building, amounted to 406 tons and required 42 boxcars to haul from Philadelphia to Washington. The Smithsonian building, already overcrowded, was entirely inadequate to accommodate the vast amounts of newly acquired material. While most went into temporary storage at the Washington Armory, Baird and Henry began a campaign on Capitol Hill for a new museum building.

In the meantime, the assistant secretary had temporarily to dampen his accumulative instincts. Although retaining a special interest in American anthropology as "the most interesting subject of research at the present day," he no longer had at his disposal the extraordinary sums of money occasioned by the Centennial Exhibition. He was reduced to making "every possible effort . . . to invite contributions of facts and materials on this subject."[48] Baird returned to the voluntary services of Swan and people like him.

The interest of his Washington Territory correspondent was undiminished by the frustrations and disappointments of 1875–76. Swan wanted particularly to get to the Queen Charlotte Islands. They had become somewhat of an obsession to him ever since he had worked with Kitkune and his friends in 1873, and what he had seen of their Kaigani kinsmen in Alaska increased the allure of "the unknown islands." Secretary Henry tried to interest Major Powell, director of the U. S. government's Rocky Mountain Survey, in sponsoring an expedition by Swan to the Charlottes. Powell asked for an estimate of costs, but nothing came of the idea.

Baird did arrange for another Alaska voyage on the *Wolcott* in 1878, but the cutter had already left Port Townsend by the time his letter reached Swan. With no opportunity for travel and no money for purchases, Swan's collecting was minor. He sent nothing to Washington in 1877, only some fishes and small Haida pieces in 1878. In the next year he was back in Neah Bay, now as customs collector for the Treasury Department and sending east what Makah material — fish lines and nets made of nettle, fishes, and shells — that could be procured at little or no expense.

In 1881 Baird could authorize only fifty dollars for purchases, allowing Swan to buy a fine Clayoquot sealing club and a few other pieces. Swan pleaded to be allowed to go with Powell on the commissioner's cruise that summer, but was told that inadequate appropriations made an expedition impossible. Swan had to "be content to wait as Mr. Micawber did, 'for something to turn up.' "[49] The Charlottes remained "unknown islands."

With such a lean budget Baird was fortunate that year to find another enthusiastic volunteer for Northwest Coast duty: John J. McLean, a member of the U. S. Signals Service and just posted to the new station at Sitka. Motivated, much like Swan, by a sense of contribution to science, McLean was honored "to have my name enrolled in the ranks of that noble army of 'Truthseekers' " arrayed under the Smithsonian's banners. He promised Baird, "the worthy chief" of that scientific army, that he would do all he could "to accomplish the special work you have assigned to me in this portion of Alaska," a promise he fulfilled with enthusiastic alacrity. Within weeks he had disposed of the $30 allotted him, sending a collection of mortars, shamanic charms, pipes, and a deerskin dance headdress.[50]

McLean's parcel was greatly welcomed on the Mall, but his letters, filled with news of intense collecting activities in southeast Alaska, were very disquieting. The Rev. Sheldon Jackson, McLean reported, had paid a flying visit to Sitka and, laying out some two hundred dollars, had bought nearly everything available. The new Presbyterian missionary to the Chilkat, Eugene S. Willard, whom McLean had hoped to enlist for the Smithsonian, was already engaged with Jackson to collect for their Princeton alma mater. Rev. S. Hall Young at Fort Wrangell was accumulating a fine collection. Captain John M. Vanderbilt of the Northwest Trading Company had a small but unique one; Paul Schulze, the company's president, was making a collection for the Berlin museum through his Alaska agents. More ominous, McLean reported that two Germans — "scientific gentlemen, connected with the Berlin Museum" — were to spend the winter among the Chilkat Indians and make extensive collections. "Such is the present outlook," McLean wrote, but he was certain that, given authorization and an advance before the sailing of the Northwest Trading Company's *Favorite* in October, he could at least be "in the field before these German gentlemen."[51]

Baird was concerned but hardly alarmed by these reports of competition in the field. He was certain that the Institution in the long run could outdistance the efforts of Rev. Jackson and his Presbyterian missionaries, but he nevertheless wrote Jackson to secure his aid in the National Museum's cause, stressing that "nowhere so well as in Washington will these things come under the notice of our law-givers and the best portion of the American population" and serve as resources for "extended treatises." He wrote similarly to Captain Vanderbilt. As for the two Germans, brothers Aurel and Arthur Krause, Baird had met them in Washington in the spring and understood that they were to winter in northeast Siberia. They would probably not be an interference. He nevertheless authorized McLean to act immediately, instructions which enabled the Signals officer to secure a fine 142-piece collection on the fall voyage of the *Favorite*.[52]

Baird was in fact behind in his information about the Krause brothers. After two months in Siberia, they gave up the idea of wintering on the barren Chukchi Peninsula and headed for Alaska, where they had been invited to stay as the guest of Schulze's Northwest Trading Company at the Chilcoot post of agent George Dickinson and Sarah, his native wife. When Aurel appeared in Sitka in the spring, "with the special object of securing all the Ethnological specimens he could purchase in town," McLean had anticipated him by using a further hundred dollar authorization to purchase the largest collection of stone and bone implements and carvings he had ever seen at one time. Naturally Krause, who became McLean's guest, "seemed to regret very much that he was not in time to secure the collection."[53]

At about the time Baird realized that he had been in error about the Krauses' plans, he heard of the expedition to British Columbia of J. Adrian Jacobsen and of Commissioner Powell's large collection for New York City's American Museum of Natural History. Baird's limited resources on the Northwest Coast were further curtailed by McLean's bitter dispute with the customs commissioner at Sitka, William Gouverneur Morris, which forced the Signals Office to transfer McLean to California, then to Nebraska. Baird was short of money and without his valuable southeast Alaska correspondent just at a time when the scramble for Northwest Coast Indian specimens was most decidedly on.

Baird, with Swan and his government service personnel in Alaska, had had almost unchallenged possession of the Northwest Coast for so long that he regarded it as almost a proprietary region of the Smithsonian and its National Museum. Some collections had escaped — Lieutenant Fast's as early as 1869, and there had been the Pinart threat of 1871–72 and 1875–76 and Swan's mutterings about Dutch interest and Steindachner — but the Smithsonian's priority in time, its advantages in opportunities, and its preeminence in the United States had allowed it an easy near-monopoly of the field, which Baird assumed to be an almost natural position. In fact, the Smithsonian, relying on its old correspondent, donor, and surveys system, was quite ill-equipped for the challenges of the 1880s, a decade of rapid growth of ethnological interest and sophistication and of museums backed by funds for acquisitions and even for expeditions.

The Northwest Coast scramble, so dramatically discussed in Baird's 1881 correspondence, will be viewed more thoroughly in chapter 3. It had been anticipated in 1878 by G. M. Dawson, a geologist for the Canadian government, who collected a fine assortment of specimens from the Queen Charlotte Islands. The following year Commissioner Powell made a collection for Ottawa's Indian Affairs Department, and two years later contracted to make a collection for the American Museum, the first commissioned collection since Swan's Centennial commission. Powell's work was of greater importance than Sheldon Jackson's efforts on behalf of Princeton Theological Seminary and Princeton College, but neither matched the significance of the sudden appearance in 1881–82 of German collectors into the region.

The Bremen Geographical Society's Krause expedition collected ethnological and natural history material from Alaska, and the Berlin Museum für Völkerkunde sent J. A. Jacobsen solely in search of ethnological materials. While Baird was vexed with competition from Princeton and New York, those rivals at least kept the material for American repositories. The Canadian collections were small and taken from their own territory. European collectors, however, were a different and wholly undesirable kind of competition.

Baird had always been sensitive to foreign collectors. He had fretted about Pinart in 1873 and as recently as 1879 had again been alarmed by what had to be quite out-of-date reports of the

Pinart–de Cessac expedition to the West Coast. He wrote in his annual report that some of the most interesting archaeological locations in the United States were being systematically explored and their "finds" removed by foreign governments. The French were singled out as being diligently occupied in collecting prehistoric remains in California with plans to extend the work into New Mexico and Arizona and into Oregon and Alaska. Already "many tons of the choicest objects" had been shipped to Paris.[54]

Removal of irreplaceable material from American territory was a cause of regret, and Baird reinforced the message in a letter to the speaker of the House of Representatives which asked for support for the new Bureau of Ethnology's plans for a comprehensive investigation of North American Indians. Amply provided foreigners were carrying away American materials — "almost in shiploads" — to foreign museums. It might be neither practical nor desirable for the United States to follow the example of Denmark, Greece, Mexico, and other countries in establishing antiquities export legislation; "we may, however, prevent it in the future by our pre-occupying the ground." An appropriation of ten to twenty thousand dollars annually would enable the National Museum "to defy foreign competition." Unless some action were taken soon, he wrote in 1880, it will be necessary "to depend upon European museums for investigating the antiquities of the United States." Now in 1882 he was exasperatedly angry. "I wish there was some law," he wrote to Swan, that prohibited foreigners from "coming in and carrying off all our treasures." He had no objection to their taking sketches and photographs, but "the specimens themselves should come to American establishments."[55]

The wrath of Spencer Baird at Jacobsen's immense collection and the smaller but significant collection of the Krause brothers spurred him to action. He regretted that the National Museum had lacked the means to anticipate these foreigners, but he intended to find better opportunities in the future. "What is past is gone," he wrote, but now "we are somewhat better off" and could "try to recover as much as possible in lost ground."[56]

Two things had altered his circumstances. As chairman of the U. S. Fish Commission, Baird had received a significant appropriation to prepare an exhibition for the 1883 International Fisheries Exposition in London. Since establishing the Fish Commission in 1871, he had taken its work as seriously as his responsibilities to the Smithsonian, but often the two roles were complementary and even interchangeable. The exhibit that he and G. Brown Goode had prepared for the 1880 Berlin Fisheries Exhibition had contained a small number of items demonstrating aboriginal fishing practices — spears, hooks, lines, and nets. More important, the U. S. display had been so overwhelmingly impressive that the exhibition judges had awarded the Emperor's prize personally to Baird. With such a precedent, Fish Commissioner Baird was determined to sustain the reputation gained at Berlin and to spare no effort in creating a display second to none for London.

Congress, with the national pride involved and a subject so practical as commercial fisheries, succumbed to Baird's argument that he could hardly redisplay his earlier Berlin effort; it allowed $20,000 for the creation of a new and comprehensive installation. While Baird was intent upon surpassing both his own effort and that of any other maritime nation, at the same time he intended to use the appropriation to recover some of the "lost ground" on the Northwest Coast. The keen and frustrated Swan could be employed to collect fisheries material, including native examples.

The second favorable alteration was Major Powell's creation of a Bureau of Ethnology and its transfer from the Interior Department to Smithsonian auspices. While Powell claimed that his Bureau was "only a nominal branch of the Smithsonian," Baird, now secretary since Henry's death in 1878, had a different conception of its status. He felt no compunction in using a portion of Powell's comparatively large appropriation, soon $40,000 annually, for his own collecting purposes. In 1882 he reserved $5,000 for collecting in Alaska and elsewhere "where foreigners are engaged in competition with our own collectors," and was even more emphatic the following year on his right to a piece of Powell's money. He had found, he told the Major, that Congress was interested only in increasing the National Museum's ethnological collections and his "most potent argument" to the appropriations committees "has been the assertion that unless we occupy the field at once, we shall find ourselves anticipated therein by the emissaries of foreign governments." The Bureau's work in the Southwest was very gratifying, but "the region which hitherto has not received enough of the attention of the Bureau of Ethnology is that in the extreme north-western part of the continent, — one more interesting, perhaps, than any other, and now being most rapidly depleted by foreign emissaries." Swan, he concluded, would be given $2,000, possibly even $3,000, from the reserved funds.[57]

Swan was put to work in September 1882 as "Assistant and Collector for the Fish Commission" (he had, of course, his own official stationery) at a salary of $125 a month. He quickly discovered the impact which increased tourism and other collectors had made upon conditions since his last commissioned collecting seven years earlier and complained that what the tourists had not swept up, foreign agents had. He had heard by now of both Jacobsen and the Krauses, but he had the latter jumbled into "August Krause or Krawser" and responsible for shipping fifteen tons of choice articles from the Queen Charlottes (the Krause brothers never touched the Charlottes). This bit of misinformation provoked the usual expression of regret that he had not been able to go with Dawson or Powell to the Charlottes; instead of Haida material sitting in unopened cases in Ottawa or added to the treasures of the Berlin museum, he would have secured a splendid collection for Washington.[58] The depletion of artifacts and the exhorbitant prices paid by foreign collectors and summer tourists made collecting more difficult and it took him an inordinate length of time to gather his first installment.

Baird's priority in 1882 was for specimens relating to whaling, sealing, and fishing and he instructed Swan to collect all such articles as was possible to procure. "I should like to show at London," he wrote, "a more complete collection of Northwest coast fishing equipment than Canada will have on the occasion." That rival, in any case, was easy to outdo, but Baird was also looking after the interests of his museum. It did not matter greatly if all the collections did not reach Washington in time to be forwarded to London; they would in any case be put to use in the general display at the National Museum. Nor did he limit acquisitions to fisheries. "Get all you can of other illustrations of the Ethnology and Archaeology of the Northwest."[59]

The Fisheries Exposition appropriation was merely the first phase of Baird's response to foreign incursions: with his lien on Major Powell's Bureau of Ethnology appropriation, he could authorize Swan to make that long-delayed summer cruise to the Charlottes. "It is," he wrote, "better late than never." Swan's Fish

Commission salary was extended until July 1883 when he was allotted $300 a month from Powell's Bureau funds, though this amount had to cover all expenses and purchases as well as his salary. The initial authorization was for three months, though Baird hoped, should results justify it, that it might be extended to a total of $2,000. His instructions for the Bureau-funded expedition mixed Fish Commission with National Museum: "You will understand that we want the fullest collection of all kinds, especially of objects connected with the fisheries and with hunting."[60]

Swan could at long last make his expedition to "the unknown islands" of the Queen Charlottes. He had been making itineraries for such a trip since 1875 and his plans were by now fully matured to include a canoe voyage to every village in the group. Earlier in the year he had taken on Johnny Kit Elswa, a Haida from Tanu, as general assistant. Kit Elswa was "the most faithful[,] intelligent and reliable Indian I have seen"; he could show him things on the islands to which foreign collectors had never had access and take him to archaeological sites where few Indians now lived. A group of Kit Elswa's Haida friends, who visited them in March, gave assurance that they would arrange their valuable articles, now stored away in large wooden chests and boxes never opened to tourists and collectors, to be available for Swan's selection, with Johnny as authorized agent "to shew me all their other secret treasures."[61] Under such favorable conditions, Swan was certain he could make a sweep of the Charlottes.

He departed Victoria on June 18 aboard the HBC's *Otter* for his first and only visit to the Queen Charlotte Islands. After brief stops along the Inside Passage where he picked up a few pieces, especially from Rev. Crosby and R. H. Hall, he arrived with Kit Elswa at Masset on June 25. There he remained at quarters provided by Alexander McKenzie of the HBC for far longer than he had intended. He puttered around with fish and marine collections, sketched poles, gathered legends and tales, and made "a fine collection." Kit Elswa was of great service in enabling him to buy at low prices. Of greatest interest to Swan was a set of five copper dancing figures, "very like the copper images of the Aztecs." (The Aztec connection was his pet theory, tolerated but frowned upon by Baird.)[62]

Old chief Edenshaw, whom Swan was to hire as canoesman and pilot to the North Island and around the west coast of

"*James G. Swan and Johnny Kit Elswa, his Haida interpreter, taken after their return from Queen Charlotte Island, B. C., October 1883.*" *Spencer & Hastings, Victoria, photographers. Courtesy of the Jefferson County Historical Society.*

Graham Island, arrived from Fort Simpson on July 9. The party, now including old coast hand James Deans of Victoria, Edenshaw's wife, three men, and two boys, did not leave Masset until August 6. Swan left five cases with over two hundred ethnological and natural history specimens for McKenzie to ship to Victoria.

The first call was the Parry Passage–Cloak Bay area. Both Kiusta and Dadens were long deserted. Edenshaw knew them well; he was chief of the peoples who had migrated from there to Masset and some of the remaining poles and a house were his own. In one house he found a shark's head mask and two fins which he gave to Swan. Swan and Deans found few shell heaps in which to rummage, but Edenshaw pointed out a burial cave on North Island, nearly sixty feet long, in which lay twenty-eight or thirty burial boxes, each containing mummified remains. Near Kiusta was another burial cave in which fragments of boxes and bones were scattered. Edenshaw also identified the gravehouse of Koontz, a shaman. There was little, however, that Swan could take: "the prejudices of the Indians and my overloaded canoe" prevented what "I could easily have done if I had been in a steamer."[63]

Objects were very tempting at the "Skungo" burial cave but more especially at Koontz's gravehouse, where Swan saw a five-foot sceptre carved in the image of a killerwhale, the dorsal fin itself being twenty inches long. But he could hardly chance offending Edenshaw and the other six Indians who were his crew. With Edenshaw's consent, he extracted two tusks from the burial house, expecting to find them to be those of the Mexican wild hog (they turned out to be Asiatic). Deans, however, "took a specimen which was considered the personal and private property" of the shaman and to this desecration the Indians attributed all the bad weather that the party later experienced. Whatever its cause, the difficult weather meant that the navigation of Graham's west coast took twenty days, "made the more tedious by the blatant boasting of our Indian pilot, who by constantly asserting that he is the most powerful chief on the Queen Charlotte Island[s], sought to convince us of the great condescension on his part that he was willing to convey the party to Skidegate."[64]

At Skidegate Swan stayed at the oilworks operated by William Sterling and Alexander McGregor, was reunited with Ellswarsh, a Haida silversmith who had worked with him in Port Townsend two years previous, and spent several days buying artifacts. Again he secured a "fine lot" of Indian objects which left him "well satisfied." On September 4 he and Kit Elswa went with Ellswarsh and four others to the east coast villages of Moresby Island. At Koona Chief Skedans showed them a fine carved chest, but would not name a price. Other things were procurable — dance hats, bows and arrows made of copper and used for dances, and a wood carving of an eagle's claw holding a salmon.

At Tanu or Klue village, he found that Kitkune, the chief who had visited him with the Haida party of 1873, was now dead. A nephew had married old Kitkune's widow and now reigned in his place, heir to his name and property. Swan was welcomed as an old friend. The young chief took him to his unfinished new house, one of the finest and best native-style dwellings Swan had seen, and honored him with a display of ceremonial paraphernalia.

> Young Kitkane opened a secret door skillfully framed into one side of the house so as to be unnoticed even by the careful search and disclosed a chamber or building place where were stowed away for safe keeping the sacred emblems of the old Chief. These are the finest of any I have seen but the young man was not willing to part with many of them and for these he asked a large price. I purchased a few rare and curious masks.[65]

One purchase was more than a mask; it represented Oolalla, a demon who came from the mountains to devour men. The head-piece was a skull and from it descended a perfectly jointed skeleton of wood, the whole so ordered by strings that teeth would gnash and an arm would stretch out to point a bony finger toward an intended victim. So well executed was the piece that "it must have been an object of terror to the savages when used in their midnight incantations by the dim light of the lodge fires."[66]

Although the weather turned bad again, Swan did not mind being storm-bound among the numerous houses, poles, and posts of Tanu. There was more of interest here than in any village he had seen. Indeed, he would have stayed even longer "but the people are not anxious to sell their curiosities, as they have not yet come under missionary influence." Similarly, he had at first little

luck at nearby Skedans, then, just as he was leaving, the natives —
"Indian like" — began to bring their things for sale and he secured
"quite a lot."

Young Kitkune now wanted to back out of the sale of the
things from the hidden closet at Tanu. He was, Swan wrote,
"influenced by his mother, and an old man to whom the dancing
masks I had purchased had a sacred meaning and he disliked to
have the emblem of their secret performances sold to a white
man." But Swan was determined to keep them, thinking them
very similar to Guatemalan pieces. In the end, "young Kitkune let
me have the lot."[67]

Swan returned to Skidegate after his successful tour of Skedans
and Tanu and spent a day on Maude Island, site of New Gold
Harbor village, where he bought some fine masks and an enormous kelp fish line equipped with thirty hooks. The little steamer
Skidegate, used by the oil company, was preparing to go to Victoria, and Swan decided to take her there as he might not have
another chance until spring. He was, moreover, nearing the end
of his appropriation and, as every day new things were coming
in, he was afraid of exceeding it. He arrived back in Victoria on
September 27, having been away over three months. The balance
of his purchases came down on the *Otter* and he shipped all
twenty-nine cases to Washington in mid-November, most of
them too late for the London exhibition.

With his collection on the way to the D. C. Mall, Swan settled
down to his correspondence with Baird. He told the secretary that
he regarded the summer visit as "a mere reconnaisance." He
hoped he would be allowed to return to Tanu for young Kitkune's
big feast in September when he could fully observe the dying
"Tamanowas" dances and he certainly would like to get back
with a steamer to that mummy cave on North Island. He would,
he wrote, have liked to have extended his visit through the winter, but he dared not linger. "I saw so much to purchase that I fear
I have already far exceeded my appropriation."[68]

Indeed he had. His accounts were hopelessly overspent. He had
been given $2,100 and had spent $3,247.82, with most of the
difference owed to the HBC and the Skidegate Oil Works. Part of
the overrun was due to the zeal with which he had collected black
cod at Skidegate; a part was invested in a large argillite collection
he bought from R. H. Hall.

Argillite carving was one of Swan's weak spots. When he received a letter in Masset from Hall, from whom he had already bought a sizable argillite collection for $351, stating that the Fort Simpson trader had located what he considered to be the finest carved stone collection he had ever seen, Swan could not resist. The temptation was made all the greater by McKenzie telling him that the earthquake of October 1880 had buried the island's only slate deposit. This erroneous report caused Swan to believe that these articles, already eagerly sought after, would become increasingly scarce and valuable. Swan, grasping the "rare opportunity," ordered this new Hall collection, sight unseen, for $207. Nearly all of it arrived in Washington broken.

Baird was not very sympathetic to Swan's indebtedness. He had, he reminded him, expressly stipulated that the collection must come within the appropriation. Swan continued to complain about what he considered money due him, suggesting that Baird sell some of the slate carvings to balance the accounts (out of the question, replied Baird; they were entered as government property and, if sold, the funds would go into the Treasury). Baird relented, however, and continued Swan's salary payments until February 1884, thus giving him almost enough to settle his debt. After a few months' lapse, Swan was back on the government payroll once more.[69]

Swan's collection had scarcely arrived in Washington when Baird was suggesting the possibility of yet another summer's expedition, this time for the Cotton Centennial Exposition in New Orleans. When the appropriation materialized in July, Baird was able to authorize another $2,100 for Swan. Although Swan made his usual plans for several excursions, he did not this time travel beyond Neah Bay and Victoria. Instead he secured collections from agents in Bella Coola, Bella Bella, and Alaska. From Capt. C. I. Hooper of the USS *Rush* he bought a scaled-down Cape Flattery whaling canoe, complete with gear of suitable size.

He claimed that the crowds of tourists had run up prices by 200 to 300 percent above the previous year's prices, but, since he had made no trip north, the actual cost to the government was about the same. He again complained of the lack of advance funds (part of his New Orleans salary had to be used to clear his previous year's debt). People on the coast and especially Indians would sell nothing unless for cash, and he was no longer willing to make advances for the government and then be unable to get his pay. "The want of that amount still due me has so crippled and embarrassed me that I have been unable to do what I otherwise could have done."[70]

Swan's most significant pieces in this collection were probably ten carved posts, eight from Bella Bella and two from Bella Coola, and a number of Bella Coola and Haida masks, the latter apparently being those bought (and held back?) the previous year from Kitkune at Tanu.[71] Baird was struck by the Makah canoe, made entirely new and specially painted, and was moved to enquire about the authenticity of the whaling material that Swan had sent him. It all looked so clean and new that it gave an impression of being made expressly for the Smithsonian. Swan explained that whaling gear which had been successfully used became highly prized. An old harpoon staff broken and repaired might be valued at forty-five dollars, while an unused new one could be bought for five dollars. "As the Indians are constantly making all kinds of gear they use, I prefer, when I can, to get the best looking specimens rather than take a lot of old stuff at an enhanced price." Baird could be sure, he continued, that everything sent was actual Indian work and made for use, except, of course, models which were generally made to order.[72]

The Cotton Centennial was Swan's last real work for the Smithsonian and the National Museum. He sent a number of small lots in subsequent years, but after Baird's death in 1887, he began to be passed over by the new men at Washington. Ensign Albert P. Niblack, a young Annapolis graduate who worked for the museum on secondment from the navy, wanted to use Swan's expertise for extensive coastal explorations, but his proposals in 1885 and 1887 came to nothing, as did his 1888 project of having Swan and Kit Elswa come to Washington to help organize the collection. Niblack's own museum publication, *The Coast Indians of Southern Alaska and Northern British Columbia,* an ethnological survey with emphasis upon material culture, gave prominence to Swan's collection and acknowledged his work.[73]

Swan's efforts to obtain further commissions met no response from Washington. He wrote of the opportunity to secure valuable Bella Coola material through Johnny Kit Elswa and announced that the Tanu ceremonial material he could not buy in 1883 was now available. The Indians understood, Swan explained, that their things would be kept in a sacred receptacle and put "in a glass house."[74] But his letters went unheeded in Washington and Swan never returned to his islands. He collected a little for the Chicago World's Fair in 1892 and 1893, partly on behalf of the Washington State exhibition and partly for Franz Boas, who was in charge of the exposition's own Northwest Coast display. Not surprisingly, he again had financial problems: when the state was slow in paying, he spent Boas's advance on its collections. But this was his last effort. He died seven years later, in May 1900, at the age of eighty-two, broke and in debt.

Swan would have like to have been successful, prosperous, and respected. Fortune and character denied this to him, but his contribution to knowledge did bring him a modest share of recognition even in his own lifetime. The praise did not always come undiluted. In 1890 the historian Hubert Howe Bancroft's autobiography gave a short tribute to Swan's work. With no sensitivity, however, he included an account of an 1878 visit to Port Townsend in which he told that he had to wait for Swan to "get sober" before they could meet. "Poor fellow! The demon Drink had long held him in its terrible toils." Swan read Bancroft's *Literary Industries* with mortification.[75] Unfortunately, it was true. He had been an "habitual drunkard" (as the court twice declared) for years, using alcohol, perhaps, to exorcise the disappointments that haunted him.

Swan was a prodigal son of science. He was frequently profligate and sometimes silly.[76] But he had his merits, not least of which was an appreciation of the customs, if not always the manners, of the Northwest Coast Indians, and a willingness to take them seriously. And he left the National Museum with a magnificent collection.

Chapter Three

The French and German Competitors

"ANTHROPOLOGY," Secretary Henry remarked in 1877, "is at present the most popular branch of science."[1] Such an interest could not be confined to Swan and the other friends of the Smithsonian Institution. While the Smithsonian and its U. S. National Museum had a deserved preeminence in American science, it was becoming but one museum among many. Other museums, some old, some new, were responding to the increasing popular and scientific interest in anthropology and to the urgency of salvaging what could yet be saved of primitive man's possessions.

Civic or national pride, combined with capitalist philanthropic affluence, brought new museum foundations or the reorganization and expansion of existing institutions. In Berlin, Paris, London, Vienna, and New York, new dimensions were given to old cabinets or struggling divisions; in Leipzig and Hamburg, in Stockholm and Oslo, even in Seattle, Victoria, and Sitka, new museums were founded in the decade of the 1880s, and others would soon follow. The scramble for Northwest Coast artifacts was an epiphenomenon of this much larger movement, the "Museums Movement" or "Museum Age" of the nineteenth century. Museums of paintings and decorative arts, of natural history

48

and medicine, of folk customs and national history, flourished, established and funded by governments, learned societies, universities, or men of wealth.

Collections of the Classical Age were, of course, as old as the Renaissance, and "artificial curiosities," the odd and arresting productions of exotic peoples, had entered the cabinets of royal, aristocratic, and wealthy connoisseurs for centuries. Anthropological museums frequently grew from such cabinets, and in them, as well, lies the origin of the museums in Leningrad, Madrid, Copenhagen, Vienna, and Berlin. Sometimes museums grew up in capitals of mercantile exploration and trade as institutions to exhibit the curiosities brought back from the far-flung networks of commercial empire. In many ways the ethnological collections of the British Museum belong to this category and the very names of the East India Marine Society Museum, the Congo Museum, and the Übersee Museum announce a major factor of their origin.

The ethnological museum, as a consciously distinct idea, can be traced to the published discussions of Edmé-François Jomard and Phillip Franz von Siebold in the early 1840s, while credit for the earliest foundation has been variously awarded to Leiden (c. 1837), St. Petersburg (c. 1837), and Copenhagen (c. 1841). The idea became a movement in the 1870s with foundations, for example, in Leipzig (1873), Rome (1875), Bremen (1876), Hamburg (1878), and Dresden (1879). The following decade saw a rapid expansion of museum anthropology, a development that was "without parallel even in our own age of museums."[2]

In almost every country of Europe, America, and the British Empire, institutions were founded, reorganized, or expanded. The enormous Christy collection was installed in the British Museum, Oxford University acquired the eccentric ethnological material of General Pitt Rivers, and Baron Anatole von Hügel began to add ethnological specimens to the fledgling Cambridge University archaeology museum. The Rijksmuseum voor Volkenkunde in Leiden was reorganized, and new museums established in Amsterdam, Rotterdam, and The Hague. The Musée du Trocadéro was established in Paris, and others begun in Munich, Oslo, and Stockholm. In Berlin Adolf Bastian opened his separate building, and in Washington the National Museum found expansive new quarters. New York's American Museum and Ottawa's government museum received their core ethnological collections in that decade. Within the Northwest Coast region itself, Seattle, Victoria, and Sitka started new, albeit quite modest, local establishments.

On the Continent there was a tendency for anthropology museums to develop separately or to become distinct foundations. This was true in Berlin, Hamburg, Leipzig, Cologne, Rotterdam, Leiden, Rome, Florence, and Paris. At Bremen, Dresden, Copenhagen, Brussels, and Vienna such collections shared a museum with other departments, most often natural history. Independent anthropological museums were much less common in the English-speaking world. The encyclopaedic British Museum encompassed ethnology along with everything else. So, too, did Bloomsbury's sister institutions at Dublin, Glasgow, Liverpool, and Manchester. The North American tendency was for ethnology to be a part of natural history museums, as at New York, Ottawa, and later Chicago and Brooklyn.

At universities, however, anthropological museums developed as separate institutions. Harvard's Peabody Museum of American Archaeology and Ethnology, founded in 1866, was the first, followed by others at Yale, Oxford, Cambridge, and Pennsylvania. Most museums were universal in their scope, but a few almost naturally limited themselves to their own country or locality. Harvard was American in a hemispheric sense, the Canadian federal museum restricted its collections to those from within its own territories, and the Provincial Museum in Victoria and the Sheldon Jackson Museum in Sitka stuck to ethnic stocks within their own politically defined regions. Washington State was less provincial, encompassing the world, but with an emphasis upon the Pacific region.

The effort of these museums in harvesting the works of primitive peoples around the world had a double impetus behind it. Joined to a growing fascination with primitive mankind was the realization that civilization was rapidly destroying the subject of that interest. "To the general interest in ethnological studies," wrote a Danish museum ethnologist, was added the insight that "it is necessary to use the time to collect before it is too late." As early as 1863 George Gibbs had written of the importance of making immediate collections. From his post in Berlin Adolf Bastian made constant iteration of the most urgent need for the promptest possible actions while Daniel G. Brinton, doyen of American anthropologists, repeated the warning that "the time is short and the opportunity fleeting." Museum officials everywhere felt that "a museum which does not utilize the current moment dooms its further development."[3]

Moreover, many museums began to realize that they could no longer depend upon donations. As long as the goods of primitive peoples had been plentiful, articles often found their way into collections as gifts. With the increased scarcity of ethnographic objects and the consequent competition for them, these pieces began to assume a higher market value and, with that, donations tended to dry up. Museums were finding it necessary to have acquisition budgets, even to launch expeditions to distant parts of the earth, at the same time as the increased sophistication of the new science demanded more methodical collecting policies. While the bulk of museum acquisitions still came from travellers, scientists, naval officers, consuls, and merchants, people with a warm interest in science and at least a modicum of understanding of the purposes of museums, museum professionals realized increasingly that the most valuable material came from specialists able to pursue their studies among the people from whom they collected the objects.[4]

Spencer Baird's major concern about foreign collectors encroaching on the Northwest Coast had been with the French expeditions, to which he called the attention of Congress on more than one occasion. In fact, he need not have worried about the French. The threat to American (or Canadian) antiquities from that source had been the single-minded enthusiasm of amateur Alphonse Pinart, a young man of inherited means.[5] Pinart had met the Americanist Abbé Brasseur de Bourbourg at the Paris International Exposition in 1865, and through this chance meeting Pinart developed a fascination for the natives of America that resulted in extensive travels to the Americas and Polynesia.

In 1871–72 he visited Alaska, spending most of his time in the Aleutian and Kodiak islands. His extensive collection from this area went to the Musée de Boulogne-sur-Mer (and agitated Spencer Baird). In 1875 he set off again, this time with the assistance of the distinguished Léon de Cessac and a plan for extensive exploration of South America and the American Southwest and Northwest. Although endorsed by the French government and given a promise of transportation by the French navy, the expedition was financed by Pinart.

After slowly making his way across the American continent and meeting de Cessac in California, Pinart went to British Columbia in early 1876, where, with the aid of James Deans, a local amateur antiquarian, he dug up some burial cairns and shell heaps in the vicinity of Victoria. After a trip to Cowichan and Nanaimo, he returned to California to join de Cessac on a voyage to Alaska in 1877. The French naval vessel which was to take them was ordered suddenly to Polynesia, and de Cessac was left stranded in Peru while Pinart worked in Tahiti. Pinart's fortune collapsed soon afterwards and he was never able to resume his ambitious anthropological plans.

The archaeological and ethnological collections abandoned in California were retrieved for the ministry of education by the French consul in San Francisco in 1882; storage charges cost the ministry some 3,000 francs. The collection contained, when eventually received at the Trocadéro museum in Paris, thirty-eight Tlingit pieces, as well as odd Umatilla, Klickitat, and Makah items, possibly obtained in San Francisco, but more likely collected by Pinart in the north.

Pinart never returned to the Northwest Coast. The collection he had carried with him, mostly South American and Mexican items, he presented to the Paris museum in 1881. It included two small argillite poles and an intriguing — but now lost — stone mask with a perforated mouth, which had come from a Vancouver Island tumulus. Another mask, acquired the same year from "Mission Alphonse Pinart," is the incredible "sighted twin" stone mask.[6] The catalogue lists its provenance as "a protestant pastor" at "Meqtlakquatla," no doubt the missionary William Duncan (though he was not ordained) at the model village Metlakatla. The Musée de l'Homme's mask is Pinart's major legacy to the Northwest Coast. Supporting himself upon a fragile fortune, unconnected with any institution, Pinart was a self-propelled dilettante and not, excepting always that haunting stone image, a major factor in the collecting process.[7]

Pinart was for a time, it is true, a threat to Baird's American preserve and even a useful foil in his congressional pleas. Shiploads and tons of material did not go to France. Though the total quantity of Alaska and California material was not negligible,

Baird's apprehensions about French expeditions in the 1870s were exaggerated, probably deliberately so. His anxieties about German collectors were not.

Baird's first intimation of German interest had come from McLean's Sitka letters, which reported that Northwest Trading Company president Paul Schulze was collecting for the Berlin museum and that two scientists connected with the same institution were to winter among the Chilkats. These were in fact two separate initiatives. Schulze's was a casual collection, auxiliary to the major Jacobsen expedition being sent out by Berlin, while the two Krause brothers represented the polar research fostered by Bremen's scientific and mercantile interests. Unlike Pinart's effort, these were institutional expeditions supported by the advanced resources of Imperial Germany. Science in the new German Empire was organized and ambitious, backed by the same rapidly accumulating wealth and vested with similar national aspirations as in America.

The Krause expedition was sponsored by Bremen's Geographical Society, a scientific body which, under its earlier name of Verein für die Nordpolarfahrt, had established a reputation for the support of polar and sub-polar research expeditions, notably to East Greenland and western Siberia. Though based upon a large subscribing membership, its financial support came principally from the Hanseatic city's rich commercial middle classes.

The Bering Strait expedition was made possible by the generosity of George Albrecht, partner in a major tobacco trading firm and a council member of the society. He declared himself ready to stand the cost of an exploration of the Chukchi Peninsula and its surrounding coasts. Drs. Aurel and Arthur Krause, instructors in the natural sciences at one of Berlin's most advanced *Gymnasia,* were chosen to undertake the expedition.[8] Their broad scientific knowledge and especially their recent field experiences in Norway made them suitable choices for an expedition expected to be in the field for up to a year and a half. Its purpose was broadly scientific: to explore the coasts of the Bering Sea as far as circumstances might permit, to investigate the interior of the Chukchi Peninsula should that be possible, and then to extend their research into northern Alaska. The weight of their work would be directed toward natural science and ethnographic collections.[9]

The brothers left Bremen on the *Rhein* in April 1881, stopping over in Washington, D. C., for discussions with Baird and Dall, then proceeding to San Francisco. There they found transportation to the Siberian coast difficult. More important, their nagging doubts about the plan to winter on the Chukchi were fully confirmed by what they were told of local conditions. They quickly realized that they could not properly organize and maintain a collection while living in a tent and having no external communications. At this juncture Paul Schulze offered them facilities for the winter in Alaska at one of his Northwest Trading Company posts. Thus, when their work on the Asian side of the straits was ended by the season's close, they arrived at Haines, near the head of Lynn Canal, via San Francisco, on December 23, 1881.[10]

The Krauses were put up by George Dickinson, the company's resident trader, in a warehouse beside his cabin. Sarah Dickinson, his wife, was a Tsimshian schooled at Duncan's Metlakatla mission. She had been commissioned by Sheldon Jackson's U. S. Board of Education to open a school for the Chilkats with whose language and customs she was intimate. Despite Mrs. Dickinson's Christian education, she actively participated in the affairs of the local Chilkat Tlingits. The Krauses found her knowledgeable about the Indians of the entire region and obtained from her a very great portion of their information on behavior, customs, traditions, and particularly clan and tribal divisions. There was no Indian village at Haines, though nine houses and as many as two hundred natives had been attracted by the store and canneries of Portage Bay; four old villages were not far away, three up the Chilkat River and another up the Chilcoot. Klukwan, the largest of the Chilkat towns, was presided over by the ancient Chief Shotridge.

While the Krauses spent much of their time in natural history collecting and some of it merely shut up in their quarters during the exceptionally cold and snowy winter, they were able to learn a great deal. In January they visited Klukwan with Presbyterian minister Eugene Willard and for eight days were honored guests in the house of Shotridge. They were fortunate to witness both the sacred celebrations proclaiming a new shaman and the secular brewing of hootchinoo — part of the preparations for a commercial expedition to the interior Dené. They were presented a staff as a gift and collected a number of household items.

Arthur Krause remained the summer, collecting in natural history and pursuing geographical research, especially with the Indians of the "grease trails" to the Yukon. Aurel left Haines in early April, travelling with the company steamer. He visited Heena village, then went to Killisnoo where he spent several days as the guest of Carl Spuhn, Schulze's brother-in-law and another German official in the company. Arriving at Sitka late in April, he received a welcome from McLean, generously friendly now that he had preempted all likely purchases for the Smithsonian. After a few stops south of Sitka, Krause made his way back to Germany, arriving in Bremen late in July.

The Krause collection was a compact one of about 178 items, mostly made up of clothing, spoons, knives, bowls, paint brushes, and other household items. There were a number of rattles and musical instruments, but no masks. Perhaps the prizes were the armour suits and helmets — five cuirasses of thick leather, one of which reached the knees while others covered only the upper body. Some of the Tlingit collection remained in Bremen's museum, but portions were sold to Hamburg and Berlin.[11] These last joined the enormous shipments being received by the Prussian Museum für Völkerkunde and its expansive director, Adolf Bastian. In Bastian one finds a counterpart to Spencer Baird and an ethnologist whose acquisitive instincts matched those of any nineteenth-century museum director.

Adolf Bastian was one of that breed of prodigiously energetic and productive scholars and organizers whose achievements leave one in breathless awe.[12] He studied law, then medicine, travelled for eight years as a ship's surgeon to Oceania, South America, Asia, and West Africa. The experience turned him to ethnology and he published his discoveries almost immediately upon his return to Germany. From then on frequent publications alternated with equally frequent travel, yet Bastian found time and energy to found the journal *Zeitschrift für Ethnologie,* to help organize the Berlin Society for Anthropology, Ethnology, and Prehistory, and — more important here — to establish the Museum für Völkerkunde as a separate entity within the Prussian state museums.

He had joined the staff of the royal museums in 1869 and began both a personal and a museum campaign for more ethnological specimens. The archaeological and ethnographic collections were then housed in the lower floor of the Neues Museum on Museum Island in the Spree River, but that building, erected in the 1840s, was far too confining for the growing collection and for the ambition of Bastian, who became chief of the ethnology section in 1873. By then his collecting proclivities were omnivorous and insatiable. He personally collected almost two thousand pieces from South Asia alone, but he made the museum the recipient of an avalanche of ethnographic materials from all the islands and continents of the world. His sources were the Foreign Office, the Imperial Navy, and other government agencies, but as often private German travellers, missionaries, merchants — compatriots from the farthest corners of the earth.

Bastian's great achievement was the building of a separate museum of ethnology, begun in 1880 and completed only in December 1886. The first major museum building dedicated solely to anthropology and ethnology, it housed extensive and ever-increasing collections, partly inherited but largely gathered under Bastian's direction. The building was on Königgratzerstrasse, only a hundred steps from Potsdamer Platz. The four-story early Renaissance pile attempted to display its contents to their best advantage by generous light sources and by a minimum of interior decoration. The ground floor of this almost personal monument to Bastian was occupied by the archaeological collection, most particularly Heinrich Schliemann's spectacular Homeric discoveries. The next two floors were dedicated to ethnological collections, the first to *naturvölker,* the second to *kulturländer* (a peculiar German distinction roughly equivalent to primitive and semi-civilized; North America belonged to one, Mesoamerica to the other). Osteological materials — skulls and skeletons — had their place on the top floor.

The dedication of the building was a state occasion. Crown Prince Friedrich Wilhelm, in the uniform of his Second Silesian Dragoon regiment, represented the Kaiser. Prince Wilhelm, Princess Viktoria, and the Princesses Friedrich von Hohenzollern were on hand. Count Bismarck was present, though the minister of culture presided. The speeches by Minister Gustav von Gossler and the crown prince were redolent of scientific dedication and patriotism. Gossler praised the new museum as a milestone in the development of knowledge. It closed, he said, that deeply felt gap between collections dedicated to art and those devoted to the natural sciences. At the same time, with its creation, the German Empire stepped into the first rank in its engagement to anthropological research. He dedicated the museums simultaneously "to the service of science and the honor of the Fatherland."[13]

Bastian's ambitions required a building dedicated solely to anthropology. By the end of the century his museum contained the largest ethnographic collection in the world and possibly a greater number of specimens than any other two museums combined.[14] Bastian was an obsessive collector, not merely because of a personal acquisitive instinct, but also because of the urgency demanded by the science of man. Everywhere primitive cultures were being deluged by advancing civilization; of that he was personally aware from his own travel. Unlike Troy or Nineveh, the past of these peoples, once it was gone, could never be reconstructed; "it was lost forever, submerged and forgotten." His appeals were filled with an urgent desperation. "Each year, each month perhaps, can decide the difference between Being and Non-Being, between winning and losing, and in the latter case, total loss." Ethnology dealt with unlettered people and if their objective traces were lost a great lacunae would forever exist in the scientific view of the earth. Collections were ethnology's documents; an ethnology museum was as dependent upon its specimens as a natural history museum. Their loss was, like some extinct invertebrate which left no fossil, irreplaceable. Ethnological items were the building blocks for a comparative ethnology that would be able to supply significant elements to the knowledge of mankind.[15]

Through the accumulation of extensive collections and with the assistance of that inductive method which was conquering all branches of science, Bastian hoped to build up a science of the psychology of man. He was not only a dedicated museum builder, but also the founding father of German ethnology and its leading theoretician. The similarities in human productions were so strikingly frequent even among widely separated and vastly different peoples that one could not but be impressed with the commonality of their basic ideas. The museum's collection offered a repository of examples of what he called *elementargedanken,* the basic ideas of mankind, as well as their expression in multiformed *völkergedanken* in various geographical areas of the world.

When Bastian first assumed the directorship of the ethnographic section of the Neues Museum, the collection possessed a few Northwest Coast items, the most important of which were nine pieces dubiously attributed to Cook and a portrait mask collected on the *Princess Louise* expedition of 1834.[16] Bastian's interest in the Northwest Coast area was not stimulated until 1880 when he stopped in Portland on his return from Polynesia. Along the Columbia River he observed the almost complete destruction of native culture by European contact, but he heard reports of more northerly people not yet annihilated though imminently in danger.

A conversation with Dall of the Smithsonian Institution, just returned from an Alaska trip, confirmed Bastian's impression of the ethnological significance of the northern coast as a meeting place of the two great continents, as well as his fear that civilizing influences were rapidly altering native life in that region. This experience in Oregon impressed him deeply. It left him, he said, "without peace, anxious as I was about how things might be with the more northern tribes." Too little was known of them and his curiosity was made all the more painful by the blank spot in his own museum's collections.[17]

The little material that could be found in American museums only made the European poverty more conspicuous. The Northwest Coast, he wrote Dall in July 1881, "presents to my eyes *one of the richer fields* for ethnological studies, and I often feel the wish returning, to send there a special collector for our Museum." He asked Dall for advice on good places to collect even though he doubted that the museum would have the means to undertake such an expedition; nonetheless, "I should like to be prepared, *if* by chance an opportunity *might* offer, as sometimes happens, unexpectedly."[18]

In fact, Bastian was on the eve of putting together both means and man. Finding a person to send to the coast was the lesser obstacle. A seasoned collector, Johan Adrian Jacobsen, sat idly in Hamburg awaiting a call from Berlin. The problem was money. The size of the Prussian state grant to the museum, like the congressional appropriation to the Smithsonian, did not allow for the travel expenses, salary, and purchase money of a long expedition. Bastian found the solution in private philanthropy, adroitly combining the advantage of a private museum's trustee system with that of a state-funded institution.

As a museum director and university professor he moved in the right social stratum, his Society for Anthropology, Ethnology, and Prehistory allowed a self-identification of those interested in such subjects, and he was particularly fortunate in having in Berlin the amateur ethnologist August von A. Le Coq, a man of wealth who knew others of like means. Working with banker Isador Richter, Le Coq assembled a group of rich Prussians, almost all of them Berlin bankers and businessmen, into the Ethnologisches Hilfscomité or Ethnological Assistance Committee. Full membership was open to those contributing 3,000 Reichsmarks or more: consequently, the committee was originally composed of only eleven members who subscribed fully 40,000 marks among them. (One of the members was Bismarck's banker, Gerson von Bleichröder.)[19] Two days after its formation on July 22, 1881, Bastian summoned his collector to Berlin. By now he had on hand the Hilfscomité's money, 11,000 marks of which he intended to entrust to J. Adrian Jacobsen.

Jacobsen was a thirty-four-year-old Norwegian, a fisherman's son, bred to an arduous life well within the Arctic Circle. As a youth he had followed a brother from Tromsø to Hamburg, had a spotty career at sea, then worked a while in Valparaiso. Returning to Hamburg, he fell into the service of Carl Hagenbeck, proprietor of Hagenbeck's Tierpark, wholesale dealer in animals and, most recently, impressario of ethnic exhibitions (völkerschauungen).[20]

Hagenbeck's business, inherited from his father, had fallen into bad days in the mid-seventies and, to arrest the decline, he expanded in a new direction by importing in 1874 not just a herd of reindeer but six Lappland herders and all their household goods. When put on exhibition in Hamburg, Berlin, and Leipzig, the Lapps were a tremendous success. "Our guests," Hagenbeck recalled, "were genuine primitives, unfamiliar with the glossy politeness of Europe," a condition illustrated by the Lapp mother unembarrassingly breast-feeding her child in public.[21] Hagenbeck continued his ethnic shows with a summer tour of Nubians and their dromedaries, and his desire for another winter exhibition led to Jacobsen's commission to obtain six Eskimos from Greenland to tour Paris, Brussels, Cologne, Berlin, and Copenhagen. Jacobsen secured a second group of Lapps, toured with some Patagonians, and in 1880 voyaged to Labrador for more Eskimos. Then tragedy struck at the Jardin d'Acclimatisation in Paris: one of the Eskimos died.

The Labradorian's death was a severe blow to a larger and already crippled enterprise. Jacobsen and Hagenbeck had put money into a ship, the *Eisbär*, for the Labrador voyage, but things had gone badly. Terrible weather and serious illness had prevented any seal hunting, a necessary adjunct for covering the trip's costs. The plan had been next to use the ship for a long collecting voyage to Patagonia, Easter Island, Polynesia, British Columbia, and Alaska. Now the death of the Eskimo cast a pall over the entire scheme; Hagenbeck, no doubt feeling the double effect of guilt and adverse publicity, had lost heart for further ethnic expositions. His family, moreover, was hostile to Jacobsen, blaming him for the whole Eskimo-*Eisbär* imbroglio. It was plain that Hagenbeck had little future need for Jacobsen.[22] It was at this point that the Norwegian offered the *Eisbär* expedition to Bastian.

Jacobsen had known Bastian for some years, principally because some of his Eskimo collections had ended up in Bastian's museum. In May 1881, following a written proposal, he visited the director. Bastian expressed interest and Le Coq indicated to Jacobsen that he and Bastian were attempting to assemble the means to send the ship on a two- or three-year expedition to the Pacific. It was not long before the Hilfscomité came into existence and Jacobsen was called to Berlin.

One other factor seems to have played a role in the concatenation of circumstances that led to Jacobsen's expedition to the Northwest. Certainly Bastian's estimation of the ethnological importance of the region and his concern at the impending disappearance of the natives were major considerations, but a more proximate event must have increased Bastian's urgency: the news that the Bremen Geographical Society was sending Aurel and Arthur Krause to Siberia and Alaska. For any nineteenth-century museum director, competition in a prized area was motivation enough and Jacobsen reported that Bastian feared that the Krause party "might gather up almost everything.[23] The collector was instructed to leave quickly and proceed directly to British Columbia. The leisurely *Eisbär* voyage was dropped.

Bastian's urgency and Jacobsen's own eagerness enabled the newly commissioned collector to depart Hamburg aboard the *Australia* on July 21, 1881, one week after receiving definite word of his engagement. Jacobsen travelled directly to San Francisco, took the *Dakota* from there to Victoria, and then the first available boat north. The Port Essington trader Robert Cunningham happened to be a fellow passenger on the *Grappler*. Cunningham had been trading on the coast for almost twenty years and could introduce the novice collector to coastal commerce by acting as purchasing agent for him as the boat stopped in Alert Bay and Bella Bella. Then, turning vendor, he sold Jacobsen a number of his own curios at Port Essington.

Jacobsen went with his host to Kitkatla, his first "real" Indian village, where he was able to hire a canoe and crew for the trip across the strait to Skidegate. At Kitkatla he found artifacts very expensive, partly because Israel Powell had been there less than two months before and partly because the Indians conspired to keep the prices high. Similarly, his crew demanded a high fee for the trip and, with the village united for the purpose, he had to submit to the extortion. After a very difficult trip across Hecate Strait, he reached Skidegate, then proceeded to the villages of Klue, Skedans, and Cumshewa. It was September and most of the Indians were still away fishing or at the canneries. At Skidegate, New Gold Harbor, and Masset he did better, though again prices were high after Powell's tour. Alexander McKenzie, the HBC factor, was helpful, as he would be to Swan in 1883, though it was Jacobsen himself who bought a six-year-old pole from Captain Jim or Stilta.

While the Charlottes had been his express goal, he moved on to Kwakiutl country after less than two weeks among the Haida. Fort Rupert became his base, with Robert Hunt, the HBC factor, providing housing and assistance. From him Jacobsen rented the sloop *Mystery* that gave him unusual mobility, and Hunt's two sons, George and William, served as guides, crew, and interpreters. George Hunt was especially valuable. He was twenty-seven years old and, though his father was English and his mother a Tlingit, had been virtually raised a Kwakiutl. With the young Hunts' assistance Jacobsen sailed to all the Kwakiutl villages he could — to Nuwitti, Alert Bay, and Mamalillikulla. A trail led across island to Koskimo and Quatsino on the far northwest tip of the island. There, after making friends with Chief Nagretze, he bought a "number of good, rare and original items," including cedar bark blankets and a lovely Chilkat blanket.[24]

After sixteen days among the Kwakiutl, Jacobsen headed back to Victoria in order to find a way to the west coast of Vancouver Island. The *Thornton* took him to Barkley Sound, but he then had to resort to canoes manned by natives who insisted upon high wages if they were willing at all to go out into the winter sea. Because of weather and the transportation problem, the west coast trip took Jacobsen over two months, but the large collection he brought back justified the time and expense. Now in January he was ready to return to San Francisco.

His plans, when he left Victoria in February 1882, were to spend the remainder of the winter collecting in Arizona. Upon arriving in the Bay City, however, he found a letter from Hagenbeck asking him to return to Vancouver Island to engage some "longhead" Indians for an ethnic exposition in Germany. The Hamburg zoo-keeper-cum-impressario had recovered from the setback caused by the death of the Labrador Eskimo and had already begun a touring exposition of Fuegians. The inspiration for a "longhead" exhibition had come from Jacobsen's description of the intriguing head deformation of the Koskimo and their isolation from corrupting European influences. The Quatsino Sound Indians, according to Jacobsen, continued to paint their faces in red and black, some still wore nose and lip rings, and most wore cedar bark blankets (though preferring nakedness). Jacobsen was certain that they would *"go immediately to Europe"* and he had already suggested it to them. Hagenbeck was taken with the idea. He instructed Jacobsen to recruit some Northwest Coast Indians, preferably "longheads," and bring them directly to Europe.[25]

Jacobsen left San Francisco immediately for Koskimo, where three men and two women initially agreed to go to Europe. They were scarcely engaged, however, when, under the influence of relatives and friends, the five began to waver. With great difficulty Jacobsen managed to get four to Fort Rupert. Here he found a telegram from Hagenbeck telling him to "Stay await orders." As he sat in Fort Rupert, his Koskimo troupe came under increased pressure to abandon the trip — it was, they were told, an eight-month voyage round Cape Horn. "They tell my con-tracted Koskimo Indians such lies here," wrote Jacobsen, and he was angry that the Koskimo would believe the Fort Ruperts, who had always been their enemies, more than him and Robert Hunt.

One Koskimo deserted while Jacobsen waited for the *Otter* to bring further word from Hagenbeck. Its arrival brought a telegram to "Engage nothing. Particulars letter," as well as an earlier letter which told of the death of two of Hagenbeck's Fuegians. Jacobsen tried to hold the Koskimos until he received definite instructions, but he watched, albeit now with "incomparably greater calm," as all but William Hunt's wife disappeared. They left, he reported, "without saying a personal Adieu."[26]

Jacobsen then returned to Victoria where he picked up Hagenbeck's explanation for the cancelled orders: five Fuegians had died in the previous week. Hagenbeck once again had lost interest in ethnic expositions.[27] The *Colonist* gave a variant on Jacobsen's failure:

> The Indians there scared the "specimens" with raw-head-and-bloody-bone yarns so that they decamped during the night. The Fort Ruperts offered to supply the places of the fleeing Quatsemos with round-headed Hydahs, but the offer was declined with profuse thanks, as round-heads are common in Europe.[28]

The mission to Quatsino Sound had failed. No party of "long-heads" went to Hagenbeck's Tierpark in 1882. But Jacobsen's disappointment and Hagenbeck's abandonment of ethnic expositions were not final. The idea would be resurrected on Jacobsen's return to Germany in November 1883.

Jacobsen's primary mission had been to collect specimens and in this he was quite successful. He consciously sought bone and stone objects — a general ninteenth-century preference implying antiquity and one not fully appropriate to the Northwest Coast. He was delighted to be able to procure all three of the whalebone Nootkan clubs that he saw, and he bought stone "slave-killers" and mortars and pestles whenever he could. Bone charms and ornaments were well represented in his collection lists.

A second very strong preference was for religious and ceremonial material. He sought dance masks and aprons, rattles, cedar bark rings, drums, and whistles, and his collection was rich in objects of this type. He procured a quantity of small sculpture and from his references to many of them as "idols" or "old gods," it appears that these belong partially to his religious category. He also prized shaman pieces, referred to as from a "doctor" or "medicine man."

Technological items were less well represented. There were adzes, odd nets, a kelp fishline or two, drills, fishing spears, and hooks. Household items, however, were conspicuous — spoons and dishes of all sizes. It is obvious that he had an eye for what was attractive, *"hübsch"* or *schön,"* for decorative material of all kinds. Basketry, including hats, was somewhat under-represented though he did go out of his way for old mats and blankets. These fitted, however, into a preferential category for "old" and traditional material of all kinds.

Jacobsen seems not to have distinguished greatly between old and traditional. A bias toward antiquity is implied by the bone and stone priority and by a search for mats which were no longer made, but apparently the culture seemed yet close enough to its pre-contact conditions that Jacobsen willingly accepted recent productions of a traditional kind. He bought argillite pipes and plates and new basketry; in March 1882 he regretted that the Fort Rupert Kwakiutl had not been able to make much new material since his purchase from them the previous autumn. He was willing to commission the duplication of old things that were not for sale, such as a Bella Bella chief's seat.

He constantly worried about the costs he was incurring, and suffered doubts if he was doing the right thing and buying the right pieces. What would the people back in Berlin think? Everything in British Columbia was so expensive — so much "that I do not know what they will say in Europe." Yet he had no choice: "if one wants to have something, one has to pay for it and, once I have undertaken this long trip here, I must keep at it as much as possible; I know for certain that it will not get cheaper but more expensive over time." He worried that he was buying too much, "but it is that way when one is first in this business — one wants to take away everything one sees."

He was curious (and a little worried) over how his first shipment, from Skidegate, would be accepted in Berlin.[29] Even without assurances from Germany, he quickly gained confidence in his success. A turning point was the Haida pole purchase. Everyone was astonished, he reported, because a Haida would sooner sell his wife or child than part with his forefather's pole. This was a slight exaggeration, but it bolstered his self-assurance, even more so when he learned that Governor-General Lord Dufferin had been unsuccessful in obtaining a pole in 1876. After that he was confident that he was collecting well, gathering "things which people who had lived 20 years among the Indians have not seen — especially dance objects such as masks and rattles." Aurel Krause, who met Jacobsen in San Francisco, found him "very satisfied" with his collecting.[30]

The museum was more than pleased with his results. When the first shipments arrived in January 1882, the Berliners were amazed at the uniqueness of the material. The ethnic character of the Northwest Coast Indians had previously been indicated by sporadic pieces in European museums, but "now it stood forth with all the impressiveness of reality, as hundreds and thousands of objects came to be arranged in long series." Aurel Krause praised Jacobsen's intelligent selection, encompassing not only ancient bone and stone implements, but also artfully worked objects of warfare, hunting, fishing, and household industries, symbols of shamanism, and characteristic examples of crests, all in great variety. Writing with the authority of one with experience in the same field, Krause judged that this first comprehensive Haida collection would, in all probability, be the last one brought together in a manner useful to science. The Haidas were dying and so much more thanks were therefore due to Jacobsen who, with a sharp eye for the right thing, had salvaged in the last hour a residue of a dying culture.[31]

As a tribute to the collection — and doubtless to the members of the Hilfscomité — the museum hastened to publish a sample of the collection, *Amerika's Nordwest-Küste,* which handsomely illustrated in well-drawn color lithographs some of the choicest pieces.[32] Another probable reason for publication was the museum's inability immediately to display the collection. The new museum building would not be ready until 1886. Jacobsen's crates were unpacked in the Egyptian section of the Neues Museum, but there was no space for exhibition. The collection was there when Jacobsen arrived back in Berlin in late November 1883.

Jacobsen spent the winter of 1883–84 working on cataloguing and ordering his collection. Meanwhile, Bastian had arranged for the publication of his journal as a travel book, to be put into

J. Adrian Jacobsen's collection as displayed in the Berlin Museum in 1926.
Courtesy of the Museum für Volkerkünde, Berlin.

proper German by the scientific journalist Adrian Woldt. Jacobsen
recalled the time as pleasant: "I spent this winter quite peacefully,
days in the museum and evenings at Woldt's."[33] By the end of
March the book was ready. So too was the collection: it had been
moved to the second floor of the old stock exchange, otherwise
unoccupied, for a special exhibition. A private viewing was
arranged for the Anthropology Society on March 21, 1884, and
eight days later Crown Prince Friedrich and the Prussian minister
of culture were present for a gala opening. Jacobsen and Bastian
directed the crown prince and Minister von Gossler on a tour of
the exhibited collection.

Jacobsen's assembled Northwest Coast collection totalled 2,036
catalogue entries and probably at least 2,400 pieces.[34] He considered his special prizes to be the large Haida pole, a "beautifully
carved and painted" Bella Bella canoe, a small room from an
Indian house, and the Nootka bone clubs. The larger of these
items took pride of place in the *lichthof* or glass-roofed courtyard
when the new museum building opened in 1886. The remainder
of the collection was installed in a Northwest Coast section where
it provided the richest single area collection of the American
naturvölker division.

Over the winter of 1883–84, as Jacobsen worked in Berlin on his collection and book, he and Hagenbeck decided upon another attempt to bring Northwest Coast Indians to Europe. In the spring they sent B. Fillip Jacobsen, Adrian's youngest brother, to the coast to collect ethnological objects. Adrian would follow and together they would bring back an Indian troupe, hopefully "longheads." The plan changed only slightly when Adrian agreed to make a Siberian collecting expedition for the museum; he would be free to go on to British Columbia to collect artifacts and, together with his brother, bring back a party of Indians.

Departing Berlin at the end of May 1884, Adrian Jacobsen spent 363 days travelling overland to Korea and Japan, gathering an enormous collection. Arriving in Victoria via San Francisco on June 8, 1885, he hired a group of "unpleasant" Indians with canoe to travel the same west coast of Vancouver Island that he had visited in the winter of 1881–82. This time he was gathering a private collection, one which could be displayed with the anticipated Indian *völkerschauung* and then sold to museums. He planned to circumnavigate Vancouver Island by canoe as far as Fort Rupert where he had scheduled a rendezvous with Fillip for July.[35]

Fillip, ten years younger than Adrian, had his own adventures as he travelled by hired canoe up the Inside Passage in the summer of 1884, collecting from the Kwakiutl, Bella Bella, and Bella Coola. He wintered in Port Essington, from which he could collect Tsimshian, Bella Coola, and even some Tlingit material.[36]

Meeting at Fort Rupert in early July 1885, the brothers recruited a party of eleven Kwakiutl, including two 'longhead" wives, for the European tour. George Hunt was to accompany them as interpreter. While waiting for a steamer, the Jacobsens and Hunt went in search of more collectibles and their absence allowed doubts to set into the minds of the eleven recruits. An English missionary, probably Alfred J. Hall, fostered the Indians' fears of a distant and unknown land. The Koskimo fiasco was repeated: most of the party had disappeared when the collectors returned.[37]

On July 21, the *Colonist* offered this account:

> The Indians seem to be loyal subjects to their first faith and fatherland quite as much as the Germans; indeed their love of country was found so great, that the most flattering inducements held

out by the professor [Jacobsen] failed to secure one of their number to accompany him to Europe. . . . The dusky natives were not very much taken with the proposition, especially when the missionary told them that they would be sold as slaves in Europe and never see the shores of their native land again.

All was not lost, however. Fillip told Adrian that on the steamer he had taken to Fort Rupert there had been a number of Bella Coolas on their way to the hopfields of Washington Territory. "There was nothing else to do but to make an attempt in this direction."[38] The Jacobsens caught up with the Bella Coolas in Victoria and induced nine to sign on for Europe.

In a contract drawn up by the law firm of Davie and Pooley, Jacobsen undertook to pay each Indian $20 per month plus food, lodging, clothing, and medical expenses, and personally to supervise and care for "the welfare and reasonable comfort of the parties" — who were not to be separated. On their side, the Indians contracted that, between 8:00 and 12:00 A. M. and 1:30 and 6:00 P. M., including Sundays, they would engage "before the Public in the performance of Indian games and recreations in the use of bows and arrows, in singing and dancing and speaking and otherwise in showing the habits, manners and customs of the Indians." They bound themselves to behave "reasonably and respectably" and to submit to Jacobsen's "lawful and reasonable orders." Jacobsen promised to return the Bella Coolas to British Columbia by August 1, 1886, and deposited a $1,000 performance bond with Indian Commissioner Powell.[39]

The Jacobsens and the Bella Coola left Victoria on July 27 on board the *Olympian* bound for Tacoma where they would take the railway to New York. The *Colonist* again offered its observations: "they will be quite civilized when they return a year hence."[40] In New York they boarded the *Werra* on August 5, landing in Bremen on August 15.

The exposition tour began in Leipzig where the Bella Coolas opened a month's engagement at Pinkert's Zoological Garden.[41] They erected a wooden plank house decorated with a painted killerwhale and two bears, before which stood two poles; they performed on an elevated stage which included a hollowed-out cedar block as a fireplace. The normal program included Hamatsa, Nutlamatla,[42] and several other dances, interspersed

"The Bella Coola Indians from America's Northwest Coast in the Zoological Garden at Leipzig: A Cannibal Dance." Original drawing by Fritz Waibler, in Leipzige Illustrierte Zeitung, *no. 2207 (17 October 1885), p. 387.*

with demonstrations of bows and arrows, and gambling stick games, and a mock potlatch. The dances were accompanied by box drums, and singing.

The shaman and Hamatsa dances were the most sensational. The full shaman show, reserved for special evening performances, featured the public burning of a shaman. The shaman, after half-delirious dancing, stepped into a wooden box, which, with the lid secured, was carried to the fire. "After a time it went up in flames among the crackling and glowing fuel. What a strange sight! In the shimmering glow a charred head and skeleton!" As the astonished crowd stared at the gruesome spectacle, with a sudden yell the shaman reappeared among his compatriots and, almost as quickly, disappeared into the darkness.[43]

From Leipzig the troupe moved on to Zwickau, Halle, and ten other cities, concluding their tour at Aachen in late July 1886. They followed the same general routine, though a snowshoe demonstration was added when conditions permitted. They played invariably in private establishments, often in zoological gardens, sometimes in hotels, occasionally in halls such as Berlin's

Kroll'sche Etablissement and Castan's Panopticum in Cologne. Everywhere, the Jacobsen's ethnological collection accompanied them, normally exhibited on walls and tables of an adjoining hall or room.

It was the exotic cannibalism of the Hamatsa that attracted the most notice both in popular and learned circles. The "rather attractive" young Pooh-Pooh was "a genuine hamatsa" and wore a dance cloak with carved-wood skulls to represent the eight times he had eaten flesh.[44] Descriptions of the Hamatsa and what it represented seldom failed to be highlighted in public notices. Most of the other members of the troupe had bite scars on their arms or chest; Kakilis carried seven (five on his right forearm and two on his left), each about the size of a two-mark coin. A joke was told of Herr Kommissionsrat Engel, in whose hotel the Indians lived while in Berlin. "Do you give the Bella Coolas complete room and board," he was asked at the *stammtisch* at Seichen's. "Of course," Engel answered, "they receive everything they want." "Even human flesh?" "Certainly," replied the innkeeper, "every day I need two extra kitchen boys."[45]

A minor sensation was created in Berlin when the following incident was reported:

A highly exciting scene, which could nearly have resulted in the death of a man, occurred on Wednesday night, after the end of the performance of the Bella Coola Indians at Kroll's Etablissement. After the audience had left, the Indians began, probably in honor of a religious festival, the notorious Winter or Eagle Dance which occupies the highest place among the religious ceremonies (and therefore is seldom or never profaned by public performance). It is also among the Indians the most feared since the command of the medicine man condemns to death anyone who stumbles or falls during this dance. The young Pooh-Pooh, the so-called "cannibal," stumbled during the dance, fell to one knee and, before he was able to pull himself together, the chief rushed toward him, arm raised with tomahawk ready to strike a fatal blow. One minute later and he would have gone, with split skull, to the happy hunting ground, there to propitiate the enraged eagle of the Manitou. At this moment Captain Jacobsen, who knows the practices of the Indians and who had been ready since the beginning of the dance, threw himself between the two and by his unquestioned authority prevented the deathblow.

Pooh-Pooh recovered slowly from fright, but remarked with the stoic calm of the Redskin that he would have to die for this offence to Manitou — either here or later at home.[46]

It is difficult to give full credence to this episode. The day previous the *Berliner Tageblatt* had carried an article by Franz Boas which mentioned "the terrible Eagle dance in which anyone who fell was immediately killed." The coincidence is suspicious. The full report enlarges the possibility that the whole incident was staged, even fabricated. The seriousness of falling during such a dance is indisputable, though the fatal consequence, at least by the 1880s, is less certain. Among the Kwakiutl a decade later death was faked.[47]

The Bella Coola show was not a financial success. As a European exhibition the troupe suffered some serious deficiencies. In the first place, they were all male, and the German public was accustomed to (and quite preferred) family groups with mothers and children. An even heavier handicap was that the Bella Coola simply did not look the way Red Indians were supposed to look. Their skin was the wrong tint, their noses not Roman enough, and they did not have the stereotypical tomahawk-and-headdress. One newspaper columnist commented that the nine were not very impressive: "if you are not to be disappointed, you must put away all preconceptions, formed perhaps by Cooper, of Indians." One young lady in the audience, he reported, cried out, "I'll be hanged if they are real." Even their bow-and-arrow demonstration was unconvincing — perhaps understandably, since these weapons were not often used on the coast, especially in recent years. In Breslau a satirical journal wrote of humbug and swindle. As Fillip Jacobsen later told the *Colonist,* "the uneducated classes would not believe that the men were in reality wild Indians of the west, but insisted that they were either Chinese or Japanese."[48]

The scholarly reception was much better. In Halle they performed before the Geographic Society, and the linguist and psychologist Carl Stumpf became interested in their songs. He spent four sessions with Nuskilusta, transcribing Bella Coola songs. Nuskilusta patiently repeated his songs, never losing his soft and passionate tone. Stumpf managed to overcome the difficulties of a quite strange music to note seven songs and he later got two more that Franz Boas recorded in Berlin, all published in a fascinating article.[49]

In Berlin the Bella Coolas underwent more extensive scholarly examination. A special performance was given before the Society of Anthropology, Ethnology, and Prehistory, with introductory lectures by Rudolf Virchow, Bastian, and Aurel Krause. Boas, an assistant in the Museum für Völkerkunde and preparing for his *habilitation,* a kind of second doctorate required for university teaching, studied their language and legends as well as their music.[50] Virchow took minute measurements of every possible physical feature. As a result, though we know otherwise very little about the nine, we do have forty-seven different physical measurements for each, from cephalic indices (80 to 89.3, decidedly brachycephalic) to the height of their *symphyses pubes.* Virchow, like the public, was impressed with their resemblance to the Japanese. He selected the best students from among Japanese who were studying medicine in Berlin and asked them to see if they could recognize any reminiscences of their mother tongue in the Bella Coola's speech. There was no communication: "even the most common words were completely different."[51]

The Bella Coolas were lodged in hotels where they occupied themselves with woodcarving and cards. They quite accustomed themselves to German food, though Jacobsen permitted each no more than a single glass of beer. Frau Maria Cronau of Leipzig had them to dinner and reported that, though they did eat quite a lot, they had the best of manners and were quite able with knife and fork. While decidedly a curiosity to the Germans, the Bella Coolas seem to have taken their foreign tour easily in stride. They wore well-cut European clothing, learned at least some German, and reportedly made friends among the ladies. If Frau Cronau may be trusted, "they adapted themselves completely to our customs and usages."[52] There were no difficulties of deportment and both troupe and managers appear to have respected each other and to have acted with mutual loyalty and decency.

With the tour concluded, they took a steamer from Hamburg and, escorted by Fillip Jacobsen, arrived in Victoria after an uneventful trip on August 16, 1886 — slightly after the contracted date. "All the troupe say they spent a 'nice-time,'" reported the *Colonist,* "and intended to 'live like white men' in the future."[53]

The Krause and Jacobsen collections of the 1880s were major expeditionary incursions into the Northwest Coast region. They also, and perhaps strangely, were almost the last major collections to go to Continental Europe. The world was too wide for interest to remain on any one small area of North America that was rapidly being exploited by American museums nearer the field. More importantly, the scramble for colonies, partially unleashed by Bismarck's policy change of 1884, focused European interests toward their own newly begotten natives. German ethnological concerns remained broad, but when not concentrated on New Guinea or its new African territories, looked more often to the *kulturländer* of Asia and Central America. French attention had never been upon North America and Pinart's solo expeditions had no successors. The accessions of the Musée du Trocadéro tended to follow the French flag to Africa and Oceania.

Chapter Four

The North American Rivals

THE "FOREIGN EMISSARIES" worried Spencer Baird. Yet they provided him with a persuasive argument for congressmen, and that in turn was a trump card for a piece of Major Powell's Bureau of Ethnology appropriation. In his reports, in testimony before con-gressional committees, and in correspondence with Swan and Powell, Baird expressed his concern about the French and German collectors on the West Coast. He wrote in hemispheric rather than national terms, seldom betraying consciousness that the Smithsonian's agents were themselves foreigners in British Columbia. He could scarcely complain about Canadians collecting within their own territory nor could he expect Congress to feel that a federal agency ought to view with hostility the rise of museum collections elsewhere in the United States. While declaring a kind of ethnological Monroe Doctrine against Europeans, the competition of collectors from Princeton and New York museums was also irritating to Baird's ambitions for making the Smithsonian into a great national museum.

The Princeton collections were almost wholly the result of the zeal of Dr. Sheldon Jackson, a superintendent of Presbyterian missions and later U. S. education agent in Alaska, who on several occasions had beaten Baird's Sitka representative, John J. McLean, in the pursuit of native pieces.[1] Ever since his first visit to Alaska in 1877 Jackson had been keenly interested in the natives and in their spiritual and educational advancement. He managed an intense campaign to further school and mission work in the territory, planting missionaries at Sitka, Wrangell, Howkan, and Haines. At the same time he began sending ethnological objects from Alaska and from the western tribes within his Rocky Mountains mission superintendency to his alma mater, the Princeton Theological Seminary. There they formed part of a "Missionary Cabinet" intended to illustrate "the present condition and needs of Pagan lands" as well as "the Archaeology of the Bible and early Christian archaeology and history."

While the material was appreciated by the faculty, the seminary's trustees felt that the institution had higher priorities for its limited funds. Since some of the more influential seminary trustees were also members of the board of neighboring Princeton College, they voted to transfer the collection to the college, whose funds were more adequate "for the proper exhibition and increase of a Museum of this character." Jackson's consent was perhaps expedited by Judge Caleb S. Green, who sent him a $500 check for further collections on behalf of the college.[2]

Jackson continued sending collections with his customary and indiscriminate vigor. His primary concern remained the promotion of the religious and educational needs of Alaska, especially its natives, and this necessitated continuous publicity and fund-raising among Presbyterians in the East and pressure upon government departments and congressmen in Washington. Indian articles were part of his campaign; Alaskan baskets and jewelry went as gifts to benefactors and friends among mission society workers and to influential Washingtonians like Senator H. L. Dawes, as well as to Presbyterian ladies for sale at mission fairs. Jackson collected only a fraction of the material personally.

While he never lived in Alaska, he travelled there almost annually and was in constant communication with his network of missionaries, teachers, and supporters. Each helped Jackson with articles gathered in their localities — J. Loomis Gould at Hyda Mission in Howkan, Eugene S. Willard at Haines, and James G. Brady at Sitka. Not all were constant, nor did Jackson demand it. Gould sent pieces to the Smithsonian in 1884, and Brady, who had sold to the American Museum in 1883, began to keep the better articles for a collection of his own. Jackson even contributed a few pieces to Baird's museum, but most of his shipments went to Professor Arnold Guyot's Geological Museum at Princeton College.

In 1882, 324 specimens from Alaska, Arizona, and Washington Territory arrived, followed by further donations in 1883 and 1885. Jackson was a capricious collector for whom "new wood carving [was] as good as old."[3] Much of the collection consisted of poor tourist pieces, probably made by native students at Sitka's Sheldon Jackson Institute workshops.

Princeton was thus of little serious concern to Baird. Although its collections were increased by Professor William Libby, a geologist who accompanied the *New York Times* Mount St. Elias expedition to Alaska in 1886,[4] within a year Jackson had ceased sending his collections to New Jersey, preferring to place them in a new museum he had helped to found in Sitka in association with the native school there. Aside from some very fine pieces, the Princeton collection retains an historical interest because of the number of tourist-type pieces in it from the early 1880s. A later anthropologist evaluating the collection found little in it worth listing, but thought the pieces were nevertheless "very interesting" as demonstrating "that such poor work should have been done so early."[5]

Similarly, Baird perceived no threat from Canadian collectors. They scarcely existed. Montrealer George Mercer Dawson, a geologist with the Canadian Geological Survey, had examined the eastern and northern shores of the Queen Charlotte Islands in 1878 and in the process made a representative Haida collection. The diminutive scientist — victim of an undiagnosed childhood disease that left him dwarfed but unimpaired in physical vigor — fitted into the Gibbs and Dall models for whom anthropology, despite a position subsidiary to professional concerns, had an important place. At Tanu, Cumshewa, Skidegate, and Masset villages, Dawson purchased a respectable assortment of Haida material, about 115 items in all. Some he described and illustrated in an important essay on the Haida published by the Survey in 1880. Although made while in the field for the Canadian government, it was a private collection which Dawson put on loan to the Peter Redpath Museum at McGill College. His father, Sir William Dawson, was both curator of the museum and principal of the college; it is not improbable that the collection was made partly at Sir William's request.[6]

That Dawson's small but valuable collection, the earliest substantial one to come from the Queen Charlottes, was not placed in the Geological Survey's own museum is readily understandable. An 1877 act of parliament had extended the Survey's terms to include natural history, but aside from some botanical specimens, mostly newly acquired, its museum was devoted almost exclusively to rocks, minerals, and fossils. A few ethnological objects, incidentally obtained from Indian graves or by other casual means, lay about its premises on Montreal's St. James Street because there was nowhere else for them. This was Canada's only federal museum of any kind. The Dominion possessed no analogue to the Smithsonian Institution and no counterpart to the U. S. National Museum, let alone anything as comprehensive as the London or Berlin museums. Geology was a practical concern to a young country, ethnology was not. It held no significant place in the Survey's program or in the consciousness of its director, Alfred A. C. Selwyn.

Selwyn, who came to the position after sixteen years in a similar role in the Australian colony of Victoria, was necessarily concerned with demonstating the Survey's practical effectiveness to the public and parliament. His work in British Columbia on Pacific railway surveys did prompt him to take a modest gesture toward securing "Indian work" for the museum. He asked Israel W. Powell, the federal Indian superintendent for coastal British Columbia, if he might make a collection. Selwyn did not suggest that the Survey pay for it. He seems to have understood that money was frequently "given as alms to the distressed Indians" and so thought it better to employ them to make or collect specimens. So vague a request did not move Powell to action. He was responsible to his own deputy superintendent-general, even if Indian Affairs and the Geological Survey were within the same ministry; equally significant, aid to distressed Indians was always in kind, not in cash. In any case Selwyn seems to have forgotten his impulsive and inexpensive gesture. Few Indian pieces came into its museum even from the extensive expeditions of his own Survey employees.[7]

Four years later Powell did make a collection for the Canadian government, one which ended up in Selwyn's museum. The impetus seems to have come from Powell himself while on a five-week tour of coastal villages. Departing Nanaimo on June 30, 1879, aboard H. M. S. *Rocket,* a double-screw, four-gun ship "specially intended for Indian service" (she had bombarded Kimsquit to charred ruins in 1877), he visited virtually all the major native centers of the British Columbia coast. At Fort Simpson the chiefs presented him with some old stone implements and other articles and he was asked to purchase more by "those who could not afford to give them." He decided not to let such opportunities pass. Artifacts were "now becoming very scarce"; it was "a pity that already so many unique and finely carved articles have been bought up to enrich foreign museums, and the scattered collections of occasional tourists," so he collected what he hoped would "form the nucleus of a most interesting collection of great ethnological value." Powell was putting himself out on a limb. He trusted that the opportunity presented by his visit to distant tribes would have the approval of his deputy minister in Ottawa. In time, he argued, the collection would yield "a highly prized and instructive return for comparatively a small outlay." Privately, he may have invoked Selwyn's 1875 request to help justify his purchases. In any case, Col. J. S. Dennis, deputy minister in the department, sanctioned the expenses, including $129.51, which had come directly from Powell's own pocket. The collection of 239 catalogued items, probably close to 350 objects, was sent to Ottawa.[8]

For unaccountable reasons, the cases were put in the cellars of Dennis's office instead of being sent on to the Geological and Natural History Museum in Montreal. They came to the museum only when the museum came to them, in 1881 upon the museum's removal to the old Clarenden Hotel on Ottawa's Sussex Street. Powell was understandably annoyed at the neglect of his collection, complaining, according to Swan, that it lay moulding in the cases with many perishable pieces utterly ruined. Powell had another complaint: despite acknowledgment of responsibility, the Survey could not get Treasury Board authorization to reimburse his $129.51. Only after fifteen years of patient correspondence was G. M. Dawson finally able to send him a check.[9]

Selwyn, profuse in apologies about the strange loss of the cases in an Ottawa basement, officially welcomed Powell's material as "the nucleus of a collection to illustrate the history, manners and customs of the aboriginal Indian races of the Dominion." He hoped, he wrote, that similar collections might come from east of the Rockies and from the Hudson Bay littoral. "The time when it will no longer be possible to accomplish this is at hand," he wrote, but quite another reason dictated urgency. Prompt action was necessary or Canada would be "forever dependent upon the museums of the United States for information relating to the life history of her own aboriginal races."[10] It was not only Spencer Baird who worried about foreign collections. Yet Selwyn, having voiced his official concern, lapsed back into inactivity.

George Dawson, an increasingly important figure within the Survey, took more interest in building the museum's anthropological collections and, his special survey field being British Columbia, obtained for the Ottawa institution collections from Dr. W. F. Tolmie and Alexander McKenzie, both former HBC men resident in the province. James Richardson, a colleague who had made a preliminary survey of the Queen Charlottes in 1871, contributed fifteen argillite carvings, selected by him as typical or fine. The carvings had a particular appropriateness since it was Richardson who had first surveyed Slatechuck quarry, the single source of argillite on the islands, and had given it that name. Dawson himself brought back a large Kwakiutl collection from his 1885 Vancouver Island survey. Indeed, Dawson was becoming the main force in directing the Survey's museum toward anthropology, and its most significant ethnological collections were the Pacific coast material associated with him and Israel Powell. The Ottawa collection was not large, Dawson reported in 1889, but its importance lay chiefly "in British Columbia ethnological and Ontario archaeological specimens."

The museum had no pretentions to universality. "We are endeavouring," Dawson wrote, "to collect & preserve merely Canadian ethnological objects in which we can hope to do some good"; were they to extend into non-Canadian areas, "we could hope to be able to do nothing in comparison with larger museums." Even in its own domain, the results were meager. Selwyn had disliked parliament's addition of natural history to the Survey's title and charge, instructing his field geologists to collect naturalist specimens only "when the doing will not interfere with the main objects of the exploration." Despite, or probably more accurately because of, the Survey museum's modest effort,

Dawson keenly resented the exportation of Canadian Indian material to the United States or abroad, but he could secure only limited appropriations for purchases that might forestall it.[11]

If Princeton and Canada were but small threats to Washington's leadership, New York's American Museum of Natural History was different. It received a major Northwest Coast collection from Superintendent Powell in the early years of the eighties and then purchased an enormous Tlingit collection from Lt. G. T. Emmons in 1888. Although Baird was by then dead, his successor as director of the U. S. National Museum, S. P. Langley, saw New York's acquisition of the Emmons collection as a mortifying example of the inability of the Washington museum to buy material "almost indispensable for the completion of the national ethnological collection."[12]

In many ways the American Museum was a conscious rival to Washington's National Museum. The motivating agent for its founding in 1869 was Albert Bickmore, a former student of Louis Agassiz. Inspired by civic concern and European example, Bickmore wanted to see a Manhattan museum worthy of the city and the nation. It was he who suggested the name "American" for the institution, a symbol that the founders expected their museum to hold the same central position in American scientific life that the British Museum occupied in the United Kingdom.

From its inception, the American Museum had the support of a number of New York's economic and social elite. Though it existed as a private foundation supported almost entirely by its trustees and friends, these had easy access to the political power which ensured that the New York state government would build and then maintain its building, the first portion of which was completed on Central Park West in 1877. Salaries and acquisitions, however, had to be covered entirely by private subscription.

Bickmore's leadership and the support of a wealthy set of Gotham trustees did not prevent the museum from experiencing grave difficulties in the decade of the 1870s. Its location at 79th Street, at that time far north of the populated sector of the city, was discouraging to visitors and benefactors alike. Its decision to purchase a collection of invertebrate fossils for the astonishing price of $65,000 in 1874, just at a time of financial panic and depression, brought the museum to a crisis of budgetary over-commitment. At this juncture, the institution's board turned to one of its members, the financier Morris K. Jesup, for an investigation of museum conditions. His report brought a reorganization of fiscal operations, the beginning of an endowment fund, and an emphasis upon more attractive exhibits. More important, the investigation confirmed and intensified Jesup's own interest in the museum. In February 1881 he accepted election to the presidency, a position he was to occupy for more than a quarter century.[13]

Jesup's career in banking and railway finance had made him wealthy at an early age. In his middle years he turned increasingly from business to public service and, in 1884, not yet fifty-five years old, he retired almost entirely from business. He could not, he felt, sustain his absorbing interests in both private and public spheres and so he decided to devote himself to public causes. He was active in a number of philanthropies, but the museum's presidency had first claim upon his immense ability and extensive fortune. With an imposing presence fortified by his six-foot height and iron-grey whiskers and possessing a familiarity with museum affairs resulting from continuous attention to detail, Jesup dominated the decisions of the board of trustees as easily as he imposed his will upon the staff.

At the advent of his presidency, the museum's position was extremely insecure. "The site of the new building was remote from its natural constituency; its surroundings were unattractive, and indeed desolate. Its collections were imperfectly mounted and only partially displayed. Its staff was inadequate in numbers; its financial support was insufficient and uncertain." Jesup's active presidency — almost until his death in 1908 — changed much of that. The city spread rapidly up Manhattan toward the museum, and Frederick Law Olmsted's Central Park design made the museum and its environs an urban oasis of recreation and learning. Under Jesup's more direct control was the museum's expansion. New wing was added to new wing and each stocked with large, showy, and important collections from all scientific areas. Its professional curatorial staff grew from six to twenty-eight. While supportive of the research interests of his scientific staff, he insisted upon good labeling and attractive displays. "We ought to have more lions and other big animals," he wrote in his 1880 report, "because they are what interest the public the most."[14]

Jesup's vigor and authority gave the museum a secure base for acquisitions and he would later have a direct impact upon the anthropology department. During the eighties, however, the division suffered under a lack of direction from Bickmore. He had taken charge of anthropology from the virtual origin of the department in 1873 until 1891, but his energy was dispersed in so many directions, especially to museum management and public lecturing, that it received far from full attention. Acquisition procedures were erratic and fortuitous: the trustees bought whatever was offered that was spectacular or rare, as they could afford them. They aimed at exhibition rather than toward a research collection and acted according to the whim of persuasive trustees or the fancy of a generous benefactor. One such friend of the museum was Heber R. Bishop, age forty, who had accumulated his fortune as a young sugar planter and refiner in Cuba and then, when insurrections on the island threatened his enterprises, retired to New York and launched a second successful career in gas, iron, and railways. His business took him west in 1880, and he decided to bring back to New York a Northwest Coast ethnological collection for the museum and to find a local agent who could expand it.

Director Bickmore was more than receptive. It had been, he averred, a favorite part of the whole plan since the founding of the museum "to obtain an exhibition of the Ethnology and Archaeology of our new American continent on a complete and exhaustive scale." If, through Bishop's generous assistance, a representation of the Northwest Coast tribes were obtained, it would be both interesting in itself and of increasing rarity and importance. The museum's existing collection was small. From the whole coast north of California, it possessed only a series of Chinook skulls from the mouth of the Columbia. Bishop returned to New York in the autumn, bringing with him a small collection from British Columbia and Alaska, mostly tourist trade items — silver bracelets, horn spoons, canoe models, and basketry-covered bottles — probably overvalued at $155. More significantly, in Victoria Bishop had contacted Superintendent Powell, who agreed to make a complete collection for the museum on Bishop's behalf. Bickmore was made responsible for the arrangements with Powell and sent him a general list of desiderata ranging from desiccated bodies and skulls to games and objects of worship, as well as more particular preferences, such as old stone implements ("the articles we value most highly"). Generally, wrote Bickmore, "we seek objects that have been used and perhaps blackened with age but not chipped and broken. The bright, new, clean carvings have too much a shop-like appearance as if not made for worship or other use but only for sale."[15]

The instructions were probably redundant. Powell was no novice to the collecting world. He was an old friend of Swan and had helped with "the big canoe" for Philadelphia. More important, he had the previous year made his large collection for the Canadian government and had some things already to hand. Indeed, by the time Bickmore sent his guidelines, Powell had already shipped a canoe and a post which the curator quickly installed in the third-floor gallery.

Powell collected most of his New York material the next summer during an official northern cruise aboard the *Rocket,* which took him to most of the coastal villages, though not to the west coast of Vancouver Island. He did, however, stop at Fort Wrangell in Alaska to interview Chief Shakes about a fishing dispute between Shakes's Stikeens, in American territory, and the upriver Canadian Tahltans and Sticks. It was from Shakes, according to Swan, that the finest portion of the collection came, especially masks and headdresses. The bulk of the collection arrived in New York toward the end of the year and was placed on exhibit in January 1882. Powell continued to work toward "perfecting" Bishop's donation, although he found it difficult owing to the large number of curio hunters who had visited during the previous year, no doubt an allusion above all to Jacobsen, and he had to pay more. Only in January 1885 did he ship off the last lot. Some of these he had intended to keep, but he found that many had become so damaged by moths that he decided to send them to New York.[16]

The collection, as finally received in New York, totalled 791 pieces at a cost, including photographs commissioned from Edward Dossetter, of $2,174.09. The next year a shipment of Tsimshian articles from the Skeena, including also some Nass items, valued at $90 was sold to the museum by J. Isaac's Indian Bazaar, probably at Powell's arrangement. This is one of the earliest curio dealer invoices to appear in a museum file.[17]

The most sensational object Powell sent was unquestionably his own "big canoe," which at 64½ feet surpassed Swan's Centennial contribution. Often called a Haida canoe, though her decorative carving is in Bella Bella style, she was reportedly made on the Skeena River near Port Essington. This canoe is likely the one Powell saw in 1879 near Bella Bella and described as 68 feet long and capable of carrying one hundred people. She was brought to Victoria, reportedly from Killisnoo, Alaska, by a Haida crew. Powell, as fearful as Swan of the dangers of sun and carelessness, installed ribs for protection, but remained afraid that considerable damage might be sustained before the craft arrived in New York. James Terry, an archaeologist connected with the museum and in the West at the time, found the canoe damaged by the ship's boom while merely crossing the strait to Port Townsend. Enlisting Swan's aid, Terry put her aboard the 250-foot-long *George W. Elder* for San Francisco. From there Terry was able to ensure safe arrangements through such friends of the museum as Henry Villard of the Northern Pacific railway and Trenor W. Park of Pacific Mail steamships. (Businessmen trustees had, in such cases, a wider and more useful network than political or scientific regents.) The canoe was bolted into a cradle, taken carefully by steamer to Panama, gently mounted on two platform cars so as to swing loosely on greased guys on the rear carriage (just as Swan had desired for his big canoe in 1876). She arrived safe and whole in New York in 1883.[18]

Powell himself judged the collections as "extraordinary as well as valuable" and was being honest rather than immodest when he said that they would delight Bickmore and constitute a feature of the museum. He did have reservations, which echoed his 1879 reference to the pity of articles bought up to enrich foreign museums. "I should not like to undertake another work of the kind," he told Bickmore, "and when looking at them this morning I rather felt guilty of want of patriotism in sending the collection out of the country."[19]

James Terry, who aided in shipping the canoe, was in British Columbia and Alaska seeking archaeological material. Although associated with the American Museum — his huge collection, eventually totalling over 25,000 items, was on loan to the New York museum — he was essentially a private collector. He spent most of his time travelling, buying objects, mostly stone items such as pestles, pipes, chisels, and argillite, from individuals. In British Columbia he secured artifacts from the HBC, from Powell, from the Victoria dealer A. A. Aaronson, and from a John Bryclen of Wellington Mines.

In Alaska he bought from Carl Spuhn and Captain Vanderbilt of the Northwest Trading Company and from John G. Brady, the Sitka missionary turned storekeeper. All these "archaeological" items were added to Terry's American Museum loan collection, eventually purchased in 1891 for the quite incredible sum of $38,000. At the same time Terry was put on staff to catalogue and label the collection. He was dismissed two years later, with the catalogue incomplete and useless, for stealing jade from the Terry collection.

In 1888 an enormous Tlingit collection joined the Powell-Bishop collection. Again Heber Bishop was instrumental in securing the collection, gathered in Alaska between 1882 and 1887 by naval lieutenant George T. Emmons. Bishop brought Emmons into contact with Bickmore, negotiated the terms with Emmons, saw to it that the exhibition cases were emptied of his own collection so that Emmons's material could be installed in their place for inspection by trustees and friends, and then helped to raise the purchase money. All the trustees, as well as Collis P. Huntington, Cornelius Vanderbilt, John D. Rockefeller, and J. Pierpont Morgan, contributed toward the purchase price. The Emmons collection, which cost a tidy $12,000, was a major coup for the American Museum.[20]

George Thornton Emmons, the collector and purveyor of this large and costly collection, was born in Baltimore in 1852, the son of George Foster Emmons, a career naval officer who had been a member of the Wilkes exploring voyage to the north and south Pacific in 1839–42.[21] Tradition has it that ethnological pieces adorned the family home and served as prompters to the son's collecting impulse. Certainly there were Pacific pieces in the family for Emmons later gave Princeton University a Fijian war club and a South Seas shark-toothed sword from the U. S. Exploratory Expedition and he donated his father's Wilkes shell collection to the American Museum.

The Emmons family moved to Princeton and young George attended private and church schools in Pennsylvania and Connecticut before receiving a presidential appointment to the U. S. Naval Academy. The years following his 1874 graduation

George T. Emmons and the young Louis Shotridge. Courtesy of Frances Emmons Peacock, via Jean Low and Robert de Armond.

(twenty-eighth of thirty in the class) are obscure; he was for several years on Mediterranean shore duty and a small augury of the future was a stone implement from Troy, picked up personally in 1879 when Schliemann was excavating Hisarlik. In 1882 he was posted to Alaska aboard the USS *Adams,* then virtually the entire American presence on the sub-continent.

As an officer, later executive officer, on the *Adams* and its 1884 replacement vessel, the USS *Pinta,* he shared various law-enforcement and peace-keeping responsibilities which placed him in frequent contact with the Tlingit. One can assume, though with little direct evidence, that he began collecting native material soon after his arrival in Alaskan waters. It was an avocation of many of his fellow officers and he was, as senior officer next in command, particularly well placed. He was with the *Pinta* as it escorted the *New York Times* Mount St. Elias Expedition up the coast and was doubtless among those "officers who were making collections," purchasing briskly from the ship-side Indians at Yakutat. These items would largely have been tourist curios and spurned by the more discerning Emmons, but "some one went out in a canoe and made a great 'find' of some boxes in the grave of a medicine-man in a retired part of the bay." That evening two sacks full of material were spread out on the floor of Captain Nicholl's cabin: among other things, a quantity of painted wooden masks, a leather shawl ornamented with puffin bills, and a crown of wild goats' horns. Someone else had bought a small, charm-like body-scratcher. Professor Libby preserved a large share of the boodle for Princeton's Guyot Hall museum, and it can be only presumed that Emmons, an old friend of Libby and perhaps the sagacious discoverer of the "find," was able to keep a share of the material.[22] Whatever the circumstances of the gathering of Emmons's first major collection, by August 1887 when he shipped it to New York it numbered 1,284 catalogued specimens.

On leave from the *Pinta,* Emmons came personally to oversee the installation of the collection in the west side of the museum's gallery. Bickmore, reporting at President Jesup's request, found that the specimens were all old and original, with "a standard and increasing value." "They have not been brought together by chance," he wrote, "but in regular thoughtful sequence." Each was carefully numbered with a description, "generally very full and of permanent value," given in the accompanying catalogue.

Bickmore judged the collection's value might "be fairly stated to be in the vicinity of twelve thousand dollars" and, should such an amount be able to be raised, "the Museum should by all means make such an addition to its already attractive Exhibition in the Department of Ethnology."

Bickmore, under pressure from Bishop not to allow his lectures and other occupations to prevent his giving all the time required to obtain funds for the collection, despatched a letter to prospective donors asking them to become museum patrons or fellows-in-perpetuity and thus aid in adding "this unique collection to our present means for popular instruction and for permanently preserving the works of the aboriginees of our land, who are rapidly passing away or changing their primitive habits." He followed up this letter with personal visits to explain "more fully the rarity and completeness of this collection." Emmons pressured the museum for a decision within sixty days, alluding to "a substantial offer for the whole collection." Whether the Chicago buyer actually existed might be a matter of doubt, but Bishop believed it. "You may count upon it," he wrote Bickmore, Emmons "will not give you one day's delay . . . it is sold to the Chicago party, if not taken by us on the 14th." A more compelling time factor to Emmons was the pending lapse of his naval leave. When, by February 12, he had obtained an extension to that, his pressure relented and he was able to secure from the mysterious Chicago buyer a time extension. "I wish the Museum to obtain the collection as I can make it the finest Indian collection *from one people* that is known, and in your Museum I can always have access to it which would not be the case should it become the property of an individual."[23]

Despite the dropped deadline, the purchase was made on time and New York acquired almost 1,500 items, including 39 stone mortars and dishes, over 50 rattles, and at least 100 masks. Emmons had not ignored less showy items. One of the more unusual pieces was a small box containing only human excrement, a son's first stool left by the mother in the forest so that the boy might grow up strong and powerful. As a collection, it was worthy of praise. Bishop thought it "the finest one in existence in this country" and quite impossible to equal. Franz Boas judged it probably the most complete collection ever gathered from southern Alaska and praised Emmons for the care he had taken in its cataloguing, with each specimen fully described as to usage or associated legend.[24]

The New York acquisition caused shock waves in Washington. A. P. Niblack, a navy man whose intimate knowledge of the U. S. National Museum collection had enriched his newly published survey of north coast groups, felt that "in ancient or old time material Emmons' collection knocks us out badly," though he felt Washington still retained a clear superiority in other types. "In the collections illustrative of the arts, industries and ceremonial institutions," he wrote, the American Museum's new collection still "can't hold a candle to those in the Nat'l Museum." Emmons thought differently. After a look at the Tlingit collections at Washington, he judged that "my collection stands alone [as] the only one from the country." While not agreeing, the director of the National Museum recorded publicly that the Emmons collection was another example of the loss of almost indispensable collections because the museum "had no money."[25]

The end of the eighties is a convenient time to pause, to mark some endings, some beginnings, and some transitional aspects of Northwest Coast collecting. The decade was a boom period for the region. In 1870 settlements of any size had existed only at Seattle, Tacoma, Port Townsend, Victoria, and Sitka. Agricultural settlement was confined almost entirely to small areas of Puget Sound and to the southeast coast of Vancouver Island. Trading posts and stores were scattered at numerous places along the coast, many in British Columbia still managed by the Hudson's Bay Company, but increasingly by independent traders.

Spectacular growth began in the 1880s, the decade opening with a gold rush to Juneau and the beginning of western construction of Canada's Pacific railway, completed in 1885. By that time Tacoma was already joined to Henry Villard's Northern Pacific. Immigrants and capital, attracted by the burgeoning timber trade, by the development of the salmon canning industry, by rich agricultural land on Puget Sound and in the Fraser valley, and by the commercial opportunities of growth, poured into Washington, British Columbia, and Alaska. Forestry, fishing, and mining caused intensive intrusions into previously remote locations like Port Essington, Skidegate, Killisnoo, Haines, and Klawak. There was mineral prospecting almost everywhere and gold rushes to the Stikine and the Cassiar. Juneau outpaced Sitka, Seattle boomed from 3,533 people in 1880 to 42,837 in 1890, and Vancouver was called into existence as the terminal city of the Canadian Pacific.

The labor market in the fishing and canning industries and for harvest workers in Puget Sound and the Fraser valley drew natives rapidly into the cash economy as did the rise of the new urban centers. While economic development attracted Indians into the European economy and toward an increasing dependence upon trade goods, missionaries and teachers arrived in growing numbers to bend their spiritual and cultural life to Christian and European standards. Catholic, Methodist, Presbyterian, and Anglican missions dotted the coast, though many met with very indifferent success. The most notable work was done by William Duncan among the Coast Tsimshian at his community of Metla- katla, by Thomas Crosby at nearby Fort Simpson, and by Shel- don Jackson's missions and schools in Alaska. The native popula- tion, after having suffered an incalculable numerical decline earlier in the century, stabilized, and most groups benefited from eco- nomic enrichment and the enforcement of peace.

Trade, mining, canneries, agriculture, missionaries, and even tourists had a major impact upon many natives, their traditional culture, and their productions. The impact, however, was extremely uneven over the region extending from northern Wash- ington Territory through provincial British Columbia to politi- cally unorganized southeast Alaska. There was great variety both in the extent of contact, in the Indians' accommodation to it, and in their retention of traditional and modified material culture. Even the groups, such as the Klallam and Songhees, most inten- sively in contact with Europeans, still had artifacts of value and most continued to produce at least some types. More remote groups like the Chilkat, the Quatsino, and the Nishga, retained much of their material culture.

The eighties also brought to an end the Smithsonian's most dramatic collecting on the coast. The Cotton Centennial of 1884 was virtually the close of Swan's Smithsonian work; indeed, it was almost the last commissioned National Museum collecting on the coast. Spencer Baird died in 1887 and, though his death did not end the Institution's interests in the north Pacific, fur- ther collections were largely accidental bequests or small-scale commissions related to the construction of single life-groups. The New Orleans exhibition was, then, a kind of capstone to the Northwest Coast work of Baird and Swan for the Washington museum.

In a more decisive way the eighties marked not only the crest, but also the end of organized European collecting on the coast. Bastian felt his Berlin museum had quite enough from the area and was exceedingly reluctant to divert more of his resources into new acquisitions.[26]

The late eighties brought several beginnings, too. The British Columbia Provincial Museum was founded in 1886, the impetus for its inception coming explicitly from the activity of foreign collectors depleting the province of indigenous artifacts. This nativist response, akin to Baird's concern about French and German incursions and Selwyn's about the Americans, brought into existence the first museum within the cultural region itself and, while of limited initial significance, was pregnant of future development. The following year saw the beginning of an Alaska museum at Sitka, brought about by similar motives.

The nativist or patriotic element made itself first felt in British Columbia for quite simple reasons. The province, unlike Alaska or Washington territories, was self-governing and had been since 1871. Washington received statehood only in 1889 and, while it had institutions of higher learning long before British Columbia, it was tardy in developing museums. Moreover, Indian art and artifice were less spectacular on most of its coast and collections gathered there did not usually leave the United States. When museums were founded in Tacoma and Seattle, they depended very largely upon the Indians of Alaska and even British Columbia for their ethnological collections. Alaska's governmental institutions remained rudimentary, but Sheldon Jackson and some of his associates founded a private museum to save for the region — and its natives — the indigenous patrimony.

British Columbia's museum was a direct offspring of the 1880s scramble. Swan had noted in 1884 that there was "a deal of complaint" in Victoria about the collection he had shipped to Washington, "which the authorities said should have been sent to Ottawa or London." While there was talk in town of prohibiting foreigners from collecting, he thought it more likely that the provincial legislature would make appropriations to purchase for a museum of their own the articles that collectors and tourists were "taking away in such great quantities."[27] No such action occurred, but the departure of the Jacobsen and Powell collections to Germany and New York brought renewed concern and prompted a group of Victoria's distinguished citizenry to attempt to do something to save for the province a modicum of its native legacy.

Meeting on the evening of January 14, 1886, thirty Victorians, including the city's members of parliament, Judge Matthew Begbie and Dr. W. F. Tolmie (both collectors) and Superintendent Powell, put their names to a letter petitioning the government to establish its own museum. While the petitioners asked for the foundation of a museum which would exhibit minerals and other natural resources for practical benefit and to pursue investigations into the imperfectly known natural history of the province, their most prominent concern was about the loss of ethnological antiquities. "It is a source of general regret," read the petition, "that objects connected with the ethnology of the country are being yearly taken away in great numbers to the enrichment of other museums and private collections, while no adequate means are provided for their retention in the Province." Since the quantity of such articles was limited, "their loss is frequently irreparable, and when once removed from the locality of their production their scientific value and utility to the country are greatly lessened." The proposal met with the approval of the William Smithe government. Naturalist John Fannin, a local man, was appointed to begin his duties as curator on August 1.[28]

Fannin commenced with a small room, about fifteen by twenty feet, located in the government buildings known as the "Birdcages." Because Fannin's own interests were in natural history and because of the limited space and resources given him, little was done toward fulfilling the petitioner's ethnological aims. The public accounts list only nine dollars expended upon Indian material before 1893.

A somewhat different foundation to that in Victoria was the establishment in 1887 of the Alaskan Society of Natural History and Ethnology, organized by Sheldon Jackson and Sitka residents at the urging of a touring group of scholars, businessmen, and politicians. The Society included Senator C. B. Farwell of Illinois, D. C. Gilman of Johns Hopkins University, Nicolas Murray Butler of Columbia, and Edwin Hale Abbot of the Wisconsin Central

Railroad as non-resident members, and John G. Brady and John J. McLean as Sitka members. The Society's purpose was to collect and preserve information relating to the ethnology and natural history of the entire Alaskan territory. Associated with it was a museum which was later named after Jackson.[29]

The motivations behind the new Sheldon Jackson Museum were mixed. Jackson, the moving spirit, seems to have become concerned about the drainage of native artifacts from the territory, a process to which he had been contributing by his gifts to Princeton. The museum, he wrote in retrospect, had been founded after some of the distinguished visitors had brought home to him how the curios of the country were being bought up and carried away by tourists so "that in a few years there would be nothing left to show the coming generation of natives how their fathers lived."[30] If this attribution of motive is at all true, it shows a remarkable consciousness. Ottawa, Washington, and Victoria might bewail the loss of the artifacts from their territories and take measures to preempt that, but neither Selwyn and Baird nor the 1886 Victoria petitioners conceived of saving materials for the benefit of future generations of Indians. Most thought, if they considered the matter at all, that there would be few future generations.

While Jackson must be conceded a prescience far removed from the main lines of his age, the descendants of his young wards were not his only concern. He saw the museum as a useful adjunct of the Sheldon Jackson Institute's industrial school and its current cohort of Indian children. E. H. Abbot, one of the inspiring visitors, had offered to sponsor a school department oriented "to teaching your Mission children to carve and weave and practice the native arts which the Thlinket Indians show so much skill." Such work had long been done at the Institute and offered for sale to tourists at Sitka. It had even been widely exhibited, notably at the Cotton Exposition of 1884–85. The new museum would display the finest student work from the "Abbot Foundation of Wood Carving and Weaving" as well as "have on hand for study of the students the best Specimens of the old work of their Ancestors." Others had ideas more comparable to those of the Victoria petitioners. F. E. Frobese, who was to become curator of the Jackson Museum, noted that Alaskan curios were being bought up in such quantities by eastern tourists that they were becoming scarcer every season.[31]

*The original building of the Sheldon Jackson Museum, Sitka. The Tsimshian
student, Edward Marsden, provided the decoration. Alaska Historical Library,
Vincent Sobolef Collection.*

A frame building to house the museum and curio shop was
completed for formal inauguration in 1890. About fifteen by
thirty feet, it was decorated on the exterior to resemble a native
house. Executed by Edward Marsden, a Tsimshian student at the
institute, one side was painted with a killerwhale, "a gigantic
monstrous representation in true totemic style." In the center of
the gable, Marsden painted a flat board in imitation of a pole,
complete with "an oval spot" to indicate the customary entrance
to a native house — the actual door was a hung one beside the
decorative pole. In 1897 this modest edifice was replaced by a
remarkable concrete building, octagon-shaped with a dome and
cupola. Designed by John J. Smith of Boston, who came to the
coast to supervise its building, the structure was permanent and
fireproof.[32]

The museum did not keep regular hours, but opened for special
occasions, particularly when a steamer called into town. Jackson's
instructions to Frobese were quite clear: "whenever you hear the

gun notifying you that a steamer has arrived, you will go home and dress up for the reception of tourists at the Museum." The museum curator was to be sure to take a lunch so he would not have to be absent from the building and a boy was to be trained to make change and act as doorkeeper. Above all, the museum was not to be opened under any circumstances on the Lord's Day, "no matter who or how influential the parties are who may wish to have access to it."[33]

With his own museum in Sitka, Jackson no longer shipped material to Princeton. His gifts and services, such as a Chilkat blanket sold to Abbot for forty dollars, however, continued to flow southward to those who were or might be of use to him. But his collecting of both Eskimo and Northwest Coast materials was now focused wholeheartedly on his Sitka museum, and into it he poured his own acquisitions, those of his Presbyterian collaborators and of a network of friends and correspondents.

The first acquisitions were twenty-two Haida argillite carvings, soon joined by others that were locally assessed "as works of art [that] will not suffer in comparison with the carved stone mantel ornaments of the East." He also secured two poles in 1888 and brought them by boat to Sitka. They were loaded onto a small trailer and pulled by thirty-seven boys from Metlakatla and seventy from the Sheldon Jackson school. Accompanied by the school's brass band, the Tsimshian poles made "a sort of triumphal entrance into Sitka."[34] Emmons gave three items, and while other objects trickled in from local sources Jackson remained by far the largest donor. Because his own travels and interests had shifted northward, Eskimo accessions greatly outnumbered Indian.

The establishment of museums at Sitka and Victoria made little impact. Most collections were destined still for places far from the cultural region itself. Assisting in this process was another important development of the 1880s, one which helped to call into existence both regional museums: the dramatic increase of tourist traffic, especially on the Inside Passage to Alaska.[35] Pleasure travel developed spectacularly after 1880, primarily from San Francisco; then, after completion of the Northern Pacific in 1883–84, from Portland and Tacoma. Regularly scheduled cruise ships were put on the voyage to Alaska, journeying as far north as magnificent Glacier Bay. Except for a coaling stop at Nanaimo, most of these

Natives selling curios at Sitka. Case & Draper, photographers. Alaska Historical Library.

excursion steamers missed the British Columbia coast. Some called at Bella Bella or other villages, either with the required permission or merely in awareness of lax customs enforcement. As early as 1881 Jacobsen had found Skidegate greatly affected by the tourist trade; the next year Swan was impressed by tourism's effect upon his collecting. Soon Duncan was operating a Metlakatla gift shop that catered to the summer tourists.

Tourists found that "a round trip ticket to Alaska means more unalloyed enjoyment than can be crowded into a similar two-weeks' trip in this country or any other." Miss E. Ruhamah Scidmore travelled on the *Idaho* in the 1883 season and on the *Ancon* the following summer, then published in 1885 the first of many tourist guidebooks to southern Alaska. In 1884, 1,650 passengers took excursion on the ships of the major steamship company. Their numbers increased to 3,889 in 1887 and to 5,432 in 1889, with an uncounted number who reached the Panhandle by other lines.[36] Indians and their curios rivalled scenery as the major attraction of the tour. A chief and seemingly infectious activity of the summer visitors was curio collecting.

The arrival of a ship in Wrangell in 1880 would occasion "a grand rush on shore to buy curiosities and see totem poles. The shops were jammed and mobbed, high prices paid for shabby stuff manufactured for tourist trade." Silver bracelets hammered from dollar and half-dollar coins were the most popular items, then baskets, toy canoes, and paddles. Three years later Frederick Schwatka found that the same village offered all kinds of Indian curiosities, from mountain-goat spoons at twenty-five cents to "the most elaborate idols." When one line of goods was sold out, "the natives will immediately set to work to satisfy the demand."[37]

Steamer day at an excursionist port-of-call became a market and festival day with hectic movements of vendors to the streets and wharf, and tourists spilling off the gangway in search of prizes. At Sitka the shrewd Mrs. Tom, far-famed for her mercantile skill and flamboyant social presence, would sail down to the wharf in her costume of "yellow kerchief, pink waist, magenta shawl, white stockings, and purple parasol." Below the old Russian fort, on both sides of Lincoln Street's dilapidated wooden sidewalks, "a score or two of old squaws and decrepit men squat on their haunches and expose for sale the curios with which they hope to tempt the tourist." Miss Scidmore's descriptions imply that the tourists were easily tempted. At Kasaan the first sound of a steamer's paddlewheel, heard for miles on the calm fiord, would send the Indians rummaging through their houses and chests to sort out their things, "and when the first ardent curio-seeker rushed through the packing-houses and out towards the back huts, their wares were all displayed." Kasaan John had silver bracelets, and a sharp-bargaining Indian was selling medicine-man's charms "and kindred relics of a departed faith." An old man, blind, with battered hat and dirty blanket, sat before a hut with a score of carved mountain-goat spoons sitting in a wood bowl beside him. But the ship's amateur curio buyers "found themselves worsted and outgeneralled on every side" by a Juneau trader who bought up everything wholesale and then resold it on shipboard "at a stupendous advance." " 'No more spoon,' said the blind chief as he jingled the thirteen dollars that he had received from this trader for his twenty beautifully carved spoons, and the tourists who had to pay two dollars a piece for these ancestral ladles echoed his refrain." In Juneau Indian women crouched on the wharf with their wares spread before them or "wandered like shadows about the ship's deck, offering blankets and mats woven . . . of cedar, and extending arms covered with silver bracelets to the envious gaze of their white sisters." After the tourists had done the shops, the native women came tapping at the windows of the ship's cabin, engaging in keen trading and sharp bargaining with the ladies from the South.[38]

Such an influx of visitors avid for souvenirs, when added to the market demands of sojourners and residents like Captain Vanderbilt and John Brady, and to the insatiable museum demand, inevitably meant near exhaustion in many localities of genuine old carvings and stone specimens. Indians were quick to supply the deficit with new carvings, baskets, and jewelry made expressly for sale to visitors. Such a reaction was not new. Indian production for a white market had long existed. The entire manufacture by the Haidas of argillite carving was for an external market.[39]

Collections made in British Columbia in the 1860s contain many items obviously made for sale. While these could retain both artistic and ethnological integrity, Swan wrote of some Sitka carvings he owned in 1873 as "of no more ethnological value than the Dutch toys carved for childrens playthings." Certainly much of the new material, as Dall commented in 1885, showed "singular modifications from the aboriginal types." Miss Scidmore bemoaned the debasement of silver work. "Anciently," she wrote, the natives had pounded a single heavy bracelet from a silver dollar and ornamented the broad, two-inch band with heraldic carvings "of their strangely mixed mythology." Now the silver workers had "become corrupted by civilized fashion," using narrow bands from half-dollars and carving them with scrolls, floral, and geometric designs. The best silver work at Wrangell was done by a lame Indian, "but unfortunately for the integrity of Stikine traditions, he has given up carving the emblematic beasts of native heraldry on heavy barbaric wristlets, and now only makes slender bangles, adapted from the models in an illustrated jeweller's catalogue that some Philistine has sent him." Worse yet, he copied "the civilized spread eagle" of the half-dollar. "One can only shake his head sadly to see Stikine art so corrupted and debased."

Another visitor, a decade later, wrote of "American flags, E Pluribus Unum eagles, clasped hands, and other borrowed atrocities. They might as well come from New Jersey!" Miss Isabel Shephard caught the buying infection at Sitka despite her realization that "these curios lose their value in one's mind when one reflects they are made by the Indians simply for sale, after the most approved patterns."[40] Carvers, both in argillite and silver, would later learn that native motifs sold better.

Although Miss Scidmore found all the stores amply stocked with curios, the better but highest-priced being at Sitka, local production could not always meet the intense seasonal demand. Sheldon Jackson found the stores at Sitka, Killisnoo, Juneau, and Wrangell almost empty at the end of the 1885 summer. He had tried to get material for church ladies' bazaars, but found that Alaska had become "so popular as a summer trip, that the tourists purchased all the baskets, mats &c" and none were left for him to send down. The only time to secure material, he advised, was in the spring before the commencement of the tourist season. One Juneau storekeeper had no intention of allowing a shortage to interfere with the lucrative summer trade. He planned "to import a good stone-cutter for the winter, to supply his shop with stone implements for the summer trade of 1885."[41]

Women at every village made baskets for the trade, but those of the Yakutats were considered the finest. These were imported into the Sitka market by Mrs. Tom, who operated a regular shipping service between the two towns, initially using a large canoe, later her own little schooner. Every steamer stop had its local silversmiths — "a lame Indian, who has quite a local reputation" at Wrangell, Kasaan John at Kasaan, Kinowen at Klemmakowan, Jack and Kooka at Sitka, and so on. The bracelets, rings, or teaspoons began as American coins. Converted into trade goods, they retailed for about three times the value of the original coin, with the wholesale price usually twice the coin's denomination. Gold was not often used, though it could be had on order, made similarly from gold coins. Duncan's Metlakatla Cooperative Store sold argillite carvings in singular and gross, and its silversmith specialized in teaspoons, securing orders for three dozen from Colonel J. W. Dawson and for eighteen from Sheldon Jackson.[42]

The tourist invasion of the coast had strong effects on the availability of artifacts. The summer's rush of 1882 had, Swan

Alaska women selling baskets and other curios to tourists, about 1900. Oregon Historical Society.

reported, "cleaned out the Indian market entirely and the agents of foreign Governments have swept away what the tourists have left." While most of the visitors bought "toys" and were not interested in the kelp line and other fishing implements which Baird at that time particularly wanted, they undoubtedly bought up good as well as dross, old as well as new. Swan worried that tourists "pick up all the Indian manufacturers they can get and advance prices."

Prices certainly rose rather substantially in the 1880s as the demand grew and the relative supply of good and accessible material declined. While tourists and casual visitors had their effect upon availability and the terms of trade, so too did the conscious and commissioned ethnological collectors and the museums behind them who scrambled after collections. So great was the demand for artifacts, it was reported in 1889, "that the natives had commenced to despoil the graves of their own relatives."[43]

In many ways the most important event in the collecting history of the eighties was not the collections of Dawson, Powell, Jackson, and Emmons, the founding of local museums, the Alaska tourist trade, the winding down of organized European and Smithsonian collecting or even the scramble itself. On September 16, 1886, a young German with a face scarred by university duelling disembarked at Victoria. It was Franz Boas's first visit to the coast, but he was not without friends. He had met Jacobsen's Bella Coola in Berlin and studied their language and music and, arriving a month after their return from Germany, he found pictures of "my Bella Coolas everywhere" (a dealer had reproduced them). Two were still in town, so he sought out "my good friend Alkinious" in the small house of a Bella Coola woman. "It amused me to see the astonishment of the women when they heard me talk their language," though he confessed that he had forgotten almost all he had learned in Berlin.[44] Boas's short trip to British Columbia that fall, his first research on the coast, was auspicious with repercussions that would last for decades in the region's ethnology and America's museum scene.

Chapter Five

Museums, Expositions, and Their Specimens

FRANZ BOAS WAS BORN in Minden in Prussian Westphalia in July 1858, the son of parents who were Jewish and liberal. At an early age he showed interest in science and geography, and, at the universities of Heidelberg, Bonn, and Kiel, continued an interest 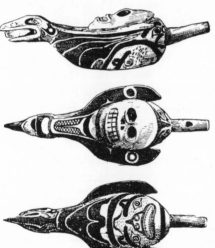 in geography while specializing in science. His Kiel thesis was in physics and he published a number of promising papers in the related psychophysics field, but his focus had already turned to geography.

In October 1882 he moved to Berlin in order to prepare himself for fieldwork on Baffin Island, where he would investigate the influence of environment and its perception upon peoples and their movements. This period in Berlin — from October 1882 to June 1883 — was a time of intense and exhilarating preparation.[1] He made arrangements with Georg Neumayer of the German Polar Commission for travel and with Rudolf Mosse of the *Berliner Tageblatt* for pay in exchange for fifteen newspaper articles. His self-training was extensive — cartography, linguistics, and the techniques of magnetic, meteorological, and somatological measurements.

He now had no time for and almost as little interest in his psychophysics work, and when he left for Baffin Island on the *Germania* in June 1883, he had become a geographer with a special interest in the study of people and their environment. He had developed a competence in physical anthropology and in linguistics, knew something of folklore and ethnology. It might have been premature to call him an anthropologist or an ethnologist; those fields were still inchoate as separate disciplines — indeed, geography had only emerged in the 1870s as a definable academic area. Moreover, Boas was himself undecided. "I am still considering," he had written in January, "whether I should let myself be taken up by the anthropologists or not. It will do no harm in any case and it puts me more frequently in touch with different people."[2] He was still a geographer and would be for several years.

His twelve-month Baffin Island expedition, made with his servant Wilhelm Weike, brought Boas into intensive ethnological fieldwork and into specimen collecting. At the end of the long and lonely sojourn, Boas returned to Germany by way of New York. He had several reasons for stopping in America. His uncle, Dr. Abraham Jacobi, a distinguished physician, lived there. Jacobi was a close intellectual patron, exchanging with him detailed letters and engaging, whenever they met, in conversation that allowed the young scholar to share his earnest plans with the older savant. More important was Marie Krackowizer, the daughter of an emigré Austrian doctor, whom Boas had met when the Jacobis, Krackowizers, and Boases had holidayed in the Harz Mountains in 1882. Boas and Miss Krackowizer had become engaged just before Boas's departure for the Arctic. The engagement helped prompt him to survey career opportunities in the United States. He was already dubious about his future in Germany where the universities were surfeit with young doctorates and lecturers *(privatdozenten)* struggling for paid positions and where he felt his Jewish birth and liberal politics would be a handicap. In America the field was open. Geography was only in the making there while at home it seemed almost finished.

He spent some weeks in January in the Smithsonian, looking over the Hall, *Polaris,* and other Eskimo collections and arranging for the publication of his work on the Central Eskimo by the Bureau of Ethnology, before he returned to Germany. Assured by his friend and mentor Theobald Fischer that anti-Semitism would not affect his university career and surprised that he was already known and respected among German geographers, but unable to find a non-academic post, he decided to qualify himself for a teaching position by registering for his *habilitation* at the University of Berlin under the geographer Heinrich Kiepert (whom he quickly came to detest). Bastian provided him with a temporary assistantship at the museum.[3]

The museum was a difficult place. Bastian was much better at accumulating than at organizing, and work patterns were chaotic. Boas nevertheless threw himself into the work and into that for Kiepert, enjoying the preparation of the American material for the new museum building as much as he hated the *habilitation* ordeal. It was now that his attention was captured by the art and imagination of Jacobsen's British Columbia material and, coincidentally, by the visit of the Bella Coola to Berlin. He worked very hard with the Indians during their two short visits to the city. Initially, his interviewing was by way of Fillip Jacobsen's Chinook, but with his facility with languages, he was soon able to engage in some direct conversation. The language was very difficult, a "terrible headache," but he was *"wie in Himmel"* at being able to work on something besides his eternal Eskimos. There was, he privately noted, a non-scientific purpose to this work: he wished to demonstrate to American scholars his competence in Indian as well as Eskimo studies. "I will do everything to force the people over there to recognize me." A paper for the New York journal *Science* would soon be ready. He was desperate now to return to America, to his American fiancée, and to America's career possibilities.[4]

By a particular blend of opportunities and enticements, Boas was being introduced and drawn to the Northwest Coast. Jacobsen's collections, the work with the visiting Bella Coola, and fascinating conversations with Aurel and Arthur Krause provided an invitation into a new ethnological field, exciting in itself and also offering an opportunity to expand his breadth as an Americanist and thus make him more marketable in the new world. His Eskimo work had made him attentive to their southern neighbors. "My fancy was first struck by the flight of imagination exhibited in the works of art of the British Columbians as compared to the severe sobriety of the eastern Eskimo." From Jacobsen's fragmentary notes he "divined what a wealth of thought lay hidden behind the grotesque masks and the elaborately decorated utensils of these tribes." When Adrian and Fillip exhibited their Bella Coolas in Berlin, "an opportunity was thus given to cast a brief glance behind the veil that covered the life of those people, and some of the general problems of the region began to loom up."[5]

Even before Boas met the Bella Coolas, he had formulated an ambitious plan for a four-season expedition that would take him through arctic and sub-arctic areas to Vancouver Island, there to supplement for the museum Jacobsen's too-cursory artifact descriptions. Bastian refused (quite rudely in Boas's opinion) to recommend the plan to his finance committee. Now with his *habilitation* successful and his introductory lectures (he suggested that one be on the Northwest Coast Indians) concluded, with the work at the museum too frustrating and uncertain to keep him, Boas left for a summer's visit to New York. There was a possible position with the Geological Survey in Ottawa; in any case, he felt the broad American opportunities were preferable to the eventuality of a German professorship.

Once in New York he decided to make a research trip to the Northwest Coast, the area he already knew so well through Krause, Jacobsen, and most of all the nine Bella Coolas. Through his uncle's friends he secured a rail pass to Tacoma and Uncle Jacobi lent him five hundred dollars. The loan, he calculated, could be repaid by collecting cheaply in British Columbia and selling dearly in the United States or Germany. Armed with travel hints and letters of introduction from G. M. Dawson, Boas arrived in Victoria in September 1886.

The overriding object of his first field trip to the coast was to further his reputation as an Americanist. He intended to learn enough about languages, ethnic distribution, and mythology to qualify as an expert in the field of Northwest Coast anthropology, which, when added to his already recognized expertise in arctic geography and ethnology, would give him undeniable credentials. He wanted primarily to use language and myth as instruments to investigate the complicated ethnological relationships of the coastal region, and he worked extremely hard to accomplish as much along these lines as was possible in his short September to December stay.

As a supplementary purpose, he carried with him photographs and drawings he had made in New York from the Bishop-Powell collection and others of the Jacobsen masks in Berlin for which he hoped to secure mythological explanations — the "stories" to which the pieces belonged. His success in this was indifferent. Only in rare cases did the Indians recognize the masks and, while he learned about some of them, this was not nearly as much as he had hoped and expected. The task, he discovered, presented extraordinary difficulties because Powell and Jacobsen had recorded neither the family nor the lineage from which they had come and such information was vital to securing explanations. Moreover, the meanings of articles belonging to secret society dances were known only to the initiated. The circle of possible informants was thus severely circumscribed and different for each ritual piece.[6]

While Boas attempted to increase the ethnological value of the Berlin and New York collections, he was also intent upon securing a collection of his own, one that he could resell for a sum large enough to offset the credit extended by his uncle. The task occupied his mind from his arrival in Victoria until he had expended all the money he could spare for the purpose. His first day's observation convinced him that he could easily recover his travel costs: there were things to collect and they were valuable. He avoided buying anything in Victoria, quite correctly anticipating lower prices and better goods farther north. His first purchases were at Nuwitti, by which time he knew "exactly what I want to buy and assemble into a very compact collection."[7]

Boas brought to his Nuwitti collecting the sensitivities of a seasoned fieldworker and the discriminating taste of an experienced ethnographer and museum man. This latter was a new element to coastal collecting. Swan had had sensitivity and Jacobsen a hardy ingenuity, but neither had the respect for artifacts as scientific specimens and ethnological examples which Boas, as one of Bastian's bright young men, possessed. This affected both what and how he bought.

He began cautiously. He probably knew that five years earlier Jacobsen had found these Indians so tied to their aboriginal ways that they were unwilling to sell; indeed, their traditionalism is likely one reason why he selected the Nuwitti for initial research. He spent a full eleven days at this remote Kwakiutl village, but did not broach the subject of buying until the seventh day, spending the first week in intensive ethnological work — recording stories, sketching poles, observing shaman healings, watching dances and potlatches. On the fourth evening he gave his own potlatch to pay for a dance he had asked to be performed for him. His respectful patience secured the confidence of the villagers as probably no previous collector had. The Nuwitti chief praised him for his kindness and for the potlatch; he was "not like the other whites who have come to us." Should Boas want anything, "we shall do our best to do what he asks."[8]

Boas was thus well established to begin to buy. He had seen almost all the ethnological objects in the village, especially dance paraphernalia, knew their uses, and had recorded the stories associated with them. He knew what he wanted, had acquired the trust of the Nuwitti and a self-confidence of his own. Ned Harigon, the local trader, was enlisted to bargain for him "because I am supposed to be too aristocratic to do any trading." This meant, Boas wrote, that "in other words I would be cheated right and left," or, more accurately, that his assumed and accepted status would hinder him in the hard bargaining required to come to a proper price. All the circumstances were right and Boas was remarkably successful. He bought all the best masks, except two he was not allowed even to see, and many other good pieces, and he also put two women to work weaving mats and blankets for him. It was "a quite splendid collection."

In the next few days he gathered more, acting like "a real businessman" — "as though I had stood behind a counter all my life." He was delighted to have obtained the complete paraphernalia — masks, cedar rings, and whistles — of the winter ceremony, proud that this was the only collection from Nuwitti that was reasonably well labeled. Boas's patient ingratiation of his prospective vendors was not only a new and quite successful trick-of-the-trade in artifact collecting, it was also a means of retaining for those articles their ceremonial, religious, and mythological meaning, with the whole context of the object. Boas brought away with him virtually an entire dance complex, so far as it was material and portable.

In this first purchasing exercise can be seen two distinguishing marks of his general approach to ethnology: his concern for the particular phenomenon and his absorption in the mental processes of people. He collected these pieces, quite obviously, for speculative reasons, yet they reflected his ethnological concerns, first, for the importance of the specific (in this case the precise winter ceremonial as observed among the Nuwitti Kwakiutl of Vancouver Island), and, second, for the psychological (in this case the mythology and meaning of the ceremonialism). The objects were not curios; they were objects whose significance, as he later wrote, came from "the thoughts that cluster around them."[9] He was concerned that his masks have stories and he continued to search for "meanings" in Jacobsen's Berlin masks for decades after they had been collected.

Although highly satisfied with his Nuwitti collection, it was a small one, not exceeding 65 pieces. He added to it, more indiscriminately, in Alert Bay so that he judged its worth to be at least $250, though he had laid out only $70. He had bought cheaply and felt a mixture of surprise, delight, and embarrassment at his actions. Though he felt "just like a merchant," he knew it was a good collection for which he might make "a tidy profit." Early in November he lost his purse; the $35 it contained left him short of money and he bought little else. The loss did not prevent him from scouring an old graveyard in Quamichan where he picked up two well-preserved deformed skulls and more from middens at Comox. The entire collection, now some 140 pieces (not counting the skulls), went off ahead of him to New York. He intended offering first refusal to the American Museum where he also hoped to secure a curatorial position.[10]

The collection now took on a further purpose. Primarily a speculative venture to pay his costs, he also hoped it would be a useful instrument in his pursuit of the New York job. He had heard of a possible opening before he left and, even while in British Columbia, he had exploited all avenues in his pursuit of it, especially his connection with Jacobi and Jacobi's close friend, the influential Carl Schurz. Boas hoped, too, that Heber Bishop, now a museum trustee, would be attracted not only to his collection but to having a curator of anthropology who was an expert in the Northwest Coast. He would offer the New Yorkers his collection, but "if I do not get a position, it will probably go to Berlin."[11]

On his return to New York Boas exhibited the collection to Bickmore and others at a gathering to which he lectured for two hours (Schurz complimented him on his English). He had asked $600 for it, but Schurz and others urged him to put the price higher, to $1,000, which he did. Bickmore regarded the collection as "very interesting," felt Boas would happily take $500 for it, and called it to Bishop's attention. But Boas was disappointed. Bishop did not come forward with the purchase money, nor did the museum decide to hire a new curator. His consolation was a contract with Bishop to label and arrange the Powell collection, for which he would receive $300. The largest part of his own collection went on to Berlin. "The interest of the Berlin Museum really lie in my heart," he wrote Bastian, but it was New York's indifference, especially to hiring him, and Bastian's promise of $500 which sealed the bargain. Bastian claimed he could afford no more, soon regretted even this commitment, and tried to delay payment until 1888. For the $500 Boas sent ninety-four pieces, holding back another twenty to exchange with the U. S. National Museum on Berlin's behalf. For these Bastian was obliged, it seems, for another $100.[12] The whole business went on to wearysome length, leading to unpleasant letters between him and Bastian and difficulties with Otis T. Mason in Washington over the exchange. It appeared harder to dispose of a collection than to acquire one. But there were profits in the end.

Boas had paid $120 for the collection; he realized $600 from it (and still retained some valuable pieces). While hardly a bad profit margin, the trip had cost him $900, making the gain from the collection only slightly more than half of his expenses. Fortunately, he found congenial employment as an editor with *Science,* the New York weekly published by N. D. C. Hodges. The $150 a month from that, the Bishop contract, 150 Marks from Bastian for an Eskimo collection, and the promised $500 for the Northwest Coast material allowed him to repay his uncle and, more important to him, to marry Marie Krackowizer and to commit himself to a North American career.

In the meantime, Boas travelled to Washington to study the Northwest Coast collections in the precincts of the National Museum. To his consternation he found them not displayed together, as were the Eskimo collections he knew from his earlier visits, but scattered in various parts of the building, exhibited among articles from dozens of different groups. It was not a random scattering, but a deliberate display technique that grouped articles by purpose and use rather than by tribal or cultural origin. There was, moreover, an attempt to display an evolutionary sequence of development within each type. To Boas this method of display was both strange and wrong: it tore the individual object from its only meaningful context and put it into artificial categories imposed upon it by the curator. His attack, published in the new forum which his *Science* position gave him, touched on more than museum display techniques, and the subsequent controversy revealed some fundamentally different conceptions of the nature of anthropology.

In the emerging ethnological museum of the nineteenth century, directors and curators had had to find their own ways as best they could. Natural history and other fields with longer antecedents gave ethnologists models or examples but no certain solution to the oldest and most controversial question of nineteenth-century museum practice. Divergent views of how ethnological objects should be arranged and classified emerged as early as the first proposals for ethnology museums and thus before even the museums themselves. E.-F. Jomard urged that a museum ought to present "a progressive tableau of the industry of man from those which meet his most basic needs to his most luxurious development," essentially a statement of what was to become the classification by type-and-evolution of the U. S. National Museum. Jomard's friend P. F. von Siebold argued for an arrangement based exclusively upon the ethnic origin of the specimens.[13]

In continental Europe the tendency was toward von Siebold's view, that is, the installation of exhibits by geographical area or ethnic association. The examples of classical archaeology, art, and decorative art museums may have been an influence; perhaps it was merely that such an arrangement "was basically so simple and natural" that it was adopted without reflection.

At Dresden, Gustav Klemm, librarian and director of the porcelain collection, as well as author of a multi-volume study of "the cultural history of humanity," assembled his own collection on the basis of type of specimen to show developmental sequence, and its 7,939 numbered items were so arranged when installed in Leipzig's new Museum für Völkerkunde in 1873. Within the decade, however, the Leipzig officials altered the arrangement to a standard geographical-ethnic one. On the Continent, after 1878, only Dresden maintained any displays according to type or sequence. There A. B. Meyer, whose museum, like his own research, incorporated both anthropology and zoology, arranged the general collections according to geographical area, but had type collections for knives, fire implements, money, musical instruments, and several other categories.[14]

Type collections had their greatest favor in England. The British Museum used a tribal or regional scheme, as did most of the smaller provincial and municipal museums, but the collection of Col. A. Lane Fox, opened to the public at Bethnal Green in 1874 and subsequently donated by its owner to Oxford University, used a very thorough evolutionary scheme of classification by type. Lieutenant-General Pitt Rivers, to use Lane Fox's later rank and name, came to ethnological collecting in part through preparing a collection to illustrate the history and development of firearms. Noting how progress from the simpler to the more complex forms often came about as the result of a succession of very slight changes, it struck him that this kind of evolutionary progress might be applied more generally to all arts and industries. With the idea of evolution, progress, and development in mind, he made an extensive ethnological collection on this arrangement and then, by Deed of Gift, imposed the order upon his Oxford museum in perpetuity. Evolution was "the one great feature which it is desirable to emphasize in connection with the exhibition of archaeological and ethnological specimens," he told a British Association audience in 1888. While a geographical or tribal arrangement had its advantages in highlighting the *ethnological* features of each group, his system possessed "greater *sociological* value" because it made apparent "the development of specific ideas and their transmission from one people to another, or from one locality to another."[15]

In the Pitt Rivers collection the stress was upon ordinary and typical specimens arranged "so as to trace, as far as practicable, the succession of ideas by which the minds of men in a primitive condition of culture have progressed from the simple to the complex, and from the homogeneous to the heterogeneous." His favorite example of evolutionary development was the boomerang; in his cases he laid out Australian examples in series to show how the most bent shape was merely an elaboration of a straight stick, which, in other lines of descent, had also evolved into the throwing stick, the lance, the club, and even from a parrying staff into the shield.[16]

Pitt Rivers's arrangement was not a personal crochet. Henry Balfour, curator after 1891, extended its range and sophisticated its arrangement. The inspiration was as much biological as sociological (Balfour was trained in zoology). The museum's exhibition "is like that employed in the arrangement of most natural-history museums," he wrote, with "the objects being grouped according to their morphological affinities and resemblances (as it were), all objects of like form and function being brought together into groups, which again are subdivided into smaller groups — into genera and species, as one might say." When the ethnological collections of tea merchant Frederick J. Horniman were given to the London County Council in 1901, along with a new £40,000 Forest Hill building done in an impressive variant of *Wienersezession* style, the advisory curator, A. C. Haddon (also a zoologist by origin), recommended that it become the one London museum "definitely set apart to illustrate the evolution of culture." The Horniman Free Museum installation was thus "designed to throw light upon the evolutionary process by which the changing present has been derived from the unstable past," and "to suggest the general line of advance in arts, crafts, and ideas from the time of early man."[17]

In the United States, arrangement by geographic area or by tribal groups was adopted at Harvard's Peabody Museum and elsewhere. The American Museum's few collections were exhibited by collector or donor, which usually meant a geographical result; after 1894, they were arranged systematically by ethnic group.

Arrangements at the National Museum in Washington were quite different. Here the installation had increasingly followed the lines advocated by Jomard and Klemm and used by General Pitt Rivers. Items were placed with like items: musical instruments were exhibited with similar kinds of musical instruments irrespective of their geographic and tribal provenance, while weapons went into a "series" with other weapons. Within each series, the specimens were ordered into a supposed evolutionary sequence so as to demonstrate the history of human progress from savagery to civilization. Such an installation system had been used at the museum in a limited way as early as 1873. In the same year Otis

T. Mason, an instructor at the city's Columbian College and anthropological assistant in the museum, published a description of the evolutionary organization of Klemm's collection, just acquired by Leipzig. What appealed to Mason in the Klemm system was its seemingly scientific character, so analogous to natural history's systematic classification. A typological classification arranged by developmental sequence offered "a systematic arrangement of the facts respecting the human race."[18] Installation of the museum's collections according to this system gathered impetus after G. Brown Goode's appointment as assistant director of the museum.

Goode, an ichthyologist, turned his scientific mind to museum administration with extraordinary thoroughness. He was, an acquaintance noted, "a deviser of methods and systems." The chief requisite to the success of a great museum, he felt, was a "perfect plan of organization and a philosophical system of classification." To these he gave much thought in his first years under Baird. After considering the methods of the large European museums while abroad for the Berlin Fisheries Exhibition, he announced in 1881 a comprehensive plan for making the entire National Museum into a museum of anthropology in "a broad sense." Man was to be the focus of the plan, the central pivot around which all was to revolve. Goode decided, doubtless in collaboration with Mason, "that the ordinary classification by races or tribes" was less satisfactory "than a classification based upon function." Exhibits would be organized to show the evolution of any given industry or class of objects by a series that began with the simplest types and ended "with the most perfect and elaborate objects of the same class which human effort had produced."[19]

It was an audacious scheme which justified its claim of placing together in continuous series objects "which had never before been placed side by side in any museum."[20] By embracing not merely the usual archaeological or ethnological material, it provided a continuum of prehistory and history, of primitive and civilized. At the end of a series on land transportation would stand a steam locomotive, representing the nineteenth-century culmination of a development that had begun with tump-lines and skids.

Implementation of the generic classification was cautious. Musical instruments and costumes were put into a type sequence, but Goode still regarded the method as provisional and engaged in a good deal of experimentation.

Otis Mason, ever since he had edited the texts of Gustav Klemm, firmly believed in museum ethnology by biological analogy. He announced that his department would follow "all the lines of investigation pursued by naturalists," considering "the whole human race in space and time as a single group" and all the arts and industries of man as if they were genera and species. Exhibitions would be arranged "to show the natural history of the objects." Mason's research strategy followed the same principle as his exhibition series: he published monographs dealing with types of specimens — throwing sticks, basketry, cradles, harpoons, and bows and arrows — rather than ethnographies of single tribes. He nevertheless admitted that the museum's collections "should not be forcibly strained into subjection to any one scheme." The same object could be arranged by tribe, material, structure, function, evolution, or geographical distribution, and no perfect scheme could omit any one of these. Indeed, an ethnic basis of display would be followed in the National Museum whenever its collections justified it; but when these did not offer enough for a "total life history of a tribe or race," the best practice was to use the material "to show the elaboration of the various human arts" and ultimately "to exhibit the progress in culture of the whole race."[21]

The Eskimo collections were sufficient to install on an ethnic basis, though even within that scheme, function and evolution of each implement were the criteria for installation in the tiered boxes that traced them through fourteen arctic locations. Other installations would follow the series principle: arrow-makers' tools, weaving, pottery production, North American gambling, and narcotic indulgences.

It was at this point that Franz Boas, just back from his first trip to the Northwest Coast, entered the Smithsonian's precincts to study the National Museum's collection from the area. He found items scattered in a dozen different typological exhibits. His anger at this method of display, in which "the marked character of the North-west American tribes is almost lost," was released in a courteous but outspoken public attack upon the National Museum's ethnology display. In a sweeping condemnation of both the arrangement and the assumptions that lay behind it, he charged that the evolutionary method of classification created a rupture between the artifact and its natural setting. In Boas's view, the meaning of an artifact could be understood only within the context of its surroundings, among the implements of the people to whom it belonged and with the other phenomenon of that people and their neighbors. The specimen, then, was best understood when seen within a collection representing the life of but one group. "We want," he wrote, "a collection arranged according to tribes, in order to teach the peculiar style of each group. The art and characteristics of a people can be understood only by studying its productions as a whole." Mason went greatly astray, Boas charged, when he regarded ethnological phenomena as biological specimens and when he classified them according to the abstractions of species, genus, and family, because he thereby missed the essential points that "in ethnology all is individuality" and that "classification is not explanation."[22]

Boas went beyond axioms and aphorisms to accuse Mason's arrangement of being unfit for scientific research: by basing itself upon deductive arguments from analogy, it did not allow for application of the inductive method. The outward appearances of two phenomena might be quite identical, yet their "immanent qualities" could be altogether different. All rattles were constructed to make noise, but they could be quite varied in psychological intent and in usage, one the outcome of religious conceptions and utilized for sacred events, another representing childrens' pleasure in all noises. The important principle overlooked by Mason was that "unlike causes produce like effects." The only fact which Mason's collections of implements taught was that different men make similar things, that drums were used by savages and by modern orchestras; it told nothing about the character of the music of each, the very thing that was, after all, "the only object worth studying." In all of this the National Museum was fooling both itself and its visitors. It was creating patterns that did not exist in the nature of the material, but were imposed by the curator. The museum created "classifications that are not founded on the phenomenon, but in the mind of the student."

Mason replied to the attack, coolly explaining that there were a variety of ways in which curators might classify and exhibit their specimens and his museum had chosen to give prominence to one which it thought most important. Ideally, he would construct a museum in the form of a checker-board so that in one way the cases would show a single tribe, while at right angles they would exhibit a single feature across cultures. Though conceding diverse possibilities in exhibition, Mason was not swayed from the primacy of biological analogy. "I think it is a growing conviction," he wrote, "that inventions of both customs and things spring from prior inventions, just as life springs from life," and that "we must always apply the methods and instrumentalities of the biologist" if ethnology were to be properly constituted. Finally, Mason absolved both himself and his system from responsibility for the diffusion of Northwest Coast material within the museum: he had not touched that region's artifacts since his appointment.[23]

Support for Mason's general position came from Major J. W. Powell, who deemed a tribal arrangement quite impossible both by nature and in practice, while Boas's views were tepidly backed by W. H. Dall and more vigorously elsewhere by F. W. Putnam of Harvard. At the latter's Peabody Museum "a natural classification" was used in which objects belonging to each people were grouped together. "By this method is brought out the ethnological value of every object," Putnam wrote. "There is no forcing into line, no selection of material, in order to illustrate a theory. Every object falls into its place with its own associates, and tells its part of the story of the efforts of man and the results which he has reached at in different times and different places."[24]

Neither side won the 1887 version of the controversy. Probably Boas made the weaker case with his diffuse and often incoherent arguments, his insistence upon only a single way in which specimens ought to be exhibited, and his statement, questionable even today, that "the main object of ethnological collections should be the dissemination of the fact that civilization is not something absolute, but that it is relative, and that our ideas and conceptions are true so far as our civilization goes." Mason had no monopoly on tendenciousness, of exhibits to illustrate a theory. Mason's own reasoned flexibility, his contention that different students were interested in different things, was probably more persuasive than his biological assumptions. Certainly he was not deflected from his classificatory schema, pursuing his plan for "elaborating series of specimens on natural history principles" by arranging for new exhibitions of cradles, scrapers, and human packing apparatus.[25]

Yet Mason and his colleagues at Washington remained open-minded in their arrangements, adaptable to various methods and sensitive to outside trends. In 1887–88, alongside displays of land transportation and bows and arrows, Mason began other installations following his Eskimo precedent, that is, arranged according to "definite and well-characterized areas." Among these, perhaps partially in deference to Boas, perhaps merely because of the richness of the museum's holdings, was the Northwest Coast.[26]

Goode and Mason, without altering their intellectual allegiance to type classification, did not strongly pursue it in practice. As early as 1888 Thomas Wilson, their archaeological colleague, threw over developmental series for "the unity of neighborhoods." In 1893 Goode wrote of the idea in the past tense, as an "at one time" intention, not abandoned, but unrealized because of practical difficulties of installation and space. Mason retained a similar commitment to the method. When visiting European museums in 1889 he was extremely disappointed that Leipzig's museum, with its Klemm collection, was closed. (He seems not to have realized that the director, Hermann Obst, had rearranged it on ethnic principles more than a decade earlier.) Dresden, still partially committed to a topical system, he found to be the best administered museum in the world. The Berlin museum was remarkable for the immensity of its collections, but, by using a simple arrangement by regions, nationalities, or tribes, it made little attempt "to work out any of the finer problems of ethnology." The new Pitt Rivers Museum, on the other hand, was a "gem" where his own methods were perfectly implemented in one functional series after another. Oxford was the only museum where "every piece has a raison d'être." While seemingly satisfied, even confirmed, in his method, Mason soon moved toward a conception of ethnology in terms of geographic areas. To a large measure this was a consequence of his suggestion that the Smithsonian's anthropological exhibition at the World's Columbian Exposition in Chicago be a joint effort of the National Museum and the Bureau of Ethnology, using as its guiding feature Major Powell's "great linguistic map" of North America, just published and "the crowning result of ethnological labors on our continent during fifty years." This decision was consistent with his flexibility, but it did undermine his commitment to developmental typologies. The shift from tech-

nological types to linguistic stocks as an organizing principle propelled Mason toward a geographic determinism.[27]

Mason intended the display to investigate the relationship
between climate and natural resources and the arts, industries,
language, and races of the North American Indian. The Chicago
exposition offered an opportunity to test those questions and he
was very pleased with the results. The great diversity of stocks
crowded into the homogeneous environment of the Pacific coast,
for example, allowed fruitful ethnological studies which showed
that while languages might be "radically different" and tribal
organization "entirely unlike," in the satisfaction of their material
necessities, the divergent tribes had "yielded to regional or geographical forces." Material culture, he concluded, was controlled
by the environment while spiritual or metaphysical expressions
"were overwhelmingly ethnic and linguistic."[28]

While Goode and Mason were moving toward a geographical
exhibition method, their position still differed fundamentally
from that of Boas. They were moving in the direction from
which he had departed, although, as he might have said, unlike
causes were producing similar effects in actual exhibition appearance. Mason's preoccupation was with "arts and industries," with
the material culture which was the basis of museum collections
and exhibitions. Boas was also a collector and interested himself
in museum exhibitions, but he was more interested in the idea
behind the material phenomenon, in the mental processes of the
people, and more especially in what this might show of the history of the culture.

Boas had begun his career with an environmental hypothesis for
the Baffin Island Eskimo and was unconvinced by the efficacy of
that approach. Geographical and climatic explanations were too
patent and obvious and did not touch on the origins of cultural
traits or their distribution. Many traits were found beyond the
geographical region and seemed to predate a group's migration to
its present environment. "Anthropogeographical considerations"
could not be a sufficient basis for the study of the origins of any
culture, he wrote in 1888, "as their influence is only secondary in
determining, to a certain extent, the direction in which the culture
develops." Study of cultural origins must begin, he continued,
with investigation of ethnology and physical character.[29]

The attack by Boas on the Washington establishment had been audacious, even presumptuous. He was in 1887 still a very young man scarcely established in the United States. He had, it is true, already made a mark for himself for his work on the Central Eskimo, but his reputation was slender and his position as yet far from established. It had been a bold step to use his *Science* columns in so direct an attack upon the National Museum's exhibition pattern, one of its most cherished ideas.

Boas was able to fortify his standing in American science by further fieldwork in the West, this conducted under the auspices of and with funds from the North-western Tribes Committee of the British Association for the Advancement of Science. The opportunity had come at the beginning of 1888 when Horatio Hale asked him to undertake field research in British Columbia for the Committee.

Hale and Boas had met at the 1886 Buffalo meetings of the American Association for the Advancement of Science. Now a man of advanced age, Hale had worked on the Oregon tribes as a young philologist with the Wilkes expedition in 1842. Long deflected from ethnological work, he had lately returned to it in his retirement. Resident in Ontario, he had taken charge of the ethnological survey of the northwest tribes of Canada funded by the British Association and the Canadian government and nominally under the chairmanship of Oxford's E. B. Tylor. Finding that he could arrange summer leave from *Science,* Boas accepted the offer with alacrity and departed on his second Northwest Coast visit in May 1888.

Boas's instructions were to make a general survey of British Columbia tribes, with emphasis on language and physical anthropology, and to prepare an ethnological map of the province. As he had already done linguistic research and prepared an ethnographic map for *Petermanns,* he devoted much of his energy on this trip to physical anthropology, to measuring Indians (usually those in jail), and more especially to collecting skulls and skeletons. This he pursued with his usual zeal and, as with his ethnology collection in 1886, with speculative intent.

Stealing bones from a grave was "repugnant work" and even prompted horrid dreams, but "someone has to do it" and, he emphasized, skeletons were "worth money." He dug in a burial ground near Victoria, on an island near Port Essington (while a photographer distracted the Indians), in Saanich, and, on his way home, at Lytton. He could collect only a dozen or so skulls himself and about the same number of skeletons, but he heard of a Cowichan collection of about 75 skulls that James and William Sutton had gathered for the American phrenological market. The collection proved exciting. Boas spent an entire day measuring it, finding to his surprise considerable variation within a single linguistic group. When he received assurance from Washington that there was a market for such material, he bought the entire Sutton collection, bringing his British Columbia total to some 85 skulls and 14 complete skeletons. The Sutton brothers were willing to gather more and Boas, telling them of some sites he knew of, left an order for whatever they could find. Working both by land and sea, the Suttons gathered 48 skeletons complete with crania, one without, and 74 skulls — a total of 123 individuals in all. A recount reduced the number to 119, perhaps "a few more" than Boas had wanted, but the collection should be kept whole, the Suttons thought, "as it makes along with what you already have a complete collection from one end of the island to the other." At Boas's rate of $20 for a complete skeleton and $5 for a skull, the value of the collection was about $1,300; certainly, wrote William Sutton, it was worth at least $1,000 and he had laid out in cash about half that amount.[30]

The collection had cost "a great deal more trouble & expense" than Sutton anticipated. The bones were "in caves and such out of the way places" that he had had "to buy some of the indians" at a dollar each to show him the sites. That had let the word out and "some half breeds at Fort Rupert started quite a disturbance and tried to incite the Indians to shoot them." Then S. A. Spencer at Alert Bay had laid a complaint before the provincial police, causing William "quite a lively time to prevent an investigation." The bones were a possible embarrassment and "I would like to get them off my hands as soon as possible." He was "afraid of the authorities confiscating them, there has been such a disturbance over them, they may be compelled to take action." The matter became even more urgent in January when the Cowichan Indians found that some of their graves had been molested and raised "quite a rumpus." Information was laid against James Sutton and a warrant obtained to search his Cowichan sawmill for the bones, but nothing was found.

Nevertheless, the Indians hired a lawyer to proceed with the case.[31]

While the Suttons worried in British Columbia, Boas delayed in New York. He dearly wanted the bones but did not have the money. He finally made an arrangement to pay in installments, and Sutton shipped the skeletons and crania to the American Museum, invoiced with a falsified origin and labelled as natural history specimens — "an incognito that answered well." There were about a dozen fewer pieces than Sutton had earlier mentioned "on account of not being able to go after some we had stowed away, owing to the rumpus with the Indians." Most came from Discovery Island, from the environs of Victoria, and from among the Cowichan in the Koksilah River area. Boas's total physical anthropology holdings thus amounted to about 200 crania, of which 100 belonged to complete skeletons. These, secured "by the help of some friends," had cost him $1,600.[32] He quickly looked for purchasers, trying to interest, without success, the New York museum, Virchow in Berlin, and Dawson in Ottawa. In any case, he wanted to keep the collection together at least until he had finished work on it. In the meantime it was stored, first at the American Museum and then, with his appointment as docent at Clark University, at the university's laboratories. Over the next few years it grew by about another hundred, a few skulls gathered on the coast in 1889 and 1890, but most of them non-Northwest Coast purchases and gifts. He finally disposed of the collection, partly to Virchow's Berlin museum and the remainder, with some difficulty, to Chicago's Field Columbian Museum in 1894.

While osteological collecting occupied much of Boas's energy on his 1888 trip, he also made a small collection of about fifty-seven pieces — mostly dance material, but also a shaman's outfit — for the American Museum. This latter collecting irritated G. M. Dawson, a member of the BAAS committee which was financing the larger part of Boas's field work and the man in Ottawa most interested in the Geological Survey's museum and in the Northwest Coast. Dawson saw to it that on Boas's next field trip any collecting would be for the Ottawa museum. He secured authorization of up to $300, from which Boas was able to buy such "very nice pieces" that he was sad to have to pass them on so quickly. A few, worth $48.30, went to Oxford on order from E. B. Tylor. Tylor particularly wanted a shaman's "soul catcher," a piece of great interest, he wrote, to the history of religion.[33]

Dawson secured another $300 for Boas in 1890, but Boas literally missed the boat that summer and did not get north of Victoria, New Westminster, and Ladner. Before going to British Columbia, he did research, supported by Major Powell's Bureau of Ethnology, on Oregon and Washington state tribes, and there gathered a dozen items from the Quinault, Tillimook, and Chinook for the National Museum.

Early in 1891 Boas accepted an assignment to work on the anthropological exhibits planned for the 1893 Chicago World's Fair, the exposition to be held in honor of the 400th anniversary of the discovery of America by Columbus. In charge of "Department M," somewhat mislabeled as the Department of Ethnology, was Frederic Ward Putnam, director of the Peabody Museum at Harvard.[34] Putnam, who, like Horatio Hale, had met Boas at the AAAS meetings in Buffalo, asked the young immigrant scientist to serve as assistant in charge of physical anthropology and to supervise a special display of Northwest Coast tribes. As part of his duties, Boas entered into correspondence with hundreds of schoolteachers, missionaries, and administrators to arrange the measurement of over 90,000 North American school children and 17,000 Indians. Simultaneously, he set in motion a scheme for a comprehensive Northwest Coast Indian exhibition that would focus on the Fort Rupert Kwakiutl.

A trip west in the summer was largely consumed by ethnological work for the Bureau of Ethnology along the Columbia and Yakima rivers, but Boas also made arrangements for World's Fair collections with a number of coastal acquaintances and particularly with George Hunt. Upon his return east in September, the outlines of the fair display were firm.

The Fort Rupert Indians would be the "standard tribe," with additional collections from the Haida, Tsimshian, Nootka, and other neighboring tribes. The Kwakiutl were made the pivot of the display because, Boas wrote, they were central to the region's culture, which had its origin among these Fort Rupert tribes whose influence had been exerted over the other tribes on the coast. The evidence of this was in the borrowed Kwakiutl names given to all those ceremonies which played so important a part in the customs of their neighbors. Boas had arranged with Hunt for a collection of the necessary specimens to ilustrate Kwakiutl life and culture and, moreover, had arranged that Hunt bring to Chicago a group of Kwakiutl "to show whatever is asked of them in relation to their customs and mode of life particularly the ceremonies connected with their secret religious societies." Hunt would bring a large house, canoes, the outfits of daily life, and all that was necessary for the performance of ceremonials.[35]

For his collections Boas enlisted the assistance of experienced people he knew on the coast. James Deans, the old HBC man from Victoria who had assisted Pinart in his shell-heap collecting in 1876 and had toured the Queen Charlottes with Swan in 1883, and who was a frequent contributor of ethnological miscellania to the *American Antiquarian* and other journals, he commissioned to make a Haida collection. Fillip Jacobsen, who had stayed on the coast after bringing home the Hagenbeck Bella Coolas, was to make a Bella Coola collection. Mrs. O. Morrison, native wife of Charles Morrison, the Fort Simpson trader so helpful to Swan, was to collect at Port Essington and on the Skeena. Swan himself, now seventy-three years old and already working for Washington State's exhibit, was to collect from Cape Flattery. Myron Eells, a Congregational minister also engaged in the state display, was charged with gathering a representative collection of the Puget Sound Salish, while others were asked to collect at Shoalwater Bay and in the British Columbia interior.

The Boas team began their work in earnest in the spring of 1892. Their collections began arriving in Chicago in the fall, stored in the acres of warehouses specially erected for the exposition. From Deans came three boxcarloads of Haida material. "The wide world will stand in amazement" was his confident assessment of the beauty of Haida art as revealed by his collection. Ceremonial and shamanistic material was included, along with an entire Skidegate house and its forty-two foot pole. It was, he admitted, "a rather poor specimen of a Haida house but then, as so few of the old houses were left & I could do no better." At least as unusual was a set of models which accurately reconstructed Skidegate village at its 1864 prime: twenty-five houses and poles, ten memorial columns, six grave posts, and two burial houses.[36]

The model Haida village collected by James Deans, with other exhibits from the Chicago Fair as initially installed in the Field Columbian Museum. Courtesy, Field Museum of Natural History.

Jacobsen sent a Bella Coola collection costing $554 and particularly strong in clan and secret society material and in stone implements. From Mrs. Morrison came almost $500 worth of Nass and Skeena pieces, some of which, including two large poles, had been bought through merchant Robert Cunningham. Swan sent a small collection of sixty-five articles from Neah Bay, and Eells a good sampling of everyday articles from Puget Sound, as well as a collection of models illustrating every canoe type to be found between the Columbia River and Cape Flattery.

Last to arrive — delayed by storms at Fort Rupert and Alert Bay — was Hunt's collection. It was easily the largest: in addition to a whole house, it had some 365 pieces heavily emphasizing the winter ceremonials. Hamatsa, Grizzly Bear, Nutlamatla — virtually every Kwakiutl (and some Bella Coola) secret society — were represented.

Boas felt that his collaborators' efforts had resulted in the most systematic collection every presented. Putnam judged the collections as "the most complete and important ever brought together from this, ethnologically, most interesting region." The assessments were exaggerated, but qualifiedly true. On the other hand, items were frequently poorly labeled since Boas had put aside his usual concern with stories and explanations.[37]

To this collection was added the loaned Tlingit collection of Edward E. Ayer, a Chicagoan who had made his fortune supplying railway ties, first to the Northwestern, then to the Union Pacific roads. "A natural born collector," his accumulation of ethnological artifacts became his chief recreation and delight. He had begun as a young man on a trip to California and continued while on army service in Arizona and New Mexico. Once in business, he collected as he travelled across the Plains, realizing that native life would soon be a thing of the past. With his wealth he bought everything he could lay his hands on, almost entirely from Indian traders in all parts of North America. His Northwest Coast collection came largely from an 1887 Alaska trip on the *Ancona,* which called at every cannery. At each stop he bought what he could, "and I had good luck, for I had two cabins full of Indian stuff." As usual it came indirectly: "I very rarely purchased relics through chiefs, though; mostly through dealers." Carl Spuhn, the Northwest Trading Company's agent at Killisnoo was on board the ship and, observing Ayer's purchases, told him that "up in our loft we have any quantity of these things, and you can have all you want." At Killisnoo he "got all that three or four men could carry." Spuhn would take nothing for it. Ayer later reflected that the loft collection "would be worth several thousand dollars now. He was a very fine chap."[38] Before taking it to the World's Fair, Ayer had displayed the collection at his Lake Geneva, Wisconsin, summer home — in a converted bowling alley. The poles were piled up against the barn.

The Northwest Coast exhibit, along with hundreds of others brought to Chicago by Putnam's assistants, by private collectors, by states and foreign governments, was intended for installation in the gigantic Manufacturers and Liberal Arts Building. The clamor of numerous exhibitors for additional space, however, pushed Department M out of that centrally located building and into a special one, belatedly begun for Putnam's department and a Liberal Arts spillover. Inevitably, construction was delayed and the Anthropological Building was finished a full month after the opening of Chicago's Great White City. Despite efficient installation by department staff, the exhibits were open to the public only on July 4, nine weeks late. Even then visitors had difficulty finding the building.

The Anthropological Building, shoved into the neglected and badly treated southeast corner of the grounds, inaccessible and distant from the central buildings, and hemmed in by the lake, the dairy barns, powerhouse, and train lines — "by what might be called the kitchen and back yard of the exhibition" — was "likely to be overlooked by nine out of every ten visitors." A plain and unpretentious structure whose only asset was that it contained the necessary space, "the Anthropological Building is the furthest in the rear, the most forlorn in its exterior and interior, and pre-eminently the one with the most promise of being a failure." The sorrowful fact was that Putnam had been squeezed out — "buffeted about by more worldly and self-assertive chiefs of departments" and disliked by Director Harlow N. Higinbotham.[39]

The department's outdoor exhibits were not hampered by building problems and were ready for the opening. Putnam had arranged reproductions of Yucatan ruins in front of the building and the portal from Labna and the Serpent House of Uxmal shared pride of place with a Southwest cliff dwelling replicated to natural size. On the ethnographic grounds north of the building, along the shores of South Pond, were the habitations of the native groups, most particularly two Northwest Coast houses occupied by the Kwakiutl.

Reminiscent of the unfulfilled ambition of Swan and Baird for the 1876 Philadelphia exhibition, and following a direct precedent established at Paris in 1889, the Chicago exhibition would display native groups living in their own habitations and demonstrating their crafts, customs, and ceremonies. The thrust of the Columbian Exposition was to honor America's pioneers and to celebrate the accomplishments of four hundred years of American progress. Putnam's aim was even more retrospective: to show the inhabitants of pre-Columbian America. The government's office of Indian Affairs would exhibit civilization's work upon the American aborigines in model schools.[40]

Boas arranged for Hunt to bring as many as fourteen adults (of which four should be married couples). The consent of the Canadian Indian Affairs department was secured and early in April 1893, fifteen adults and two children, led by George Hunt and escorted by James Deans, arrived in Chicago. William Hunt and his Koskimo wife, the only longhead of the party, were with the group. They were all housed temporarily in three small rooms in the stock pavilion, with mattresses and bed-clothing, six chairs, and two stoves being requisitioned for their comfort until they moved into the traditional beam and plank houses on the ethno-logical grounds. The construction of these, threatened by delays in the confusion of the last days before the fair's opening, was completed when Boas himself procured some missing timbers.

The Haida house, standing behind its immense pole, was small but impressive. The Kwakiutl house, formerly belonging to the Nakumgilisala of Nuwitti, was typically painted with a Thunder-bird over the door and moon crests to each side. Arranged nearby were canoes, poles, and posts, most gathered by Boas's collectors, but several loaned by Ayer. The beach in front of the houses was eventually graded for easy canoe access. The actual occupation of the houses in May became the occasion for "the first of a series of ceremonials" since the Indians "never enter any home without elaborate ceremonies." A requisition went in on the next to the last day before the fair's opening for 39 yards of blue and scarlet flannel, 232-dozen pearl buttons, and other material needed at once to complete the outfit of the Fort Rupert Indians.[41]

Despite the effort at systematic and authentic representation, the expeditions to Mexico and South America, and Boas's indefatig-able anthropometrics and Northwest Coast work, the fair's anthropology exhibit was something of a failure. It was significant enough in its own right (though probably not matching the impressive Paris display of four years earlier), but when pushed to the remote edge of Jackson Park, literally at the end of the railway track, it became marginal to the exposition. Moreover, the sheer size and diversity of the fair overwhelmed the department.

Chicago's was by far the largest world exposition yet under-taken, with more exhibits in an incomparably larger area than Paris and well over the Philadelphia Centennial's area, number of exhibitions, and attendance. Even the Kwakiutl made very little impression. It was not merely that they shared the ethnological grounds with an Apache craftsman and a Navaho family in their hogan, with four families of Penobscots in their birch bark wigwams, with representatives of the Six Nations in a traditional Iroquois bark house, and with British Guianese Arawaks in a thatched hut; the exoticism of these official exhibitions simply

*The Kwakiutl troupe at the Chicago World's Fair, 1893. American Museum of
Natural History.*

could not match the enormous color and panache of the ethnological exhibition "run riot" on the Midway Plaisance. This mile-
long "open mart and caravansary of nations" was a free-wheeling
entrepreneurial sideshow which almost overshadowed the exposition itself. Nominally the Midway was under the administration
of Putnam's department of ethnology — appropriate enough,
wrote the fair's official historian, for here the ethnologist could
study the actual daily life and customs of "peoples of every clime
and continent, typical representatives of all the varieties and races
of mankind." Crowded under G. W. G. Farris's 250-foot-high
wheel were 280 Egyptians and Sudanese in a Cairo street, 147
Indonesians in a Javanese village, 58 Eskimos from Labrador, a
party of bare-breasted Dahomans in a West African setting,
Malays, Samoans, Fijians, Japanese, Chinese, as well as an Irish
village with both Donegal and Blarney castles, and a reconstructed old Vienna street. The official ethnological exhibition
with its handful of Kwakiutl, Navaho, and Arawak was reduced
to insignificance. Only the most unusual or bloodcurdling Kwakiutl demonstrations could match the erotic Egyptian dancers and
other *succès de scandale* of the Midway.[42]

On May 24 the Queen's birthday was officially celebrated at the Canadian Building with an afternoon reception for all British subjects. At the same time a Kwakiutl canoe pushed off from the South Pond beach and, propelled by a dozen paddles, came round the canal and entered the Grand Basin through the classical peristyle. As it passed under the arch, the entire boatload stood up and "howled and danced to the jingle of the tamborine." The noise quickly drew several thousand spectators to the colonnaded waters, there to puzzle over "why the British flag should be floating over such a fierce, savage-looking lot."[43]

A far more horrible scene reportedly transpired one sweltering mid-August evening. In a gruesome enactment of what a journalist called the "Sun Dance," George Hunt cut two pairs of gashes through the skin of the backs of two Indians. While the two stood motionless, Hunt raised the flesh and passed heavy twine beneath the loose strips and tied the ends firmly together. The low monotone chant and the dull drum beats of the other Indians now became wilder and more violent as the two Indians, rivulets of blood trickling down from the cuts in their backs, raced round the platform driven like steeds by two more natives who seemed to take a wild pleasure in the act. "Around and around they ran, leaping, twisting, and diving till it seemed to the horror-stricken spectators that each instant would see the flesh torn from their bodies." The other Indians became frenzied and then, with eyes like wild animals and faces like famished wolves, the two tore the ropes from their fleshy fastenings, each "snapping and snarling like a mad dog" at the other Indians on the platform. Hunt walked over to one and extended a bare arm which was fastened upon with teeth that met in the flesh. When finally released, a piece the size of a silver dollar was missing from his arm, but he merely smiled, showing no signs of pain. In the hour or more that had elapsed a large part of their audience of five thousand had left, "sickened by the horrible sight."[44]

The Rev. Alfred J. Hall learned of the atrocious performance from the lurid *Sunday Times* account. He had only just arrived in London from Alert Bay and what he read of the pagan behavior of his Kwakiutl flock outraged him. He protested to Ottawa and demanded the cancellation of the Kwakiutl's engagement if that were at all possible. Before leaving Alert Bay he had, he said, done all he could to persuade the Indians not to go to Chicago and he confessed to having had some influence so that those who went had been gathered almost wholly from other villages. (It will be recalled that Hall had been quite successful in keeping the Fort Rupert Indians from leaving with Adrian and Fillip Jacobsen for Germany in 1885.) At Chicago on his way to London, he had personally observed that the U. S. government was proudly exhibiting civilized bands from their industrial schools, while from Canada came "only this display of paganism, chosen by Dr. Boaz because the most degraded he could find in the Dominion."[45]

Lawrence Vankoughnet, the deputy superintendent general of Indian Affairs and the recipient of Hall's outraged letter, responded immediately. He asked the Canadian commissioner at Chicago to have such exhibitions stopped at the earliest possible moment. A. W. Vowell, Powell's successor in Victoria, was told to ascertain from Kwakiutl agent R. H. Pidcock if he had known of Hunt's object in asking the Indians to appear at the fair and, if so, what measure he had taken to frustrate the endeavor. Pidcock replied that he knew Hunt had been commissioned by Boas to make a collection of curios and to persuade about a dozen Indians to go to Chicago to illustrate their mode of life, but he had had no idea that Hunt contemplated any such dance as reported. He had discouraged any Indians who had asked his advice. He had been led to believe, he wrote, "that the party were in [the] charge of Dr Boaz or his agent and that Hunt was only employed as Interpreter, as I should not consider that he was at all a fit and proper person to have charge of a party of Indians." From Chicago J. S. Larke confirmed the event. Although "the barbarism I think was not as great as described," some of the cruel and revolting scenes as reported in the *Sunday Times* had occurred. So much repugnance had been created that exposition authorities promised to halt any repeat performance.[46]

Like the Bella Coola's performance of an "Eagle Dance," it is difficult to determine how much of this "Sun Dance" was real and how much hokum. Boas described a similar dance, the *hawi'nalaL,* a few years later and, though he usually was careful to mention the special effects used to simulate bloody scenes, his account contains no mention of theatrical devices. Charles Nowell described a similar ceremony, which he called the "Warrior Dance," in which there was no fakery — it "hurted a little bit" when the flesh was pierced, but during the dance "I didn't hardly feel any pain at all." Larke's letter, too, seems testimony that the newspaper reports, though exaggerated, had a basis in fact. Another incident involving apparently vicious and bloody beatings turned out to be pure folly: the clubs were made of kelp and filled with red paint.[47]

While the presence of fifteen Kwakiutl in Jackson Park for the better part of six months occasioned difficulties (there were, for example, some liquor problems), the group did not in other ways produce as much interest as Boas might have liked. Moreover, he found himself too busy with administrative work to advance greatly his own Kwakiutl studies. He was able, however, to teach Hunt to record linguistic texts in phonetic script, preliminary to the thousands of pages of myths, descriptions, and other texts that Hunt would send to New York in the following years.

In one respect the fair was a reunion. Capt. J. Adrian Jacobsen was at Hagenbeck's Arena on the Midway where he exhibited the unsold portion of the British Columbia collection which he and Fillip had made in 1885–86. George Hunt, Jacobsen's very useful assistant back in 1881–82, and his brother William and his wife were, of course, in Chicago. All three had intended to go with the Jacobsens to Germany eleven years before. Boas discovered that almost all the Kwakiutl material in Berlin had been bought from members of the Chicago troupe and that he could get full descriptions of the specimens for Bastian. Jacobsen even claimed partial credit for the Kwakiutls' presence in Chicago: the favorable reports made by the returned Bella Coolas of their trip to Europe had helped Hunt in convincing his Kwakiutl friends to make the Chicago visit.

Jacobsen's collection, inappropriately displayed among Hagenbeck's trained animals, was only one of a number of Northwest Coast collections which supplemented the Boas-supervised material in Department M. In the Anthropology Building itself, not far from Boas's display, was a large collection gathered and exhibited by Captain Newton H. Chittenden, "the picturesque explorer and investigator" who held official appointment as a British Columbia special commissioner to the exposition. Next to Chittenden's artifacts were "collections of ethnological material from British Columbia and Baffin Land" exhibited by Mrs. Franz Boas, material collected by Boas, perhaps largely in 1886, and not sold to Berlin or elsewhere. Not far away was Ayer's large North

American collection, including a considerable selection of Tlingit basketry, and the Alaska collection of E. O. Stafford that had been gathered by A. P. Swineford while governor of the territory. In the physical anthropology section, located on the building's north gallery, were Boas's Vancouver Island skulls, systematically displayed in glass cases among other cranial examples.[48]

Northwest Coast displays could be found elsewhere on the grounds. The British Columbia room of the Canadian Building, itself guarded at its main entrance by two Haida bear sculptures, contained "a handsome collection of curios" gathered by Indian agents under the supervision of A. W. Vowell. Superintendent Vowell had made the collection reluctantly, feeling that the $4,000 he understood Boas to be spending was enough to "carry out the object desired." The $500 advanced him by the Department of Indian Affairs could fetch "but little of interest" since "all the best things that were available are pretty well exhausted by the drains constantly made upon them by tourists and by the said agents of the World's Fair." Ottawa would hear of no such thing and, learning that the fair's collection would not be "exhaustive," insisted that every effort had to be made to see that the Indians and their manufactures were fairly represented. Vowell shipped material costing $495.40, mostly minor items like mats and spoons, but certainly enough to prove to British Columbia's own commissioner in Chicago that his province's aborigines were "of higher artistic development than any of the Indians to the east of the Rockies."[49]

Washington State's pavilion contained an Eells–Swan collection. In the U. S. Government Building, about a thousand yards from the Anthropology Building and much more central, Lt. G. T. Emmons displayed his huge collection of Alaskan Indian material, some 2,474 items supplemented by another 500 collected by Sheldon Jackson from Point Barrow Eskimos. Gathered since his 1888 sale of 1,350 pieces to the American Museum, the size, quality, and careful cataloguing of this collection established Emmons in first place as a Northwest Coast collector.[50] More comprehensive was the Smithsonian exhibition, jointly organized by the National Museum and the Bureau of Ethnology and based on Powell's linguistic map.

Among the language stocks selected to explore the relationship of language, ethnicity, and environment were the Koloschan (Tlingit), the Salishan (Bella Coola and Salish), the Skittigetan

(Haida), and the Wakashan (Kwakiutl, Nootka, and Makah), each represented by costumed figures and wall cases of artifacts. Unlike Putnam's exhibit, the Smithsonian's was ready for the opening of the fair. It was, wrote a visiting French anthropologist, "extrêmement belle dans toutes ses parties."[51]

The Columbian World's Fair closed in October and the process of winding down this largest of expositions began. The Kwakiutl troupe went back by Canadian Pacific rail. Putnam carried on a long argument with the railway company that they "be returned free like other exhibits, as they were exhibits in every sense of the term." Boas was glad to see them go. Nothing had ever caused him more worry and trouble; he swore "never again to play circus impressario." Deans, left behind at a dinner stop on the Prairies, wired ahead that the Indians be put off at the next stop, there to await him on the next day's train. Thereafter, according to Hunt, Deans "acted Bad to us. I did not like his way at all." The old Scotsman apparently lorded over his charges, not letting Hunt know what he was doing and telling everyone that Hunt was "one of his Indians." Indeed, Hunt felt that Deans "was wors than Indian." Putnam had arranged for $2,100 to be placed on deposit at the Bank of British North America in Victoria in Hunt's name. Hunt paid off "the boys," $150 to each, then returned to Fort Rupert to suffer from a serious measles epidemic that laid him low and, to his great sorrow, brought the death of his youngest son.[52]

The collection in Chicago went various ways. Captain Chittenden packed up his "Collection of Relics and Antiquities" for shipment to the California Mid-Winter Exposition. The explorer and guide had given it to the Province of British Columbia in 1891, but took it on the exhibition circuit (he had already been to London for the Colonial and Imperial Exposition and to Antwerp) before depositing it in Victoria in 1894 after the close of the California fair. The Washington State collection returned to become part of a state museum in Seattle. The Canadian Department of Indian Affairs intended to sell its collection, but, finding that Indian curios were a glut on the market, decided to send it back to Ottawa where it might form the nucleus of a museum at the department offices.[53] Eventually it ended up at the Geological Survey's museum.

Department M's collections were kept in Chicago. Partly as a result of Putnam's prodding, the leaders of the fair and the city decided to make exhibits from the exposition the basis of a permanent museum on the grounds. The collection of Hunt, Morrison, F. Jacobsen, et al. were moved to the Palace of Fine Arts, the building chosen to house the new Columbian Museum. To those collections were added, by gift, the Ayer collection, and, by purchase, Hagenbeck's Jacobsen collection, the Stafford-Swineford collection, and, at least provisionally, Boas's skull and skeleton collection.

Boas intended to stay with the collections. He expected to be placed in charge of the anthropological department of the new museum. That was certainly Putnam's recommendation. As he wrote to Ayer, the moving force behind the new museum, "Dr. Boas is the only person besides myself who is qualified to take charge of the anthropological material" and the only one left in Chicago who could bring order from the chaos of stacked boxes at the former Fine Arts Building. Putnam wanted very much that Boas be kept so that the "vast amount of exceptionally important and valuable material I have brought together should be placed in the proper charge of one who not only knows all about it, but who is the best man the museum can get to take charge of it."[54]

It did not happen so. Putnam, never popular with the dominant forces of the exposition's administration and no more so with their successors in the Columbian Museum, found his influence thin and his advice ignored. Boas was kept on temporarily, but when the trustees found they could secure W. H. Holmes of the Bureau of Ethnology as curator, they hired him. Boas properly felt himself the victim of an "unsurpassed insult" and departed Chicago on April 15, as soon as his installations were in place.[55]

He had long left his position at Clark University, part of a general revolt of the faculty against President G. Stanley Hall. Virtually all the others had been snapped up by Chicago University's W. R. Harper, but Boas had been passed over. The increasing demands of Putnam's department at the fair had turned his assistantship into full-time work and seemed to promise permanency at the successor museum. Now that had suddenly disappeared. He was too proud to accept an inferior position and his professional standing demanded that he should not. He was again unemployed and dependent upon contract work.

In the meanwhile he would spend the summer in Germany, then travel again to British Columbia to work toward the completion of the British Association's Northwest Tribes Committee research that had been left in abeyance because of his duties for Chicago. He could combine this with special assignments from Putnam for the American Museum and from Mason for the U. S. National Museum. Both wanted to have Northwest Coast figure groups for their displays and no one was better qualified to supervise their construction than Boas.

The life- or lay-figure group had been an innovative feature, at least in American terms, of the Smithsonian's Chicago fair exhibition. Going far beyond mere costumed manikins, the display included a number of groups of figures arranged into a representative scene and surrounded by appropriate objects.[56] W. H. Holmes, an artist before he turned ethnologist, supervised an impressive group of Powhatan Indians quarrying stone implements, while Frank Cushing was responsible for displays of Navaho and Plains women in life-like scenes and for five Zuñi groups employed in various typical occupations.

The figure group developed directly out of the life-sized manikins in use for decades, initially merely as a frame upon which an aboriginal costume could be hung. The earliest ethnological manikins at the U. S. National Museum were "Eskimo Joe and his wife Hannah," crude figures made in 1873 in imitation of the heroes of the *Polaris* expedition. By that time Moscow's Dashkov Museum was using natural-sized papier-mâché figures to represent thirty of the peoples of the Russian Empire.

European museums were far advanced in the use and, even more, in the techniques that would produce the sculptured verisimilitude initially desired. French and Japanese virtuosity was much admired for its trompe-l'oeil effects in plaster, wood, or papier-mâché and the National Museum imitated those effects as best it could. As well, it investigated the manufacture of figures at Castan's Panopticum in Germany, the races of man display at London's Crystal Palace, and even Madam Tussaud's. The next step, again pioneered in Europe, was from single figures to groups of figures engaged in some representative endeavor or action. The lead came from folklore museums, notably Stockholm's Nordeska Museet where Artur Hazelius combined Swedish peasant folk-groups with reconstructed period rooms. One was shown at the Centennial Exhibition in Philadelphia where it provoked the admiration of all. Hazelius extended his range to ethnology at the 1878 Paris International Exposition and exhibited a Lapp tableau at the Palace Trocadéro that was a sensation.

The use of groups in realistic settings spread quickly in Europe. The full, mature use of groups was demonstrated with outstanding success by E. T. Hamy at the Paris Exposition in 1889. In the Liberal Arts Building Hamy, together with his artist-modeler Jules Hebert, reconstructed families representing different prehistorical cultures in what was "probably the most interesting and instructive" anthropological exhibit of the fair and certainly the one that attracted the most attention. Four family groups represented mammoth, cavern, Neolithic, and Bronze Age man, as well as their contemporary counterparts of Russian reindeer herdsmen, Sudanese blacksmiths, and others. The effectiveness of this type of group was carried to an even higher level of mimesis by Emil Holub's Bushman, Matabele, and Zulu groups for the South African exhibition at the Prague Exposition of 1892.

The group concept had exciting advantages. It showed, like the zoologist's environmental group (which doubtless influenced it), the specimens in a realistic imitation of their original setting and use. The viewer saw how artifacts were actually employed and in what association they were placed among other implements. Groups changed the idea of figures: they "were no longer pieces of sculpture but pictures from life."[57]

The haste and confusion of preparing the Chicago display did not allow the National Museum to sculpt their figures as carefully as the models from Europe and Japan that inspired them, but the prepared groups were nonetheless effective in their novelty and interest. Confessedly imitative of achievements abroad and less ambitious and successful than Holub's Prague groups, the Chicago experiments did cause the National Museum to feel that "something has been done which was never before attempted for the American Indian" and with a result which seemed "to more than justify the effort." Carefully made figures, "absolutely expressive of the bodily features and general appearance of the people," and arranged in groups demonstrative of the progress of their industries, were to become parts of the permanent exhibition in Washington.[58]

Otis Mason wanted a Northwest Coast group for the museum, one that could first be shown at the up-coming Atlanta Exposition. Boas accepted the assignment eagerly. He would combine his British Columbia fieldwork for the BAAS with a collection for a Kwakiutl Hamatsa group and then supervise the group's construction in Washington. It turned out that the American Museum also wanted a Northwest Coast group. A shake-up there had resulted in Putnam being appointed curator of anthropology, a position he held concurrent with the directorship of the Harvard museum. Putnam had, like Mason and Holmes, been impressed in Paris with the creative possibilities of figure groups and, though at Chicago he had imitated the French exposition's use of live natives in their habitations rather than Hamy's sculptured figures, only the latter was conceivable for permanent museum installation. Boas could prepare two groups for the American Museum, which might also provide an entré for him into permanent association with the New York institution.[59]

Boas left for British Columbia in September 1894. This was his fifth trip to the province, but the first one (excepting his initial hurried visit of 1886) to include a part of the winter, the season when the Indians were settled in their villages and engaged in their elaborate ceremonials. For the first time he saw the winter dances and secret society ceremonies as they were actually performed.

Wrapped in a blanket and wearing a cedar bark headring, he watched the Hamatsas, the Nutlamatlas, the Seals, and the Tsonokwa dance round the overfed fires at Fort Rupert. It was all quite different from the impression he had gathered from hearing of these rituals and even from what he had seen of the mock performances of the Bella Coolas in Berlin or the Kwakiutl at Jackson Park. Here was the real thing and he worked himself to near-exhaustion watching, listening, and recording. He made casts of faces and took photographs of poses and ceremonies (through the assistance of O. C. Hastings, a professional hired from Victoria).[60] He bought what masks and cedar bark rings he could obtain, purchased more from John J. Hart at the Indian Bazaar in Victoria, and left instructions with Hunt to obtain more masks and rings at the end of the season.

For Washington his Hamatsa scene would feature the new initiate emerging from the yawning mouth of the painted ceremonial

Franz Boas posing for the modelling of his U. S. National Museum Hamatsa group. Smithsonian Institution photo #MNH 8302.

screen. He could not too closely duplicate this in New York, yet intended to stick to the Hamatsa theme by showing the initiate outside, returning from his spirit quest. Another group would focus on industries, on men carving and painting and on a woman weaving a basket while ingeniously rocking a suspended cradle. It was invigorating but exhausting and he was still without any definite prospects of permanent employment. He was depressed and frustrated, hated being so long away from Marie and his children. He was able to return in time for the year-end holidays. It had been a very useful trip, even if Putnam was reprimanded for the size of his accounts and the interior exposures taken by Hastings did not develop.

He now went to Washington in January 1895 to oversee the preparations for the National Museum figures. The most accurate way for preparator Theodore A. Mills to work was for Boas himself to pose before a photographer. He did several poses in coat and tie, but in most of the photographs he appears clad only in exercise pants, barefoot, and stripped to the waist. He emerges from a hoop, used to represent the round mouth of the ceremonial screen, with an animated facial expression and a silent howl emerging from his lips. Elsewhere he is the drummer beating on a non-existent box drum, and yet again he solemnly holds the neck ring of the emerging initiate.[61]

The seven-figure group was almost complete at the end of March, but details — especially the late arriving cedar bark rings from Hunt — were added when the figures returned from their Atlanta debut the next year. A Tlingit chief in ceremonial regalia was a less complicated construction and needed only a sculpture and the abundant Alaska materials already in the museum's collection.

Boas, still unemployed, but with possibilities mooted both at the Bureau of American Ethnology and from Putnam in New York, spent another summer in Europe, primarily to study continental museums' use of life-groups. On his return to New York, he began work on the American Museum groups for which he was under contract. The work went slowly, probably because of other commitments, especially his massive Kwakiutl report for the Smithsonian. At the year's end President Jesup complained that, though Boas had been paid $600, no group was complete or even "any approach to that result" in spite of every assistance which had been offered to him.[62]

Boas's dilatoriness and Jesup's perturbance did not hamper Putnam's efforts to bring Boas on the museum's staff. That had been part of Putnam's plans for the museum from the time he had accepted the curatorship. There was no immediate opening, but Putnam assured Boas that "it will come by and by, and of course I shall do all I can for you." The Northwest Coast groups would serve as "a wedge for you." Putnam kept up pressure on both sides; he had on the one hand to create a position and on the other to keep Boas from taking something else before he could make that arrangement. He negotiated with President Seth Low of Columbia for part of Boas's salary to be paid by the college, and secured an offer from Abraham Jacobi, Boas's uncle, to contribute secretly a portion of Boas's museum salary. This, Putnam hoped, would make the museum's actual outlay so insignificant that Jesup would agree.[63]

To convince Boas to delay accepting an offer from the Bureau in Washington, he wrote of his ambitious plans for anthropology at the museum — of great ethnological displays with groups and lodges and a physical anthropology division complete with laboratories. Assisted by Marshall Saville, George Pepper, and Harlan I. Smith, Putnam and Boas would make an unbeatable team. "I have a deep affection for Dr Boas," he wrote his daughter, "and there is no man for whom I have a greater respect and whose learning I most greatly admire. I only hope he will decide to cast his lot with me in New York." Boas was not so certain. He did not think highly of William Ripley and Livingston Farrand at Columbia and he sought a position at Stanford, closer to his Pacific Coast interests, but he held off the Bureau until a definite offer could come from Putnam.[64]

In December Putnam had arranged things in New York. The Columbia side was almost certain, Jacobi's check was on deposit at the museum, and Jesup's opposition (on financial grounds and "because he is so young") had been overcome by Putnam's assertion that his appointment would give the museum first place among American museums.[65] Boas made a last quibble about title and status, then agreed to take the position. On January 1, 1896, he began as special assistant curator.

Chapter Six

The American Museum and Dr. Boas

ANTHROPOLOGY HAD NOT BEEN the American Museum's strongest department. Albert Bickmore had had the department as one of his several responsibilities. A non-professional in any case, he had spent the greater part of his time on public lectures and general administration. In 1891 the department was given over to Frederick Starr who soon left for the University of Chicago. James Terry, whose archeological collection the trustees had just bought for a princely sum, succeeded him. Terry's special charge was to catalogue and label his collection; he was dismissed two years later for stealing from his old collection.

This unhappy sequence determined President Jesup to secure for the much-abused department the best man in the country. His adviser suggested either W. H. Holmes of the Bureau of American Ethnology (soon to oust Boas from Chicago) or Frederic W. Putnam of Harvard's Peabody Museum. Jesup was told that Putnam, as a museum archaeologist, might be more suitable than Holmes, whose background lay in geology and art and whose curatorship at Washington was merely honorary. Putnam agreed to take the proffered head of department on condition he retain his directorship of the Peabody and reside in Cambridge. While thus spending only one week each month in New York, he at last brought strong direction — as well as prestige and distinction — to the museum's anthropology program.[1]

The accumulation of anthropological collections before 1894 was as erratic as the department's leadership. The Pacific Island holdings, primarily the Appleton Sturgis collection purchased in 1891, were unsurpassed among American museums, but collections in other areas, including the Americas, were whimsical. Mexican and Peruvian expeditions were giving substance to those pre-Columbian areas and the museum already possessed great, if uneven, strength in Arctic Alaska and Northwest Coast material.

At the core of the Northwest Coast holdings was the Powell-Bishop collection of British Columbia and the Stikine specimens, including the great canoe sent across Panama. To this had been added the large Emmons collection gathered between 1882 and 1886. That purchase had put Lieutenant Emmons and the American Museum in a close and continuing relationship. He secured an extended leave at the time of the sale and, with museum encouragement, busied himself with working up his notes into "a creditable monograph of the 'Tlinkit' tribes illustrated largely from my collection." He returned to Alaska where he intended making "quite a collection during my canoe travel through the Alexandria Archipelago" and which the museum would have "the first opportunity to procure at satisfactory terms." By the end of his 1888 season he claimed to have covered over six hundred miles by canoe, gathering information and specimens.[2] Only in the summer of 1890 did he return to active service on the *Pinta,* duty which allowed him some freedom to collect, but made it difficult for him to work further on the promised "creditable monograph."

He was soon negotiating with the Columbian World's Fair administration and the Navy Department to show the "fine exhibit" he had accumulated since his 1888 sale. The fair's director-general thought the idea a good one, but Putnam and Boas would have nothing to do with Emmons and his collection. Their reasons, that his collection had already been offered for sale and that the government should have some control over objects secured by its naval officers, seem so punctilious as to make them suspect. Perhaps Putnam and Boas merely wanted reason to secure additional fair funding so as to extend their departmental collecting into Alaska — the whole territory, Putnam wrote, could be covered for about $3,000. In the end Emmons showed his new collection among other Alaskan exhibits in the U. S. Government Building, where, with its "intelligent system of labeling," it received favorable notice as drawing the visitor "into sympathy and friendship with the wild children of the glaciers as no monograph, however well written, could do." Putnam and Boas's Ethnology Department had no Tlingit exhibit. Irony, in fact, overcame Boas and Putnam: in December 1893, Emmons sold this new collection to the American Museum, only months before Putnam became its curator. Boas was to come to it two years later. The 2,474 Northwest Coast pieces cost the museum (along with some 500 Point Barrow Eskimo items) a full $25,000, paid over five years at 5 percent. The trustees' reluctance at adding so large and expensive a collection in an area already covered was overcome by the report that the new Columbian Museum in Chicago had made an offer to Emmons. Faced with this possibility, "only one course was open, and that, to buy it."[3]

With the second Emmons collection purchase, the American Museum's Northwest Coast holdings were now huge and, for the most part, well catalogued. They were overwhelmingly Tlingit and north coast, with the central and southern areas thinly represented. The Emmons material, supplemented after 1894 by further purchases from the lieutenant, gave the museum a prominence in the region that could only be heightened by the distinction of Putnam as curator and by Boas's Northwest Coast scholarship, now becoming acknowledged as preeminent.

Putnam's New York position was enviable. President Jesup's interests were turning increasingly to departments like vertebrate paleontology and anthropology, areas which could collect and display spectacular physical objects like dinosaur skeletons or Inca monuments and totem poles, attractive to the public and donors alike. Anthropology was getting a new wing, already under construction, and the museum had three expeditions in the field in Latin America. New displays and life-groups were being assembled and now Putnam had the most impressive side in American anthropology. "Boas and myself make a pretty strong team and with Saville, Smith and Pepper to help," he wrote his daughter, "you see I have the best equipment of any anthropological museum in the country." He regarded himself as being "called" to New York to put its department into first rank among museums in America. Much of his work at the American Museum would be done with an eye back to the shores of Lake Michigan and with a bitterness, both on his own account and on behalf of Boas, toward the Chicago trustees. "I'll show Chicago I can go them one better," he wrote with obvious relish.[4]

Some edge was taken off the elation when Jesup informed him that there would be no acquisition budget for 1896. "The financial outlook, together with the present unsettled condition of business generally" — freely translatable as the financial collapse of 1893 and the spectre of populism and free silver in an election year — made it unwise to solicit the trustees, although he hoped 1897 would be better.[5] (As it turned out, 1897 would be vastly better.)

In the meantime, Boas busied himself with settling into this his first really secure and responsible museum position and in developing plans to forward Putnam's effort to put the American Museum unquestionably "at front rank." His ideas on effective exhibition methods were laid out in a November 1896 memorandum to Putnam. In it Boas described the techniques which should be used in the new wing's displays and warned against an extension and over-elaboration of life-groups. The figure group, he wrote, was the most effective of all museum display methods. "No other means can be devised to attract the visitor so forcibly and to bring out certain points so clearly as a group." But some museums, notably Bremen, Hamburg, and Prague, had gone too far in their use, losing continuity between the group and the rest of the exhibition and striving after effect rather than elucidating specific leading ideas. Groups ought to remain simple, representing only one thing and bringing that out as forcibly as possible; they should be closely related to the cases around them; and they should be small and enclosed so as to be visually self-contained. Most important, they should not attempt to imitate the visage of man. Skin color ought not be absolutely true and hair should be indicated by paint or plaster, not using real hair. They should be shown, not at the height of action, but in a moment of rest. When figures looked absolutely life-like, the lack of any movement caused "a ghastly impression such as we notice in wax figures."[6]

In the same paper Boas recorded his views on the department's collections and their future development. The museum's strength was in the South Seas, Eskimo and, quite unevenly, in North American Indian material. The South Seas and Eskimo collections were very good; like other early collections, however, they emphasized beautiful pieces and needed to be supplemented with ordinary objects. Other continents were hardly represented at all. On the North Pacific Coast (a phrase which Boas preferred to Northwest Coast), the Tlingit and Haida were well represented in

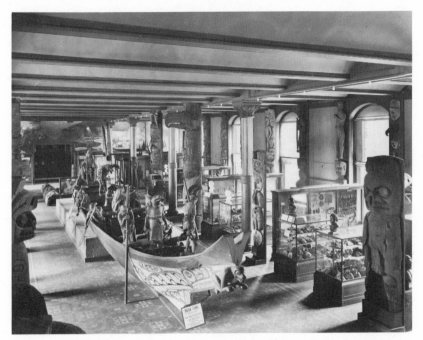

The North Pacific Hall at the American Museum of Natural History in New York. In the aisle is the big canoe collected by Israel W. Powell; the Tlingit figures were prepared with the assistance of George T. Emmons. American Museum of Natural History, no. 33003.

the Emmons and Powell collections, but there was virtually nothing from the area between Milbank Sound and the Columbia River. Since this, the area of the Kwakiutl, Bella Coola, Salish, and Chinook, was his special interest, he hoped for funds to repair the deficiencies. An accidental event not five weeks later enabled him to take the first step toward increasing the North Pacific Coast collections and breaking Jesup's ban on purchases.

Samuel Kirschberg, a partner with Frederick Landsberg in the pawn and curio business in Victoria, had shipped a collection of central coast and Thompson River specimens to New York where he hoped to sell them at prices advantageously above those prevailing in Victoria. The steamer carrying the collection caught fire, however, and the shipment having suffered some damage, the whole of it was put up for sale as salvage. After a good deal of bargaining, Boas bought all but ten pieces for $800, rather a bargain, he thought, for 180 items, some of which, notably a Chilkat blanket formerly the property of Mrs. Pidcock, the Kwakiutl agent's wife, and a particularly fine Nootka rattle, had entirely escaped damage in Kirschberg's trunk.

This fortuitous salvage purchase was a mere tidbit. Boas had his eyes on much better things. He had realized from the very first the value to research and collecting which the wealth of the American Museum's trustees and friends could allow. Late in 1896 he drafted a letter to Henry Villard, sponsor of A. F. Bandelier's Peru and Bolivia expeditions, proposing that the former president of the Northern Pacific, now proprietor of the *Evening Post,* contribute toward filling the museum's central and south coast collections gap. With several thousand dollars over the next two years, he wrote, "we should have the most thorough and I may say a complete collection from the region between Columbia River and Mt. St. Elias." The letter proved unnecessary. By this time he and Putnam had interested President Jesup in Boas's north Pacific schemes.[7]

Jesup had always been sympathetic to grand designs and large-scale ideas. He had underwritten the Jesup Collection of North American Woods, some ten years in acquisition, the Jesup Collection of Economic Entomology, and was at this time supporting the Arctic explorations of Commander Robert E. Peary. Putnam and Boas put before him a vast north Pacific research and collecting project dressed in the tempting guise of research on the fundamental question of the peopling of America over the Siberian-Alaskan route. Jesup had long felt that research and collecting could go hand in hand and that both scientists and laity could be satisfied under wise museum administration.

Most of the trustees had gradually been converted to the importance of research for a museum of New York's standing, although collections amenable to striking exhibition remained supremely important in their conception of a museum. "We should leave research to the Germans," one trustee grumbled, but that was not the president's own view and his imagination was struck by the great problem of the origin of the American Indian. He "got very much interested in that question" when it was placed before him by his anthropological curators and, in his 1896 report to his trustees, Jesup wrote that "the theory that America was originally peopled by migrating tribes from the Asian continent" was a subject of great interest to scientists in several fields. "The opportunities for solving this problem are rapidly disappearing," he wrote, and "I would be deeply grateful to learn that some friends of the Museum might be disposed to contribute the means for the prosecution of systematic investigation" into this intriguing problem. When no one came forward, Jesup took his own suggestion and offered to underwrite the entire project himself.[8]

The Jesup North Pacific Expedition, announced in March 1897 (coincident with McKinley's inauguration), was an ambitious undertaking. Its main object, Boas announced, was "to investigate and establish the ethnological relations between the races of America and Asia." "There are few problems," he said, "of greater importance to our knowledge of the early history of the American race than its relations to the races of the Old World." While often a matter of speculation, the subject had never received systematic investigation, all the more urgent now because of the danger that Siberian tribes, about which very little was known, were rapidly being affected by European culture carried along the lines of the new trans-Siberian railroad.[9]

The scale of the Jesup Expedition surpassed any previous research and collecting on the Northwest Coast. While archaeological and anthropological expeditions were very much a part of the late nineteenth-century relationship between museums and scientific philanthropy, the only regional precedent was the British Association's North-western Tribes Committee, which had existed for a decade and which had maintained Boas in the field over four seasons. Indeed, for Boas the Jesup Expedition was a continuation of the systematic work of the Committee and in the summer of 1897 he was both on his last field year for the BAAS and his first for Jesup.[10] The BAAS Committee's precedent paled, however, in comparison to its successor. The Committee's annual £100 grant, sometimes matched by $500 from the Canadian government, and its ability to place only one, at most two, researchers in the field seasonally, was small in comparison to the full resources which Jesup's pocketbook and the American Museum's personnel and experience could provide.

Over the six years in which fieldwork was actively pursued, professional archaeologists and anthropologists were sent to both sides of the north Pacific, often for seasonal work, but also for extended research periods. Work on the Northwest Coast was most intensive in the first year, 1897, when Boas directed the fieldwork and was accompanied by Harlan I. Smith and Livingston Farrand. Locals James Teit, George Hunt, and Fillip Jacobsen were enlisted for assistance. Boas, occupied at the museum and with other projects, came only once more, in 1900. Smith spent four seasons investigating ethnological questions as well as the archaeology of British Columbia and Washington.

North American research concentrated on the Indians of the British Columbia interior, much of that entrusted to Teit, the Spences Bridge Scotsman who increasingly gained Boas's respect for his trustworthy recording and intelligent collecting, on the Kwakiutl and Bella Coola of the central coast, and on the Salish, Quinault, and Quileute of the south coast. John R. Swanton, a member of the Bureau of American Ethnology staff, was seconded to Boas's service to study the Haida, among whom C. F. Newcombe also rendered some valuable assistance.

For the expedition whose raison d'être was the Siberian connection, it seems odd that relatively little work was done in Alaska. Late in the expedition Swanton did work among the Tlingits but made no significant collections. That the museum already possessed an unrivalled Tlingit and an excellent Alaskan Eskimo collection was a factor. While regretting the omission of the Aleuts, Boas justified restricting the North American work principally to British Columbia and Washington on the grounds that the Eskimo had been studied by E. W. Nelson and others and that Emmons's manuscript on the Tlingits might still be forthcoming.

The Emmons manuscript was a delicate issue. For Jesup and the museum it was an unfilled promise for which they had waited since 1888; for Emmons it was an incubus, the kind of work for which he now realized he was not suited. The monograph had been a reason for securing naval leaves in 1888–90 and Jesup had moved mountains to secure yet another leave in 1897–98, only to have Emmons's health collapse. Then, just as he recovered and reported that he was "fairly launched on the writing," the Cuban crisis brought his sudden recall for duty aboard the Atlantic Flying Squadron. He shipped all his notes and drafts to New York and prepared for battle: "I will say good bye," he wrote, "we are not going out for any fun I can assure you." Although the squadron cruised to Nova Scotia rather than into the guns of the Spanish fleet, his health again broke and he returned to Princeton too ill to work. He resigned from active service the next year, but the incomplete manuscript remained a festering point in his relations with the museum. He never published it.[11]

Boas did secure a forty-five page article on Tlingit basketry from Emmons in 1903, but was otherwise quite disillusioned with him. Working closely with the specimens in the Emmons collections, Boas revised his 1888 opinion on the value of the catalogue and labels. Now, he felt, the information on the masks was not trustworthy and the catalogue contained very little material of scientific importance.

After 1897 the museum bought very little from Emmons. The coolness toward the collector was partly the unfinished manuscript and partly Boas's generalized distrust. Emmons, he felt, treated collections less as scientific specimens than as trading material, and he had the feeling that "the Museum is 'being done' by Mr. Emmons." The serious amateur and collecting entrepreneur was simply not scientific enough to meet Boas's professional standards.[12]

The chilling attitude that now emanated from Central Park was noted by Emmons. He was partly responsible for it. He could not be bound to a single institution because he required more outlets for his collections than merely the American Museum. Although he had given or sold the Smithsonian a few items, nothing very important, since 1890, he had never been particularly close to the anthropological establishment in Washington. On an 1899 visit, however, he had discovered the "vast repository of magnificent old collections" that was the Smithsonian. The Wilkes material was "most astonishing" and Swan's Haida pieces fine. The Tlingit material, left essentially as Niblack had studied it, was good, but incompletely catalogued and arranged, a deficiency he volunteered partly to remedy. "I find as much work as I feel inclined to do." W. H. Holmes seized the Emmons opportunity and asked him to do some buying for the museum on his next trip to the coast, then went further, commissioning him to equip and install a Chilkat Tlingit life-group, one of twelve the curator was putting together for Buffalo's 1901 Pan-American Exposition. The most important figure was a woman at work weaving a Chilkat blanket. Emmons soon had a line on a partially completed blanket, secured during the summer of 1900 on a trip to the

Upper Chilkat, along with carvings, basketry, and clothing for the group. "I have procured everything complete," he wrote from the steamer homebound, "and I am particularly well pleased with the result." The group was assembled over the winter of 1900–1901 and after exhibition at Buffalo, found a permanent home in Washington as a striking representation of the laborious process of blanket creation. Holmes and Mason appreciated the capabilities Emmons showed as a collector: feeling "that the Lieutenant's friendship is worth a great deal to us," they humored him along with mutually beneficial purchases.[13]

The continuation of the exposition tradition, especially the World's Fair in St. Louis, provided the museum with acquisition funds and allowed a healthy succession of purchases of Emmons's material from 1902 to 1904, much of it secured from Victoria's curio dealers. The Smithsonian's mature collection of Tlingit and other Northwest Coast specimens and its restricted appropriation, even when supplemented by special exposition funds, still did not make the Smithsonian a potential buyer for Emmons's newest major Tlingit collection, now grown to some twelve hundred pieces.

Emmons, the collector in search of a museum, was therefore ripe and willing bait for the Field Museum's George Dorsey, who was in the midst of his high-spending campaign to match the American Museum in coastal material. He arranged for Emmons to exhibit his collection for three months in Chicago to provide a persuasive argument for his trustees of its importance. The strategy worked. Dorsey was able to purchase the collection in April 1902, paying $10,000 plus exchanges to a value of $2,000. Emmons stipulated that the Field's new accession not be called the Emmons Collection, that designation being reserved for his huge, two-installment collection in New York; this was the Spuhn Collection, named for Carl Spuhn, the German-born official of the Northwest Trading Company who had given Alaska artifacts to Edward Ayer and who provided a base at his Killisnoo station for Emmons's summer trips.

The Chicago sale had a tone almost of a wholesale transaction. Dorsey once described the terms as $1,000 per 100 pieces. It was soon followed by yet another large Emmons sale, this time of 253 baskets, mostly Tlingit, for a further $2,500. Like all of Emmons's major collections, the baskets were a remarkable set.

All were old, many rare and unique, "the whole forming undoubtedly the only complete collection of baskets ever collected from one tribe," Dorsey trumpeted. "I believe it will never be possible to duplicate this collection."[14] Dorsey now had Emmons in his Chicago museum stable and sent him off to Alaska to complement the field collecting of C. F. Newcombe.

Emmons was doing quite well, but this did not impress Boas in New York. The collector's offer to work for the American Museum at the same time as he was to travel to Chilkat in Dorsey's interest was simply too much for Boas, already impatient over the lingering monograph and unimpressed with Emmons's scientific qualifications. "I take it that he is simply trying to get as much as he can from both of us." Emmons's knowledge about the Tlingit might mean "that we have to stand him," but he was "a very slippery customer." Boas would have preferred, in 1903 as when he was collecting for the Chicago Fair, "to send a man who knows ethnology to Alaska and let him do the whole thing over." However good Emmons was at industrial and historical material, Boas felt that he could never provide valuable information on religion, mythology, and language, some of the primary aims of Boasian ethnology.[15]

In the Jesup Expedition's work, Boas was willing to use non-professionals if he felt they met his own standards. He had confidence in Teit and George Hunt, whom he had personally trained in verbatim reporting and whom he trusted to carry out a very large part of the Jesup fieldwork under his distant supervision. Both Teit and Hunt would secure the stories that went with the artifacts. On the other hand, Boas did not feel that C. F. Newcombe possessed the scientific knowledge necessary for the proper explanation of specimens; he preferred to get his Haida material through his own man, Swanton, though he accepted Newcombe's services in securing pieces which Swanton could not. While he felt unable to place full confidence in the naturalist Newcombe, he unhesitatingly asked his old friend Fillip Jacobsen, now in Clayoquot, for a Nootka collection. The rationale for this capriciousness revolves, no doubt, as much around Boas's personality as it does upon the scientific abilities of the residents. Despite Newcombe's strong admiration for Boas's methods, he was already tainted by his work for George Dorsey and the Chicago Field Museum.[16]

Boas's team devoted most of their time to mythology, to survey archaeology, and to physical anthropology, especially to making plaster of paris casts of Indians' heads (a new practice and judged at this, the height of its popularity, as "the only feasible method of permanently preserving the vanishing type of America natives"). Research on the question of intercontinental ethnic affinities was the expedition's fundamental object, but Boas used the opportunity to explore a number of subsidiary interests, especially decorative art. From the beginning he had insisted that, while "such antiquities as are found to have any bearing on the subject" would be collected, the accumulation of museum specimens was "merely incidental to its main object." He was reluctant to commit Jesup funds to "purely collecting work" which was "not absolutely necessary for the object of the expedition." Nevertheless, he utilized the collecting opportunities afforded by the expedition as fully as he could and was ready to use Jesup's money if other funds could not be found.[17] One incentive to collecting was the installation of the Northwest Coast collection in the new north wing of the Central Park building; another was the deficiencies in the existing collections.

Boas was, of course, acutely aware of the central and south coast hiatus. Progress was made quickly toward filling the gap. Attention was paid immediately to the British Columbia interior: to the Chilcotin and Salish. At the same time Harlan Smith made some significant collections among the Coast Salish and Livingston Farrand contributed the results of a season's work among the Quinault and Quileute. Since the museum had "no collections whatever" from his own Kwakiutl, he told Hunt that "any thing that you may obtain will be welcome." Similarly he wanted "everything" that Fillip Jacobsen could supply from the Nootka. While this seemed almost indiscriminate, he gave his customary emphasis to ceremonial objects and continued his usual concern with "explanations." Masks, rattles, and ceremonial objects of cedar bark, along with carvings and paintings, were singled out in his initial instructions to Jacobsen and Hunt. Swanton was told that "every thing that you can get fully described will be highly desirable." He enjoined Hunt that "it is far better for us to get a few pieces less and the stories belonging to each. We do not want to grab every thing, and then not know what the things mean." While he emphasized ceremonial material, he tried also to ensure that the unique or unusual did not overwhelm the common. From the Bella Coola, he wrote Hunt, he wanted "just as many masks and rings as you can get, but also the ordinary every day things, — fish traps, blankets, hammers, pestles, etc." Reviewing the situation after two years, Boas more strongly emphasized the commonplace. "On looking over the collections that we have made among the Kwakiutl," he wrote, "it strikes me that we have not yet a full collection of the simple every day implements." The collections lacked such things as towels, glue, canoe calk, sharks-kin "sandpaper," and canoe-builders' wedges. "The best thing you could do would be to sit down and think what the Kwakiutl used for cooking, including every thing from beginning to end, then what they used for wood-working, for painting, for making basket-work, for fishing, for hunting, etc."[18]

Each area might have its peculiar desiderata for Boas's enquir-ing mind — hammered copper figures and model poles with sto-ries, for example, from the Haida — but he also wanted to rem-edy the museum's almost complete deficiency of monumental sculpture. As he wrote to Hunt, "we cannot get enough of these and the older they are the better." Hunt sent a large number of Kwakiutl poles and posts. Newcombe proved his usefulness in securing poles from the Haida, in getting a mortuary column and houseposts as well as a fine frontal pole. Harlan Smith did impor-tant pole-gathering among the Salish at the Fraser delta and at Comox. He secured two houseposts at Musqueum near Van-couver in May 1898 and in August he found the Comox anxious to sell and bought eleven posts for $90. "I daresay this lot fills your desire for posts from this region at less expense than you contemplated," he proudly wrote his chief.[19] Dr. R. W. Large, the missionary doctor in Bella Bella, bought him two houseposts in November 1900.

The accumulation of collections was rapid. By the time the new North Pacific Hall opened late in 1899 the *New York Times* could boast that the museum's collection put an end to the old reproach that the finest ethnological collections from Alaska and British Columbia were in Europe. New York's collection was now superior to any (possibly excepting Washington's, it allowed), especially in exhibitions which were "unique and of the highest interest." A year later Boas assured Jesup that the expedition had acquired 6,626 ethnographic artifacts and 1,896 physical anthropology specimens for a mere $14,072.91, compared with the more than $37,500 paid for only 3,825 in the two Emmons collections.[20] Even allowing for exaggeration and the inclusion of archaeological material among the sums, the growth of the Northwest Coast material was prodigious.

Gross numbers might be as misleading as they were impressive; it was the diversity and comprehensiveness of the museum's accession as much as its sheer quantity that made New York's collection so valuable. The Nass and Skeena Tsimshian were still thinly represented, but the central and south coast gap in the collections was filled with Bella Coola, Kwakiutl, Bella Bella, Nootka, Salish, Quileute, and Quinault collections, supported by neighboring Interior Salish and Athapaskan materials. Showy ceremonial items and impressive statuary were abundant, but almost equal emphasis was given to the ordinary, the obvious, and the petty. The moss for wiping salmon, the puff ball to cauterize cuts, the kelp and dried huckleberry samples happily coexisted with mortuary poles and a Bella Bella canoe.

Boas also retained his strong interest in physical anthropology. His own collection, acquired by means fair and foul, had been left behind in Chicago. He now worked at building the American Museum's collection, buying skulls and bones from C. F. Newcombe ("the more you can let me have, the better")[21] at the usual five dollars per cranium rate, though Hunt got somewhat less. Hunt paid two dollars each for the ones he bought, but he found most in burial caves which had once been used by the region's inhabitants.

Hunt's cave visits were as much for ethnological objects as for heads. He insisted that the caves were at least fifty years old and were largely unknown to the Indians. "What I am looking for is the old thing," he wrote, and some of the wood pieces were so rotten that they would not bear their own weight. In one cave he could find nothing else of value "so I took these five Heads for there came in my way." More often the caves produced "some find old thing" and he reckoned that cave hunting was sometimes cheaper, even after paying a guide, than buying from the Indians. Aside from skulls the caves yielded copper and stone pieces as well as wood carvings. He found two of the best masks he had ever seen and some old dishes in one pair of caves, while from another he extracted five pairs of copper neck and knee rings.

*Franz Boas and the George Hunt family at Fort Rupert, with Franz Boas at
upper right and George Hunt second from upper left. American Philosophical
Society.*

Carved coffins, some bracelets, a stone pile-driver, two carved eagles and a raven, a bone knife and awls were among the cavern booty. The natives, for the most part, did not seem to mind Hunt's troglodytic searches since, as Boas wrote to Superintendent Vowell, the relationship and identity of the people buried at these places were "no longer known." On the other hand, "the mission People" opposed Hunt's activity and 'would like to get me on another trouble if they can find out me Brecking into the graves." (He had been arrested for cannibalism in March 1900 and, though acquitted, it had cost him $400 in expenses.) To minimize the danger from "the mission People," both white missionaries and their native flocks, he asked Boas to arrange things with Vowell. Vowell made clear that he had no objection to collections made from graves so long as the skeletons were neither cared for nor claimed by any Indian. This gave Hunt the desired official license, though there remained "much talk from Mr Halls People about me going into the old caves with graves."[22]

It was in this Jesup Expedition period that the collaboration between Boas and Hunt solidified. Although Boas had worked with Hunt since 1888, most particularly for the World's Fair and then in the winter of 1894–95, and thereafter Hunt had been recording Kwakiutl stories for Boas at fifty cents a page, Boas had never had full confidence in him. At both Chicago and Fort Rupert he had found Hunt "hard to deal with" and "too lazy to use his brain." In 1897, however, Hunt had, as asked, come to Bella Coola ahead of Boas, worked hard, and prepared things well for Boas's arrival. The New Yorker still found Hunt "unbelievably clumsy" with the Rivers Inlet dialect, but he had time to improve Hunt's general orthography and fully entrusted him with collecting and money transactions.[23] The relationship always retained a faintly patronizing air, but then Boas was *le patron*.

At this time Hunt was forty-three years old and had been assisting collectors since interpreting for Commissioner Powell in 1879. The son of an English Hudson's Bay Company factor and his Tlingit wife, Hunt occupied an interesting position. In the village of Fort Rupert, where his father was normally the only white man, he grew up virtually a Kwakiutl. There was no qualification to his knowledge of the Fort Rupert language. He was an initiate in the Hamatsa, the highest Kwakiutl secret society, and even acquired shaman credentials. He twice married Kwakiutls and raised his large family within the Indian society. His occupations in fishing and canning were those usual to an Indian though often at a more responsible level.

He seems to have considered himself Kwakiutl and certainly suffered the legal penalty for Kwakiutl ceremonialism. On the other hand, he was the son of a European father (though himself one who had gone rather native) and his sister married S. A. Spencer, a white trader at Alert Bay. He earned the trust of Europeans and was given by them responsibilities which almost no Indian of his time ever enjoyed; indeed, he seems to have been regarded as possessing as much reliability as was average in European society. He may have been more "lazy" intellectually than Boas would have liked and was probably never overweeningly ambitious. What marked him out, as much as anything else, from the Kwakiutl around him was his literacy. His spelling was uncertain, but his writing was clear and his style plain. He was not a comfortable writer but he did not avoid it.

In a collaborator on the coast Boas had three requirements: easy accessibility, especially linguistic, to native material, literacy for communication and for recording information, and the reliability of a "European mentality." Hunt possessed all these. So did Teit at Spences Bridge, a European whose accessibility came through marriage and residence, and whose Scottish nativity and upbringing ensured literacy and reliability. Anthropological collectors might be Indians like Henry Moody, Charles Edenshaw, Charles Nowell, or Louis Shotridge, half-bloods like Hunt or William Beynon, or whites like Teit, but they all required those three attributes of access, literacy, and reliability. Hunt stood high in each.

The collaboration was not always easy. The Kwakiutl were among the most conservative of Northwest Coast groups and became easily suspicious of what Boas and his Fort Rupert assistant were doing. At the very beginning of the Jesup Expedition Boas gave Hunt money for a feast and sent a letter for him to read to the assembled Kwakiutl of Fort Rupert. In it he flattered the Kwakiutl and praised his own efforts on their behalf, especially in trying to show "to the white men in Victoria that your feasts and your potlatches are good. . . . that your ways are not bad ways." It was a shame, he went on, that the old laws were not obeyed by

the children and that many young men did not know the history
and stories of their people. He himself knew more than did the
Kwakiutl children for he kept their laws and stories in a box
where they would not be forgotten. "Friends, it would be good if
my friend, George Hunt, would become the storage box of your
laws and your stories."[24]

The feast and flattery seem to have worked, but misunderstand-
ings were easily created. Hunt was in difficulty the next year, for
example, with the Kwakiutl of nearby Alert Bay. "Here is he
Who is finding out all our Dances then he gos and tell it to Dr.
Boas," Hunt reported it said of him. His detractors claimed that
Boas wrote that the Hamatsa still ate human flesh. Even in Spencer's store Hunt was attacked for a picture of a Hamatsa mask
which Boas had published to explain the dances and rites. The
same year Harlan Smith and Mrs. Smith gave interviews to the
Victoria press after having been guests of Hunt's sisters in Fort
Rupert. Mrs. Smith reportedly said some quite unflattering things
about Sarah and Jane Hunt — "the names she called them there, I
am shame to talk about." Hunt was no longer being spoken to by
his sisters, who retaliated further by informing the Indians that
Smith had also collected skulls: they had told "the Indians What
Mr. Smith Done to there Daid, and that I was Helping them."
Smith would never be allowed to come to Fort Rupert again,
never be permitted the opportunity "to still there grave again." If
all this was not enough, Chief Hamasaka had heard in Victoria
that Boas had said that everything around the world was changing
for the better except for the Kwakiutl tribe who were "still living
on the Daid People." Poor Hunt had been summoned to a feast
and there flatly informed that "they Dont want you or me to see
the Dance of any kind again." Things seemed quite desperate: "I
have know friend Even Mr Spencer and sisters are against me
now. the only thing I am wishing for is for my life Be spared."[25]

Boas acted immediately to quell the discontent and to protect
his source and his own reputation. He sent another letter for Hunt
to read at a feast to be given at his expense and enclosed portions
of his writings which refuted the calumny spread against him. He
could not understand what could be said against the Smiths unless
it came from meddlesome newsmen twisting things for excitement. He wrote Chief Hamasaka to deny that he had ever said
that the Kwakiutl still lived on the dead. "I do not say what is not

true." The Kwakiutl, Boas insisted, "have no better friend than I."
"Wherever I can, I speak for you." He had many times told the
chiefs in Ottawa and in England that the potlatches and dances
were not bad.[26] The affair seems to have blown over.

Boas occasionally felt obliged to keep his collaborator up to the
mark. "I thought you were going to send me a lot of stuff before
the close of December," he wrote early in 1901. "I suppose you
are doing your work all right, only you must keep me informed
more fully as to what you are doing." He could not get money to
continue Hunt's work "unless I can show results of your labors."
The irritation continued when no word arrived. Boas suspected
lethargy and curtly informed Hunt that "I beg to remind you that
under our present arrangement you must continue to collect."
Hunt's next shipment reassured him since it contained what Boas
regarded as the best old pieces yet obtained. Nevertheless, "you
must," he insisted, "do your level best to send to the Museum
material enough to justify our continued expenses in this direction." The pressures were obviously fierce if Hunt were to keep
his $75 a month salary. He accepted the challenge: "I am going to
try to get all I can to Please you and the Museum this year."[27]

Earlier Hunt had been reprimanded for buying some specimens
which Boas considered not "genuine." A stone bowl was obviously newly made, Boas wrote, and some of the masks made him
suspicious "that the Indians may try to impose upon you to a
certain extent in giving explanations of masks, and connecting
them with the stories that you are writing down." Hunt defended
himself; he was there to see the masks used just before he bought
them and he doubted that Indians would have bothered to make a
stone piece. He accepted the reprimand, however, as well as
Boas's instructions to collect only things of unquestionable age
until they had a chance to discuss the problem on Boas's pending
visit.[28]

Hunt developed his own tricks of the collector's trade. Cave
collecting was one, a patient sense of timing another. He knew
better than to pay high prices during the winter ceremonials when
he could get the same pieces for a fraction of the cost at their
close. On one occasion he told Boas of how he had obtained some
ceremonial cedar bark rings. Seeing that a man from Nuwitti
owned a set, he got the man's creditors to reclaim their loans.
These "Pressed him so much that he Had to come and Beg me to

The Whalers' Washing House of the Nootka before George Hunt collected its contents in 1904. American Museum of Natural History, no. 104478.

Buy the sect [sic: set] for 40.00 Dollar But I told him I can't pay more than 8.00 Dollar for it." They compromised at $8.75. Only an insider could force a sale in this way.

Hunt's advantage as a collector was this insider's position. Fort Rupert remained a center for ceremonial life and he usually spent summers working at Alert Bay, increasingly the region's economic pivot and fishing port. Although the Kwakiutl were distributed widely in the bays and inlets of the straits, islands, and channels of Vancouver Island and the mainland, and their villages reached round the northern tip of the island, they mixed intensively amongst themselves in the summer fishery and then in exchanging feasts and ceremonies during the long winters. Hunt knew most of the Kwakiutl personally and his relatives and friends provided an extensive information network throughout the area. Others might collect in the region: Rev. Hall for people at Home and Dorsey and Newcombe for Chicago, but Boas could be assured of Hunt's superiority. "You see," he wrote New York, "I have lots of friend and that is Where we get the Best of all."[29]

As an insider, he could raid the old caves with comparative impunity. An outsider would have caused greater resentment, as Smith did, than merely that of Hall's people. As a member of Kwakiutl society Hunt could call a feast for Boas to scotch rumors circulating against them. With such advantages and with the opportunities which Jesup's funds and Boas's terms gave him, Hunt proved a capable collector. During the five years of the Jesup Expedition he sent over twenty-five hundred ethnological pieces, ranging from everyday material to houseposts and figures.

Oddly, Hunt's most important single purchase was not Kwakiutl but the Whaler's Washing House of the Nootka, a west coast group whose language was only distantly related to their Kwakiutl neighbors but whose culture, especially its ceremonial element, was partly shared and even borrowed from them. Even at Nootka Sound Hunt's membership in Kwakiutl society assisted him.

Boas had known of the existence of the Whalers' Washing House for some years, but its location — on an island in Jewett's Lake near Friendly Cove — was secret. What was known of it made it an alluring prize and he asked Hunt to secure it for the museum. As it turned out, the plank and beam house was filled with human images, some ninety-five, with whale sculptures and human skulls.[30]

Hunt visited Friendly Cove in the winter of 1903–4 and soon found that credentials were required even to be shown the sacred Whalers' House. As one initiated into shamanic knowledge and with some happy luck he passed muster. His own account best conveys the flavor:

> They Brought a sick man to me to *Heleka* or to get the sickness out of him, for they say that I could not go to see the Whalers Praying House onless I was PExala [a shaman]. Wel I told them to Bring the sick man to me after medle night then I well show him that I was *PExala*. so they did, and I was Lucky to get the man Wel, and as soon as he was Made Wel, I was aloud to go But nat known By Every Body only the Head chief and his speaker.

Having seen it, he had yet to buy it. There was dispute about the right to sell between the chief and a second chief. The former claimed that his great grandfather had built the house, while the second chief, an old man, said that it belonged to him, that his people had put up the house six generations before. The first chief threatened to lay charges if Hunt gave money to the old man and the latter threatened to stir up trouble among the people if Hunt did not give him half the purchase price. That had long been set at $700, but the head chief altered his demand to $500 and ten

Kwakiutl Hamatsa songs, certainly a coin only an initiated insider could pay. Hunt agreed to the demanded price, but the next day the deal collapsed. The chief said he could not sell the Whalers's House "for he said that his People said that if he sell it that he will Die in a short time."[31] Obviously the old man's threats of stirring up the people had been effective.

Hunt was very disappointed: "and now my Dear Friend," he wrote Boas, "if you New How Bad I felt you would Be Either Be sorry or laugh." He would persist, try to get the two chiefs together, and get them to divide the money and the dance songs. "I am In hopes that the Meeting of the two chiefs will Be godd for our side for I think that I will get it yet." It was over a week before he was able to bring them to friendly terms about splitting the price. On his part, Hunt had to promise to leave the house alone until all the people were away to the Bering Sea sealery and at the canneries in New Westminster. He was to leave Nootka "so as the Indians think that I have not Bought to Keep things Quiet." The two vendors promised "that they will work to Bring it out in the night time," and left in charge a man named Lewis, who would be able to ship out most of the material in July. The secret was not well kept and by August Hunt learned that 'all the Indians is angry about their chief selling it to me."[32]

Part of the pressure Boas put on Hunt to keep him up to the mark was motivated by the pressure which he himself was under from Jesup. The museum president and expedition patron had been initially "amazed and delighted" with Boas's energy, but by 1900 he was growing restive and wanted more results. Boas assured him that everything possible was being done, but by 1902 only two volumes of the expedition's memoirs had appeared and the now elderly Jesup urged Boas to write up a summary volume that would give "proof of man's migration from Asia to the New World." While Boas was prepared to announce that the expedition had found ample evidence of "an intimate relationship" between Pacific coast Indians and the people of eastern Siberia, and even that the Chukchi, Kamchadal, and other Siberians 'must be classed with the American race rather than with the Asiatic race," he felt unable to comply with Jesup's desire for a summary publication. In turn Jesup notified Boas that he was withdrawing financial support.[33]

Boas was thunderstruck and he feared for his scientific reputation. Fortunately, Jesup agreed to sustain publication of the expedition's memoirs and Boas remained involved in that and in similar research for another half-dozen years. He never missed an opportunity to pay tribute to Jesup's generosity, but the warm and easy confidence that once existed no longer ran between them.

The end of the expedition was less calamitous than it might sound. Publication of research continued, but no museum personnel were sent into the field. Funds for Teit and Hunt were less available, but the effect was more noticeable on research than on acquisitions. Regular acquisition funds remained available and Hunt went on sending in Kwakiutl collections in 1903 and secured his very important Nootka collection, including the Whalers' Washing House, in 1904.

Boas bought a small but choice Tsimshian collection from Henry Tate of Port Simpson, a half-blood who began taking texts for him in the Hunt manner. That same year, 1905, Adolph Lewisohn of New York donated a significant collection of Tlingit material, especially baskets and shaman articles, that had been collected by Louis Levy, a fur trader at Juneau. It was a splendid collection of Tlingit objects, full of what Emmons called "choice pieces" and especially notable for its one hundred decorated baskets and a shaman's box filled with rattles, ivory necklaces, and other shamanic articles.[34] A smaller collection of Alaskan material, a part of the results of the Harriman Alaska Expedition, was transferred to the museum from the Zoological Gardens in 1905 and Emmons presented a number of Tlingit charms and other small items.

Under Boas's auspices the American Museum's Northwest Coast collection had grown to immense size and, while still possessing a Tlingit bias, developed a comprehensiveness which any institution might envy. And, it must be noted, while Boas naturally had a special interest in the North Pacific accessions, it was not the sole area of his responsibility. He supervised the growth of the museum's important collection of California tribes. In 1901 he extended the museum's concerns to the Philippines and was soon responsible for work in Africa and Asia financed by Jacob Schiff and others. The liberality of the museum's friends was astonishing. The Hyde brothers paid for the museum's enormous collections from the Southwest, Mrs. Jesup aided Arapahoe research, while others continued the generous support of the Central and South American interests of Putman and Saville.

The greatest tribute to the work of Putnam and Boas in these years came from the pen of their rival, George Dorsey of the Chicago Field Columbian Museum. During the decade between 1895 and 1905, Dorsey wrote in *Science,* American Museum anthropologists made "a systematic attempt to carry on investigations over an ever-increasing large area as fast as means would permit. As a result of this intelligently directed series of field operations there grew up in the American Museum one of the greatest departments of anthropology to be found in any museum in the world." It was doubtful, he continued, "if any institution ever acquired in the same period of time collections of such magnitude or ever accumulated material with such intelligence or exhibited it in an equally sound manner."[35]

Dorsey's tribute to the department was written after Putman, Boas, and Saville had all departed from the museum. Putnam was the first to go, resigning in 1903 and moving on to establish a new museum at the University of California for Mrs. Phoebe Hearst. He left satisfied that he had elevated the American Museum to front rank among American anthropological collections. Jesup, now feeling his age, that same year named a director to assist in the museum's administration.

Boas never quite accepted H. C. Bumpus, an invertebrate zoologist, as his superior. There was no Putnam to mediate when Boas and Bumpus clashed in 1905, and it was probably a relief to everyone when Boas resigned. Although he continued to edit the Jesup Expedition memoirs, his curatorial work was over. He could devote his energies to his Columbia University duties, to writing, and to dozens of other professional responsibilities and ambitions. He had lost much of his interest in museum work and had begun seriously to question many of the assumptions behind museum anthropology.

Chapter Seven

The Field Museum
and Dr. Newcombe

THE ESTABLISHMENT of the Field Columbian Museum in the burgeoning, ambitious city of Chicago had been a major new foundation, blessed from its inception with a healthy endowment, interested patrons, and a hard-working staff. Edward Ayer, whose Indian collection had been loaned to Putnam's Department M, was the businessman catalyst behind the conversion of the Columbian Exposition into the Columbian Museum. Assisted by George Pullman, Philip Armour, and others, Ayer seized upon the idea, suggested initially by Putnam, of founding a great new museum upon the basis of the exposition collections.

With the depression cast upon the city by the Panic of 1893, Ayer's committee could raise only a few hundred thousand dollars. Marshall Field, the department store magnate and far the richest man in Chicago, had repeatedly expressed his lack of interest in the museum idea. In the crisis, Ayer renewed pressure upon his fishing friend, appealing to the millionaire retailer's vanity for immortality and personally showing him the Fair's enormous quantity of exhibited material. Field capitulated magnanimously by pledging a full million dollars, easily enough to launch the new museum, which took on the name of its major benefactor. Ayer became the Field Museum's first president, donated his collection to it, and over the succeeding years sent rich material — Egyptian and Oriental as well as American — paid for by his wealth and often collected by his hand.[1]

The new Chicago museum possessed all the ambition of its city. Putnam had foreseen an ethnological museum "that would be without rival" and one of the institution's early supporters spoke of the wonderful possibilities of Jackson Park becoming another British Museum. As heir to Putnam's Department M and other fair exhibits, the museum began with an extensive anthropological legacy. "An almost overwhelming mass" of objects from Egypt, Peru, Paraguay, Colombia, and the Yucatan, as well as North America, became part of the new museum. From the Northwest Coast were all of the fair acquisitions gathered by Boas, Hunt, Eells, Deans, Fillip Jacobsen, Mrs. Morrison, and Swan, supplemented by the purchase of Hagenbeck's Jacobsen brothers' material, Ayer's collection, and Boas's osteological material. These were housed in the exposition's huge Fine Arts Building, an impressive Ionic edifice whose graceful proportions, imitative of the Athenian Erechtheum, masked the horrifying fact that it was a wooden tinderbox. (Despite elaborate precautions to minimize its vulnerability, insurance costs were three times the normal rate.)[2]

The anthropological collections had been arranged hurriedly and often provisionally in the new building by Boas before he left. The next few years were devoted primarily to reorganization, a process not assisted by a rapid turnover of curators. Holmes had ousted Boas, but decided to return to Washington in 1897 and was succeeded by George A. Dorsey, a young man just hired as assistant curator for physical anthropology. Despite Boas's initial work with the collection, much of it remained in a state of confusion, with collectors' lists "more or less tangled," and a variety of incongruous case styles in use. The settling-in meant that energy was directed more toward "working over old rather than in purchasing new material": labeling, numbering, cataloguing, and changing the installation from that of an exposition to "an arrangement on museum lines." Once acquisitions began, the museum quickly utilized its financial resources to gain international importance in a number of areas, including anthropology. Especially under Dorsey, the department rapidly expanded the museum's holdings of Classical, Oceanic, East Asian, Benin, and American material.[3]

Dorsey was an Ohioan. He attended Denison College, then went to Harvard for another degree in 1890. He stayed on for post-graduate work in archaeology under Putnam who simultaneously employed him for the Chicago fair. Dorsey did fieldwork in Peru, Equador, Chile, and Bolivia for the exposition, then received his doctorate in 1894, Harvard's first in anthropology. He remained at Harvard as instructor in anthropology before taking the assistant curatorship at the Field Museum in 1896, becoming curator the next year. He was only twenty-nine and, with his smooth-shaven face and athletic frame, looked even younger. He wore his learning lightly and was already becoming known for "his energy, self-reliance, competitiveness and hard-boiled man-of-business manner.[4]

Dorsey's energy, the interest he aroused in his work, and the appropriations he commandeered for his department allowed the anthropological section to overshadow all other museum departments. The trustees had determined that the department's immediate energies should be expended on making the North American section especially strong, and by 1903 a visiting curator could write (with only some travesty of the truth) that Chicago's North American Indian collections, "filling hall after hall, arranged stock by stock and tribe by tribe, are absolutely the finest ethnological collections in existence" and, without consideration of quality, "surpass all other collections combined from North America, in all museums of the world."[5]

The abrupt departure of Boas in 1894 had not meant that Chicago would ignore the Northwest Coast. Dorsey gave particular emphasis to that area, perhaps because of its inherent interest, perhaps because of the museum's inherited strength, perhaps because of the American Museum's pretentions in that region. For whatever motive, his Northwest Coast collecting shared fully in the aggressive and ambitious character which he brought to his curatorial role.

Dorsey's promotion came at almost the same time as Boas was beginning his career at the American Museum and convincing President Jesup to contribute tens of thousands of dollars to Northwest Coast research. The coincidence was entirely fortuitous, but it pitted two of the most ambitious men in American anthropology into direct competition for the collectible resources of the North American Indian. Dorsey consciously aspired to rival the older eastern institution at the same time that New York determined to be a great center of anthropological research. That Chicago's new museum would measure itself by New York's was inevitable. The Illinois city aspired to national and international status; as the railway hub of the north and west, it hoped to equal, even to overtake, the elder metropolis. While the American Museum had an almost quarter-century start, the Field began with resources any museum might envy.

The New York-Chicago museum rivalry was intensified by the personalities involved. F. W. Putnam had been hired in New York to take charge of its anthropology department in 1894, just at the time when he had become thoroughly disgusted "at the turn things have taken at the Columbian Museum."[6] With his advice ignored and then his protégé, Boas, passed over for the curatorship, Putnam felt very badly treated by the Chicago museum and its trustees. His annoyance was all the greater because he justifiably claimed paternity to the idea of utilizing the exposition to create a great museum on the shores of Lake Michigan. Boas was even more bitter toward Chicago, a bitterness that festered in the protracted argument over the physical anthropology collection he had left at the Columbian Museum.

The difficulties over Boas's osteological collection presented the least attractive aspect of the bad feeling between Boas and his "dear enemies" in the Chicago museum administration.[7] His personal collection of skulls and skeletons had been gradually accumulating since 1886, and, even after he sold a large collection to Virchow in Berlin, it totalled some 238 items at the time he left Chicago. Three quarters of these, 179 catalogued entries, were Northwest Coast, primarily Salish and Kwakiutl. The bones and crania had been, as described earlier, acquired partly by Boas himself, but largely through the Suttons. Others had come from his photographer, O. C. Hastings; some from James Deans. To these he added skulls from a variety of sources as disparate as New Zealand and British Guiana. In the winter of 1893–94 Boas had been installing these, though they remained a personal collection, in the east court of the Field Museum. Putnam had recommended their purchase, but no action had been taken when, on February 19, Boas heard that Holmes and not he was to become curator.

Before he left Chicago, he named his price as $2,800. He held tenaciously to the figure, refusing offers of $2,000, then $2,500. Director F. J. V. Skiff capitulated and paid the full price on October 24. Six months passed before it was noticed that there was no catalogue to the Boas collection, a matter which Dorsey, when he became assistant curator for physical anthropology, took up with Boas. As a student of Putnam's and an exposition colleague of Boas's, Dorsey secured from Boas, after his initial refusal of any cooperation, an agreement "to do for you personally what I will not do for the Field Columbian Museum." Although Boas promised "all the information I have" in exchange for duplicate ethnological specimens, the museum never received its catalogue, a matter of continuing regret.[8]

The catalogue was victim of the less than cordial relations between Chicago and New York. Friendly relations were made more difficult by Boas's unwillingness to admit Dorsey to his growing circle of disciples and colleagues. Dorsey bore considerable responsibility. His entrepreneurship outreached his scholarly concern and the rapidity of his work easily opened him to charges of superficiality and to the use of methods not professional enough for Boas's punctilious views. Overshadowing this was Dorsey's connection with the perfidious Field Museum, his ambition to raise the new museum to high rank among anthropological institutions, and his special determination to rival New York.

The competition of the Field and American museums — reflective of the metropolitan rivalry of their seats — was most intense in North American ethnology, the area to which both museums devoted particular attention in the late 1890s. When Dorsey, acting under formal instructions from Holmes, decided to collect on the Northwest Coast in 1897, he stepped upon the very sensitive toes of Franz Boas, just departing himself for the inaugural season of his ambitious Jesup Expedition.

Dorsey's first expedition on behalf of the Field Museum was a rapid survey of much of western North America — tribes of the plains, plateau, coast, and desert — all in four months. His stated purpose was to secure collections illustrating physical characteristics and to gather materials for life-groups, rapidly becoming standard features in American museums. He took with him museum photographer Edward P. Allen, not only for the photographs considered necessary, but also to assist with plaster facial casts.

After securing a large amount of osteological material from the Blackfeet and, at Bonners Ferry, what he believed to be the only two Kootenay skeletons ever collected (the Kootenays kept a close watch over their grounds), Dorsey arrived in Victoria on June 19. There he engaged James Deans as a guide for work among the Haida and Tsimshian. Deans was particularly familiar with the Charlottes, having circumnavigated Graham Island in Edenshaw's canoe with Swan in 1883 and then securing the Columbian Exposition Haida collection, including the complete model village and Haida house. Dorsey intended to benefit from the old Scot's north coast knowledge. Although the record is not clear on the point, it seems almost doubtless that Dorsey's plans were focused on the Skungo burial cave seen fourteen years before by Deans and Swan. Deans remembered its precise location and this time there would be no inconveniences such as Edenshaw or a full canoe to frustrate collecting.[9]

No steamers were scheduled for Masset so the party boarded the first available ship north, hoping to find at Port Simpson a means to cross the strait to Graham Island. Luck was with them: the storekeeper at Masset was visiting Port Simpson and together they hired the *Janet,* a former survey vessel easily remade seaworthy. Battling wind and tide, it took a full three days of tacking to cross the seventy miles of sea to what Dorsey described as "this half-modern, half-barbarian, half-dead, half-alive village" of Masset. After photographing, taking head measurements, and purchasing specimens — including three carver's tools bought from Charles Edenshaw — the Chicago pair and their Victoria guide departed Masset to sail westward along the north shore of Graham. They made stops at the village sites of Yan, Kung, and Kiusta, places "long since abandoned and given over to solitude, to moss, and to cedar trees." At Yan they found a skeleton and two crania. A shaman's grave house at Kung yielded up its contents: a long coffin box where the shaman's remains lay, atypically at full-length, and surrounded by masks, rattles, and other magical material, much of it crumbled to dust.[10]

These stops were mere preludes to the expected riches of Kiusta. On a tiny egg-shaped island was the shaman's grave house

("Gorgie's Coffin House," Dorsey called it) from which old Edenshaw had allowed Swan to take only the tusks. Fourteen seasons had tumbled it into ruins; "two hats were all that remained to tell of the former glory of Gorgie," Dorsey wrote, but he did scavenge the man's bones. Skungo Cave, eroded from the conglomerate and lying at the head of a steep gully about five hundred feet from shore, had not been relieved of its contents. Swan had never returned and his naval friends, Niblack and Bolles, had also been frustrated in their desire to collect the cave's rich contents of bones and boxes. That it still remained in 1897 was, even considering its remoteness, something of a miracle. Its existence had become widely known among the cognoscenti. Swan had shared his knowledge with the Smithsonian and its Alaskan naval friends, and Deans had reported on it to Boas at the Chicago fair. Dawson in Ottawa had known of it for some years, "informed on what I thought good authority" by someone who had himself seen the place. Even now, C. F. Newcombe of Victoria was collecting on the islands and, acting in part on Dawson's information but also on Swan's, intended to visit the cave.[11] He would be too late.

Dorsey and Deans rapidly scavenged the cave for all that was worth taking, extracting "a large collection of complete skeletons of both sexes and of various ages" along with "many objects of ethnological interest." The total haul was at least sixteen individuals and probably more. Having secured their major prize, they turned back, first to Masset where they found Newcombe visiting the village for natural history and ethnology purposes. They admired his small collection, claimed that, though they had bought a few things from Edenshaw, they had been "quite unsuccessful in collecting." Dorsey asked Newcombe to collect some skulls or skeletons for him, agreeing to pay from five to twenty dollars for skulls and up to twenty dollars for skeletons.[12]

From Masset Dorsey and company sailed north to the abandoned Tlingit village of Old Tongass, where they found little "except the totem poles and the old ruined houses." Dorsey very much wanted to find a shaman's grave since, because of the Tlingit practice of cremating all but shamans, "it is no easy matter to secure osteological material from the Tlingits." Leaving Old Tongass "we espied one of these little houses perched far up on a rocky point" of Duke Island. The grave house was about thirty

The mummy of the woman shaman found in her grave house on Duke Island,
Alaska, in 1897 by George Dorsey, and unwrapt for the photographer.
Photographed by E. P. Allen. Courtesy, Field Museum of Natural History.

years old, they judged, and stood some five feet high and six feet
square.

Removing a portion of one of the walls, we could see the body,
which had been carefully wrapped in several cedar-bark mats, and
tied into a neat bundle with stout cedar-bark rope. Over the bundle

were branches of bog myrtle, and under the head was a box. Removing the wrapping still further, we disclosed the desiccated body of a woman doctor. In one hand she clasped a long knife, its steel blade entirely wasted away, leaving only the handle. In the other hand was a beautifully carved wooden pipe inlaid with finely polished abalone shells; but her real title to distinction lay in the immense wooden plug or labret which she still retained in her lower lip.[13]

This was photographed, step by step. What was salvagable went into the *Janet,* to become part of Field Museum accession 592.

The boat sailed on to New Tongass, normally inhabited, but now they found that every living soul had left for the canneries. The emptiness allowed for prowling — and the procuring of a carved image from a grave. The *Janet* was taken back to Port Simpson, then left there as Dorsey, Deans, and Allen boarded the *Islander* for Port Essington on the Skeena River. Dorsey found Robert Cunningham's store a useful source for Haida as well as Tsimshian pieces.

The Chicago party did not stay long. "Desiring to visit those villages which are least contaminated by modern influence," they went up the Skeena to Hazelton on board an HBC steamer whose frequent refueling stops lengthened to six days the 152-mile voyage to Hazelton. The villages along the way, places like Kitwanga and Kitsegukla, were deemed "disappointing both in their smallness and modernness, and none seemed worthy of any extended visit." This was a judgment based more upon the *Caledonia*'s itinerary than from on-site investigation; Hazelton, which was hardly a native village at all, but where the vessel's journey terminated, Dorsey found "sufficiently primitive to be of interest." He bought some articles of native clothing and "by a bit of good fortune we were enabled to secure the complete paraphernalia of a shaman" who had just converted to Christianity. Rattles, charms, blankets, masks, and headdresses went into his case, soon joined by the full costume of a member of the "Dog Eaters" society. After a visit to the new cemetery (Dorsey seems to have left the grave houses alone) and a horseback ride to Hagwelget, the expedition returned downriver on the *Caledonia*. Dorsey was not yet done. Before boarding the steamer for Victoria, he raided a grave house on an island in Port Essington harbor for a skeleton, and later in Bella

Bella two burial grounds yielded skeletons as well as a coffin box.[14]

On its way south, the steamer stopped at Namu where Dorsey and Deans found Boas impatiently waiting for transportation north to Port Essington. The boat halted long enough for them to come ashore where they exchanged "very friendly" greetings with Boas. For Boas the friendliness was forced. He had been told in Chicago that Dorsey would not be in British Columbia at the same time as he; even more, he resented the Chicagoan's incursion into his own territory without the slightest consultation. He was sure he would have informed J. W. Fewkes or Frank Cushing, for example, of his plans were he to invade their Southwest field. He was mad that Dorsey had not shown a similar courtesy. "This trip of Dorsey's annoys me more than I can say," he told his wife, "this Chicago crowd simply adopt our plan and try to beat us to it." This was his country and anyone seriously intending to study the area "should seek and take my advice and not just run out here at random." Dorsey had the inconsiderate effrontery even to speak of going to Fort Rupert and Deans capped it by asking the whereabouts of George Hunt. "I was mean enough," he admitted, "not to tell them where he was, and I have written George Hunt that he should not do anything for Dorsey." The whole affair made Boas furious, not only with Dorsey, but with himself for being so bothered by it and then resorting to deception. He wanted to think of himself as unselfish, but "I must do that for my own protection." He did find consolation in the suspicion that Dorsey had been to so many places in so short a period that "half of his time must have been spent travelling" and with the conviction that, in any case, "little Dorsey won't have achieved much with the help of the old ass Deans."[15]

Dorsey, on the other hand, was quite pleased with his operation. Arriving in Victoria on August 10, he shipped twenty-two boxes to Chicago, then read in a Victoria newspaper the quite false report that all his material — collections, notes, and instruments — had gone down off Masset on the *Mexico*. (Boas, initially taken in by the newspaper error, reported sourly to his wife from Rivers Inlet: "by the way, Dorsey's collection was *not* on the sunken *Mexico*.") Within a day, Dorsey and Allen were off for the Columbia River, California, and Arizona.[16]

Boas's suspicions about the superficial character of Dorsey's trip were quite right. The expedition had the character of a fervid rip-and-run operation and Dorsey probably had spent at least half of his time travelling. The "terrifying superficiality" that so often characterized his work was seldom shown to worse advantage than on this trip. While Allen did secure some quite superb photographs — "the finest photos ever taken along the coast," Dorsey claimed — the expedition was otherwise little more than poorly disguised plunder. Dorsey was briefly arrested for desecrating graves on the Columbia — the charge was dismissed upon an assurance of restitution — and so flagrant was the pillage on the Queen Charlottes that the Anglican teacher and missionary in Masset, Rev. J. H. Keen, was moved to angry remonstrance. There were, he reported privately, loud complaints from the Indians about graves disturbed and houses sacked at Kung and elsewhere. "They tell me that bones & other things have been removed wholesale, & that the perpetrators had not even the grace to cover up their excavations." Dorsey "must have handled the graves most unmercifully." Keen intended to see the devastation at Kung for himself and, if the tales of Dorsey's "wholesale plunder" were true, he intended to "expose the rascal." His investigation confirmed the depredation and brought a letter of condemnation in Victoria's *Daily Colonist*.[17]

The Indians, Keen wrote, had found almost every grave in the neighborhood of Virago Sound and North Island rifled and the coffin boxes strewn about. "In one case some hair, recognized as having belonged to an Indian doctor, and a box which had contained a body, were found floating in the sea." Keen quite pointedly laid the blame on "a party of Americans" gathering material for the Field Columbian Museum. James Deans had accompanied that party and Keen asked that the Scotsman name the men "who, however laudable their object, could so mercilessly ride roughshod over the susceptibilities of the Indians."[18]

Deans, outraged and anxious to reply, sent a copy of the paper to Dorsey, who counselled quiet. The Victorian came round to the view "that the best dose of medicine, for that teacher, was silent Contempt." Keen's letter travelled farther than Chicago. Boas was predictably contemptuous of Dorsey's shocking carelessness. With evident delight at his rival's discomfiture and a measure of self-congratulation, he wrote of having done the same kind of grave robbing hundred of times, but "I have never come into conflict with the feelings of Indians." (He did not mention his agents, the Sutton brothers, who had.) G. M. Dawson heard of the episode and was outraged. "I sincerely trust that his interests in British Columbia Indians may wane if it is likely to continue to take the form indicated." Dorsey's Toronto friend, David Boyle, informed him: "there is a good deal of 'feeling' down there about the opening of certain *recent* graves." Boyle had tried to defend the Chicago curator, but he was told that "the evidence was too strong."[19]

C. F. Newcombe seemed undisturbed by Keen's evidence. He had innocently mentioned the cave to Dorsey at their meeting in Masset and, though detecting in Dorsey what he later realized was a "rather guilty appearance" at hearing of "a certain mummy cave," he had not then realized that Dorsey had already raided it. Only when he had then taken his boat round Kiusta expecting to make his own haul, did he realize what had happened. "Alas," he wrote Dorsey, "another ghoul had anticipated my visit & my hopes were doomed to be disappointed." (He had, Deans reported, "found nothing to bring away but one foot.") There were also, Newcombe noted, "rumours of a discovery of certain evidences of crime on one of the rivers, followed by, I fear, only a partial restitution," a reference to Dorsey's arrest at The Dalles.[20] Newcombe's tolerant friendliness was doubtless appreciated by Dorsey and contributed to the fruitful relationship that was developing between them.

Despite Dorsey's twenty-two cases from the coast, his Field Museum was considerably behind the American Museum. The life-groups were only just begun, he had a much smaller staff, and few contacts on the coast. With Jesup's generous benefaction, Boas was sending out several men a year and had George Hunt permanently on the spot. Marshall Field's endowment did not provide the same singularity of purpose which Jesup's grant gave Boas for the Pacific coast and Deans was no substitute for trained collectors or for Hunt's inimitable location, experience, and ability.

Unsuccessful in an attempt to hire Harlan Smith away from New York, Dorsey had to rely on his personal expeditions, and these were spread over much of the western half of the continent. In 1899, as part of another whirlwind western trip, he visited the Nisqually, Puyallup, and Muckleshoot reservations of Washington

State. There, among the Duwamish, he secured a complete Salish spirit canoe, a series of decorated boards set upright in the ground to simulate a canoe and used to assist a shaman in his dramatized voyage to the spiritual underworld to recapture a lost soul. On a quick trip to Victoria, he was able to get Nuwitti Tom, a Kwakiutl from Hope Island and one of the Chicago fair troupe, and several fellow Kwakiutl to submit themselves to plaster-of-paris poses in Hamatsa attitudes for his Kwakiutl group. He recorded some of their songs on a gramophone, which he replayed for the benefit of the members of Victoria's Natural History Society.[21]

While the casts and recordings worked out splendidly, Dorsey still lacked sufficient Kwakiutl material for the four groups he now had planned in the reorganized Northwest Coast halls and he was anxious to have a Kwakiutl pole and other large sculptures. He asked C. F. Newcombe to help with both tasks. The next month the collector was off to Hope Island on behalf of the Field Columbian Museum. In Newcombe Dorsey had found his man on the spot, the invaluable resident collector required for the systematic accumulation of collections. Chicago's effort to match New York in Northwest Coast holdings would rest upon the energy and ability of Dr. Charles Frederick Newcombe.

Newcombe was by training a medical doctor. Raised in Newcastle and educated at Aberdeen, he practiced a few years in British asylums and then privately in the Lake District before migrating to Oregon in 1884 with his pregnant wife and three children. In the beautiful rugged country at Hood River, on the south shore of the Columbia where it flows through the Cascade gorge, he established a home and practice.[22] Medicine was not his major interest; it was at most complementary to his enthusiasm for the life sciences. The emigrant doctor was a passionate field naturalist, an example of the Victorian "heyday of natural history" when the collecting of plants, shells, insects, and spiders was a fashionable hobby for a multitude of amateurs and a serious one for thousands of field and closet naturalists. The transplantation to the western new world gave impetus to Newcombe's avocation. The flora and fauna were unfamiliar and the discovery of a new species, the goal of every field man, was more likely on the slopes of Mount Hood than along Windermere's ancient shore.

Equally interesting were the arrowheads and celts which could be found in relative abundance along the Columbia River, especially upstream toward The Dalles. To his collections of the animal and vegetable kingdoms, Newcombe added the productions of aboriginal man. When he moved his growing family to Victoria in 1889, the thirty-eight-year-old physician was soon active in founding the city's Natural History Society and spent much of his free time among the Provincial Museum's growing collection of regional specimens. The move also allowed a broader scope for his interest in Indian antiquities. Across Victoria's harbor was the Songhees Reserve and Victoria was a center not only for that resident Salish band, but for all the Indians of the coast. A sailboat — at first a simple, open eighteen-footer — increased the collector's mobility and allowed him to explore the myriad of islands in the Gulf of Georgia.

Newcombe's practice was never demanding and he became all but retired. He was comfortably off, worth some $68,000, largely invested in solid, interest-bearing British rails. It was a nearly perfect life: rearing five intelligent young children, living in the mild climate of a small British city that was away from some of the gaucheries of the Yankee frontier, and possessing a natural history society and a young museum. There were abundant collecting opportunities and a rich correspondence with scientists in Washington, Montreal, and Britain.

The idyll was soon shattered. Marian Newcombe died in her bed after giving birth to their sixth child. Newcombe's 1891 diary sparsely records the long, sleepless agony as he watched his wife slowly passing away, her seven days of pain so blunted by opium that she could not recognize her own children. He found limited solace in long walks along Victoria's blustery beaches. Two months later he left the immediacy of his sorrow for a year's trip to Britain and the Continent, the distractions of travel being better than bleak mourning in a half-empty home. On the way he called on G. M. Dawson in Montreal, studied the Washington collections, and met Goode and Dall at the Smithsonian. In Britain he renewed old friendships and made new ones, attended a few lectures and scientific meetings, and presented a collection of Columbia River arrowheads to Cambridge lecturer John Marr.

In May 1892 he was back home in Victoria, prepared to renew his life as father and naturalist. He sailed often in the waters of the

C. F. Newcombe with Henry Moody at Tanu, 1923. British Columbia Provincial Museum.

strait and gulf, concerned largely with mollusks and birds, plants and fossils. The summer of 1895 took him farther afield, travelling with Francis Kermode of the Provincial Museum on a three-month visit to the Queen Charlotte Islands. Natural history remained the dominant concern, for the Charlottes were as remarkable for the singularity of their biology as for being the homeland of the Haida. The following summer brought a trip to Barclay Sound, again mostly for botanizing, but Newcombe picked up the odd stone hammer and other Nootka relics to add to his growing collection. In 1897 he was back to the Charlottes, accompanied by ten-year-old Arthur acting as assistant naturalist, and with his new covered sailboat, a Columbia River fishing type, shipped with him as deck cargo on the *Danube*.

Naturalist work remained part of Newcombe's purpose, but this 1897 expedition was the first in which ethnological collecting was a primary motivation. He had his own collection to supplement, but he also carried four separate commissions. Dr. Hugo Schauinsland had passed through Victoria on a world trip and sought a totem pole for his Bremen museum. British Columbia's Premier J. H. Turner asked for a Haida pole to present to the

Royal Botanical Gardens at Kew. G. M. Dawson, now Selwyn's successor as director of the Geological Survey, had advanced $300 toward a Haida collection. And Boas, whom he had met in 1894, put up $150 toward securing a pole and other large items for the American Museum.

Originating from different countries, the four commissions ought not to have conflicted, but Newcombe had not calculated on Dawson's hostility to exports and his special suspicion of Boas, whom he felt was using the British Association committee to advance himself and his American Museum. Newcombe, just after he had agreed over dinner to assist Boas, received Dawson's warning that the New Yorker, though still funded partly by the British Association and the Canadian government, was collecting "entirely in the interests of the American Museum" and "whatever he may get in that way is lost to us."[23]

Newcombe set off in mid-June, the *Danube* calling at Alert Bay and Fort Rupert on the way north. He disembarked at Skidegate and launched his twenty-four-foot *Pelican* there. In a small notebook he recorded (not very systematically) some of the details of his navigation, many of his experiences, and some of his purchases. At Skidegate, for instance, he met Josephine Elswa, wife (or perhaps widow?) of Swan's 1883 helpmate, Johnny Kit Elswa, who told him that Judge Swan had bought her dance hat for thirty dollars sixteen years before. (The price was, of course, somewhat of an exaggeration.) At Maude Island he relocated the shaman's grave he had noted in 1895 and took its skull; at Cumshewa he found several "mummy boxes" but took nothing. From Jane Shakespeare of Skidegate he bought some baskets and seal spears, and elsewhere in the village he obtained a bow and six arrows and a puffin-beak rattle. Many of his dealings were with the elderly and the distaff, those unable to partake in the summer's fishing and cannery labor, and his notebook lists unbought or "reserved" items as often as it records actual purchases. As Newcombe discovered to his cost, it was a "waste of time" to collect during the summer season; the villages were nearly as deserted as Jacobsen had found them in 1881.[24] Still something of a novice at expeditionary field collecting, he was learning the tricks of the trade.

Despite the unpropitious season, Newcombe was able to send a respectable collection to Ottawa — Dawson thought it "a considerable quantity of good material."[25] He bought a pole from Tanu for Kew Gardens and a fifteen-foot inside pole from Skidegate's "Daagu-kunklin House" for Bremen. He sent nothing to New York. Dawson's strong opinions of Boas and exports may have been a cause; perhaps it was merely the season and the difficulty of securing enough of the kind of monumental work that Boas wanted.

The trip had a significance larger than the filled and unfilled commissions, the objects reserved, and the lesson of summer collecting's frustrations. At Masset, when Newcombe was about halfway through his itinerary, he came across Dorsey and Deans, just returned from their Kung and Kiusta raids. Newcombe knew Deans as "the old prospector from Victoria" and as a colleague in the Natural History Society, but this was his first contact with Dorsey. Newcombe's guests "looked over my small collection of Indian curios & said the prices given were extremely moderate." They indicated that they had, excepting their Edenshaw purchases, collected little. Such talk was merely the wariness of the first meeting of two collectors, each suspicious of a possible rival. Newcombe did allude to the mummy cave of Skungo which was on his future itinerary, but Dorsey later claimed not to have caught it, only a reference to west coast villages containing hundreds of skeletons.[26]

Despite the caution, more on Dorsey's part than Newcombe's, the men spent several hours together and the initial friendship was confirmed by Newcombe's amused toleration when Dorsey's body-snatching became a subject of public controversy. When the Chicagoan again visited Victoria in September 1899 to make his plaster casts and cylinder recordings, Newcombe was quite happy to be asked to help in completing the Field Museum's Kwakiutl group.

After years of casual collecting for his own cabinet, Newcombe was now a part of the museum scramble. It had begun modestly enough, with the orders from Premier Turner, Schauinsland, Boas, and Dawson. A collection of artifacts for Kew, selected to illustrate native uses of local plants and taken with him on an 1898 trip to England, had been a marriage of his botanical knowledge with his developing ethnological interests. Dawson, having "some prospects now of a new and more extended Museum" in Ottawa, wanted "anything connected with the Indian population of the country." He asked Newcombe for more material as well as an expert appraisal, then supervision of packing, of the collections of A. A. Aaronson, one of the Victoria curio dealers.[27] Now Dorsey needed him to complete the Chicago Kwakiutl groups.

Boas's unfilled order for Haida poles had also to be considered. With the usefulness of a resident collector obvious, Newcombe's growing experience and expertise were in demand and he was prepared to supply his services. Initially he worked as a commissioned freelancer, collecting for Dawson and Dorsey in 1899, for Dawson, Dorsey, Boas, and Stewart Culin of the University of Pennsylvania Museum in 1900, and for Dorsey and Boas in 1901. The problem of freelancing and multiple commissions was a sometimes complicated nuisance and he was later relieved to settle down with a three-year engagement, extended into 1906, which put him exclusively in the service of the Field Museum and on a regular monthly salary.

His 1899 trip took him to Kwakiutl country for a month. Dividing the spoils between Dawson and Dorsey illustrated some of the difficulties of playing off the demands of two or more museum commissions. He worked the area fairly thoroughly, visiting Dorsey's chosen area for the group, Hope Island and Nuwitti, as well as Alert Bay, Fort Rupert, and Village Island. At Fort Rupert he found the Indians engaged in a potlatch and "too busy to talk business." It was his first experience of winter potlatching and, having read his Boas, Newcombe was disappointed at "the tameness of the dances and the squalid dress & surroundings of the performances," and shocked "that nearly all wore white man's clothes & very often without any of the stage accessions" so fully pictured by Boas. The dances only slightly affected his collecting errand: he bought "about $250 worth of stuff." The prices were "way up" compared to far-finer Haida pieces, he thought, but he secured a fair selection of masks and rattles, a number of old boxes, but only two carved dishes. At Xumtaspi on Hope Island he bought four small poles, all carved single figures, including one depicting Tsonokwa, the wild woman of the woods.[28]

In his enthusiasm, Newcombe wrote simultaneously to both Dawson and Dorsey to tell of his successes, then decided to reserve most of the material for Ottawa. Having an idea of what Dawson particularly wanted, he sent to Dorsey a list of "remainders," including ceremonial items suitable for the Chicago Hamatsa group. Carelessly enthusiastic, he offered two unusual pieces to Dorsey, then shipped them off to Ottawa as soon as he had a favorable response from Dawson.

The articles in question were examples of the bawdy frankness that entered much of Kwakiutl oral literature and humor, but was more rarely depicted in their sculpture. "One of these is a kind of house totem pole representing a man about 12 or 14 feet high, with legs separated & holding his sexual organ in his hands." The "second impropriety" was an ancient potlatch dish. "At one end a man's hand & arm are shown; at the other his legs with knees drawn up & his heels support his testicles from which springs his erect organ." The indecent pole had once stood at Nuwitti, where the open legs had been the house entrance. While the pieces "may not be thought suitable for a moral show," the man's offending organs "could easily be obliterated" from the sculpture, and the dish, if set at the back of a museum case, was "not so obtrusively indecent as might be supposed." The grease dish was a fine piece of work "& illustrates a certain phase of Indian character" so he thought that "some comprehensive museum would not despise it." Dawson was anxious for "any good carved work," and these pieces, "notwithstanding their somewhat compromising character," were articles he wanted. The Canadian National Museum could "scarcely afford at this date to lose anything old and characteristic." Dorsey, too, wanted all the material, especially the Xumtaspi posts and was disappointed that he lost them to Ottawa. He overlooked the loss, but the area for misunderstanding was wide and dangerous.[29] In 1901, working in the Queen Charlottes for both Boas and Dorsey, Newcombe was more circumspect in dividing the purchases, though he promised Dorsey a beaver coffin support, intending a similar frog figure for Boas — then sent each the others'. The switch seemed to go unnoticed.

Soon after Newcombe's return from the field, Dorsey turned up again in Victoria, this time with Stewart Culin in tow. Culin was curator of American archaeology and general ethnology at the University of Pennsylvania's Free Museum of Science and Art (later renamed The University Museum) and a great admirer of Dorsey's energy and acumen. The two curators came from a whirlwind tour of Sac, Fox, Shoshone, and Arapahoe groups, then a visit to Puget Sound (where Culin secured a Duwamish spirit boat almost identical to the one already in Chicago) and to Neah Bay for Makah fishing implements and some ceremonial items.

In Victoria their first step was to call on Newcombe. He showed them his recent Kwakiutl collection, and took them through the Provincial Museum and on a visit to the local dealers. Since the Philadelphia collection was almost bare of Pacific coast material, Culin selected from Newcombe's 1899 collection to the value of $200 and then $262 worth of material from Frederick Landsberg's shop. Newcombe, after partaking "somewhat freely" of Culin's luncheon hospitality, took his guests across the bridge to the Songhees Reserve. Among items of interest were three large carved and painted posts of Lk u'ñen house seen lying on the ground. These were Salish posts, quite different from the northern poles. Carved in relief, they showed the image of a man holding an animal against his body. The two curators were departing the next morning; Newcombe, again the convenient man on the spot, was commissioned to negotiate with the old woman who owned them. (At ten dollars, one went to Philadelphia and two to Chicago.) Back in his museum office, Culin asked Newcombe for more: a good representative collection from the coast and at least one pole.[30]

Newcombe's 1900 Charlottes' trip was thus in the interests of Culin and the University of Pennsylvania and it turned out to be very profitable for the Philadelphia institution. Although "the finest carved specimens have long disappeared," Newcombe was surprised to find more artifacts than he had expected. He bought a nice Masset collection, some eighty-four items, which he valued at $300, as well as some rather rare specimens: a "very ancient" twisted copper neckring belonging to the family of Chief Klue of Tanu for many generations, certainly an unusual piece and perhaps as old as the maritime fur trade; a ceremonial leather armour; a chief's headdress with ermine skins; and a large old copper, fine "but doubtful whether of native copper" (in fact few, if any, were of native copper). Newcombe also got Culin the poles he wanted — two Masset "sticks," one thirty-six feet high, the other a smaller memorial column.[31]

At Skidegate, Newcombe met John R. Swanton, a Bureau of American Ethnology anthropologist seconded to the Jesup North Pacific Expedition for the year. The Victoria physician had come across Boas at Alert Bay on his way up and learned of the Swanton mission. He feared that the Washington ethnologist would be a rival, but when the two met at Skidegate, they got on well, with Newcombe's anticipations of competition ending in collaboration.

Swanton, who had no experience as a field collector and rather dreaded it, went out of his way "to say a good word for Dr. Newcombe" to Boas and hoped that he might use Newcombe, who "is strong just where I am not, i.e., in collecting." Boas, however, would have little of it. He expected Swanton to study the Haida language, religion, and social organization and also to double as collector for the American Museum when his informants became "tired of telling" and when he was making his routine enquiries into Haida technology. Moreover, Newcombe was not a trained ethnologist. Despite Swanton's plea that Newcombe was an "enthusiastic collector" aspiring to "real scientific work" and one who attempted "to preserve and represent everything as accurately as he knows," Boas was unmoved. "I do not like to get specimens through Dr. Newcombe, because he has not the scientific knowledge that you have, and your specimens will be well explained, while his will not be explained." Despite these reservations, Boas thought Newcombe might usefully act as a supplemental collector on his trip to the Charlottes. For one thing, Boas wanted anatomical specimens and Swanton's linguistic and ethnological enquiries, which required that he "get on as closely as possible with the Haidas," precluded him from rummaging for bones and mummies. Moreover, Boas wanted a pole or two, as well as memorial columns and grave posts, and Newcombe could secure such large pieces much easier than Swanton, inexperienced and tied to his Skidegate and Masset informants.[32]

Boas's offer of a short engagement arrived almost simultaneously with a letter to Newcombe from Dorsey holding out the prospect of a two-year contract with the Field Museum. Newcombe ignored Dorsey's offer and responded immediately to Boas's. Doubtless he was flattered: he "strongly admired" the thoroughness of the German-American anthropologist's work and was "proud to be associated in any way with it." He wanted Boas to know that he had "never been disinclined to render you such assistance as is in my power" and, even when collecting in the same field, "indeed, when it was in my power to get things that I thought by your own work you ought to have, I refused to purchase them." Newcombe seems to have been aware of Boas's prejudice against him. "I quite realize," he wrote, "that my work has not been up to the present in the higher levels of Ethnology," but he hoped that, through working with a professional like Swanton, he might be able to secure both the artifacts and the kind of data which Boas wanted.[33]

In any case, he could still do some work for Dorsey and postpone the long-term contract for a few months. Despite its uncertainties and difficulties, he liked his freelance independence. He wanted, for example, time to complete his own Queen Charlotte Islands program. He had not entirely forgotten his natural history interests on the islands and had long intended a description of the relatively unknown Ninstints, an abandoned village near the southern tip of the group, as well as a detailed study of the almost entirely unstudied west coasts of the islands.[34] First, however, he had another Kwakiutl assignment to fill for Dorsey.

When Newcombe undertook, as part of his 1901 trip, collections for Dorsey's seemingly never-complete Hope Island group, the territory of the Kwakiutl had already been extensively collected. Dorsey and Newcombe had worked it, Boas had been there the previous summer "buying *everything* in sight," and Hunt was more active than ever on behalf of the American Museum and its Jesup Expedition. Rev. A. J. Hall, who had sent a few shipments back home to the Church Missionary Society and to Superintendent Vowell, was a collector and used his local agents to assist him. Yet another collector was Capt. D. F. Tozier, commander of the *Grant,* an Alaskan revenue cutter based in Port Townsend. Tozier had recently twice visited the Kwakiutl, reported Newcombe, and "bought lavishly, expressing his intention to have a specimen of everything acquired by Dr. Boas if possible." A compliment to Boas, perhaps, but it would not have been appreciated: the Revenue Service collector was notorious for skimming material from villages by dubious means and stowing it away in Tacoma's Ferry Museum almost entirely unlabeled. Hunt reported that Tozier offered $100 for a huge feast dish, employing this as a defense when Boas reprimanded him for paying $65.50 for a similar one. Another, unnamed collector had come to Alert Bay in 1899 "collecting all Kind of specimens."

Asking to see Hunt, he told him that Boas would not be back to the coast. "Then he said I hope that you Dont Expect to see him come out here again, for the museum people Would not send him out here again for they say is to Expensive man to them, and now he said I am send in his Plase." Hunt's letter went on to mention Newcombe and Hall: "so you See we got Enimey all Round us." Hunt himself was Newcombe's most serious competitor and the rivalry in the field was sometimes intense. Newcombe reported that a letter sent to his Kwakiutl assistant, Charlie Nowell, had been detained at the Alert Bay post office by Hunt's sister and, Newcombe supposed, opened and read, "for G. Hunt went soon after to *Karlokwis* & bought the Sisiutl seat" that Newcombe was asking Nowell to collect.[35]

Newcombe intended to avoid Xumtaspi, already "well-worked" by Boas, Hunt, Dorsey, and himself, by visiting Blunden Harbour, a village "quite off the beaten track" which had not been "nearly so kicked over by Dr. Boas & his agents." On investigation, however, he found that it had just been visited by a trading schooner and "all valuable things gathered up."[36]

Despite these problems and disappointments, the trip was a productive one. Nowell was able to find a killerwhale seat, "fairly good," but carved from cedar, not the harder yew of the Sisiutl seat to which Hunt had beaten him. He was able, during and after the winter dances, to buy Hamatsa neckrings, rattles, batons, masks, games, waterbuckets, and several baskets. Dorsey was "perfectly delighted" with Newcombe's acquisitions and "most proud of the carved seat."[37]

The success of Newcombe's Kwakiutl collecting was dependent in large measure upon Charlie Nowell, Newcombe's counterpart to Hunt. Born in 1870 at Fort Rupert into a high-status family of the Kueha tribe, he had, like all Kwakiutl, a succession of names — he was given the name Charles James by Rev. Hall when he attended the Anglican school at Alert Bay. In about 1895 he married the daughter of Lagius, chief of the Nimkish.[38] Through his inherited and acquired status and his wide circle of relatives and acquaintances, Nowell was well placed to assist Newcombe, who began using him in 1899.

Like Hunt and other native intermediaries, Nowell's value lay in his being a part of Indian society, his literacy, and his reliability. Although the relationship was fruitful, it was also not without difficulty and Newcombe never extended the responsibilities and trust which Boas gave Hunt. In 1905 Newcombe suspected that "the begger charged me twice" for some articles. "He has been pretty good so far, but is always liable to break down, I feel." When Newcombe called him to task for the double charge, collaboration lapsed for a time, but Newcombe succeeded in renewing it when he was again in need of the Kwakiutl's assistance. At times Nowell revolted against the lack of full confidence; he protested vehemently when Newcombe entrusted a local native merchant, Stephen Cook, with money and gave instructions that Nowell was not to be paid until the goods were actually shipped. "If you cant trust me to have the money," Nowell wrote indignantly, "dont ask me to do anything for you, for it made me shame when Cook told & shewed me the note you gave him." Within Kwakiutl society, Newcombe's and Cook's actions constituted a grievous insult.[39]

Having satisfied Dorsey with the Kwakiutl material, Newcombe left now for his Queen Charlottes trip, again taking his tidy little boat aboard the *Danube* and accompanied by young Douglas Scholefield as crew. Since Boas was paying only expenses, Newcombe felt "at liberty to collect for others" and accepted Dorsey's proposal to work on a salary of $100 a month, expenses, and $600 for purchases.[40] Both curators knew that he was working on a double commission.

Large sculptures were Newcombe's first priority. Both Dorsey and Boas wanted them and so, immediately upon his arrival at Skidegate, he made known his desire to purchase poles at Cumshewa, Skedans, and Tanu, the principal deserted villages along the east coast of Moresby Island. Newcombe by now had experience in pole purchases and knew the difficulties of divided and disputed ownership, of tepidness toward sale, and of transportation difficulty.

After two days of talking up possible sellers in Skidegate, he left for the deserted villages, accompanied by Henry Tait, known also as Captain Klue, hereditary chief of Tanu. More Haida followed in a second boat. This was a reconnaisance journey: at all three villages he took photographs and selected a number of suitable poles — "more than actually wanted to allow for contingencies as regard title, change of mind, etc."

Then he returned to Skidegate, where he began a week of "tedious negotiation & endeavouring to clear up questions of title." This was almost invariably a complicated, almost litigious, problem. Inheritance was inherently open to controversy, if only because relatives could claim right through either the traditional Haida matrilineal descent system or through the quite opposite European inheritance law. Wills were, of course, unknown and any descendant might claim right to the property. This was particularly true when no potlatch had been given to legitimize an heir's ownership or title. Prices, too, could be a problem. Newcombe set a standard $1.00 per foot for house poles and $1.50 per foot for grave posts. This was fair market value, but it bore no relation to the original expenditure for the erection of a pole whose costs had included not only the cedar log and carver's compensation, but the feast and potlatch gifts which had been a necessary accompaniment of the pole's raising. On May 7 he noted that he was seeing some sellers "who are changing their tum-tum," but by the next day he felt he had "finished up preliminaries." Although the sellers remained "very shaky & difficult to deal with," he was ready to start south again to superintend the taking down of the poles he had bought.[41]

At Cumshewa, while his Haida crew were preparing to take down the purchased sticks, Newcombe looked around the crumbling houses and tilting poles. Suddenly he heard a loud clamor from the workmen. He returned and "found W. Woods & Abr. Moss at high words about W. W.'s pole wh. he claimed through his mother. A. M. claimed through a reputed uncle." The two protagonists had about equal support from their fellows. In the drizzling rain, Newcombe attempted to separate the disputants and to get them back to work, but "every one wanted to hear the arguments used" and some "seemed inclined to fight." Newcombe "finally got Capt. Klue to get to work & W. W. to go to his wife's pole." In a letter to Boas, he summed up the pole problems: "I have had the greatest difficulty in persuading people to sell. There are endless claimants to the purchase money & I nearly had a serious fight on my hands last Saturday — involving two leading Christians. I had to defer purchasing a very fine pole pending the decision of the Indian agent, Mr. Todd."[42]

Buying the poles was not the end of the process. They still had to be delivered to their distant destinations. Part of the bargain was that he would pay the work crew while they were en route to and from the villages, but the pole owners would be responsible for their wages while they labored to get the poles down and to the beach. Great care had to be taken in insuring that the pole did not fall so heavily as to split. The downed poles usually had to be towed to a steamer landing, but this shipment was large enough that the *Tees* came round to pick up the cargo, which had been skidded down into the water. It took five and a half hours and the hard labor of all eight Indians to get them aboard the ship. Newcombe sent word to Robert Tait, his usual craftsman, to meet this shipment in Vancouver to arrange for crating and forwarding to New York and Chicago by rail.

In spite of all his difficulties, Newcombe had in less than three weeks secured for Dorsey a house pole and grave post from William Woods, Klue's beaver sculpture, which once had supported the boxed remains of Chief Skedans, Moses McKay's grave post, and a forty-eight foot frontal pole from Abraham Moss at Cumshewa. The two larger poles had to be cut in two for transportation. A carved yellow cedar box, intended for the late Chief Skedans as a coffin for himself, but considered by his survivors as more suitable for blanket storage, also went to New York.[43]

Troublesome as was the purchase of houseposts, frontal poles, and memorial columns, buying grave posts, called *xats* from the Haida, was even more difficult because they almost always still contained their human remains in coffin boxes attached to their back or hung between two supporting pillars. Newcombe successfully secured examples for both Boas and Dorsey in 1901, but his efforts to secure more were frustrated. He had leads on several at Cumshewa, but could not conclude his negotiations until the people had interred the bodies. This they had promised to do in the fall of 1901. So Newcombe had to wait until the next spring before he could do anything. There was, he said, a great deal of sensitivity involved. "All say it would be against their own feelings and the opinion of their neighbours to take them down until the remains of their friends had been under ground for at least some months." It would, he wrote Boas, "take time to complete arrangements for burial so as to conform both to white & Indian usages as far as possible."[44]

With these large and special pieces dealt with, Newcombe was now free to pursue some of his own interests — and to fill an order from Boas for skeletal material. These specimens were "always welcome" in New York, Boas had told him, "but do not do as Dorsey did." He took his *Pelican* south to Ninstints, off the extreme south tip of Moresby Island. Chief Ninstints came along as pilot, but the old man would not be a serious impediment to anatomical collecting. "He is half blind," Newcombe assured Boas, "& I hope to acquire many interesting things in that almost wholly deserted village for you." Using his own boat, with young Scholefield as crew, enhanced his freedom: "One of us to keep the chief employed while the other collects." The village was disappointing, however; half, including the best houses, had burned down some years before and the remainder had been rifled. He found a few skeletons and skulls while Scholefield diverted Ninstint's attention, but there were few osteological items to be had. On their way back toward Skidegate, he steered the *Pelican* into Skedans and Cumshewa where, unimpeded by any natives save the old, unseeing Ninstints, he scoured the old mortuaries for bones. The foresection of the *Pelican* swallowed these up, stowed safely out of sight.[45] More were added to the collection at Kayang and Yan.

From Skidegate, the *Pelican* sailed north, first to Masset at the end of June, then across Dixon Entrance to the villages of the Kaigani Haida in Alaskan waters. This was a voyage of enquiry for Newcombe. He had never been in the country of the Kaigani, Haida who had been migrating across the strait to Prince of Wales Island for a hundred or so years. He took Henry Edenshaw as guide and assistant. Edenshaw's mother was Kaigani and his family had status on both sides of the boundary waters; though a Masset resident, he owned a house and possessed the authority of a chief in Klinkwan.

Newcombe's expectations were high: he had heard that two Kaigani villages were "just abandoning heathenism & selling off their ceremonial property." He was soon disappointed: the new converts, he found, had been taking their dance material and selling it for good prices at Ketchikan and Wrangell. Yet he found at Klinkwan, Kasaan, and elsewhere what he considered the best remaining supply of Haida things. Prices were extremely high in ·comparison to the Charlotte islands: a wooden helmet, although the only one of its kind Newcombe knew of, was priced at fully fifty dollars. Because of the prices, he did not buy a great deal, contenting himself with a survey of the situation and noting what might be bought on a return visit.[46]

Newcombe returned from the north at the end of September 1901 and spent the rest of the year and most of January tidying up his Charlottes work and more especially preparing his topographical notes and maps of the islands. The work proved more extensive and took much longer than he had expected, and he ruefully admitted that he would never have undertaken the task at the remuneration agreed upon with Boas had he realized all that it involved. The results, later published in Swanton's *Contributions to the Ethnology of the Haida,* a 1905 Jesup Expedition memoir, were maps of Haida place names and a list of the families which had once occupied the villages, the latter compiled by Swanton with Newcombe's assistance.

In February a letter arrived from Boas asking Newcombe if he would care to collect further for the American Museum. He had to say no. By this time he had accepted Dorsey's continued importunities for a full-time engagement with the Field Museum. He did plan to finish up the business over Edenshaw's Klinkwan boards, a Tanu mortuary pole, and a Cumshewa mortuary house as part of his old commission, but he felt that the interminable Haida maps for Boas and Swanton had already caused him to defer Dorsey — "and the salary!" — long enough.[47]

For almost two years Dorsey had wanted to hire Newcombe. He had written Director Skiff about the absolute necessity of a "thoroughly representative" collection from the ethnologically important Northwest Coast region: the museum's Haida collection, he wrote, was "hardly worthy the name, there being not even a single category of objects fully represented." Newcombe, "a man of scholarly attainments, worthy of all confidence and respect," and an experienced anthropological collector, could fill this gap. Now, in November 1901, Dorsey had secured the approval of the director and executive committee for a three-year engagement at $100 a month salary, plus expenses and purchasing money. Characteristic of Dorsey, it was an audacious and sweeping conception: "Simply make the best collection obtainable whether it costs $1,000.00 or $2,000.00 or what not." He wanted Newcombe to "make a clean sweep" of the Kaigani and "not leave the Haidas until you have made as full and complete a representation of the Haidas as can possibly be made at this time, getting all raw materials, foods, masks, all ceremonial objects, fishing and hunting implements, games etc etc." Skeletons were desirable, and grave posts and house poles, "no matter how large or of what dimensions," would be welcome. He intended to devote an entire hall to the Haida, showing "every phase of their life and industry" and he wanted "to do it better than it has been done by any other institution."[48]

Newcombe accepted in similar spirit. Apart from the monetary considerations, he assured Dorsey, "it will be a labour of love for me to carry out the programme you have so boldly sketched out." He retained one major reservation about the "noble scheme," one that had earlier bothered Israel Powell and more especially, George Dawson. "As a patriotic Britisher," he wrote, 'I must own that I often sigh when I think how lightly these things are regarded by mine own countrymen." But none of them were in the field and, rather than aid in the dispersal of collections among numerous individuals and museums, "I would far rather do what I can to help to make a really representative one" in conformity to Dorsey's ideal.[49]

Newcombe began his new employment with a February trip to the Kaigani. He started optimistically. The Kasaan villagers were about to move from the old town to a new village at a cannery site; since one of the conditions for their move was that all pot-latches and dances be given up, "I quite hope I have struck the right place at the right time." His hope turned to disappointment when he learned that "most of the good things have been drained away" and that the Kaigani were not anxious to sell what remained. A number of things were regarded as heirlooms to be passed on and were "not to be had at all"; what was for sale was offered only "at a *most* exhorbitant price." The ownership of other pieces was divided or disputed. It was the prices which most surprised Newcombe. Carved chests of the kind available in the Charlottes at ten to fifteen dollars were held for sixty dollars in Kasaan. Helmets, which he thought Dorsey ought to have, were priced from fifty dollars and up. He resigned himself to very selective purchasing — to buying only the most desirable at the lowest possible price. He bought only thirty-five pieces and these were mostly stone tools and fishing apparatus. From Kasaan he went on, via Ketchikan and Wrangell, to Howkan, Klinkwan,

Sakwan, and Quihanlen, remaining a month in the area. He was successful in buying everything available in the four villages, including a number of masks, rattles, and other ceremonial material. The results were not extensive, though hardly any of what he had procured was still available from the Charlotte Haida. He could buy no poles. Excepting a gift of one Kasaan pole to the government park at Sitka the previous year, none had left Kaigani hands. Newcombe hoped for a few good small poles yet. If one sold, he felt certain others would follow, but "it takes a long time to get a new idea into the heads of the Kaiganis."[50]

From the islands Newcombe sailed to Haines in Chilkat Tlingit country. He despatched two cases to Chicago, including a long feast dish, part of a monument from a doctor's grave at Klukwan. Alaska continued to impress him as "*very* expensive." To clear out merely the big things in the Whale House at Klukwan would take something like fifteen hundred dollars, one thousand being required for the chief's inside posts and carved house back alone. Such prices seemed absurd to him, but he was assured by the missionary at Haines that they had been quoted for a year or two, so had to be accepted as genuine. Again, unclear title hindered his acquisitions and added to the already high prices. Buying a Klukwan post required satisfying several owners and there were other rival claimants "who still threaten trouble to the seller & to myself." There was a set of four houseposts available, but "the necessary formalities in the way of house-building, erecting a monument to the uncle & distribution of property" had never been completed and the prospective vendor was too poor to do it. "Some near relative with sufficient means may at any time do so, but until the custom alluded to has been carried out, the title to the poles & many other interesting and valuable things, is in abeyance." It was the same sort of thing that had blocked him with various items at Kasaan. Competitors were not absent and lent additional complications: the same piece had been bidden for by several collectors and he heard that G. T. Emmons was coming back the next month for more collecting. "I am not letting my friendship for him interfere with my purchases, as I take it this is an open field." Nevertheless, he would not follow up on the expensive Klukwan material until he had further instructions from Dorsey; the prices "must be beyond the figure you intended for me to go to in this district."[51]

Dorsey was not worrying about Emmons. He had just bought that retired naval officer's fourteen hundred-piece Tlingit collection and was now accepting his offer to negotiate further for the large Klukwan pieces whose prices so amazed Newcombe. Dorsey would let Emmons, the Alaska veteran and old Tlingit hand, take care of Klukwan. "Let Chilcat rest untill I have heard from Emmons," he wrote. Newcombe should concentrate on the Haida, which Dorsey considered of greater interest anyway. He was "especially desirous that our Haida collection should be second to none." The Chicago curator remained unperturbed by prices. The Klukwan pieces were desirable "and we must have them, though they cost $1500." Such figures were, he fully realized, very high.

> The time has come, however, when these few exceedingly precious objects which collectors heretofore have not been able to purchase in the Northwest on account of prices, are to be secured, even though the price is somewhat excessive, so that when you come to objects which are exceedingly desirable you must not let the price stand in the way of your securing them.[52]

Newcombe was much more cautious and parsimonious. He was not used to spending his own or even other peoples' money on Dorsey's audacious and lavish scale. He may have feared setting precedents and driving up future prices. Back in Victoria he was obviously relieved by Emmons's assurance that he had not paid too much for the Chilkat material.[53]

The collector was not home a month before he departed again for northern waters, this time taking the *Dolphin* with him, the better for osteological and mummy collecting. The trip began auspiciously, with a very inexpensive Chilkat blanket bought from Gunia of Masset for $40 at Ketchikan, but his main object was a systematic study of traditional Haida industries which he carried out over a six-week period at Kasaan. He was delighted that Charles Edenshaw, Henry's cousin, was visiting the village and he quickly took him on, "the best carver in wood and stone now living," as informant, a role to which Edenshaw was becoming accustomed after already having worked casually for Boas and more seriously for Swanton. This was the most systematic episode of Newcombe's career as he pursued examples of native technology and the ethnological information which made it meaningful. He gathered about eighty objects, almost all of which illustrated manufacturing material or the finished products of handwork. He gathered spruce roots and cedar bark in various stages of preparation for a variety of uses. Since many things had by now been replaced by trade goods, he felt no compunction at commissioning old people to make new examples of disappeared objects — or at least models of them. In order to advance his work, he "had to employ oldish people to renew their almost forgotten occupations." Traps, cradles, nets, and mats were not always easy to commission. He persuaded one woman to make a fishing net, but the knotting was "so hard upon the fingers not in practice, she refuses to promise a full-size one."[54]

After finishing at Kasaan he spent a few days in another vain attempt to secure poles at Howkan and Sakwan. The season — it was now August — was against him. Klinkwan and Howkan were entirely deserted except for a few whites. He bought at Hunters Bay a wooden hat decorated with feathers from Joe Wallace for fifty dollars, a price that must have made him cringe. Still without poles, he determined to stop in the Charlottes, more familiar ground to him and where he had a long list of possible vendors. He got a short inside pole at Masset from Edenshaw, a thirty-eight-foot one from Yan through W. Stevens, a sixteen-foot Tanu inside pole from Paul Jones, and two eight-foot pieces from a shaman's grave. The Yan pole was destined for Charles Read at the British Museum, fulfilling Newcombe's long determination to place a pole in the great museum of the Empire.

Newcombe began 1903 with a two-month visit to Chicago. It had become imperative that he know what was already in the Field Museum's collection. On his return in February he stopped in Albuquerque to see the new museum and curio shop established by Fred Harvey, who ran the catering business for the Sante Fe railway and who was closely associated with Dorsey. In Portland he dropped in on Mrs. F. C. Frohman's basket shop, an emporium filled with western Indian basketry supplied by her husband's trading store in Wrangell and by a network of agents along the coast.

Within a month of his return home, Dorsey was in town on another of his peripatetic tours. Newcombe again took him to the

Songhees Reserve, to Duncan, and on a tour of Victoria's Indian traders. Landsberg lifted almost $500 from Dorsey's account — primarily for a Kitkatla chief's headdress and Chilkat-style leggings and apron. Dorsey put out $125 at Aaronson's store, while Stadthagen, whose material was almost invariably inferior, received only $25 in patronage.

Almost as soon as Dorsey left town, Newcombe was away, now intent upon improving Chicago's Salish collection. After an up-island trip to Duncan and Chemainus, he headed for the Fraser Valley, his first serious collecting among the mainland Salish. After visiting Harrison, Port Douglas, and Agassiz, he concluded that the old Salish baskets had become "an exteme rarity." The New Westminster Indian agent was buying "every basket in sight" for Mrs. Frohman and she and Landsberg were taking everything which Charles Inkman, another local, could provide.[55]

Newcombe was able to do better with stone items and succeeded in buying four burial posts, also very scarce. By May he had reached Spences Bridge in the dry interior where he hired James A. Teit, the Scotsman whom Boas had started on a similar career as collector, for ten days' work as guide and interpreter in the Nicola Valley and Kamloops area. After visits to Sicamous and Penticton, he returned to Victoria. Newcombe remained home for only two weeks, departing in mid-June for a three-month trip north, visiting Salish, Kwakiutl, Bella Bella, and Coast Tsimshian country before reaching Skidegate in late July. He was again on the *Pelican* with his younger son, William, as crew. At Chemainus they ran into trouble: "caught in act of removing bones from a grave by two Indians & had to bribe them to secresy [sic]." (His accounts list $5.50 opposite "Chamainus, purchase of skel's 993, 994, 995," which must represent the hush money.)[56]

On the Queen Charlottes he and Willie sailed unguided to Ninstints, Skedans, and Chaatl, where they collected a number of skulls, skeletons, and other material, but Indians were fishing at Kaisun so there they had to be cautious. Early in September, he was able to make a number of purchases in Skidegate and to negotiate for two poles. On the way home he saw Fillip Jacobsen in Port Essington and arranged for him to collect in Bella Coola and Clayoquot.

In the meantime, Dorsey had been out on another flying visit, hoping to join his local agent "on a totem pole raid," but he missed the *Danube* in Victoria, so went on to Alaska after picking out some material from the Victoria dealers. He wrote, saying that the museum now had enough Haida poles, but he still wanted monumental sculpture in other Northwest styles. For Chicago's purposes, Dorsey felt the west coast of Vancouver Island would now be the most profitable; "that seems to me," he wrote, "the only region that has not been 'combed' thoroughly." While "old Tozier had had his drag-net out" in the area, he thought that "a man of that sort never thoroughly exhausts a region."[57] Newcombe was already in Clayoquot.

He and Willie had arrived back from the north coast in the first week of October, but stayed only long enough to make the necessary arrangements before leaving for a month on the west coast, taking the *Pelican* with them. Most of the Nootka were away sealing, hop-picking, or getting winter supplies of salmon, bear, and deer. He did the best he could and made arrangements with various people to be "on the lookout for me in advance of G. Hunt, whom I left at Nootka, busy only with stories." Hunt had succeeded in fooling him with the stories story: he was also after the Whalers' Washing House, which he got the following spring. Newcombe came across another Boas associate on this trip, "a man called Sutton," who told him how, in collecting skulls for Boas, he had always "squared the chiefs of villages who told off men to accompany him & to point out those they had no objection to losing." While Newcombe made a decent collection on the west coast, he intended to return in May. The autumn, with the harvest and salmon season just finished, was not a propitious collecting time: "Now they are too flush with money to handle economically."[58]

At home again, Newcombe busied himself with consolidating and packing the collections. Charlie Nowell, taking a leaf from Hunt's practices, offered to collect skeletons from caves near the mouth of Knight's Inlet, caves where objects for winter dances were also cached. A new aide was John Humphreys of Chemainus, an educated Cowichan half-blood greatly interested in "museum matters." Newcombe had met him in March, and now Humphreys brought in a collection and explained the usage of a loom and other pieces. He had more in Chemainus and Newcombe determined to go there for them. "Am risking my skin in Chemainus, where we had the unpleasant experience over skeletons," he told Dorsey, but

Humphreys had "a few exceptionally fine Salish things which I have been after for some years."[59] Teit sent an Interior Salish collection down from Spences Bridge and Landsberg had ten west coast skeletons that Dorsey wanted. It was a busy end to a busy year. Newcombe had been home less than four months in calendar 1903, easily the most demanding collecting year for the fifty-two-year-old doctor. His expenses and purchases had amounted to $3,760.17, the largest of any year he worked for the Field Museum.

Nineteen hundred and four brought even more activity. He went down to the Ferry Museum to look over Captain Tozier's collection, and then Dorsey suggested that he take a Northwest Coast exhibit to the St. Louis Universal Exposition. Newcombe had already been in touch with W. H. Holmes of the Smithsonian about buying some Haida poles for the Institution's St. Louis exhibit and Dorsey and Fred Harvey wanted to secure one or two at the same time, but Dorsey's World's Fair proposal was a considerably larger undertaking. W J McGee, chief of the Department of Anthropology at the fair and an old friend of the Chicago curator, was trying to match Putnam's Chicago effort of eleven years before, especially emphasizing live native exhibits. "The time is ripe," he wrote, "for the world's first marshalling of the races and peoples of the earth at a single point," something that would raise the fair "to the highest place in the history of expositions."[60] Newcombe entered into the scheme with energy. He could not possibly make all arrangements by the fair's scheduled opening of April 30, but he managed to secure a party of seven Indians, a large house, two canoes, and an impressive enough collection in time to leave Seattle on May 17, barely two months after taking on the assignment.

The work was hectic: an eight-day tour of Puget Sound and Neah Bay, two trips to Clayoquot and two to Alert Bay, one of which involved a canoe trip from Fort Rupert to Hardy Bay and an eleven-mile hike to Koskimo Sound. In between he fitted in a circle trip to Klickitat and up the Columbia and Yakima rivers. Initially he had hoped to bring carvers and basketry workers from the Neah Bay Makahs and at least one "longheaded" Koskimo woman. These engagements collapsed. His greatest trouble had been persuading the Indians "that they can make enough from their basketry & woodwork to be equivalent of what they would get

*Some of the Kwakiutl and Nootka at St. Louis, 1904. Identifiable are, from
left, Charlie Nowell, Bob Harris, and Atlieu. From* The Forest City:
Comprising the Official Photographic Views of the Universal
Exposition Held in St. Louis, 1904 *(St. Louis: N. D. Thompson [1904?]);
photograph by William H. Rau.*

from fishing and hop-picking &c." They all knew that Hunt's
1894 Chicago troupe had earned twenty dollars a month and
"think they ought to get the same." In Neah Bay he had no long-
established contacts which would have offset Makah hesitancy; he
suspected George Hunt's sabotage was behind the last-minute
decision of the Koskimo not to go. Things were frustrating and
Newcombe discovered it to be "more difficult than I anticipated
to get people for the Fair."[61]

He could still count on Charlie Nowell and his friend Bob
Harris from Fort Rupert, and from Clayoquot on the west coast
came the shaman Dr. Atlieu, his daughter Annie Atlieu, his half-
brother Jasper Turner, and Jack Curley and his mother, Mrs.
Ellen Curley. Atlieu, who had served as Karl von den Steinen's
1902 informant when the Berlin ethnologist was in British
Columbia to identify Jacobsen's Nootka specimens, expressed his
concerns and expectations in a letter dictated to Newcombe.

I depend on you to have the same mind toward us as we have to you. There are those of the tribe who think it is too great an undertaking for me for they have never been far away from home. But I have no fear. I also want to see the place where we are going and meet the great chiefs who will be there.[62]

With the west coast people came a large house, about fifty-three by forty-two feet, bought through the Nootka storekeeper for a hundred dollars. Atlieu sold his thirty-eight-foot whaling canoe to Newcombe. With it was a whaling outfit, a harpoon, and as much other material as Newcombe could buy to fill the house. He had a chief's seat and sixty-three other pieces bought at Koskimo by Nowell, as well as Lagius's canoe, the one he and Charlie had travelled in to Hardy Bay. Atlieu and the other four were in Victoria by May 14 and Newcombe accompanied them to Seattle and then on the Northern Pacific to St. Louis, where they arrived on the twenty-first. Nowell and Harris came with Willie Newcombe eight days later, but the house and other things were lost in transit and arrived very late. It was August before they could move from tents into the erected house.

The fair was sited at Forest Park, an immense 1,240-acre tract five miles west of the Mississippi River. Its organizers had determined that the exposition, in tribute to the 1803 Louisiana Purchase, should rival and surpass the Chicago World's Fair (both opened a year later than their anniversary celebrations). Highlights at St. Louis were the recently revived Olympic Games, a display of one hundred automobiles, the first sizable exhibition of motor cars anywhere, and a forty-seven acre Philippine exhibition in which almost all ethnic groups from the recently acquired archipelago were represented.

W J McGee's aim in the fair's anthropology section was "to satisfy the intelligent observer that there *is* a course of progress running from lower to higher humanity, and that all the physical and cultural types of man mark stages in that course." To assist in demonstrating this evolutionary model he brought to St. Louis African pygmies, Ainu from Japan, Tehuelche from Patagonia, and, among American Indians, representatives from the Cocopa, Pawnee, Dakota, Pueblo, Pima, and Pomo groups. These far outdistanced Putnam's 1893 achievement, and, when supplemented by the Philippine pavilions and other exhibitions on the grounds and along the Pike (St. Louis's equivalent of Chicago's Midway), justified McGee's boast that "the assemblage of physical types of mankind was unquestionably much more nearly complete than was ever before brought together." Newcombe's Clayoquot and Fort Rupert Kwakiutl were seen as physical representatives of the "singularly light-colored fisherfolk" of Vancouver Island, and the Nootka dwelling as illustrative of "a native type of house designed to fix the social organization and facilitate the maintenance of law, partly by virtue of elaborate totems (or animal tutelaries)."[63]

The Indians, doubtless quite oblivious of being a part of a field school of anthropology conducted by the University of Chicago, settled down into a routine of making wages by carving, weaving, and basket-making. Dances were performed regularly and for special occasions. Nowell recalled a particularly memorable ceremony for which Bob Harris made a convincing baked mutton model of a friend from the neighboring pygmy encampment. The similacrum was complete with "blood" bladder and a whistle imitative of the small man's squeal. In the performance Harris played a crazed Hamatsa who "killed" the "screaming" pygmy in a bloody, cannibalistic scene that reportedly fooled all the spectators, Newcombe included. The real pygmy was ceremoniously brought back to life by Harris while the West Coast men danced round them. Newcombe recorded only that the "Kwakiutl distinguished themselves as Hamatsa."[64]

The coastal Indians were also represented at the fair by two houses brought from Alaska by Governor John G. Brady to flank the two-story stucco Alaska Building. Newcombe must have looked with some wonderment at the fifteen Kaigani Haida poles that stood beside the houses. These were what he had failed to persuade the Kaigani to sell in 1901 and now Brady had got them all as a gift to the government.

Brady had come to Sitka in 1878 as one of Sheldon Jackson's missionaries. He soon dropped out of the ministry for a business career in the small community, but he remained a friend and partisan of Jackson. Before starting his own collection he sent some curios to Jackson and to the American Museum.[65] Respected as a local resident and businessman, he was appointed governor by McKinley in 1897 and personally took charge of the territory's exhibition at St. Louis. Already he had been successful in securing

One of Governor Brady's poles being taken down for exhibit at St. Louis.
Beinecke Rare Book and Manuscript Library, Yale University Library.

the donation of Kaigani poles for a public park near the site of the
old Tlingit fort. On a visit to Kasaan in 1901 he secured, through
W. T. Bunard, a trader there, the gift of a frontal pole, a canoe,
and four houseposts from Chief Son-i-hat. These were to be
placed in the government park at Sitka "and remain there as
memorials to my people." In return, Brady promised a school

building, appointed Son-i-hat a native policeman at ten dollars a month, and invited him to Sitka for a ceremony in his honor. "I want him to feel that he has made no mistake in presenting these relics to the Government."[66]

The poles, after being "repaired" and painted by natives, were put up on the government reserve by a labor gang from the Sitka jail. Brady's tact and diplomacy in the deal brought its reward when he decided that Alaska should be represented in St. Louis not only by a well-designed building filled with mining and agricultural exhibits, but native houses and poles — something "with an Alaskan flavor." On a tour of the Kaigani's country in September 1903 he secured promises of poles or houses from half a dozen Haida. "We are," he wrote home, "rich in totems." In November he spent almost a month in the revenue cutter *Rush*. The only difficulties he encountered were stormy weather, poor rigging, and lack of deck space for all the donations. The natives complied completely with their promises "and have, with the utmost good will, given their totem poles." Some mortuary poles still had bones "which were taken out and put in new blankets and buried." He picked up a house, a house frame, and fifteen poles and he completed his task the next March when the *Rush* picked up from the Tongass Tlingit two more poles and enough cedar planks to complete the second house. Brady was himself surprised and deeply touched by the generosity of the Indians, which extended to donating other material he had not even sought. "Surely a great change has come over them" he wrote, but his own generosity and promise to preserve the poles in the Sitka park as memorials to their people probably had something to do with the Indians' actions.[67]

He took six natives, led by John Baronovich, to St. Louis to help put up the houses and poles, but they did not stay on as exhibits. His own and several other loan collections were on display. At the fair he found a great demand for the poles — "the whole collection would have brought a big price" — and was talked into selling two house boards to Dorsey and one of the Tlingit poles to the Milwaukee Public Museum (he excused himself by saying that it was so old that it would have fallen apart on the way home.) At the end of the fair, the poles were sent to Portland for the Lewis and Clark Exposition and then returned to Sitka for the park, which was declared a national monument in 1910.[68]

The Alaska Building at St. Louis, flanked by native houses and poles. Beinecke Rare Book and Manuscript Library, Yale University Library.

Brady seems to have enjoyed the fair, but not the criticism he received for being so long absent from the territory. For Newcombe, however, the glamor of the fair quickly wore thin. The exposition's administration remained chaotically behind in its accounts, he could find only unsatisfactory accommodation in the swollen city, and he suffered from the almost unbearable summer heat that caused such severe vericose veins in his left leg that he was almost crippled. "I lost a lot of time in St. Louis," he wrote later, "& grudged the loss of my annual cruise. Neither the cash nor the opportunity of seeing many interesting people & things quite made up for this." Dorsey was repentant for ever suggesting Newcombe's involvement: "for the fortyeth time I again apologize for having been the cause of your being mixed up with such a mess."[69]

Newcombe at last escaped to his display and cataloguing work at the Chicago museum in August, leaving Willie behind "as hostage" in St. Louis. In September he brought Nowell and Harris to Chicago for a few days' work on the collections, a visit that lengthened to a month. "On getting them here," Dorsey explained to McGee, "I at once realized that I had two of the most

valuable Indians of the whole Northwest Coast for our purpose —
namely, the proper identification of the large collection which the
Museum acquired in the early days from Hagenbeck of Hamburg."
Dorsey was pleased to find that the two Kwakiutl "recognized at
once the large majority of the specimens as having come from their
tribe" — in fact, "Bob himself made many of the pieces."[70]

Dorsey or Harris was probably exaggerating, Boas had said
almost the same about the relation between Hunt's Kwakiutl at
the Chicago Fair and Jacobsen's collection. But certainly the two
were extremely useful and were kept busy identifying specimens
and in putting the finishing touches to the Hamatsa group started
seven years earlier by Dorsey. Nowell recalled the assignment:

> There was a bunch of statues looking like men from Fort Rupert —
> we could recognize them — which they didn't know what to do
> with because they was all naked. The Museum people was just
> about to go and dump them because they didn't think they should
> show them that way. So we found the Indian blankets — cedar
> bark — that the old people used to use and put them over them,
> and we put red bark on their heads and eagle down. There was also
> a row of people that was supposed to be singers. We painted their
> faces black and red — the same way as we paint ourselves at the
> winter dance. There were two Hamatsas (Cannibals) there which
> we also clothed with a bearskin, and neck rings and eagle down,
> and the Hamatsa ring on his head. The women we made to sit
> around watching.

The next day he was asked to stand inside the glass case to answer
questions and to explain the thing to museum visitors.[71]

The Hamatsa group was almost a duplicate of Boas's U. S.
National Museum display of a decade earlier: it too showed the
initiate emerging from the painted-screen mouth of *mawi+*.
Newcombe was responsible for much of the costuming and ceremonial objects, but a surprising amount came from the Jacobsen-
Hagenbeck and George Hunt collections acquired at the close of
the Chicago fair.

Jasper Turner and Dr. Atlieu were also brought to Chicago,
working six days among the West Coast collections. By October
18 all were back in St. Louis and anxious to return home, but
McGee was slow in coming up with fare money (the exposition

The Hamatsa life group prepared by C. F. Newcombe for Chicago's Field Museum of Natural History. Courtesy, Field Museum of Natural History.

had been a financial disaster, losing over fourteen million dollars). At last, on October 24, Newcombe had his cash in hand. The next morning he discovered that the·Indians had acquired "an enormous amount" of excess baggage and it took another day "in order to overhaul it." The excess was reduced to 150 pounds and only eleven dollars in charges. The trip home — Newcombe went as he came, first class and sleeper, while the Indians went second class with four bunks in tourist — was uneventful. After a night in Seattle, they arrived in Victoria on October 30. A relieved Newcombe recorded that he had "shipped all Indians," then had to report that one of the women "was seen drunk a short time before the Steamer left & she refused to go with the rest." Atlieu, he heard from Jasper Turner, took sick on his arrival at Clayoquot and "was nearly going under through an attack of pneumonia." By January the shaman was "quite strong again" and later sent Newcombe an ancient, ritualized harpoon. It was a gift, meant "as a token of his high regard," and something no money could buy.[72]

Newcombe was soon back in Chicago working away at the installations of the coast collections. He returned to Victoria for another summer season and a resumption of his *Pelican* cruises, then again to Chicago to complete his work over the winter of 1905–6. In July his work was finished and his oft-extended contract lapsed. He had been with the Field for over four years of almost full-time collecting and was probably relieved to return to independent, freelance work closer to home and family. In any case, the museum administration was unwilling to allow any further expenses for the Northwest Coast.

The Field Museum's trustees had long been concerned with the great expenditures being poured into Dorsey's department, its American collections, and especially upon Northwest Coast accessions. As early as 1901, when Newcombe's contract and a Northwest Coast appropriation of $9,100 were approved, along with $4,500 for Cheyenne, and $10,000 for other Great Plains material, the trustees had determined that these acquisitions "will complete the Ethnology of North America, so far as the plans of the Museum shall ever extend, and that no further appropriations for this purpose will be necessary or asked for."[73] The minutes' sweeping finality proved totally ineffective. Dorsey's driving audacity, his ability to wheedle the support of Director Skiff and trustee Edward Ayer, could not be so limited and restrained. Within eight months he secured approval of $10,000 for the purchase of Emmons's Spuhn collection, and other appropriations continued to enlarge the department's American materials. He bought another Emmons collection in 1902 for $1,163 and the following April convinced the museum to buy Emmons's collection of Tlingit baskets for $2,500.

Sensitive to the executive's feelings, Dorsey gave compliant assurances and yet refused to allow opportunity to pass him by. "I shall not ask for further sums of money for this region," he wrote in 1904, except — and he kept open the catch — for special specimens or "to cover some possible contingency which is not yet in sight." Within days, he was running true to form, asking, and securing, a special appropriation of $1,100 for the purchase of Chilkat carvings. In March 1905 he received Skiff's approval to an extension of Newcombe's contract for another six months, supporting his case with the assurance that, "excepting perhaps Boas," there was no ethnologist living "who has such a comprehensive grasp of the culture of the North Pacific Coast."[74]

He was prepared to agree with Director Skiff that the museum had "reached a point where it does not seem desirable to extend the work of collecting much further — at any rate at the present time — on the North Pacific Coast." But he wanted $825 to fill in a few gaps, especially of large carvings.

> Our collection of massive carvings, such as totem poles, house posts, etc. from the Kwakiutl, Haida and Tlingit, is the most complete in existence. It is desirable that we make our collection of grave figures and Potlatch carvings equally comprehensive and interesting. These figures are among the most interesting from a Museum point of view that it is possible to obtain on the coast.

The executive committee went along, also allowing yet another $900 for the completion of Newcombe's cataloguing and installations, but pointedly noting that "it is understood that no further appropriations will be made for this work." Already the special opportunity of harvesting, through Dorsey's friendship with McGee, much of the ethnological material exhibited at St. Louis, had provided another opportunity for expansion of the collections. Dorsey could argue that the Clayoquot and Kwakiutl there had specially prepared material that was absent from the Field's collections and thus would not duplicate any of it. He was allowed $385 for the purchase. When Newcombe's contract was again near its end, Dorsey renewed his appeal on the grounds that the work was "of the very highest importance," that it would be fatal to discontinue his services. The collection now stood as "a close rival to the great collection in New York City which has certainly cost three times as much." Again he secured the necessary.[75]

Dorsey's success in moving a reluctant executive rested upon his political skills, his ability to deal with the business and philanthropic mind, and his persuasive dramatization of the anthropological world. When in November 1905, he had an opportunity to secure from Frederick Landsberg several large Kwakiutl potlatch figures and a feast dish along with a Salish stone bowl, the executive committee denied the requested $200. At its next meeting, "upon reconsideration of Dr. Dorsey's recommendation," the negative decision was rescinded. The same year, after the executive committee had turned down his request for £266 and 65,000 Marks (about $1,100 and $16,250) for collections offered by European dealers, he personally appeared at the next meeting to explain their great value. Dorsey's case, pitched in the sweeping terms that would appeal to the committee's lay mind, was based upon the primacy of anthropology as the science of man. "No other branch of science is so close to every man as Anthropology," no science was the source and inspiration to so many other sciences. "Every thought of the mind, every product of the hand, has its antecedent. The beginnings of all things lie in the past, which is the special province of the Anthropologists." The value of an anthropological museum rested upon "its ability to illustrate by abundant material the history of man" and "to epitomize and reduce to laws, by its arrangement, this history." Thus, "through abundant material and proper arrangement, a Museum of Anthropology becomes, of all possible museums, the most interesting, the most instructional, and the most valuable to the greatest number of people." The executive committee, apparently convinced of its responsibility to provide him with abundant material for such an important purpose, approved the purchases.[76]

Dorsey might push and wheedle, but by 1906 his years of Northwest Coast collecting were over. Even he could not compel the trustees to go further. He had to content himself with a collection which, while it did not "quite approach in magnitude or importance" that at the American Museum, was at least "the second best in the world." It was, as he was quick to point out, a very strong second best, comprehensive in its coverage of American groups and its illustration of industries and ceremonies.[77] In some areas it was preeminent, notably in the number of massive sculptures which towered above the eighty-eight cases in the seven halls devoted to the tribes of the coast — far more display area for the region than that allowed in any other museum.

Despite a published claim of continued North American priority for the museum, few accessions bolstered the coastal collections and these were minor gifts or purchases. In 1912 businessman Homer Sargent began donating pieces, mostly interior basketry and woven materials collected for him by James Teit, but the museum's own ethnological interests shifted elsewhere. Offered another large Alaskan collection by G. T. Emmons in 1909, Dorsey had regretfully to turn down the possibility of Chicago supremacy over New York in Tlingit material. He would have liked to have the material, but it was impossible because "we are at the present time devoting all of our available funds to regions beyond North America."[78]

That same year Dorsey took leave of absence, which stretched to four years, to write for the Chicago *Tribune*. His place was taken by Berthold Laufer, a sinologist without great interest in North American ethnology. The emphasis of the museum tilted ever more toward the Far East, the Malay Peninsula, and the Philippines. After 1912 it found its income suddenly curtailed by a failure of the bulk of the bonds in the Field endowment to pay interest. Dorsey, beset by scandal, resigned in 1915. (His expedition liaisons became too flagrant when he induced a girl "of good family" to go with him on an overseas excursion and, after the matter became public, his wife divorced him.) He continued in journalism, publishing the best-selling *Why We Behave Like Human Beings* and other popular science books.

The Field Museum's move to its permanent uptown site in Grant Park in 1920–21 meant the shrinkage of exhibition space in the smaller building. Much of the anthropology collection went into storage. Laufer refused the prospect of two Kaigani poles — the kind that Newcombe could not secure at all in 1901 and 1902. He was under the impression, he wrote, that the museum already had "too many totem poles" and certainly more than they could show in the new building. With Sargent's baskets coming in wholesale, the museum already had "too many Indian baskets" and quite enough Salish material.[79]

In 1933 the museum sold for $1,225 thirteen poles and potlatch figures. These were largely Newcombe-collected sculptures but included Ayer's thirty-foot Haida pole and two Landsberg figures. Most went to a Salvation Army boy's camp. The National Pole and Treating Company of Minneapolis bought a pole which Mrs. Morrison had sent from Port Essington for Boas's Chicago World's Fair display.[80] Similarly, six canoes, four from the Chicago fair and the two Newcombe had brought to St. Louis were lost, exchanged, or sold. (When the museum reinstalled its Northwest Coast collection in a magnificent new setting in 1982, it had to commission a new canoe.) Such attrition was a sad postscript to Dorsey's great scheme and the achievements of himself, Newcombe, and other builders of the Field's collection.

Chapter Eight

A Declining Market

"I FIND I CAN DISPOSE of any old Alaska pieces without difficulty," G. T. Emmons wrote in December 1902. This situation was misleading. After the St. Louis fair, the Northwest Coast market turned bear and Emmons was soon complaining that Indian material had become "a drag on the market" and that "a collection would not bring its cost any place."[1]

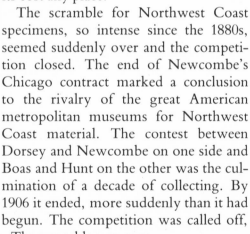

The scramble for Northwest Coast specimens, so intense since the 1880s, seemed suddenly over and the competition closed. The end of Newcombe's Chicago contract marked a conclusion to the rivalry of the great American metropolitan museums for Northwest Coast material. The contest between Dorsey and Newcombe on one side and Boas and Hunt on the other was the culmination of a decade of collecting. By 1906 it ended, more suddenly than it had begun. The competition was called off, the expeditions run down. The scramble was over.

There were several factors working in this structural change in the pattern of Northwest Coast collecting. For one thing, the importance of museum collections for American anthropology had peaked; after 1900 there was a steady decline in the attention paid to material culture. Ethnological research now meant fieldwork, but the collection and study of artifacts played a relatively

212

minor role in the fieldwork undertaken by university students and even museum scholars. Social and cultural anthropologists became less and less concerned with material culture and technology, the stock-in-trade of museums.[2]

Another factor was mere surfeit. The Field and American museums, the great metropolitan rivals of the previous decade, both decided that their collections from the region were large and representative enough. There was little point in continuing to collect material which they could never hope to display; another dozen Kwakiutl masks seemed merely redundant when they had scores already. By the turn of the century, many felt that "enough has been collected."[3] But there was a broader factor in the shift away from Northwest Coast collecting. San Juan Hill and Manila Bay marked a deep change in the current of American life, an alteration which soon affected American museums.

Anthropologists and anthropological collecting had always tended to follow the flag of national commerce and external influence. The British Museum stood as a monument to formal and informal empire, while German museums were filled with the products of the Cameroons, East Africa, and New Guinea, the Dutch with Indonesian ethnologica, and Belgium possessed its own Congo museum. American museums had collected largely from their own continental empire, extending their range outside the United States and Canada only haphazardly and then most often to Mesoamerica. The Spanish-American War and its aftermath, marking a formal conversion of the country to overseas empire, changed all that. Increased American commercial and naval interests made the Caribbean into an American lake and placed much of Central and South America under American dominance. Puerto Rico, the Philippines, Hawaii, and several smaller Pacific islands were annexed. The Pacific and Far East regions became increasingly important, strategically and commercially, in American eyes. The Field and American museums, private incorporations directed by men whose careers were adaptive to political and economic trends, were particularly sensitive to the new currents of geopolitical interest.

George Dorsey was a reluctant convert to the altered circumstances, but his trustees had long been anxious to direct anthropological attention abroad. The museum had decided to devote all its available funds to regions outside North America, and, as

Dorsey bluntly told Emmons, "pity or no pity it is the literal truth that it would be quite impossible for me to secure the interest of my Director in the purchase of your Tlingit collection." The trustees had "taken the stand that our North American collections are, in general, sufficiently representative of North American culture, and that the policy hereafter will be to extend our field of activity into South America and more especially into Asia and the Pacific."[4] In New York Boas was more receptive to the new mood and quite prepared to exploit it.

Though Boas later recalled 1898 as "a rude awakening" to the aggressive imperialism that shattered his ideal of America, at the time he happily hitched his own wagon to the ascending star.[5] "Owing to the present and ever-increasing importance of the social and commercial relations between America and Eastern Asia," he told Jesup in 1901, "it is highly desirable that the American people should have a thorough knowledge of that country [sic] and of its people." Recent political events "imposed upon our scientific institutions the duty of familiarizing the American people with the inhabitants of the countries for whose welfare we have made ourselves responsible, for whose future developments and progress we shall be held to account before the judgement of history." He was prepared to assume the anthropologist's burden, "to enlighten our people" about their new colonial wards. "No effort seems too great, no expense too high, that is required in the fulfillment of this duty." He secured the establishment of an East Asiatic Committee at the Museum and persuaded Jacob H. Schiff to contribute $18,000 for a Chinese collection. With Berthold Laufer in China for the Jesup Expedition he had a "first foothold outside of our continent" and a larger scheme of extending the museum's work to the Philippines, the Malay Peninsula, Indo-China, Formosa, and Japan.[6]

While he was "taking up East Asiatic problems" with relish, Boas still sought "to supplement" and "to round off" the Northwest Coast collections, especially in Tsimshian, Nootka, and archaeological areas. The museum was "going right ahead" with Northwest Coast material, observed Emmons in 1906. But with the collapse of the Jesup Expedition and then Boas's resignation, even the American Museum's collecting activities on the coast ran down. Clark Wissler, Boas's successor as curator, noted that the north Pacific coast was one of two North American areas "in which collecting may cease and on which no money need be spent." Indeed, anthropology was losing its favored position within the museum. The rising man was Henry Fairfield Osborn, a vertebrate paleontologist with a flair for exhibition and a winning manner with donors, trustees, and with Jesup, whom he replaced as president in 1908. "Between ourselves," Osborn observed, "much anthropology is merely opinion, or the gossip of the natives. It is many years away from being a science. Mr. Jesup and the Museum spent far too much on anthropology."[7]

Matters at the third great American museum, the Smithsonian's National Museum at Washington, were no different. For years it had become an almost incidental factor in the Northwest Coast market. Its dependence upon governmental appropriation was a major disadvantage in an era when private philanthropists were more generous to museums than congressional Republicans.

The Bureau of American Ethnology, formally tied to North American subjects, was more concerned with linguistics and mythology than with material culture; it lost much of its impetus under the ageing Major Powell and then suffered from a demoralizing quarrel over his successor. Dominated after 1903 by Secretary S. P. Langley's perception of congressional pleasures, it turned toward physical anthropology and the problem of immigrant mixtures within the country. Meanwhile, the museum followed imperial currents. It increased its work in the Caribbean and Mexico and asked for an Hawaiian appropriation. Otis Mason, the curator of ethnology and anthropology, personally abandoned North America for Malay and East Asian concerns and several colleagues similarly turned their eyes abroad.

For the Northwest Coast the days of large-scale purchases by encyclopaedic museums was a thing of the past. The collecting process did not, however, wither and die: other institutions and even some very major private collectors were entering the field to provide a continuing, though more sporadic and fragmented, demand.

In 1905, just as the bottom seemed to have fallen from his market, Emmons made his first sale to George G. Heye. It was a small, mixed collection — Tlingit and some Nishga and Gitksan Tsimshian — but the beginning of a continuous string of almost

George G. Heye on the left, with three Bella Coola acquisitions. Mrs. R. C.
Draney is at center, E. S. Robinson on the right. Courtesy of the Museum of the
American Indian, Heye Foundation, N. Y.

annual sales which would extend until 1943 and involve about
2,200 catalogued items. Few of the lots that flowed to Heye were
large scale, but Heye's reliable patronage gave Emmons an outlet
for his smaller collections, and enough money to allow him to
continue doing what he loved.

As a collector George Gustav Heye was an institution in himself. Always an omnivorous and compulsive consumer of Indian
material from North and South America, he eventually incorporated into the 'Museum of the American Indian, Heye Foundation," the largest area collection of its kind. His money came from
his father's involvement in Pennsylvania oil, later sold to Rockefeller, and he kept it active in Wall Street finance. His interest in
Indian artifacts came after he graduated in engineering from
Columbia in 1897. He was working in Arizona and bought the
deerskin shirt of his Indian foreman. "Naturally when I had the
shirt I wanted a rattle and moccasins. And then the collecting bug
seized me and I was lost."[8]

His first major purchase was a Pueblo pottery collection in 1903 and soon he was sending out his own expeditions to Puerto Rico, Panama, Costa Rica, and Ecuador and securing ranking anthropologists and archaeologists like George H. Pepper and Marshall Saville to lead them. Alongside this systematic collecting went his indiscriminate "boxcar collecting" of odds and ends from any source and any Western Hemispheric aboriginal group. Much he collected personally on flying fieldtrips or digs. A huge man reaching nearly six feet four inches and with a willfulness as large as his frame and fortune, Heye developed a monomaniacal dedication to gathering Indian material. By the time of his death in 1957, his New York museum contained over three million pieces.

Assessment of Heye's motivation varied. Pepper credited him with a single dominant idea: "the bringing together of material, not for personal gain or the mere gratification of a personal hobby, but for the use of students" and done along the most approved scientific lines. Others disagreed. "I doubt whether his goal was anything more than to own the biggest damned hobby collection in the world," commented one who knew him; "he bought all those objects solely in order to own them — for what purpose, he never said." Heye's wealth and seeming susceptibility to scholarly guidance allowed him to attract to his enterprise some of the best men available, "drawn towards Heye by the prospect of a new dream museum."[9]

Heye's Museum of the American Indian came into formal existence in 1916. Before then he had stored his growing collections in rented space in the Knabe Piano building on New York's Fifth Avenue, then on two stories of a loft building on 33rd Street, overflowing into a large collection at the University of Pennsylvania's museum. The death of Heye's mother in 1915 left him an inheritance that allowed the collector's enthusiasm to increase. After Heye had come fully into the estate, Saville confided to Putnam, he "is devoting his life to this project, and all his available means." Expeditions were planned to various locales, but the immediate need was for a new building.[10] That was soon underway when one of the Huntingtons offered a site at Audubon Terrace, Broadway and 155th Street, alongside the headquarters of other scholarly and cultural organizations. Heye accepted the offer. Incorporating the Museum of the American Indian, Heye Foundation as a charitable trust, he gathered together a number of wealthy trustees to help with construction of the $250,000 museum building, which finally opened in 1922.

The chief interests of Heye and his staff were, as befitted the tendency of the times, South America and the Caribbean, but the whole of the hemisphere was Heye's chosen province. He visited the Northwest Coast numerous times and purchased collections from every direction. Emmons was his most frequent and long-term coastal source. In 1904 and 1905 he made purchases from Landsberg and Stadthagen, probably through Emmons who was picking over the Victoria dealers at that time. A large collection was bought in 1908 from Rev. Thomas Crosby, missionary at Masset and the Skeena. A Mr. F. M. Covert seems to have been the intermediary, but few things are certain about Heye's collections; despite the scientific intentions of his employees, Heye was notoriously contemptuous of accession and catalogue records. Boas, whose own artifact gathering had almost ceased, made arrangements for George Hunt to collect for Heye in 1906 at his usual salary of $75 a month. Heye received artifacts and Boas texts, but Heye found it difficult "to do business with an Indian at a distance of over 3000 miles" and by 1910 even Boas was suspicious that Hunt was using Heye's money "for purposes other than collecting" — perhaps for potlatching — and the final Hunt collection was shipped to Heye in 1910.[11]

A large amount of coastal material, including pieces collected by Culin and Newcombe, came to Heye through the University of Pennsylvania museum. Emmons's sales to Heye, too numerous to list, include his first Tahltan collection of 1903, parts of his Nass and Skeena collections of 1905 and 1909, a large collection of jade objects sold in 1924 for $5,000, and a large number of secondary collections, most notably that of A. W. Vowell, the former Indian superintendent. The sale included three remarkable stone batons found by Vowell in a cache along the Skeena in 1898.[12]

In 1916, as part of Heye's new museum effort, Leo J. Frachtenberg was hired for two years to collect in northwestern Washington State among the Quileute, Quinault, and Makah. T. T. Waterman, another anthropologist at the beginning of his career, spent three years, 1919 through 1921, in the field among the Puget Sound Salish. Collections in both cases were thin; collecting for Heye was ancillary to their own linguistic or ethnological fieldwork and those regions were badly depleted by that time.

Captain D. F. Tozier's collection displayed in the Ferry Museum, Tacoma, Washington. From Arts and Crafts of the Totem Indians; *classified and photographed by Professor W. H. Gilstrap, Curator, Ferry Museum (Tacoma, n.d.). Pacific Northwest Collection, University of Washington Libraries.*

An important prize came in the midst of the reorganization and building program — an offer of the Tozier collection, now in the custody of real-estate developer F. E. Sander, and stored in Seattle. D. F. Tozier, it will be recalled, was an officer of the U. S. Revenue Service who had accumulated a collection stored at the Ferry Museum in Tacoma. A native Georgian, he had entered the service in 1865 and, after duty on the Atlantic, the Gulf, and the Great Lakes, was transferred to Port Townsend in 1891, assuming command of the *Grant* three years later.

It was commonly reported that Tozier had accumulated much of his mass of material by theft or "by the exercise of a show of force and authority."[13] On one occasion a complaint was laid by the B. C. provincial police alleging that the officers and men of the *Grant* had illegally traded with the Indians at Ucleulet, selling them illicit whiskey and stealing a headpiece from a native's house. No museum man or serious collector had any respect for Tozier or his methods. Culin, who had seen the collection twice, called its owner "a thoroughly dishonest man" and Emmons expressed the general sentiment when he wrote that Tozier "collects without knowledge or method and knows no more about what he has than any stranger."[14]

Despite the contempt, all coveted his collection or at least the better pieces in it. Culin thought that, excepting the large Kwakiutl houseposts and a number of fine feast dishes, the collection was not especially notable. The thousands of smaller objects, of course, "could be employed to advantage by us," but there was "little of great excellence" and nothing essential. Dorsey very much wanted at least the poles and feast dishes. Tozier, however, priced his collection well beyond any museum's estimate. It was claimed to be worth more than $30,000 in 1901 and three years later it was offered for sale at the modest price of $250,000.[15] Grace Nicholson was able to buy a few hundred dollars worth of pieces from the collection in 1905 and that sent Culin and Newcombe, acting for Dorsey, scurrying to Tacoma to see what was up. The prices asked were so exhorbitant — at least twice those of Landsberg — that they gave things a miss.

Tozier retired in 1907 and left the coast. Shortly thereafter the collection was transferred to something called the Washington State Art Association for a reported price of $40,000. The shadowy art society, headed by a former streetcar conductor, apparently intended to use the collection as the basis for a city art museum. The Washington State Museum at the University of Washington in Seattle hoped to succeed to the material, but in 1917 owner or agent Sander offered it to Heye for $17,000. George Pepper was dispatched to Seattle to inspect the collection and negotiate terms. The warehouse was crowded and cramped, but Pepper managed to inventory the contents. Though he could find practically no data for any of it, he had no doubt as to the collection's value. The twelve or so poles and posts had been blackened with oil; it was impossible to tell their age, but they were well carved and "make a fine appearance." These, along with the large feast dishes, were "worth a considerable outlay." Pepper succeeded in beating Sander down to $12,500, leaving only some basketry and argillite behind.[16] The collection was indeed prodigious, with some sixty chests, a six-foot chief's seat, two hundred halibut hooks, and a house front, among the more than ten thousand items.

George Heye provided much of Emmons's bread and butter after the end of the scramble, but even his appetite for Indian material could not digest all that Emmons, through his summer seasons and broad network of sources, was capable of providing. The collector's fourth major Tlingit collection, already numbering 1,650 pieces by 1905, could find no home. With North American material a "drag on the market," he split off portions of it to Heye and others, but could not interest any museum in the thousand-plus core. Putnam at Harvard turned it down; Dorsey refused even to bring it to his directors' attention. George Gordon at the University of Pennsylvania was very interested, then backed out. Finally, in 1908, the organizers of Seattle's Alaska-Yukon-Pacific Exposition asked that Emmons exhibit the Tlingit collection there with the possibility of purchase at the close of the fair. He was reluctant to accept; he would have to travel to Seattle and install the collection and there was a risk in shipping, but, with "Indian collections at a discount," he took it west for exhibit in the fair's Alaska Building.[17]

Officials at the University of Washington, whose campus had been the site of the fair, were impressed and wanted to keep its 1,900 pieces for the state museum which they administered. Emmons's price of $14,500 proved hard to raise. The legislature turned down a requested appropriation, but the university's regents, together with a public subscription, at last paid Emmons the full purchase price in 1912, though he had to forego most of the 5 percent interest due him. In the meantime he sold a small, then a larger collection, including thirty Salish baskets, to the growing Milwaukee Public Museum, an institution that had added an anthropological curator to its staff only in 1909.

With Boas gone from the American Museum, Emmons was able to renew his old patronage connection there, now with President Osborn and Director Bumpus. They had tentatively made an offer of $13,000 for his Seattle collection, but then decided it too much duplicated their existing material. They did, however, contract Emmons to help design and complete the three dozen costumed figures that were added to Powell's sixty-four foot canoe in 1910–11. Presented as a group of Tlingit arriving for a potlatch, the ceremonial canoe scene became the largest single life-group in the museum, perhaps the largest in North America.[18] At about the same time Emmons sold a large Eskimo collection, 764 pieces for

$2,500, and 71 Indian baskets for $700 to the Alaska Territorial Museum in Juneau. Over the next few years he sold several collections to the Peabody at Harvard, the largest a $600 Tsimshian collection.

This was, nevertheless, a difficult time for Emmons. Not only was the scramble over, Northwest Coast ethnology was, as he pronounced it, "about dead" in American museums. There was no longer, he complained, a single curator who knew or cared about the coast. New York had the finest and most complete collection, but it was "piled in cases" and "all the effort and time is given to language & folklore." There had been, as Emmons properly discerned, a significant shift not only away from the Northwest Coast and the North American Indian in general, but also from ethnology and the study of material culture to folklore, linguistics, and social anthropology. This was partly the result of the larger role that university departments were playing, often at the expense of museums, in the increased professionalism of anthropology, but it was also a tendency within the structure of the discipline itself, even among museum personnel. Anthropological writers had become too scientific, Emmons complained in 1915. "Today, they do not seem to be willing to go out and study the life of the Natives but sit in their offices and discuss theories and psychology and there then seems to be in the New York Museum men who love to praise each other." They were now all into complex theories; "out of the simplest act of primitive man they want to find some distant motive." To a collector who had cut his teeth in the museum scramble and who kept to "the plain facts" of blankets, jade, and basketry, it was all "a lot of scientific cranks" and childish discussions.[19]

Emmons's friend, C. F. Newcombe, also suffered from the market's decline, but he had other interests which could help to keep him occupied. On his return from Chicago he had been anxious to find some work. "It is necessary that I should get something on a pay basis as soon as I can. My rent has just doubled, my Chinaman is very expensive & not one of my five children is yet off my hands." Nevertheless, he turned down an offer from Boas and Dorsey's proposal for a long-term engagement in Asia. "I prefer," he told A. L. Kroeber, "to be free for a while."[20] He was willing to arrange sales and take on limited commissions, but for the next few years he was kept busy in historical studies of the early explorers of the coast, on provincial government assignment for the Simon Fraser centenary exhibition, as consultant for a federal study of sea lions, and in building a new home on Victoria's Dallas Road.

Requests for his services came largely from smaller institutions interested in building up their collections. Stewart Culin, for example, came through Victoria on a field expedition in August 1905. Culin was now at Brooklyn's Institute of Arts and Sciences as curator of ethnology and was actively building up its collections, aiming at areas which could give immediate results. The timing of his Victoria visit seemed opportune. Newcombe had his own collection up for sale, over a thousand pieces gathered since his Hood River days, as well as the results of the summer voyage from which he had just returned. These included a fine Nass River collection made by his son Willie, now twenty-one years old and an active collecting collaborator.

Culin, after viewing the material stored in Newcombe's barn, was "convinced that I could not too strongly recommend its purchase" and persuaded Newcombe, on the strength of this, to allow him some of the new, uncatalogued pieces.[21] For $752.75, Culin took 182 specimens, the more significant being a Tsimshian doctor's outfit and chief's headdress and a series of Cowichan spindle whorls. The largest and, in Culin's eyes, the most important items were three carved posts, brought down from the Quawshelah of southern Vancouver Island.

Brooklyn's trustees did not agree to buy Newcombe's main collection for which he was asking $4,500. Kroeber at the University of California's museum expressed interest, but Newcombe, on his way back from his last stint in Chicago, detoured to Ottawa and there in June 1906 successfully negotiated with the Geological Survey for the sale of the collection, now supplemented by about six hundred more pieces. The accumulation of twenty years' collecting, it comprised artifacts from all areas of the coast, most bought directly from the Indians. Naturally it was especially strong in Haida and next in Kwakiutl. He was scarcely home when Emmons dropped by, wanting to buy the collection for $7,000 spot cash, $500 more than Ottawa was paying over three years. Newcombe stuck to his bargain with the Survey; the money helped pay for his new house.[22]

Culin was back in 1908. Newcombe, busy with house building and his historical studies, had only a few things on hand, but offered Culin what there was and then happily guided the Brooklyn curator through the curio dealers' establishments and across to the Songhees Reserve. Landsberg had closed his store to join the real-estate boom and was offering his remaining stock for sale. Culin latched onto a Haida wooden helmet, which, though it looked new, Newcombe assured him he had known of since 1895. Landsberg's basement remainders provided other desiderata and Culin was able to buy some Nootka pieces and a few toys (Indian games were his special interest) at the Songhees Reserve.

In between visits to reserve and dealers, Culin had been inspecting Newcombe's stock, especially masks and a carved chest. He was undecided about buying until F. W. Putnam called into town on his way back to Harvard from California. Suddenly Culin became covetous. "The knowledge that Putnam was after these things led me to conclude this purchase."[23] There was still nothing like competition to close a sale.

Culin and Newcombe maintained close touch after this visit. The curator wanted to supplement Brooklyn's collection, particularly with totem poles. When Newcombe secured two large Haida house poles and, through Charlie Nowell, a set of Kwakiutl poles, potlatch figures, and feast dishes, he reserved these for Culin's inspection on the latter's 1911 western expedition. Culin was satisfied, then repeated the usual curio-dealer tour, getting bargains among the remains of Landsberg's unsold goods. He took two Haida helmets for fifty dollars, then learned from Newcombe that the merchant had had them made. "But, as they were correct in every particular, they were excellent museum specimens, the best that could be procured now."[24]

Having done the dealers and culled Newcombe's stores, Culin set off, with an obliging Newcombe as guide, for the mainland and a buying tour of the lower Fraser valley. While getting thoroughly lost on potholed roads amid swarming mosquitoes, they secured various items from the Salish at Chilliwack — an iron chisel with elk-horn socket, a stone hammer, a paddle, and a child's basketry rattle. From Chief Shau-kail's wife, Newcombe bought an old blanket in a red, blue, and white checkered pattern, assumed to be goat hair, for twelve dollars.[25]

The next day the Indians brought them a lot of old things, Newcombe buying most of it, before they boarded the railway for Yale. Here Newcombe picked up an old iron knife and native twine used for river dip nets. They hired Charlie Hope to take them downriver by canoe and a half-blood boy, William Lewis, to accompany them as they drifted downstream. At their first stop, Chief Pierre's wife brought out a goat-hair blanket with an interesting design worked in coiled yarn, which Newcombe took for ten dollars, along with a chief's cane, a bag of hemp fiber, and a jade chisel. A side trip to Harrison by motor occasioned a visit to Charles Inkman's store and its stock of baskets, the best assortment, Newcombe promised Culin, of new basketry to be found in the province. Culin was disappointed; all seemed to him coarse and lacking in artistic quality.

In Vancouver they looked up Rev. Crosby, whose main collection had been sold to Heye in 1908. He had a few things left in his house, including a Fraser River stone image, three Haida whistles, and a very beautiful bone labret, but these were not for sale. A collection, largely stone, was on loan to the city museum, but Culin, on viewing it, thought it so uninteresting as not worth pursuing. Even Thomas H. Allice, a commercial traveller who often acted as a basket middleman for Rhodes & Co. of Seattle, had just sold his stock to Grace Nicholson and Homer Sargent. It was a poor end to an otherwise fruitful coast tour for Culin. He embarked for Seattle, leaving behind an order for a canoe, while Newcombe caught a morning boat for his second northern trip of the year. He had a commission to collect for British Columbia's provincial museum. The anthropology collection at Victoria's Museum of Natural History and Ethnology had long been in a state of neglect, but the province was now, "at this eleventh hour," beginning "to take active steps to increase their Indian Collections."[26]

British Columbia's provincial museum was a neglected child of the 1880s scramble. Founded in large part as a response to local concern about the great exodus of ethnological pieces, it had promptly lapsed into anthropological inactivity until 1893, when, in a short outburst that took advantage of the collecting of James Deans and Fillip Jacobsen for the Chicago World's Fair, an astonishing $1,700 was spent on an "assortment . . . remarkable for its diversity."[27] By this time Newton Chittenden's 1884 Haida collection, though still on exhibition at the fair, had been promised to the museum, now housed in the former Supreme Court building. Over the next few years Deans was temporarily engaged to arrange the Indian material and a few items were added, most importantly a collection purchased in 1897 from Charles Hill-Tout, the Vancouver Salish scholar. Then, upon the occasion of the installation of the collection in much larger quarters in the east wing of the new Legislative Buildings, Newcombe was paid $330 to prepare a preliminary catalogue of the museum's holdings, including its 1,066 ethnological and archaeological specimens.[28]

By 1900 the position of the museum might be described as that of a good late-starter, with a modest and well-organized collection in adequate quarters. When Culin visited Victoria that year he commended it for its admirably classified and displayed collections: "in every way the best museum I had seen west of Chicago." There were problems, however. Curator John Fannin, in the years before his 1904 retirement, became erratic and negligent. Newcombe complained that Fannin was quite willing to dispose of ethnological material, trading it off or giving it away. Fillip Jacobsen, who at about this time donated masks to the museum, found Fannin so uninterested as to throw them out. Despite the urging of some, including the Natural History Society, that Newcombe succeed Fannin in 1904, taxidermist Francis Kermode was promoted to the position. "Nice enough in his way," Kermode lacked any scientific attainments and, according to Culin, "neglected the valuable ethnological collection which I had had much occasion to praise." Labels were loose and the whole collection was "practically uncared for"; Newcombe did what he could to assist, "but, with the present outlook, its case looks hopeless."[29]

It was not entirely so. For some years a reaction had been building, not unlike that of 1886 which had led to the museum's foundation. British Columbians were kept aware of the quantities of material being collected by American institutions, especially the museums of Chicago and New York. The Victoria papers usually covered the visits of Dorsey, Boas, and others, happily enumerating the number of cases shipped back to Central Park or Lake Michigan. The Johnson Street dealer Frederick Landsberg exploited the local press to publicize his museum sales, partly from mere puffery and partly in an attempt to whip up a local market for his material.

Landsberg's planted stories were often accompanied by comment deploring the losses to the province of rare and irreplaceable material. When he shipped "no less than five cases of Indian curios" to Philadelphia as part of Culin's 1900 purchases, the *Colonist* story lamented that some of these pieces, "of exceedingly great age and proportionately rare," would have made "a valuable addition to the provincial museum." In April 1903 Landsberg inserted a photograph of "B. C. Indian Curiosities for Chicago," adding his own promotional comment about "the great pity . . . that such valuable relics of the now rapidly disappearing Indian tribes cannot be retained in the province."[30] Others commented indignantly on Landsberg's sales. "LOSS TO BRITISH COLUMBIA Through the Depredations of United States and Other Foreign Collectors of the Province's Most Valuable Indian Relics" headlined a *Colonist* story later that year. It was a comment on a Dorsey visit and his Landsberg purchases, with the moral "that the enterprising neighbors to the South are rapidly depriving British Columbia of the very choicest specimens of native ingenuity."[31]

To the many in the province who were deeply interested in native history "the plundering of the province by foreign collectors" was a source of deep concern. The anonymous *Colonist* writer went on to catalogue the "evidences of the despoiling process which has been in progress for many years past": New York, Boston, Philadelphia, Chicago, San Francisco, and other foreign cities of the continent, while England, Germany, even Austria and Norway, had all done their share. "Today British Columbians are face to face with the unpleasant conviction that through their own neglect and lack of energy their best relics — their priceless amulets, or rarest totems and most beautifully wrought charms have been yielded up without protest and bartered for a sum representing scarcely a tenth of their real value." The government and people were urged to atone for past neglect by appropriating even a comparatively small sum for the purchase of native rarities for the provincial museum.

Another article of the same year, "How the Province is Plundered," quoted a gentleman just returned from New York where he had seen the "veritable forest of totem poles," part of the American Museum collection that was "admirable in its range and completeness." "Why, oh why have not our leading men taken an interest in this deeply important subject and done something to save for future generations something like a coherent and continuous record of the clans who peopled this Island and the neighboring coasts?" That the lament was not entirely disinterested patriotism was revealed when the gentleman went on to praise Landsberg's assiduity and to comment that Landsberg was intending to leave the country and was offering his entire collection at a price well below its real value. Certainly Landsberg was doing his best to unload his entire stock in 1903, hoping to go to a now-pacified South Africa. He neither sold his collection nor went to the Cape and the *Colonist*'s inspired stories followed along the same lines in succeeding years. The Natural History Society added its small voice to the "crying complaint that the Indian relics of British Columbia are being rapidly absorbed by the scientific institutions of the United States," but there was no response from successive provincial ministries.[32]

British Columbia's apathy to the large-scale drainage of Indian artifacts was diagnosed, probably accurately, in one of the newspaper notices:

> No man is a hero in the eyes of his valet, and close acquaintance with the unregenerated siwash renders him and all thereunto pertaining more or less of a nuisance to the utilitarian white man. Hence it arises that locally little attention is paid to the folk-lore and legends of the aborigines, and still less to the antiquities and remains of this ancient race.[33]

British Columbia was a settler's country, bound upon expansion and development. Racism was conspicuous and unabashed with little regard for the contemporary position of the Indians or for their previous accomplishments. Only a few voices were raised in favor of local public collections and these came most often from interested dealers or the small and ineffective intellectual community of the province. In Vancouver Charles Hill-Tout counted himself as "one of those who never cease to express regret" at the passing of so many treasures to the United States and felt it "a serious reflection upon the Province" that anyone wishing to study the region's aborigines "must go to New York to do it."[34]

The pressure, slowly building, finally achieved some movement of the museum and ministerial glacier. Kermode was moved to write in his 1909 report of the daily increasing difficulty and cost of procuring anthropological material. In the midst of a collecting area unrivalled in the world, little was being done to take advantage of the "golden opportunity of the present." In 1909 Newcombe was asked to rearrange the museum's collection according to tribe (it had heretofore been displayed by category of specimen regardless of origin), and later that year his new *Guide to Anthropological Collection in the Provincial Museum,* a sixty-nine page illustrated catalogue of the collections, appeared. The voice of the provincial librarian and archivist, E. O. S. Scholefield, was added to the pressure for action. In his 1911 annual report, Scholefield cited the "high importance" of the matter as a justification to go beyond his departmental purview and urge "the desirability of acquiring a really representative collection of relics and tokens covering all phases of the Indian life of British Columbia." "If the formation of such a collection is not undertaken at once, and vigorously prosecuted, it will be soon, very soon indeed, once and for all too late for the Province to acquire an exhibit worthy of the great ethnological field which it covers." The refrain of the native races fast forsaking their old and immemorial customs, of the province being for years "the happy hunting-ground" of collectors of the world, was an old one. While Scholefield mooted the equally old idea of devising some legal means of preventing the export of the best material, he confessed to the difficulty of such regulation. Instead he suggested that the government "proceed immediately to acquire by purchase all available material" that would illustrate "a people whose history can never be without interest."[35]

Scholefield's intervention was propitious. He had the ear of the provincial secretary, the Queen's and McGill educated Dr. Henry Essen Young, and was securing impressive appropriations for his archival and library enthusiasms. Young, an active and influential cabinet member, was already working toward founding a provincial university and had secured money for a new legislative library and museum building. The provincial economy was booming, buoyed by a rapid expansion of agriculture, timber, mining, and railways. Government revenues increased from just over four and a half million dollars in 1909 to almost ten and a half in 1911. The mood, moreover, had never been more positive. Local prejudices toward the "siwash" remained unchanged, but the native Indians were regarded as increasingly irrelevant to the rapidly developing

province — with their numbers in decline, the provincial government successfully secured the reduction of reserve lands and, with
compensation, moved the Songhees from Victoria's Inner Harbor
Reserve and the Kitsilano from valuable Vancouver land. Less
then ever a nuisance or an obstacle to progress, native arts could
be more readily appreciated. The Natural History Society worried about Indian children not learning blanket- and basket-making. The lieutenant governor's ballroom was decorated with sten-
cilled coppers and crests, perhaps the first application of
Northwest ornamentation to such purposes. The new Empress
Hotel's lobby sported a set of Landsberg-commissioned totem
poles, judged by Culin to be effective despite inaccurate paints.[36]

In April 1911 Scholefield and Young asked Newcombe "to take
the field" and gather as representative a collection as was possible
with the $3,000 placed at his disposal. The money came from
Scholefield's "Collecting Archives" budget rather than from
museum appropriations, Kermode being on the outs with his
minister. (Even the next year, when the money was placed in the
museum budget, Newcombe ignored Kermode, feeling "quite
capable of getting necessary curios without his aid.")[37]

Once launched, the provincial collecting program was pursued
with vigor. Newcombe brought in James A. Teit to complement
his coastal work with collections from the province's interior.
Newcombe's accounts ran to $2,646 in 1912 and $1,046 in 1913
and Teit's to $729 over the two seasons. The high cost of commis-
sioned collecting was reflected in the percentage paid for salary
and expenses; in 1911, for example, it cost the government $1,400
to collect $1,669 worth of specimens.[38]

Emmons thought that the effort was "too late." British Columbians were now "straining every nerve to make up for their past
indifference"; the province "has at last aroused itself to the fact
that it has lost its opportunity to gather a necessary collection to
illustrate its native tribes and now Dr. Newcombe has been given
ample funds and every means to gather everything remaining."
But it had delayed too long: "the old material has gone with the
old people."[39] In fact, Newcombe was surprised to find a decent
quantity of material of almost all kinds even in places, like the
Queen Charlottes, which he thought were played out.

The "straining of every nerve" was over almost as quickly as it
had begun. The provincial economy collapsed in 1913 and by the

following year revenues had fallen by almost a quarter. Museum appropriations were slashed, then cut again. "The Province is now impecunious," Newcombe reported in July, and "so my engagements with the Museum are curtailed."[40] Nevertheless, the sudden, short-lived spurt had doubled the catalogued entries at the museum from 1,390 to 2,837 and provided a solid basis which allowed the provinces to possess a collection, if certainly not of the first rank, yet of strength and significance. A trickle of material, small purchases, and donations from provincial police and surveyors, enlarged the collection over the next decades.

In his 1911 to 1914 collecting, Newcombe, as usual, took a special interest in poles, both for the provincial museum and for orders, some long-standing, from other institutions. As of 1908, no less than six museums had written him about large poles, but it was almost useless, he felt, to try to secure them by correspondence and the costs of expeditions added too much to their price. A. L. Kroeber at Berkeley's museum, for example, had wanted a Haida pole since 1907, but Newcombe had to discourage him. "There are so many individuals to be placated at different rates of compensation & it is so seldom that enough Haida are on the islands during the short spell of good weather for towing that it has become a difficult matter to procure a totem pole nowadays without an expensive personal visit."[41] Now that the provincial government was absorbing his travel expenses, Newcombe could fill his back orders.

By 1911 Kroeber was all the more anxious for "a tall and striking specimen" that would be a show piece when the new University of California museum was opened to the public in the fall. He got a large Skedans pole, purchased through the generosity of Phoebe Apperson Hearst, patroness of the museum, in time for the opening.[42] Newcombe shipped a Skidegate pole to Baldwin Spencer at Melbourne's museum and sent two more Haida poles to Culin along with some small Kwakiutl houseposts and the long-awaited canoe. Haida, Nootka, and Kwakiutl poles went to the provincial museum. The great gap in its collection, as in all collections, were Tsimshian poles from the Nishga and the Gitksan.

Like the Kaigani in 1902, the Nishga of the Nass River and the Gitksan of the Skeena River had never sold a pole. They, like the

Kwakiutl, had not stopped carving and erecting new ones. Only the coastal Tsimshian seem to have been at this time represented in museum collections: Mrs. Morrison's commissioned pole for the Chicago fair, the Fort Simpson pole collected by Swan, and another sent to the Pitt Rivers Museum by the HBC's R.H. Hall in 1900. On Newcombe's 1912 trip he had "started the Nass & Skeena people thinking over the desirability of selling their poles" and, though he had "found the people hard to deal with," hoped that he could buy several in 1913. "Once the ball starts rolling," he wrote in terms reminiscent of his Kaigani experience, "I expect it will be easier to do business with them."[43]

The Nishga proved immovable. It was partly the old problem of price: "until they get started, they are absolutely at sea as to what charge to make." They were still pricing them at their original cost, including all the value of the potlatch and gifts given at the time they were erected. This made Nishga prices "more exhorbitant than the Alaska Haida even." Newcombe reluctantly abandoned his intentions of securing Nass poles. As was his custom, he refused to overpay: "Once an abnormally high price is given that standard would be immediately set for every pole on the river." The first Skeena sale seems to have been to the American Museum in 1923. According to Marius Barbeau, that first Gitksan vendor "was forced to yield to his relatives the initial cost of the pole, that is, far beyond what he claimed to have received in payment."[44]

On the Queen Charlottes, where he was more at home and where sales had been almost routine for over a decade, Newcombe had none of these difficulties, but there remained the inevitable problem of disputed ownership. In August 1911, for example, he bought a Klue pole from Mrs. Oliver, who represented Zantise of Skidegate. Then George Green claimed it through his brother and uncle. The case was one of inheritance by Haida uncle to nephew versus Canadian inheritance by widow, with extra complications of Haida borrowing. Zantise, the widow of old Chief Skedans and claimant by that right, told the story:

> Many years ago in the vilage of Clew a man by the name of Wah des da ya married my daughter.
>
> After about five years my daughter died and as was our custom he took me for his wife.

> We lived together for twenty or thirty years when a relation of my husband Che hal by name lost his wife. Chehal was not able financially to erect a grave post for his wife and he asked my husband and myself to do it.
>
> We did so, at a cost of about $1000.

Zantise maintained that by Haida custom this act gave her possession not only of the grave post, but also the house and housepost of the deceased. Now old and without any means of support except the charity of Mrs. Oliver, she was happy to sell the post. Although George Green was a cousin of her husband, he "did not put in a cent or a days work" on the pole. "He is a big strong man, with a comfortable home, and grown family and does not need any of the small amount Dr. Newcombe will pay for the pole." Green, however, claimed that since his uncle, the same Clehal, had been the original owner, he was now "the right owner of it." Both parties agreed to abide by the decision of Thomas Deasy, the Charlottes' Indian agent, but he refused to give an opinion, merely sending a copy of the relevant section of the Indian Act. Newcombe, citing the law, sent full payment to Mrs. Oliver, representing Zantise.[45] He was, perhaps, led by the precedent which Agent Todd had established in the Woods-Moss controversy at Cumshewa years before, perhaps by his sympathies with the relative needs and circumstances of the claimants.

Pole problems might be difficult at the purchasing end; they could also be difficult at the selling end. The saga of the Cambridge-Milwaukee pole is exceptional but instructive. It all began when the distinguished mathematician, antiquarian, and ceramics collector, James Whitbread Gleisher, Fellow of Trinity College, Cambridge, visited Victoria in the summer of 1907. Long a friend of Baron Anatole von Hügel and of the Baron's Cambridge University Museum of Archaeology and Ethnology, Gleisher bought a number of artifacts for the museum from local dealers. At Stadthagen's he had seen a totem pole which, after discussions with von Hügel, he ordered from the Victoria dealer. Gleisher knew it was no great thing: "Do not be disappointed," he told von Hügel, "it is very rough, & has only 4 figures on it. All I can say is that it is *far and away* the best of the *old* ones that I saw." Von Hügel was delighted. "Your Totem post has found a comfortable place," he wrote Gleisher, "& smiles most amiably upon us." Von Hügel

"H. Stadthagen, The Indian Trader," one of the Victoria curio shops selling to tourists, collectors, and curators. Courtesy of Bill Holm.

and Gleisher quickly learned that the pole was bogus. Stadthagen claimed that it was from "the Frog Tribe of the Nootka Indians," an absolutely meaningless designation, and over one hundred years old. As Newcombe informed A. C. Haddon, it had actually been carved from a telegraph pole by "Nutka Jack" at the Songhees Reserve in Victoria. By 1913 von Hügel was willing to pay up to £120 for a real pole. He wrote a letter of enquiry to Dorsey who recommended Newcombe as the one man to get him a good pole: "You may depend upon it, that whatever he sends will be good."[46]

On his two trips to the Charlottes that summer, Newcombe examined poles in twelve villages but the "sole result" was Chief Skilkin's Yan pole. It took considerable labor to get the pole down and then to tow it to Masset where, at almost forty feet, it proved too long for the steamers. Cut in two, it arrived in Victoria in November 1913, but with the raven figure at the top broken.

Newcombe had the pole "redressed" and repainted, but Dorsey was abroad and Newcombe waited for his return before renewing correspondence with Cambridge. By then war had broken out: von Hügel, as an enemy alien, was temporarily removed from the university, the museum stopped buying, and shipping was impossible.[47] Having cost him $332.50, the Yan pole lay in Newcombe's garden through the war and armistice. Only in 1921 was he able to sell it to Milwaukee's museum, where it would cause yet more difficulties.

The Milwaukee Public Museum put the pole on its lawn in front of the Renaissance-style building it shared with the public library. The unveiling unleashed an astonishing controversy that hinged largely upon taste but also involved allegation of theft. The leading opponents of the pole founded their criticism upon aesthetics. Boris Lovett-Lorski, a Russian-born sculptor at the Layton School of Art, insisted that the pole, while an interesting demonstration of "the artistic attempts of the red man," should not be placed before a classically inspired edifice. It was "a mésalliance between savage art and the elegances and beauties of the Italian renaissance." The pole needed open air and sky. Others agreed on the incongruity, that it "simply does not fit there." A full public debate brought Lovett-Lorski and another artist face-to-face with the anthropology curator Samuel Barrett and D. C. Watson of the Art Institute. The latter felt that the pole was not only "awfully good looking" but in perfect harmony of contour with the building. Moreover, "it tells the world that the building is a museum. Otherwise one might think it is a Turkish bath." Alderman John Koerner now took up the battle against "the hideous object," while the newspapers, dubbing the pole "Ignatz," had a field day. "Wednesday was Ignatz day at the city hall," reported the *Journal* and, after three hours of verbal battle, "Ignatz could be seen smiling." An attempted intervention by the municipal art commission was thwarted by the city attorney: the Yan pole was not an art work in the statutory sense, but "a relic pure and simple." Newcombe was drawn in by an urgent wire asking for the history and authenticity of the pole, but the battle was over. "Until the sky falls down, Ignatz will remain out in front of the museum building."[48] Indeed, when the museum moved to new premises fifty years later, the pole moved too.

Newcombe's loss of the Cambridge pole sale had been just one of the tribulations which war visited upon him. His income was dependent upon dividends from British stocks and bonds, and remittances from this source, let alone his ability to touch the capital, were badly affected by exchange controls. He hung on, helped by a commission from the Peabody Museum of Anthropology and Archaeology.

Harvard's Peabody Museum was another small institution now seeking to expand and round out its Northwest Coast material. The oldest (1866) North American museum devoted solely to anthropology, the Peabody already had an unusual collection from a variety of sources. From its earliest years it had become the successor to a number of Massachusetts societies and institutes, such as the state's historical society, the Boston Marine Society, the American Antiquarian Society, and the Boston Society of Natural History, the latter itself partial heir to the Lewis and Clark and other collections which had formed a portion of Charles Willson Peale's famous Philadelphia museum. This put into the Peabody some of the best examples of very early Northwest Coast pieces stemming from New England's participation in the maritime fur trade and the whaling periods.

Among the Nootka whaling hats, slave killers, and other rare early items were such trade-influenced pieces as a basketry hat made in the shape of a European beaver hat and the well-known "Jenna Cass" Haida portrait mask, apparently collected before 1827 and one of a number of similar labreted masks probably made for the trade.[49] The Peabody's Edward Fast collection of Tlingit material, purchased in 1869, has already been mentioned. Small lots came into the Peabody in the 1880s from Alice C. Fletcher, Rev. E. S. Willard, and Rev. Myron Eells, and an exchange with the Smithsonian brought it pieces collected by Wilkes, Swan, and McLean.

Harvard graduate F. W. Rindge, a California millionaire, contributed dealer-bought collections in the 1890s, including a great many argillite pieces. As the price of his philanthropy, Rindge received a photograph of each donation, a procedure precedent for the large number of donations given the museum by Lewis H. Farlow, another wealthy Californian with a Harvard connection. Farlow bought from a number of Pacific coast dealers, but largely from Grace Nicholson, who ran a well-known Indian and Oriental emporium in Pasadena. Farlow became one of her best customers. When she had something good, Farlow wrote, "she always gives me first whack," though she often sent material to Harvard on approval without Farlow ever seeing it. Nicholson employed a buyer, but made numerous expeditions herself, such as those to Puget Sound in 1905 and 1909. She had a broad network of field agents procuring for her, including T. C. Allice among the Salish. She established a reputation as an extremely capable woman with high quality material.[50] Farlow reported that when Dorsey visited her store in 1903, "he did not have a nice time. She is darn spunky & does not bull doze for a cub."

Almost annually, from 1902 to 1915, a large amount of all kinds of Northwest Coast material, especially baskets, flowed from Pasadena to Cambridge and platinum prints went back to the Pacific. In 1914, 1915, and 1917, the ubiquitous Emmons also sold several collections, the largest being Gitksan material, to the Peabody.

The accumulated total gave the Peabody "a few good things" from all the Northwest Coast groups by 1917, but C. C. Willoughby, Putnam's successor to the directorship, wanted to round out the museum's collections from the Kwakiutl, Nootka, and southern coastal Salish and he turned to Newcombe as one who knew the region better than anyone else. On his part, Newcombe wrote Charlie Nowell, now operating a store at Rivers Inlet, and Nowell agreed to go with him by motor launch to Kingcome Inlet and other places "which have not been so devastated by George Hunt &c." They spent two weeks in early May in Kwakiutl country, securing 140 specimens, including examples of most of what Newcombe thought Willoughby would want. "It was a surprise to me to find that so many of them still existed." He attributed his success largely to Nowell's close contact with the Kingcome people during the winter. "He ran a small store at the winter village of the Kingcome Indians who gave a series of potlatches inviting all their neighbours and, so, he was able to make quick negotiations for what there was to be had." Travel and time increased the expense enormously. Purchase costs for the 140 items in the Kwakiutl collection had been only $254.10, but salaries and expenses brought the total to $621.80.[51]

Willoughby, pleased with the five cases, asked for Nootka and Salish material, which Newcombe thought could be had for reasonable cost. The trips to Port Angeles and the west coast of

Vancouver Island in April and May 1918 were disappointing; Newcombe secured a few things from the Quileute but very little from the Nootka. He returned to Willoughby over half of the $500 advance.[52]

In his 1917–19 collecting for the Peabody, Newcombe had been told to avoid buying any large carvings because of the museum's restricted space. By 1919, with the opening of a new section of the museum building, the situation was reversed. A large Tlingit pole from the Harriman Expedition, stored since 1899, was installed on the first floor of the new addition and Willoughby asked Newcombe for some Kwakiutl examples. He travelled north in May and secured two sixteen-foot Karlekwees houseposts from Chief Mountain — shipped gratis to Boston by the New England Fish Company — and in October bought yet another, this a Nimkish Thunderbird with whale.[53]

Newcombe was now entering his sixty-ninth year and, though both his eyesight and hearing were impaired, his energy remained scarcely touched by the years. In May 1922 he was in the Charlottes, and then spent June and July escorting the American Museum's Pliny Goddard, who was rearranging New York's North Pacific Hall, along the British Columbia coast. T. F. McIlwraith, who met him at Bella Coola and visited him in Victoria, reported that Newcombe "is very deaf now, but energetic as ever." "Nearly every one knew him or of him," Goddard recalled, "and greeted him as an old friend."[54] His reputation as a pole collector kept him in steady demand. When C. T. Currelly of Toronto's Royal Ontario Museum of Archaeology wanted poles for his new building in 1922, he contacted Newcombe. This meant another trip to the Charlottes in September 1923, where the septuagenarian collector made an extensive survey to enable him to know with certainty the condition of the remaining poles. There were, he reported, "*Very* few left," with Skidegate and Masset each having only a single "decayed monument." At other villages, even comparatively new poles had fallen, amongst them one put up after Dawson's 1878 photographs and the highest stick he had ever seen. Several others, perfectly sound when he had seen them a decade before, "are now rotten at the base though in good condition above." There was a finely finished specimen in Tanu, "good everywhere right down to the ground." This he thought he could buy, but it might require another trip.[55]

Using Henry Moody and the local missionary as intermediaries, he bought Matthew Williams's pole for $150, though getting it to the boat cost another $86. He charged Currelly a round $500, enough to cover his own expenses and services. The pole arrived in Toronto in early 1924 and, after display at that summer's Canadian National Exposition, was installed in a staircase of the museum.

The second pole was offered to Cambridge's Sir William Ridgeway to replace Nutka Jack's frog telegraph pole and a substitute for the Haida pole which war had diverted to Milwaukee. Gleisher, the donor of the fraudulent frog, was anxious to make up for the Stadthagen trick. When offered a choice of a Haida pole or a Kwakiutl housepost, the Cambridge mathematician, now "an old man and anxious to settle the matter," had to admit he could not distinguish between them. He wanted a full-length pole and, since the Kwakiutl post also seemed good, he decided on both.[56] Currelly also wanted a second Haida pole. It was by now too late in the 1924 season to visit the Charlottes, but Newcombe decided on an autumn trip to the Kwakiutl where he could negotiate for posts he had seen with Goddard. In October he went north. At Alert Bay he caught a chill and that turned to pleurisy. No steamer was due for three days. He died on October 19 of pneumonia aggravated by a long-standing weakness of the heart. He was seventy-three.

Ridgeway and his Cambridge colleagues were mortified at the news, their regret "the more profound because they fear that he contracted his fatal illness while journeying north on their behalf." F. A. Potts, a Trinity Hall zoologist who had cruised the coast with Newcombe in 1911, wrote a generous notice for *Nature* and Goddard did the same for *American Anthropologist*. The unfilled orders fell to Willie Newcombe. Fortunately, Henry Moody was able to buy Tanu poles from Paul Jones and James Jones and these were shipped to Cambridge and Toronto in 1925. Learning that his father had been in touch with Mrs. E. C. Hart, the wife of the city coroner, who had two Kwakiutl houseposts at their home near Victoria, Willie offered her $150 for the pair. They were almost identical Grizzly Bear posts originally from Owikeno village on Rivers Inlet. One went to Toronto, the other to Cambridge. Willie charged $125 for each of the posts, $600 apiece for the Haida poles, which gave him a good margin for his trouble.[57]

Newcombe's years of service to the Field Museum refined his collecting techniques. Although he enlarged his experience by working among the Alaska Haida, the Chilkat Tlingit, and by excursions into the interior of British Columbia and Washington State, the Coast Salish, the Kwakiutl, and the Charlottes Haida had been confirmed as his most familiar territory. The Queen Charlotte Islands were his first and greatest love.

Newcombe's collecting was successful because he had help. Even his usual beat, the Inside Passage and the Charlottes, was far too extensive for any one man to cover. There were a number of white people upon whom he could call for aid in concluding sales over the winter, for ferreting out desirable pieces, or for securing additional information on specimens already collected. Missionaries, such as Rev. P. Charles and W. Stone at Clayoquot, were of assistance. Storekeepers at Smith Inlet, Nootka, and elsewhere were willing to aid Newcombe in specific tasks for reasonable compensation. Fillip Jacobsen was a valuable collaborator. The city dealers were always useful. Newcombe willingly bought exceptional pieces from them, usually after some bargaining. He customarily showed Dorsey and other visiting museum people around the Indian traders. Mrs. Frohman in Portland, Rhodes & Co. in Seattle, and Grace Nicholson in Pasadena, traders who were especially interested in baskets — very much the rage at this time — and their local agents were more rivals than sources of Newcombe's supply.

While missionaries and traders were an important adjunct of Newcombe's collecting network, he relied much more on natives and half-bloods. Charlie Nowell was invaluable, helping Newcombe almost constantly in the Alert Bay and Knights Inlet areas. John Humphreys assisted in a similar, if less constant, way among the Vancouver Island Salish. Henry Edenshaw of Masset was helpful, both as a literate informant and by sending Newcombe "the oldest carved box I ever remembered being seeing here."[58] The Atlieus and the Turners in Clayoquot supplied Nootka pieces, including some commissioned new ones, after their return from St. Louis and Chicago.

Newcombe seems to have enjoyed easy and friendly relationships with the Indians with whom he traded. He shared some of the Euro-American assessments of Indians, judgments probably largely correct from that point of view. Natives did have different values and attitudes regarding time, cleanliness, and even honesty. Such attitudes need not interfere with friendly relationships. Travel on the coast required a measure of intimacy and an occasional night as a guest in their homes. Since both he and his native suppliers were serious traders and Newcombe was always a niggardly buyer, some friction inevitably arose over prices, but this seems seldom to have become anything more than the normal passing irritations of commerce. On Newcombe's part, aside from the Chemainus incident, he "never made note in his diaries or in letters to Dorsey of any unpleasant incidents, overt anger or dislike between himself and natives." A Skidegate Haida once told James R. Bell that Newcombe could tell him more about the uses of some stone implements dug up near Charlotte City than could any Indian because "Dr. Newcombe, an Indian, long time ago." The native thought of Newcombe as a reincarnated native who would, when he again died, become "maybe a bear, an Eagle or a big Salmon or maybe your spirit go into an Indian again."[59]

Newcombe was a middleman, an intermediary between the demand of the museums and the supply of his region. Except for the sale of his collection to Ottawa, he operated almost always as a commissioned collector, carrying out the assignments given him by a dozen museums. He worked very much in the manner of a natural history field collector. He wrote little. His job was getting what the laboratory men might use.

Newcombe's friend George Emmons worked differently. His preferred method was not the commission, but the completed collection offered to a museum. "The expending of funds for others is by no means an agreeable occupation," he wrote in declining an advance from the U. S. National Museum.[60] He liked his independence.

Like George Heye, Emmons was a compulsive collector without scientific background. Heye's millions allowed him to be a repository, an *omnium gatherum* capable of forming the biggest collection of its kind. Emmons was equally compulsive, but had to pass his material on to museums, acting as a middleman, as an entrepreneurial dealer, who nevertheles returned to his collections again and again. Both knew their material and relished it. Emmons hated to part with many of his pieces, items which "express much more to me than any one else, as they carry me back to the Tlingit as he was when I first knew him and as he will never be again." Aware that the pickings were becoming steadily thinner, he remarked as early as 1903 that his days of general collecting were past, but "when in Indian country it would be impossible to help picking up things." As he told Newcombe, "the spirit of collecting is born in us, we are not free agents." In 1943, after sixty years in pursuit of artifacts, he wrote Heye that he was ready to let all his pieces go. "At 91 it is time to get through." He was done collecting, he said; the natives were all working at six to eight dollars a day and were holding on to any old things. Yet the bug still gripped him; even now he knew of an old HBC factor's family up north who had two fine chests.[61]

Emmons remained a freelancer all his life, engaged in collecting for the love of it but financing his vocational hobby by sales. He often wrote of selling "at cost" but he probably fooled no one. On one occasion he wrote honestly of "my personal interest," but even then noted that "my Alaska work has been wholly at my own expense and it is only by disposing of my collections that I am enabled to give the Museum my writings" — his scholarly effort which never brought forth the promised monograph but did elicit a number of smaller studies for American Museum and Museum of the American Indian publications. Dorsey, who proclaimed Emmons to be "the champeen dealer," thought "he should be a millionaire by this time." Emmons, who lost much of his capital to imprudent speculation, probably made only a decent living beyond expenses. "When one takes into consideration all the labor of a collection in travel, getting together the material, learning its use, cleaning, classifying, storing and packing, not to mention the care and expense, there is little margin when finally disposed of," he complained to Newcombe. "I think the study alone keeps us going."[62] Like a philatelist turned dealer or a bibliophile tending a bookshop, Emmons was engaged in a lifetime labor of love, one at which he turned a coin, but only a modest one.

Befitting a middleman, Emmons was close-mouthed about his sources. "I like to do my work quietly," he told Newcombe, and his letters are usually uninformative about exact provenance. His catalogues are more specific, without being necessarily more informative, and may even be sometimes spurious. While there is no reason to doubt that a certain basket had been "in the possession of a very old 'Tuck-clae-way tee' woman of the Chilkat tribe living in Kluckwan," there is also no way to confirm it.[63] Provenance made a piece more saleable and there was every motive for providing one.

Certainly a great deal of his material was collected personally and directly from the natives. In his early years he collected almost exclusively in Alaska, but later extended his range into British Columbia, making sweeps of the interior Tahltan and up the Nass and Skeena valleys. He claimed in 1910 to have been in Alaska or British Columbia every year, save two, since 1882 but his collections, especially after about 1925, came increasingly from non-natives. His correspondence is sprinkled with references to factors of the Alaska Commercial Company, to "a man in my employ in Alaska," to old Indian agents, to daughters of Alaska pioneers, to a friend whose father was in Alaska thirty-odd years before, almost always unnamed. He offered the Field Museum a stone mirror from Kispiox, one he had known of for fifteen years but only now available through a friend in the country who had kept an eye on it for him. Marius Barbeau, who was beaten to a war club and a splendid flying-frog headdress, wrote, with wonder and disappointment, that Emmons "has agents everywhere, even here on the Nass, and he corresponds with people.[64]

After 1899 Emmons used Newcombe as an agent and depot for British Columbia collections: at various times Newcombe was storing parcels for Emmons from Rev. Collison of Kincolith, Joshua Henry from the Upper Skeena, and from almost all the Johnson Street curio dealers.[65] His deserved reputation as the greatest coastal collector rested in part upon his wide network of sources, both native and white. As Governor Brady noted in 1903, "he makes it his business to buy and is always on the lookout." Like Newcombe, he seemed to have had a way with Indians, especially Tlingit, who Brady wrote, "esteem him very much."[66]

As with Newcombe, Emmons's transactions continued beyond his passing. After his wife's death, he settled in Victoria, first at the Angela Hotel, then at the Willingdon Apartments. He sold several collections to the Royal Ontario Museum in the 1930s and at his 1945 death, at age ninety-three, he had a last collection awaiting purchase in Toronto. Years later the National Museum of Canada bought the A. C. Bossom collection, formed by an Anglo-American architect largely through Emmons.

Chapter Nine

Successful Collecting in Thin Country

THE GREAT HARVESTS of the museum scramble, the ravages of fire, climate, and pests, the breakdown of traditional societies and usages, meant an inevitable decline of supply. In many areas the trade in artifacts had been so intense that it had burned itself out by the turn of the century. Collecting was becoming more often gleaning than harvesting.

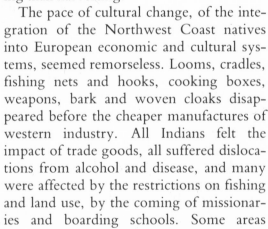

The pace of cultural change, of the integration of the Northwest Coast natives into European economic and cultural systems, seemed remorseless. Looms, cradles, fishing nets and hooks, cooking boxes, weapons, bark and woven cloaks disappeared before the cheaper manufactures of western industry. All Indians felt the impact of trade goods, all suffered dislocations from alcohol and disease, and many were affected by the restrictions on fishing and land use, by the coming of missionaries and boarding schools. Some areas remained remote from the settlement frontier and only slightly affected by land questions, by the government agents who seldom reached their villages, or by missionaries from whom they took their advantages without entering into any wholehearted conversion. While the Songhees in the vicinity of Victoria, the Klallam at Port Townsend, and the Halkomelem of the Fraser River valley were early and extensively affected by white settlement, other areas like the west coast of Vancouver Island or the Nass and Chilkat valleys were much later and more slowly affected.

The reactions of the groups to the new technology, labor market, and belief system were equally uneven. Some adapted to an entrepreneurial or industrial wage system quickly and easily; some embraced the new religion and morality with undisguised conviction. Others clung with remarkable tenacity to selected aspects of their indigenous culture and mode of life, continuing to practice the customs of their tradition and to create the ceremonial items required by it. In such places, remote from transportation, settlement, commerce, and industry, significant reservoirs and pockets of valuable ethnological material remained, often secreted away in chests and hiding places unknown to the most knowledgeable collectors or even to village neighbors.

Large clusters of poles and other monumental sculpture remained uncollected among the Haida and among the Nishga and Gitksan Tsimshian, while the Kwakiutl still retained a large number, which, despite rapid decay from a coastal climate were valuable museum commodities.

Scarcity had been a refrain of the field collector almost from the beginning. As early as 1868 E. G. Fast was claiming that the carving art was "quite lost among the natives." The collector peddling his services, or, like Fast, his completed collection, had a vested interest in premature pronouncements of the end of useful collecting. George Gibbs, who knew Alaska far better than Fast, was not fooled: he advised the purchase of Fast's collection merely because "it would cost more money to duplicate it." Heber Bishop, probably following Emmons's lead, insisted that a collection equal to Emmons's 1888 one would "be impossible" to obtain. A decade later Emmons himself claimed that "the material for collections is not to be had": "I have already gleaned the country and no further collections will ever be made by anyone." The same incantation was made by the same collector fifteen years later. His Seattle collection was now the only one "that ever can be made, as no more material is available." While iteration must be discounted for self-interest, it was becoming believable. Newcombe was finding specimens "remarkably scarce" and noted that prices had "gone up with a bound" in 1908.[1]

By 1911 Landsberg and Stadthagen had left the curio business chiefly because of the increased difficulty of supply. Aaronson was holding tight to what things he had in anticipation of yet another rise in value. Emmons became increasingly dependent upon old collections made by pioneers, early traders, and Victoria and Seattle dealers. Now it was only from such sources, he said, that "fine old specimens come into the market." Newcombe knew of nothing, except poles, that could still be found among the Haida, and Emmons was convinced that, after expeditions by C. F. and Willie Newcombe and two of his own, "no further collections will ever be made on the Skeena."[2]

Despite the increased difficulty of finding material, it surfaced under the right circumstances. When Culin visited Victoria in 1908 he searched the Hesquit encampment on the Songhees Reserve for baskets, but found only small trinket baskets and these were disfigured, in his eyes, by the use of European dyes. There was not a single basket he would put into the Brooklyn collection or even use as a personal gift. Newcombe was able to commission one woman to make a chief's whaling hat. Basketry and fishing, Culin concluded, were the only material emblems that remained of traditional Nootka culture. Nevertheless, he found among these Nootka people three sea otter bows, cedar bark mats, a wooden cradle, and a carved adze to take home to his museum. When he showed an interest in games among the Songhees, bone buzzers, wood tops, bone die, and lances and their cedar bark targets quickly came his way.[3]

This tendency, for old things to appear in places where they should be absent, surprised even knowledgeable old hands like Newcombe. In 1911 he found material, such as spoons, spruce root lines, carved halibut hooks, and stone mortars, at Masset and Skidegate that far surpassed his expectations. So much material, especially ceremonial paraphernalia, was hidden away that the outward appearance of people and their village could deceive even permanent white residents. Dr. R. W. Large, a medical missionary among the Bella Bella, noted that "when the people found I was going home [to Toronto] for a visit they brought out everything pretty much they had. I did not think there was so much in town, & some of the specimens are very good ones."[4]

Many Indians "retired" pieces which had become ceremonially devalued. "When the Tlingit realized that the method which the people had employed in building up one[']s social standing was overthrown by modern ideas," Louis Shotridge wrote, "each man quietly placed the object . . . in the bottom of the family chest with a vague hope of its recovery of the honor which it represent[s]".[5] The proper approach, a new heir, or some other factor might bring out such material to the advantage of the collector. The 1915 experience of Samuel A. Barrett is an example of the collector being in the right place at the right time.

Barrett was part of the new generation of museum curators who possessed university training in anthropology and museum practices. A. L. Kroeber's first Ph.D. at the University of California, Barrett worked initially for Heye's museum, doing fieldwork in Ecuador, then became the first anthropological curator at the Milwaukee Public Museum in 1909. The Wisconsin museum had been very active in natural history and had pioneered new techniques of presenting environmental animal groups under the hand of taxidermist Carl Akeley. Barrett adopted the environmental life-group concept at Milwaukee, using background dioramas and attempting to provide a group for each basic American cultural area. When shortage of space imposed restraints, he introduced miniature dioramas. After installing his first group, a scene of the Menomini with their rice crop, he turned his attention to the Northwest Coast. The museum possessed only a small amount of coastal material so he determined to go and collect himself. He wrote Edward Sapir, the head of the anthropology division of Ottawa's Victoria Memorial Museum, who had been recently working on the west coast of Vancouver Island, asking for advice on "where I can obtain the best and most complete series of specimens which will show the most typical conditions of life among the people of the northwest coast." Sapir, his experience limited to the Nootka, thought the Kwakiutl at Fort Rupert and Alert Bay might be the best place, but suggested that Barrett write Newcombe.[6]

Barrett went to British Columbia in the summer of 1914 but it was only a brief reconnaissance. He called on Newcombe and visited Landsberg, now in real estate but still selling from his cellar stocks, and bought from him over $300 worth of material, including a model of Chief Skidegate's house (apparently another of those commissioned by Deans for the Chicago fair) and two

coppers. He came back in January 1915. After another large purchase from Landsberg's inventory, he settled into a rented house
at the east end of Fort Rupert, only recently vacated by Edward
Curtis who had lived there while filming his "In the Land of the
Head-Hunters."[7]

Barrett hired Hunt, whose most recent work had been as a
stage director and costumes supplier for Curtis, to assist him. To
Barrett's astonishment, the collecting was so rapid and successful
that he had to send home for more money. He collected "everything that I could get my hands on," from twenty-eight shells
used in puberty rites and thirty-three cooking stones at 25 cents
and 50 cents each, to a great ceremonial screen from Smith Inlet.
With a motor launch he went to the surrounding villages and to
the mainland, extending his range as far as Bella Coola. In all, his
collections amounted to 1,010 catalogued items, some 3,351
pounds in 78 cases, at a cost of $2,152.85 and about eight weeks'
time. It was "a real killing," especially in masks, 71 of them, and
other ceremonial items. He had anticipated difficulty in buying
such material, but most of it just "walked in." "I was visited one
day by an Indian who rather timidly inquired if I would be interested in a certain mask. . . . I told him I was interested in it and
asked him to bring it in, and after we had negotiated the sale of
that, I asked him if he had any more masks or if he knew of
anyone else who had." The man not only had more, but Barrett
learned through him of many others. It was "a pretty fine lot
considering the way this whole country has been picked over."[8]

On a small budget and in a relatively small space of time,
Barrett made what he quite justly considered to be "one of the
best Northwest Coast collections that is to be found." Others
were certainly larger and possessed finer specimens, "but by-and-
large, as a complete collection of the culture, I think you will find
ours as good a collection as you find anywhere."[9]

Barrett attributed his success to having arrived in Kwakiutl
country at the time of religious upheaval, when the Pentecostals
were successful in evangelizing some of the nominally Anglican
natives. "Some new-fangled religion comes in," he said, "and
they take that up and are ready to get rid of their old things."[10]

Such religious upheaval could still be a factor in the attitude of
natives toward their ceremonial material. Sometimes it could be
devastating: a 1918 revival on the Nass led to the destruction of a
large number of poles. "The people at one time had a fit," an

Indian later said, "and chopped down the totem poles. . . . They later burnt them up." Some were torched, others sawed into pieces to be used as house foundation blocks.[11]

While Barrett attributed his unusual success to Christian revivalism, the government's efforts to eradicate the potlatch was probably a strong contributing factor. "There is a jinks on here just now," he wrote from Fort Rupert; two constables were reportedly "ready to step in at any time." Only a year before, the Kwawkewlth agent, William M. Halliday, had arrested two Nimkish for violations of the clause in the Indian Act that forbade potlatching. This successful prosecution, the first of its kind, led Newcombe to conclude that "the potlatch has been stopped and the Indians are more willing to sell."[12] This, as much as the Pentecostal's "new-fangled religion," may have allowed Barrett's remarkable "killing" a few months after the arrests. The government's long anti-potlatch campaign culminated six years later in the Kwakiutl surrender to Halliday of a great quantity of ceremonial paraphernalia that enriched the collections of three museums.

The potlatch, the seemingly profligate, even ruinous, gift-giving ceremony, had been banned by Canadian law since 1885, but enforcement had been thwarted by the courts' unwillingness to accept the vagueness of the statute, by the lack of government agents, constables, and magistrates over the widespread and mobile communities of the coast, and by the tolerant, let-live attitudes of most officials. The primary proponents of the ban were missionaries and others bent on acculturating and reforming the natives. Opponents were a few anthropologists and sympathizers, those traders in native communities who profited from the large-scale sale of trade goods used by potlatchers, and the large majority of the Indians themselves. The long truce in active enforcement was broken by Halliday's 1913 prosecutions.[13]

Those Indians of British Columbia for whom potlatch ceremonies were still meaningful, vainly protested against the threat to their institutions and social system; a number of anthropologists, led by Edward Sapir of the Victoria Memorial Museum in Ottawa, signed a circular letter with an equal lack of effect. Nevertheless, despite the conviction of two more Kwakiutl, whose sentences were suspended, things were quiet through World War I. As one Kwakiutl told Newcombe, "Mr. Halliday told us during the war, not to enjoy ourselves while the war was on. We all agree to do as he told us. And had no Potlatch as long as the war was on. And when the war was through we started again. During this time he went in to a feast and told us that the law is enforced." The Department of Indian Affairs got tough just at the war's end, ordering its agents fully to exercise their judicial powers against the potlatch.[14]

There were prosecutions in the Kwawkewlth agency in each of the next five years. One of those convicted was Charlie Nowell, sentenced to three months for paying people to come to his brother's funeral. So concerned were the Indians by the crackdown that they sent a delegation of three, including Nowell, to Ottawa in early 1919. There "they got a rather cool reception" from Duncan Campbell Scott, the stern permanent head of the Indian Affairs Department and, in his private life, a sensitive, if slightly old-fashioned, poet.[15]

In one of the 1919 cases, the four accused, as well as seventy-five other men present at court, agreed at counsel's suggestion that they would potlatch no more. In return the four were given suspended sentences by Halliday who, in his role as magistrate under the Indian Act, doubled as judge. The saw-off had an important bearing upon the potlatch cases to follow.

With a dozen convictions, Halliday was certain that things were now under control. In late 1921, however, there were several more potlatches, one of which brought five more convictions. Then at Christmas he heard of "the biggest potlatch that has ever occurred in the agency." This was Dan Cranmer's potlatch, the greatest ever recorded on the central coast. Held at Village Island, it lasted six days and involved the giving away of thousands of dollars worth of gas boats, pool tables, sewing machines, gramophones, blankets, flour, and cash in repayment for his wedding.[16]

Halliday and the local Mounted Police sergeant hit hard at this flagrant infraction of the law. Twenty-nine natives, some of them from as far north as Blunden Harbour, were charged with violations on information obtained from two native informants who had been at the Cranmer potlatch. Halliday was intent upon "killing" the potlatch; yet he was a prudent and paternal civil servant. He did not want to be left "with a very small agency to look after" where there would be "a big burden of expenses" in caring for the families of imprisoned men. Another bargain was struck. The defense counsel, after entering a guilty plea, asked for sus-

The surrendered Kwakiutl artifacts on exhibit in Alert Bay. British Columbia Provincial Museum.

pended sentences on the strength of an agreement, similar to that of 1919, that the Indians would give up their potlatching. The RCMP constable objected: the previous agreement, he said, had not been honored by the Indians; indeed, some of the Cranmer defendants had signed that agreement. He demanded tangible evidence of good faith. "I suggested," he wrote, "that the only evidence that I could see that they could give was that the whole Kwawkewlth Agency make a voluntary surrender of all 'Potlach'[sic] coppers, masks, head dresses, Potlach blankets and boxes and all other parpfanalia [sic] used solely for Potlach purposes." The court — on this occasion A. M. Wastell, J. P., joining Halliday as presiding magistrate — accepted the proposal.[17]

The Lekwiltok of Cape Mudge, the Mamalillikulla of Village Island, and the Nimkish of Alert Bay came almost entirely into the agreement. "I guess it was like paying a fine so that they would not go to prison," said Agnes Alfred: "They paid with their masks."[18] The Turnour Island and Fort Rupert people resisted. This brought a series of arrests, convictions, and detentions, including that of several women, at least one of whom was a grandmother.

The surrendered potlatch paraphernalia from those accepting the agreement was gathered in Halliday's woodshed, then moved to the parish hall where, "to pay for the use of the hall," it was put on exhibition. Halliday estimated the surrendered material at 300 cubic feet and his report lists over 450 items, including 20 coppers, scores of Hamatsa whistles, and dozens of masks. It was an impressive inventory of some of the material which remained or had been renewed in one of the most picked-over areas of the coast. "It will be a very valuable and very rare collection," Halliday wrote, "and should command good prices for museum purposes."[19]

Halliday was directed to ship the material to Sapir at the National Museum in Ottawa for evaluation, but a lack of time and the summer shortage of labor delayed its crating for several months. In the meantime, who should appear on the scene but George Heye, the peripatetic founder of the Museum of the American Indian, on one of his occasional field forays to the coast. He collected in Campbell River and Cape Mudge on his way to Alert Bay, where he naturally asked to see the surrendered potlatch material. Halliday, curious about "finding out the value of the exhibit from a museum collector's point of view," showed Heye the collection. Heye, of course, wanted to buy "a considerable amount of the stuff" and the agent, feeling that Heye's prices were "exceptionally good," sold him thirty-five pieces totalling $291. Halliday viewed his action as consistent with the object of securing as much money as possible for the Indians. "I am absolutely certain that no one but a very enthusiastic collector would have given as much for any of the articles as I obtained from Mr. Heye." He was undoubtedly right. The prices were good and he probably took pleasure in having mulcted the New Yorker. On the other hand, Heye may have used his boardroom wiles to talk Halliday into something which the agent realized "somewhat exceeded the instructions given me." Indian Affairs was angered at the sale. It found itself "at a loss" to understand his "unwarranted action," "more especially in view of the fact that they are to be taken to the United States, when they should have remained in our Canadian museum." Ottawa regarded "good value" an insufficient justification, but, feeling that "the articles are now beyond recall," let the matter drop.[20]

Halliday shipped the remaining potlatch material in seventeen cases to Ottawa where Sapir made an appraisal, arriving at a total value, without the coppers, of $1,456. This was "a very moderate figure from the standpoint of an ethnological museum," he wrote, and "more reasonable" than the prices paid by Heye.[21]

Checks were sent to Halliday in April to be given to the former owners. Some Kwakiutl remember no compensation. "I never got one cent from the money they claimed to have payed for them," said Henry Bell, who also insisted that he had packed six masks to Halliday's boat, though only three were recorded on the inventories. There can be no question that the checks were issued and sent, since the matter was made the point of an inquiry by the auditor general. How the agent distributed them is another question. Perhaps they were placed with local storekeepers and credited to their recipients; checks were not a frequent medium of exchange on the central coast. Halliday did record that the Indians considered the compensation "entirely inadequate."[22]

Certainly Sapir did not err on the high side. His evaluation of masks ranged from two to ten dollars while Heye had paid up to twenty-five dollars for his; Sapir allowed one dollar for whistles which must have been similar to those for which Heye had paid two. Of course, Heye had had first choice, but he may, as Halliday believed, have spent quite generously. Without an intensive comparative investigation of pieces and lists, it is impossible to make any firm judgment.

The coppers were another matter. Although they had a substantial museum value, no compensation was ever paid. Some had become invested by purchase and repurchase with an enormous value, but these were "artificial" values appreciated only within the social and ceremonial system that prized them. Two years earlier, in petitioning the department to be allowed "to go on in our old way," a committee of Nimkish had expressed special concern with the losses that would come to the owners of coppers and to their families if the potlatch system were abolished. Even Halliday recognized the "great sacrifice" made by the owners who surrendered their coppers. His argument, that they "must look at it in the same light as any person who had made a foolish or unsound investment," was unlikely to have made an impression. When, at Sapir's request, George Hunt investigated the history and value of the surrendered coppers, it turned out that a number were "worthless," though nominally valued at $100 each. Others, however, were valued at up to 18,250 blankets. At Kingcombe, Hunt heard that Bob Robertson, the owner of the Loch copper, had been telling people that he had given a false Loch to the police. "I believe he did this the way he acted."[23]

The bulk of the collection was kept by the National Musem in Ottawa with a portion, about one hundred pieces, donated to the

Royal Ontario Museum in Toronto. Eleven items were retained by Indian Affairs and displayed in Scott's office; all but two of these were sent to the National Museum in 1932. Over the years the National Museum exchanged a number of items, including a mask and sculpture which went to Emmons in 1928, but the collection remained fairly intact. In the 1960s talks aimed at a return of the potlatch material were opened with natives of Alert Bay and Cape Mudge. After prolonged negotiations the museum agreed to return the material to suitable museums established in the two communities. The transfers, a first of their kind, were made in 1979 and 1980. The Museum of the American Indian and the Royal Ontario Museum material was not affected.

The charges and convictions, the surrenders and the imprisonments, were a severe blow even to so resilient a culture as that of the Kwakiutl. The stripping away of four hundred-odd ceremonial items from the Lekwiltok, Mamalillikulla, the Nimkish, and others, affected nearly half of the Southern Kwakiutl and the enforcement of the law doubtless made others more prepared to sell what they had. Those who surrendered their pieces did not necessarily part with all they owned: there were no house-to-house searches and Bob Robertson may not have been the only Kwakiutl who cut a corner. But the forced cessation of the public potlatch, the feasts, and the dances was a more severe blow.

The potlatch continued but in different and underground forms that robbed it of some salient features. Much of the remaining ceremonial material must have gone similarly underground for there seems to have been little collecting among the Kwakiutl in the remainder of the 1920s, and in the next decade no museums had acquisition funds. Some of what remained or what was made as replacement may have been drained off piece-by-piece by casual collectors; a good deal was secured by the University of British Columbia museum in the 1950s through its relationship with Kwakiutl Mungo Martin.

Barrett's Kwakiutl collecting and the potlatch law surrenders occurred in one of the most often harvested regions. Collectors in the post-war period of relative scarcity and depletion looked elsewhere, among groups more remote from European commerce or whose relative isolation was only recently disturbed. One very successful collector was Louis Shotridge, working on the Chilkat, where, as Emmons once wrote, "there are still some fine old things to be had" because it was "off the beaten track."[24]

Louis Situwuka Shotridge first entered museum records in 1905 when he sold a small Tlingit collection to the University of Pennsylvania Museum. George B. Gordon, who had replaced Culin as curator at Philadelphia, met Shotridge through the ubiquitous George Heye at Portland's Lewis and Clark Exposition. The nineteen-year-old Shotridge[25] and his wife Florence had been brought to the exposition by Governor James Brady, who had met them at the Haines mission and thought it a good idea to have Florence demonstrate the weaving of a Chilkat blanket. Louis could demonstrate Tlingit dyes and exhibit masks showing face painting. Gordon, like Brady, was impressed with the couple, bought their collection, and floated the idea that the young man, scion of a high-ranking Klukwan family, make further collections for the museum in Alaska and then come to Philadelphia "to tell the history and meaning of the different things."[26]

Gordon was only beginning to take charge at University Museum, but his 1905 expedition to Alaska, made on the same western trip that he met the Shotridges, deepened his sense of the urgency of collecting ethnological information and specimens. The opportunity of using a high-born Chilkat, the heir of several generations of Klukwan chiefs (his grandfather had hosted the Krauses in 1882), fitted well into this purpose. Shotridge was, it must have seemed to Gordon, a perfect apprentice for training as a native collector. He could work from inside the culture, record myths and traditions in Tlingit as well as in English, and he seemed reliable and was certainly literate. Emmons, who had known both his father and grandfather, had a somewhat different opinion. Louis was a "nice boy," but Emmons put down his knowledge of the Tlingit past as "not altogether certain" since his sister had married a white man and he had lived with the whites at Haines more than with his own people. He spoke the language, however, and had an inherited position within Klukwan, his birthplace and the single richest remaining repository of Tlingit material.[27]

The 1907 collection that Shotridge sent from Alaska to Gordon was disappointing. There was too much new material and Gordon sent back all but ten items. The rejects were "very nice pieces, but I got from you in Portland all the new things I want." Though Gordon did not ask for another collection, he kept in touch with the young Tlingit couple, visiting them in 1907 in Los Angeles where they were working at Antonio Apache's Indian Crafts Exhibition. Then, in 1911, after Louis had toured the country with an Indian opera company (he had a fine tenor voice), Gordon hired him for the museum staff.[28] By then the museum had a sizable Northwest Coast collection, not only the material which Culin had collected through Dorsey, Newcombe, and Landsberg, but, more especially, George Heye's growing collection, much of it then exhibited and stored at the Philadelphia museum where Gordon fully expected it to stay.

Shotridge settled in West Philadelphia, began courses at the university's Wharton School of Finance and Commerce, announced his intention to try out for the freshman football team, and worked as a general assistant at the museum, initially at a modest fifty dollars a month, but soon double that. He helped in arranging the Northwest Coast exhibit, creating for it a model of his home village, a display that remained on exhibit for years.[29] This was a period of museum apprenticeship for Shotridge and, to complete his training, Gordon sent him to Columbia where he studied Tlingit phonetics with Boas and sat in on general ethnology lectures. By May 1915 Gordon considered him ready. The twenty-nine-year-old Tlingit, accompanied by Florence, was sent to Alaska where he was "to visit the different villages of his own people and to record in their own language their myths and religious beliefs and to make translations of the same in English." John Wanamaker, the Philadelphia department store magnate and member of the museum's board of managers, provided funds for the expedition.[30]

From 1915 to 1932 Shotridge was in the field most of the time, a period far exceeding that of any other museum staff collector. He based himself at Haines and Sitka, but in 1918 he collected on the Nass and Skeena rivers. For the 1922–27 Wanamaker Expedition, he purchased a small motorized fishing boat, christened the *Penn,* from which he operated along the coast. While he collected smaller artifacts such as baskets, spoons, and pendants, Shotridge was, especially after 1922, most intent upon sending back major items which other collectors had been unable to buy. His shipments were small, but the average price very high. At Klukwan in 1917 he paid $500 for three "Drum House" helmets bearing killer-whale, sea-grizzly bear, and murrelet crests.[31]

Louis Shotridge displaying some of his collected treasures. University of Pennsylvania Archives.

His 1918 shipments contained only seventy-eight pieces, but they had cost him $1,364 or an average of almost $18 each. There were spoons as low as ten cents, but the Sea-Lion House and the Eagle's Nest House collections from Sitka totalled $400 for just ten items — carved helmets and headdresses, a Chilkat border blanket, rattles, a baton, and a cannibal dance whistle. The "Land

Otter Man" canoe prow cost $100 and another carved headdress
$60. "The kinds of things we are after at this moment," he wrote
at the beginning of his 1922 fieldwork, "are those which could not
be bought with cash some years ago." He was particularly after —
and often able to get — crest hats and helmets, prominent, almost
special, and cherished features, of Tlingit culture.[32]

Such collecting, aimed at securing the most impressive prestige
items of a native culture rather than at a systematic collection of
both household and ceremonial objects, was a difficult and different kind of collecting. Gordon and his protégé were after treasures
and that could best be accomplished by the patient wheedling of
an insider, by a native of rank. Tlingit culture, even that at
Klukwan, had undergone great changes, but its most deeply held
aspects remained impervious to erosion.

Certainly Shotridge knew, after some time in the field, where
most of the important things were, but he also realized that "my
only obstacle is the everlasting esteem of the native owners for
them." He had already on his first trip experienced great difficulty
with this refusal of the natives to part with meaningful pieces.
Even when he was able to bring about a sale, he encountered the
old collectors' incubus of communal claims. He explained to Gordon some of the problems: if "other members of the house groups
that own them should learn of the proceedings with regard to
their sales, there would be always red-tape to choke the only
oppertunity [sic]."

Once he secured possession, things were easier: complaints
arising after a sale "almost always can be pacified." His purchase
of the Klukwan helmets required a great deal of peacemaking.

> I still hardly know how I ever arrived in peace. Taking these out of
> the Drum-house was something like joggling a hornet's nest,
> everybody then became the nearest kin to old Dàq-tánk for whom
> the bear helmet had been made in almost mythical time and
> searched for my shack to claim ownership on the wooden hats that
> some of them could not even identify.[33]

This kind of difficulty was often as much a case of envy and
avarice as a stubborn resistance to selling; clamor for a piece of the
action was the problem, not necessarily a high regard for the
object's traditional value. But there was, nevertheless, "the ever-

Interior of the Whale House at Klukwan, 1895. Winter & Pond, photographers. Alaska Historical Library.

lasting esteem of the native owners," and that obstacle was sometimes impossible to overcome. Patient ingratiation by a skilled and tactful insider of Shotridge's rank was indeed surely the best way, but Shotridge often failed, in large part because he was tactless.

Shotridge's chief object on the Wanamaker Expedition of 1922–27 was nothing less than the prized contents of the Whale House at Klukwan. The house itself was a relatively new structure, modern in form and two stories high. It had been constructed in 1901 and its dedication was the occasion for a great potlatch where an estimated $10,000 in property, food, and money had been distributed. It was, nevertheless, never quite finished and scarcely ever inhabited. The Whale House's treasures were actually from its predecessor, a traditional Tlingit dwelling of large size (about 50 by 53 feet) built around 1835 and "the most widely known and elaborately ornamented house, not only at Chilkat, but in Alaska." Its architectural prizes were four elaborately carved interior houseposts and the "Rain Wall," an interior screen partitioning off the chief's apartment. Standing 20 feet long and 9½ high, it had been decorated by a Tsimshian artist and, in Emmons's judgement, was "probably the finest example of native art in Alaska." These, along with the great 14-foot woodworm bowl and other crest and ceremonial objects, were stored in a cabin where they were sometimes shown to visitors for a small fee.[34]

The Whale House collection had long fascinated collectors, not least Emmons who had often sought to secure at least parts of it. Newcombe had tried to buy the four houseposts and the woodworm dish in 1902, but found not only that the quoted prices were high, but the claims so tangled or incompletely consummated that he abandoned negotiations. The prices asked then, $1,000 for the posts and carved screen and $100 for the ancient feast dish, seemed absurd to him. Emmons felt he could get the feast dish for less than what was asked of Newcombe, but he abandoned the quest when the dish turned out to be too rotten to transport. The posts and screen were, Emmons found, simply not for sale. "Another generation will have to go," he reported, before they will part with them. He succeeded only in getting a smaller and much less important house screen.[35]

Shotridge, too, had had his eye upon the Klukwan treasures for a long time. As early as 1906, soon after his first contact with Gordon, he assured the Philadelphia curator that he could get the Whale House's posts and partition, the worm dish, and many other things. He was young, naive, and cocky: "I can secure the very best of every thing there is, the real valueble [sic] ones they used to keep things that they never thought of selling before, and I am the only one to get them too, most of the totems are owned by father and some other things by my relatives, I have told them that I am going be [sic] collecting and we talked about them old things." He was still confident in 1911, telling Gordon and Heye much the same thing. Emmons, to whom Heye had passed on Shotridge's optimistic assessment, lectured Heye on the proprieties of the Chilkat. The Whale House and its posts were not part of Louis's customary patrimony, "for the Tlingit inherits through the Mother and this house was of his Fathers clan." Shotridge was, by virtue of his mother, a Kagwantan of the Eagle (or Wolf) division. That his father was born into the Ravan Ganaxtedi clan of the Whale House gave his son no inherited right to it. Even family pieces, Emmons warned, belonged also to his brothers and "could only be purchased through the consent of all and by payment to each one." Shotridge knew all this and by 1923, after his previous visits to the village, was well aware that it would not be easy to separate the Ganaxtedi from their Whale House. "The negotiation in this is by all means the most difficult in my experience, but to me it is well worth my last effort." With the great Klukwan pieces as his object, he ignored "for the time being" a number of other ceremonial things offered him — "an indifferent attitude" might serve to bring down their price — but, more importantly, "I want to handle the biggest thing first" and "I do not want small deals to interfere with my plans for going about the most important negotiation which I undertook from the start."[36]

Late in 1922 he called a meeting of the leading men of the Ganaxtedi, his father's clansmen. He tried to sell them on his idea "to allow these old things a last chance to make another good turn." He was, he said, "in a position to help them serve a double purpose, namely: the price which an important thing may bring will support a creation of something by which the whole community will be benefited" (he proposed that the purchase money be used for a memorial building). On the other hand, the old things "will stand as evidence for the Tlingit claim of a place in primitive culture." This was Shotridge's developed pitch. The significance of the old myths was about played out and the objects which represented them and acted as symbols of a past pride were increasingly meaningless. But that heritage should not be lost and the best means of its perpetuation was to entrust the posts and screens, the crests and staffs, to his museum. "It is in the interests of history that the relics which tell the tale of a vanishing people to be preserved," he wrote for European readers. "This the Museum is endeavouring to do while there is still time." Shotridge, as a museum man, embraced this collecting justification and, though he claimed to have convinced one man to part with a shaman's headdress because it "will do a good turn in the written record of his party," the efficacy of the argument was probably lost to most of his hearers.[37] Few responded to the appeal that the history of the Ganaxtedi or the Kagwantan could best be kept by a museum in Pennsylvania.

In his bid for the Whale House, Shotridge was up against that "everlasting esteem" of the Ganaxtedi for their traditional treasures. There were also a large number of local complications. While the Ganaxtedi, the most important group in Klukwan, owned the House, they had received into their clan by marriage a number of men who had descended from three other clans. Disputes of rank gave rise to such serious disturbances that the Ganaxtedi-Sinkukedi men set up a Raven House for themselves, though retaining kinship bonds as members of the Ganaxtedi clan. While Shotridge's father was alive, he had been recognized as the head of the Whale House, while Yeal-hawk occupied a similar position in the Raven House.[38] Then, with the elder Shotridge's death, Yeal-hawk assumed a headship position over both houses. As Shotridge explained to Gordon, the followers of his father recognized the other man "as their 'big-person,'" but he "was never authorized as a leader of the clan." Into "this heterogeneous state of tribal affairs," Shotridge sought to insert an uncle, Edward Shotridge, a younger brother of his father, who, "regardless of his unsettled life, is recognized as the right heir to the house and its original possessions." At the same time, however, he asserted his own prerogative to his father's rights under American law, giving him access to what he could not have under Tlingit matrilineal custom.[39]

Neither claim was accepted. By spring the affair had stirred the Chilkats into controversy and Shotridge's claims and aims commanded only minority support. "So I decided," he wrote Gordon in April, "to let the excitement quiet down a bit before my uncle and myself disturb more peace." His plan now was simply to take possession. The natives at Haines were against him, but he thought he had a Klukwan majority in his favor. Even that, however, had become irrelevant. "We have decided to ignore all community interest and proseed with our plan." The scheme went awry. Upon his arrival in Klukwan, he found his uncle had gone off to summer work. "I knew where he was employed, but since work and money are so scares around here I thought it best not to deprive him of the opportunity in making enough for the coming winter." Thus "the time of our troubles" was postponed.[40] Reading between the lines, one might postulate that Uncle Edward knew when to use his "unsettled ways" to stay clear of a situation he did not relish.

With the Whale House left to "rest" until spring 1924, Shotridge now went after the lesser prizes he had been ignoring. He bought a Hoona Grizzly Bear ceremonial hat, a Ganook hat, and other collections from Sitka. The asking prices were very high and it took patience to secure even a fraction of the valuable material, but the owner of the Ganook hat of the Sitka Kagwantan was willing to sell because the meaningfulness of its story of rivalry had become nothing more to him than "an unnecessary prejudiceness." He would not, however, give up other things of importance. Others were willing to sell, but often they held a claim only to custodianship.[41]

When spring came round again, he once more prepared to take the Whale House. He met his uncle in Juneau and they again decided "that in order to avoid immediate interference by our rival party" they would seize the houseposts and screen after the Fourth of July when most of the Indians would have left Klukwan. They still planned to take this collection regardless of all objections of the community. Even the white people of Haines were roused by the idea of their taking the old things away. He and his uncle were "only two men against the whole community"; "jealousy and greed seem to possess even those who are not directly connected with the Whale House family."[42] Once the Whale House treasures were shipped, it would be very difficult for his rivals to recover them.

When he returned to the Chilkat in the spring, Shotridge found that Uncle Edward had again gone fishing. No one seemed to know where. "I gathered that he had a bad time of it during my absence and had to leave. I do not blame him now for wanting to forget things during a brief get-away." Their plan had, he admitted, been risky: "our rival party more than once have made known to us that we take away the old things only over their dead bodies."[43]

Tensions in Klukwan and Haines had reached a point where community leaders intervened. Shotridge was made to realize that he was pushing too far. The rival party was helpless, he told Gordon, but

> there was nothing that would persuade it to let go the old things without force and blood-shed, — the old Ganah-taedi pride could not be easily put aside. Here was a splendid chance to show to my people also the Kaguan-taun quality, but unfortunately the peace party was too powerful, and then too I became aware that it was

because the white man's law was on my side that I had become the master of the affair, and I did not like it. So after the ceremony was over, in contrary to my uncle's wish, I decided to let the whole thing rest for the time being. . . . This was after all, the only way to maintain the friendship between my people and myself.

Shotridge, recorded an anthropologist a few years later, was "in the bad graces of nearly everyone because of his attempt to take something not his."[44]

Shotridge had failed in his chief mission, but he bought two other old Klukwan houseposts. When he arrived with a truck, however, there was such a disturbance among the townspeople "that it looked as if I were getting into the same kind of trouble which I experienced with the Klukwan Whale House Collection." As usual, others appeared who had a claim "of some sort"; "for the sake of peace" he postponed his acquisition.[45]

If the natives of Shotridge's own village kept him from the great treasure of the Whale House, he was successful in securing items only slightly less important. His acquisitions remained relatively few in number, but they were often major pieces of high symbolic, traditional, or aesthetic importance. The crest hats and staffs, the headdresses and shirts, were among the very best items ever available in Alaska. "He collected for you," Emmons wrote later to a Pennsylvania museum curator, "the most valuable and interesting helmets and ceremonial hats and headpieces that is or ever will be in any Museum." This was high tribute from someone like Emmons, someone who had long before put Shotridge down as "stupid naturally" and "a conceited half-educated specimen, neither Indian nor White."[46]

The ethics of Shotridge, and of Gordon, who knew exactly what his assistant was doing and how he was doing it, may be subjected to long debate. Shotridge's collecting expeditions have been seen as a plan by Gordon "to have Shotridge infiltrate his own culture to obtain its treasures." This is a harsh view but one that can be sustained by the evidence. "Most of these objects could have been secured by no one but a member of the tribe since they are prized almost beyond price," reported Gordon. It took considerable self-deception for Shotridge to convince himself that placing this material in a museum thousands of miles from Alaska would really be a tribute to tribal history, and his own feelings were not without ambiguity. In writing of securing the inimitable Kagwantan Shark Helmet, reputedly his clan's oldest possession, he confessed that "the modernized part of me rejoiced over my success in obtaining this important ethnological specimen for the Museum, but, as one who had been trained to be a true Kaguanton, in my heart I cannot help but have the feeling of a traitor who has betrayed confidence."[47]

His means of acquisition were hardly noble. He had paid a large sum, $350, for the unique helmet, made from walrus-hide shrunken over a wooden form into the likeness of a shark, and no one interfered when he took possession; "but if only one of the true warriers of that clan had been alive the removal of it would never have been possible. I took it in the presence of aged women, the only survivors in the house where the old object was kept, and they could do nothing more than weep when the once highly esteemed object was being taken away to its last resting place." In his own "House of Shotridge" (the Bear House), it was not "an easy thing" to take away the Grizzly Bear Coat and other things to which he claimed to be the only rightful heir. "I know that such act is going to hit every true member of the Kaguanton throughout the region. . . . My plan is to take the old pieces one at a-time."[48]

Shotridge's own life was filled with tragedy. He lost his wife Florence in 1917 and his second wife in an Arizona sanitarium in 1928. Customarily, he should have remarried within the clan of his dead wife, but there was no Katkaayih girl available. His second wife's mother got the notion that he would marry her, but instead he courted a married Kiksadi woman, financed her divorce, and married her, bringing upon himself the scorn of the Katkaayih and unfair slurs about the caste of his new wife. The depression-hit museum reduced his salary, then in 1932 dropped him entirely from its staff. He was left in Alaska with his third wife and four children to support. He had few savings and even these were impossible to withdraw from the bank. He had no experience in the usual native occupation of commercial fishing, though one summer he did join a fishing crew only to have it turn into a bad season.

In the winter of 1932–33 he was reduced to asking H. H. F. Jayne, Gordon's successor, for a loan. He tried to sell curios — leather and beadwork card cases, tobacco pouches, and moccasins

— through the museum, but with little success. In 1935 Jayne did help him to get a government fisheries inspector's job, a position which may only have increased his unpopularity among the Tlingit. A social anthropologist working in Alaska in 1933 and 1934 had found Shotridge almost universally unpopular because of his attempts to take the Whale House and "doubly criticized" for taking his wife from a clan other than her predecessor's. He had, moreover, received "hard words" for his unmannered immodesty in referring to his own rank.[49]

He died in August 1937, age fifty-one. Officially his death was accidental, the result of a fall from the roof of his Redoubt Bay smokehouse. His neck broken, he lay on the ground for days, alive but helpless and mosquito-bitten, before he was found and taken to the Alaska Pioneers' Home hospital. He died ten days later. The circumstances surrounding the fall are mysterious. "At Klukwan, some say he was killed for taking treasures. At Sitka, some say he was killed for ordering a fisherman off the river. . . . But, however he died, he died an 'outlaw,' unprotected by community codes." This sounds melodramatic and apocryphal and implies murder. But there may be something more and something less, even a "stranger truth." Perhaps the fall was accidental in the ordinary sense, but to many Tlingit the "real" cause might have been a cosmological retribution for his several transgressions. "Louis gave his life to the old time spirits; final payment for his part in taking what was not his."[50]

Irony had accompanied the tragic. He had spent most of his life interpreting Tlingit culture to whites in an institution which he seemed to believe offered the last chance of perpetuating the pride of his native people. He made a living at his work from 1911 until 1932. Then he was dropped. But his eye for the ethnological chance, developed by a score of years as a paid professional, remained. The same depression which caused the museum to lay him off had also affected the Tlingit, forcing them to offer "for very reasonable prices, that which they held to the last." No doubt he sought to continue to collect in order to secure money for himself and his family, though there was a genuineness to the frustration that the opportunity to buy specimens was now "better than ever" and yet there were no museum funds to take advantage of this circumstance. The museum appreciated the irony. "We realize that now is the time when it is possible to buy every thing cheap; not only the Alaskan Indian articles, but from many other countries, but it seems to be impossible to raise money for anything."[51]

In 1910, the year before Shotridge joined Gordon's staff, the Victoria Memorial Museum, successor to the Geological Survey of Canada's museum, opened in Ottawa with Edward Sapir as its anthropological division's first chief. Sapir came to Canada from the University of Pennsylvania, almost hired Shotridge in 1913 to help with museum installation and models, and the next year bought the Chilkat blanket that Florence had finished at the Lewis and Clark Exposition. Sapir was a brilliant young man, an innovating genius in linguistics, with a Boas-supervised doctorate from Columbia. He began fieldwork almost immediately, spending several summers among the Nootka; he published frequently, including the important methodological monograph *Time Perspective in Aboriginal Culture*[52]; and he built up a strong museum division, hiring Harlan Smith from the American Museum and the Oxford-trained Marius Barbeau and Diamond Jenness. At last Ottawa had a strong and permanent presence in anthropology and museum collecting. Sapir added to the Nootka collections himself, pursued a strong purchasing policy, sent Barbeau and Smith to the coast, and hired T. F. McIlwraith for work among the Bella Coola. While Smith was responsible for significant acquisitions annually from 1913 to 1929, the most aggressive collector was C. Marius Barbeau.

Barbeau spent most of his childhood in rural Quebec. After a *collège classique* education, he studied law at Laval, then a Rhodes scholarship took him to Oxford where he read anthropology under R. R. Marett and wrote a thesis on Northwest Coast totemic systems.[53] Sapir hired him for the Victoria Memorial Museum in 1911, and, after working among the Huron of Quebec and the Wynadot of Oklahoma, he was sent to British Columbia for research on the Tsimshian. His work was primarily among the Gitksan and Nishga, groups which, like Shotridge's Chilkat Tlingit, were conservative and somewhat off the beaten track. This situation was changing rapidly, however, as the Grand Trunk Pacific Railway pushed its way down the Skeena valley toward Prince Rupert.

Barbeau's arrival on the West Coast was something of a revelation to him. "I had a keen feeling of joy when I visited the Alert

Bay Kwakiutl," he wrote of his quarter-hour stop en route to Port Simpson; "real Indians I saw there. My wife was quite afraid."[54]

With the services of his informants, especially William Beynon, who later became a commissioned collector for Sir Henry Wellcome, Barbeau's work at Port Simpson progressed well. Like Swanton years before at Skidegate, Barbeau delayed collecting at first, while he settled into the situation. By the second month, however, he was well into buying and by the time of his departure he had considerably exceeded his authorization. He asked that his chief "be indulgent at my excess of enthusiasm in collecting," but "I think you will agree that my collection of specimens, nearly 300, is quite interesting."[55] Like many of his coastal predecessors, Barbeau had been bitten by the collecting bug. He returned to the coast after the war, in 1920–21, then again in 1923, 1924, 1927, and 1929. He worked first along the Skeena, then the Nass River — each time making significant collections for the National Museum. In addition, he was responsible for the museum's purchase of the collection of C. V. Smith, a fur merchant, in 1925.

Most of Barbeau's collections were made directly from the natives, their names carefully recorded in his inventories, though some came through Pat Phillipson, a Prince Rupert fur dealer. Barbeau's work was not confined, however, to Ottawa's interests. In 1924 he offered to collect for C. M. Currelly's Royal Ontario Museum of Archaeology. Sapir objected, then relented when Barbeau explained he would be buying for the ROMA only white-held collections, such as that of Phillipson, and so taking little time away from his fieldwork. Even this restraint disappeared when Diamond Jenness replaced Sapir. In 1927 Barbeau had National Museum permission to collect "in a purely personal capacity" while in the field for the federal museum. He made the most of his new liberty.[56]

Barbeau's 1927 season was spent among the Gitksan and Nishga. It was a good collecting year. The salmon fishery had been bad and he spent, besides his own museum's $500, another $1,468.75, far beyond Currelly's $500 appropriation. Barbeau sent the material to Toronto, but assured Currelly that the ROMA was under no obligation to take the overrun since he anticipated "no difficulty in disposing of the remainder" to the American Museum or Heye's Museum of the American Indian. Since the collection was "exactly the kind of thing required," the ROMA was happy to take the whole, and Barbeau was now launched as a collector in "a purely personal" as well as an official capacity. On his 1929 expedition he bought for his own museum, but sent far more to the ROMA, in addition to a medical collection for Toronto's School of Medicine and another, selected on aesthetic principles, on approval to Eric Brown at the National Gallery of Canada. When, in the last two weeks of his stay, a number of splendid headdresses and carvings became available, he simply could not resist buying them even at his own risk.[57]

The quantity and even the quality of material that Barbeau succeeded in collecting in these years is impressive. Emmons had claimed more than a decade earlier that "no further collections will ever be made on the Skeena," and yet much of Barbeau's collection came from there even though Beynon and Shotridge had collected on the river in the meantime. Barbeau's success demonstrated the deceptiveness of a "swept-over" and "cleaned-out" area. There remained pieces which collectors were unable to buy, even to learn of, and which the passage of time, a new generation of owners, or a new urgency of poverty later brought onto the market. The failure of the 1927 fishery helped create a "need for money" that made it easier for Barbeau to buy things that "have several times been bargained for by Dr. Newcombe, Lieut. Emmons, or other collectors."

> It is really surprising that there still are things available, considering the number of collectors afield, the high prices offered, the need of Indians for money, and the facilities for disposing of objects through the curio stores at Prince Rupert.[58]

Successful collecting was, nevertheless, going to be difficult to repeat. "The possibilities for further collections on the Skeena are much smaller now," he wrote of 1929 prospects. "I have collected there since 1920 and have pretty well carried away whatever was available." Yet there still remained a small number of valuable and expensive specimens in the hands of a few natives. He expected to find little on the Nass "since I may have removed most of what there still was in 1927." In fact he soon found that more specimens were still forthcoming, though "those left are among the most expensive and the owners are not looking for buyers." The last fortnight of his stay, however, brought a surge of offers: "It looks as though my activities and purchases had demoralized the Nass recently," he wrote to Toronto, "a number of splendid head-dresses and carvings as a result are now in my possession for disposal at a museum."[59]

With an inventory of material still unbought on the Nass and a network of friends there to help him, Barbeau, who did not return to the coast for another decade, could now deal from his Ottawa office. His relations with Jenness were distant and he was allowed to pursue his own work in his own way. Just when he began to take a cut for himself is difficult to determine with exactness. His ROMA purchases were accompanied by presumably genuine vouchers but with Heye he could operate more irregularly. He bought, for example, a Nishga headdress from Frank Bolton through an agent in Kincolith for $100, then promptly sold it to Haye for $150. Another headdress went to McGill for a similar price and, presumably, a similar commission. For two poles which cost $700 delivered at Prince Rupert, he charged Heye $1,200.[60]

While freelancing in coastal material Barbeau also dealt in Quebec church silver and sculpture, which he sold to the McCord, the ROMA, and other museums. His most profitable sale occurred much later when he and an in-law, both having travelled on National Museum expenses, cleared almost $1,750 from a $3,200 sale of coast material to the University of British Columbia.[61]

Barbeau bought fifteen Nishga poles for public institutions in Canada and abroad. Three of these were put into the Canadian National Railway's public park at its terminal city of Prince Rupert. More innovative was the major responsibility he took in bringing about the first totem pole preservation project that, instead of moving the poles to metropolitan museums or parks, retained them in their own locale.[62]

By the 1920s, as a result of private and museum acquisition, natural decay, and occasional wanton destruction, the British Columbia totem pole had become an endangered specimen. The largest remaining clusters were at abandoned and isolated villages on the Charlottes, on the Nass, and along the Skeena River, the last made accessible only by the wartime completion of the rail line from Edmonton to Prince Rupert.

While there had long been some concern about the disappearance of the poles, it was not until the early 1920s that any general outcry was heard in Canada. The spectacular removal of a group of poles from Alert Bay by people who allegedly had plied their native owners with drink was a minor *cause célèbre*. The press berated public and governments for sleeping soundly while Americans stole the country's heritage by fair means and foul.[63]

Public bodies, such as the Historic Sites and Monuments Board and the Royal Society of Canada, urged the provincial and federal governments to prohibit the sale and export of historical poles. Various individuals, including Sir Arthur Conan Doyle, joined in the plea for the preservation of Canada's poles. Federal agencies, too, were alarmed at the rapid disappearance of the poles. Harlan Smith of the National Museum urged that regulations be passed to forbid exports or at least to require reporting of them. Moreover, "steps should be taken to save in situ or guard until that can be done totem poles at Kitwanga, the best on the C. N. [Canadian National Railway] route or they will go as did those at Alert Bay, the best on the steamship lines." Sapir was already urging a ban on exports as well as the private purchase of poles. He even suggested the outright purchase by the museum of all standing poles. With the consent of the Indians, these would either be left at their sites or removed to Canadian museums.[64]

While the idea of wholesale purchase of poles was briefly considered, at least for the Skeena district, implementation would have been costly and would likely have encountered serious opposition from Indian owners. Barbeau, whose scholarship and fieldwork were most particularly concerned with the Skeena, also favored the preservation of those poles on site, either by the federal parks branch or by the CN Railway. Barbeau, whose claims to primary responsibility are plausible, interested J. B. Harkin of the Canadian National Parks in an "Indian National Park of Temlaham" to embrace both the modern pole sites and the legendary home village of the Skeena Gitksan.[65]

What is remarkable about these ideas was the serious proposals to preserve the poles on site. Poles had often been displayed out-of-doors, but never in their original locations. Even the Sitka National Monument consisted of poles purposely moved there by Governor Brady and none of them were actually Sitkan Tlingit poles. Most were Kaigani Haida. But railway access to the Skeena

River valley not only put the Gitksan poles in danger of sale and export, but allowed for the conception of an outdoor, on-site totem museum or park. The inspiration to preserve the totems of the Skeena rested upon a heightened perception of endangered heritage, but even more upon the poles' value for tourism. It was largely the tourist consideration which dictated the selection of the Upper Skeena as the principal focus of Canadian preservation interest.

As one of the chief carriers of the travelling public, the Canadian National Railway had a vested interest in the preservation of totem poles. Some of the best examples of poles still standing were to be found in the villages along the CN route between New Hazelton and Terrace, with the greatest concentration at Kitwanga, which the *Montreal Gazette* claimed as the showplace of northern British Columbia and, next to Niagara Falls, the most photographed spot in Canada. The railway enjoyed a receptive ear in Ottawa. The preservationist interest of the Indian Department and the National Museum in the poles as examples of native art and as ethnological specimens was quite compatible with the tourist interest of the publicly owned railway. Dr. Charles Camsell, deputy minister of mines, was urged toward preservation by his subordinates in anthropology, yet wrote of his desire to see the Skeena poles preserved "in the interests of the National railways and in consideration of the necessity of preserving these poles to encourage tourist travel."[66]

Camsell took the lead in June 1924 by convening a meeting of what became known as the "Totem Pole Preservation Committee," with Duncan Campbell Scott, deputy superintendent-general of Indian Affairs, as chairman and including himself, Harkin of Parks, and Sapir and Barbeau of the museum. The committee decided to send Barbeau to the Skeena that summer to take a full inventory of all poles in the area and to suggest the best means of preserving them. The actual work of preservation could begin in 1925, none too soon as the American Museum had bought, in the last months of 1923, the first recorded Gitksan pole sold.

Barbeau's survey was begun after his own ethnological fieldwork had been completed. He spent part of October and most of November in Kispiox, Hazelton, Hagwelget, Kitsegukla, and Kitwanga, then returned to Ottawa to prepare his conclusions. He reported that the conservatism of the Gitksan should assist the committee in its objectives. Most still considered it unworthy to sell their memorials, either to strangers or to the government. Barbeau also noted the marked suspicion of whites entertained by the Skeena natives and their lack of confidence in anything to do with government. He thought it possible, however, to persuade them to allow preservation on-site; most of the Indians were fairly friendly so long as one was patient and tactful. Provided that the consent and cooperation of the Indians were obtained and the authorization of each chief and owner was secured before any work began, he felt confident that the majority would be glad to see the government strengthen their poles and re-erect those that had fallen. He recommended that restoration begin at Kispiox, which boasted the greatest number and largest total footage of poles of any of the five villages.[67]

The committee accepted Barbeau's report and agreed that the work would be financed and supervised by Indian Affairs, with Scott in general charge. The CN Railway agreed to provide transportation for men and materials, as well as one of its bridge engineers, T. B. Campbell, to advise on mechanical work. The museum was to provide the services of Harlan Smith to act as liaison officer with the Indians and to assume overall field charge of the project, reporting to Scott. Why Sapir chose Smith instead of Barbeau can only be conjecture. Perhaps he was considered more adept at mechanical supervision, perhaps he was more willing to sacrifice his own field summers, perhaps it was Sapir's known preference for Smith over Barbeau. Smith's asset was long field experience among a variety of Indian groups, most recently the Bella Coola, and thus his understanding, as Harkin put it, of the "peculiar mental operations" of the Indian.[68]

Despite Barbeau's recommendation that work begin at Kispiox, the interests of the CN Railway determined that Smith begin at Kitwanga, since the latter was directly on the rail line, Kispiox some twelve miles from it. Seven poles were restored in the first season, nine in the second. Only two poles remained untouched at Kitwanga and for their restoration the native owner, Chief Semideck, had refused to give his consent. The third year's work, which was to be at Kitsegukla, ran into trouble immediately. On Smith's arrival he was forbidden to touch any poles, handed a protest petition, and told by Joe Brown, representing the Kitsegukla chiefs, to remove his outfit the next morning. The

A totem pole being taken down at Kitwanga by Harlan I. Smith for on-site restoration. National Museum of Canada National Museum of Man, neg. #J19268.

CN engineer and the local Indian agent suggested a withdrawal, to which Smith consented.[69]

It was difficult then to ascertain what was wrong at Kitsegukla and even more difficult now. As Barbeau had emphasized, the people of the Upper Skeena were conservative and their attitudes toward their poles remained much the same as in the past. Moreover, the Gitksan were "markedly suspicious of the white men in their dealing with them; and they profess utter lack of confidence in the Government administration." Barbeau had felt that with patience, friendliness, and understanding, the Indians' attitude toward their poles could be used to promote the preservation scheme, but "past animosities may easily be aroused again, and further collaboration about totem poles be rendered embarrassing, if not sterile." A foretaste of the difficulty had occurred late in the 1926 season when Smith reported that Tom Campbell of Hazelton refused to let him touch two fallen poles. Campbell was aggrieved, he reported, because provincial road crews had cut down one of his poles and never paid him for the damage.[70] Smith was quite conscious of the unfavorable disposition of the Indians to whites generally and government officials particularly:

> There were many grievances they could cite, some no doubt real, and some imaginary. The white man had settled on their land and were pushing the Indians more and more to the wall; they had built canneries on the coast that were destroying all the fish; they were cutting all the best timber in the country so that within a few years none would remain for the Indian; they sold whiskey in Government liquor stores and put the Indians in jail when they drank it. A few years ago, they had prohibited the erection of totem poles; why did they wish now to preserve them?[71]

The Kitsegukla chiefs' petition, signed or marked by fifteen of them, argued that no one should touch any of the poles because each was valuable to a family and were "the only honerable [sic] property that remain in our Hands." This was not sufficient reason for the opposition. Edgar Hyde, the Indian agent, could not understand the problem unless "it was through the propaganda spread by Tom Campbell," who alleged that the government intended to move villages and give the old ones to the railway "and other such nonsense." In a compilation of reasons for Indian opposition, Smith also listed Campbell as a troublemaker who "stirred things up." Smith's several other reasons were: too much home brew, the unsettled land question, broken promises by an earlier photographer, white jealousy at not being hired for the work, a missionary's opposition to preservation, and the Indians' fear that the government would own the poles if it spent money preserving them. Any one of these, added to the general suspicion of white government, was probably enough, though it could have been as petty as Smith not arranging to rent Chief Martha Malkan's house. Once the Indians resisted, Smith probably did not help his cause. "The Indians of these parts," reported Agent Hyde, "are very suspicious of a person who tries to tell them what the Government was doing for them and in my opinion Mr. Smith does talk too much.[72]

Smith abandoned Kitsegukla and "slipped down" to Kitselas Canyon, a place where no one had expected him to work and which, populated by Canyon Tsimshian, had not been included in Barbeau's report. Smith was satisfied with the location — the fifteen poles could be seen from passing trains and he was happy to be on with the work. No mind there had been "poisoned." Barbeau did not approve, telling Scott that there was not a single good pole on the railway side of the river at the canyon and only one on the opposite side, and further undermined the operation by intriguing with the engineer.[73]

Smith left the site in August, unable to get further authorizations for funds. Campbell, the engineer, continued at Kitselas, finishing eight of the poles. Although Smith had the full backing of the museum in his dispute with Indian Affairs' direction (and with Barbeau's intrigues), the archaeologist wanted nothing more to do with the project. He was succeeded by Campbell for the 1928 season's work.

Campbell was no more successful in his dealings with the Kitsegukla than Smith had been and the season was the least successful. At Kitwanga he secured an agreement to restore Semideck's poles, but only after the chief received $300 in exchange for one pole being moved off reserve land to the Hudson's Bay store. This violated the Indian Act, recently amended to prohibit sales from reserves. Agent Hyde was outraged at Campbell's disguised purchase, and lamented that the little which had been accomplished in winning over the Kitsegukla opposition was now undone. He warned that demands for payment could now be expected from most of the owners in Kitsegukla before they would allow their poles to be touched. Attempts in 1929 and 1930 to interest the Kitsegukla in restoration were without success. The new Indian agent at Hazelton, G. C. Mortimer, reported that one Indian who was anxious to have his poles restored had been threatened by the others, who informed Mortimer that the CN Railway would have to pay $1,000 for every pole on the reserve before they would agree to restoration. They were convinced that the railway was the main beneficiary of restoration work.[74]

At Kitwanga, where all poles had now been restored, a similar sentiment emerged. A village committee notified the museum "that the C. N. Ry. Co. is getting all the successful benifit [sic] out of it and us people, the sole owners, get nothing." The Kitwangas, alluding to the Semideck incident, asked for money for electric lights and farm implements for their past favors.[75]

Work ceased after the fifth season. The project had succeeded in restoring thirty poles between 1925 and 1930 at a cost to Indian

Affairs of $15,698.16. The CN Railway's costs were probably nearly as much. The restorations fell far short of the initial aim of the Totem Pole Committee, which had sought the preservation of all the seventy-one poles in Barbeau's report; in fact only eighteen of those had been restored, since he had not mentioned those at Kitselas Canyon. Even the positive achievements of the project had flaws. The work was criticized as aesthetically unsatisfactory. The poles were re-erected in rather unimaginative straight lines and were so brightly painted that W. A. Newcombe lamented that they were hardly recognizable as some of the finest pieces of native art in the province. Emily Carr felt that they had "lost so much of interest & subtlety in the process." The British Columbia artist appreciated the difficulties as well as the value of their preservation, "but that heavy load of all over paint drowns them." Much of the work was undone during the Skeena flood of 1937. The Indians cut down the Kitwanga poles to save them from the rushing water, but they were then stored without due care. The others were allowed to rot and many split along the line of the fastening bolts. By 1962 there were few sound enough for further restoration.[76] Nevertheless, despite the limitations of the Skeena project, the restoration of 1925–30 did represent a significant step in the right direction.

The impulse to preservation had come from concerned whites appreciative of the commercial and heritage value of the poles and not from the natives who owned them. Barbeau was correct when he wrote that both government and Indians had an interest in conservation "though from different standpoints." From the white view, the poles were artifacts and monuments, above all tourist attractions, the value of which was quite unrelated to the Indians who still owned them. The Gitksan were undoubtedly correct in their belated perception that only the CN Railway benefited economically from the restoration and that they, the owners, ought to share in the benefits. Finally, while restoration was seen as valuable in itself, the factor which moved it was tourist promotion. Restoration of poles on Vancouver Island and the Queen Charlottes was desirable but, being off the main line, that was never seriously considered. Smith did intend to restore poles at Kitwancool, thinking that this could help relations between that "forbidden" village and the government, but he never had the opportunity and the CNR would not have been as cooperative as with villages along its route. In the end, only poles along the tracks were restored. There was, as Carr judged, "too much catering to the 'beastly tourist.' "[77]

The Indian Act amendment, in large part a result of the government's desire to protect the poles it was paying to restore, was perhaps as significant as the project itself. After 1926 Indian Affairs had a veto on the sale of any pole on reserve land, effectively on all poles. Where enforceable, this prevented private sales, but did not seriously impede sales to public institutions. Nor did it affect exports. Indian Affairs policy — and National Museum advice — was that poles should be preserved *in situ* where they were potential tourist attractions, but where they stood far off the travel routes, as at Cape Mudge or in the Nass valley, they should be in museums. If Canadian museums could not afford them — and in the 1930s few could — they should be allowed to be sold abroad.

Ten of Barbeau's fifteen Nass pole sales did remain in Canada. Premier S. F. Tolmie protested the sale of two to George Heye and held them up on their flatcars at Jasper but dropped his opposition when assured that they were from areas remote and unimportant to tourists. His successor, T. D. Pattullo, pursued a similar policy. W. A. Newcombe joined with Harlan Smith and Barbeau in the belief that export was preferable to decay.[78] No others were preserved on site.

In the winter of 1923 T. F. McIlwraith, a sensitive young Cambridge graduate, was working under a temporary contract from Sapir on the ethnology of the Bella Coola. He was forcibly struck by the obvious alterations to the native way of life. "The manner in which the ancient civilisation has broken down here is truly deplorable," he wrote back to a Cambridge acquaintance. "Really the only native objects in common use are a few baskets, a few spoons, sticks for drying salmon, and dug-out canoes." There were a few boxes and coppers and some masks among the older people, but not a single sea-going canoe. Only two rattles, he believed, were left in all Bella Coola. He collected a few masks, though "they are deucedly hard to get" and then was given four by one of his informants. These came "with the request that I keep them forever as I was more to be trusted with them than the young Bella Coolas." He collected a little for his alma mater and more for the Ottawa museum, but made no great effort. "I found it was going to interfere with the willingness of my people to discuss the secret parts of certain rites," he wrote in excuse to Sapir, "so I made no great effort." The smallness of the collections was partly the lack of collectibles, but it was also very much because of McIlwraith's own unwillingness to take away many of the few which remained. "Practically no new ceremonial objects are being made," he wrote, "and any losses curtail the already too much curtailed sacred life to that extent."[79]

A few years later Franz Boas revisited Fort Rupert, the scene of his most intense fieldwork among the Kwakiutl. It had changed greatly since his last visit in 1900. "Civilization has badly infringed on the lives of the Indians," he wrote, but there were feasts and dances almost every day. "It is marvellous how the old life continues under the surface," "remarkable how the people cling to the form though the content is almost gone." At a feast he listened to the chief distribute the food with the traditional speech. " 'This bowl in the shape of bear is for you,' and you, and so on; for each group a bowl." The speech was the same that he had heard years before, "but the bowls are no longer here. They are in the museums in New York and Berlin!"[80]

The great age of collecting was over. Pieces could still be had and would appear from underground in the right circumstances. Even in the depths of the Depression, however, Phillip Drucker found at Nootka that "there surely aren't many specimens left on this coast." He visited much of the area inhabited by the Bella Bella, the Kwakiutl, the Tsimshian, and the Haida. "I've kinda kept an eye out for material — there isn't much any more."[81]

Chapter Ten

Epilogue

THE COLLECTING of Northwest Coast art and artifacts continues, though it has become largely a matter of old pieces recyling among collectors and dealers, of a few family heirlooms inherited from European pioneers coming onto the market or being donated to museums, or of repatriation measures undertaken by Canadian museums. In 1948 the Portland Art Museum acquired the Rasmussan collection, gathered from the late 1920s through 1945 by Axel Rasmussan, a superintendent of schools in Wrangell and Skagway. Much of it had been collected from natives, but some came from Wrangell and Seattle dealers, and from Emmons.[1]

In 1951 the Thomas Burke Memorial Washington State Museum shared with the Denver Art Museum the collection of Walter Waters, a Wrangell curio dealer, and in 1968 it received the Sidney Gerber collection, a donation rich in masks, mostly purchased directly from the Kwakiutl in the 1950s. The University of British Columbia museum greatly enriched its collection by purchases of the pioneer missionary collections of G. H. Raley, W. E. Collison, and G. H. Darby, and, through the presence of carver Mungo Martin at the museum, acquired a large number of pieces from the Kwakiutl.

Old material still comes from native sources, sometimes sought out by museum curators but as often by enterprising dealers. In 1977 a Victoria dealer made a coup at Klukwan by buying the contents of the Frog House, unleashing a controversy among curators and splitting the native community into rival factions. A legal attempt by dissidents to recover the material was thwarted because the material was already out of American jurisdiction. A year earlier an American commercial gallery's attempt to remove the Whale House treasures resulted in a roadblock, the demolition of the offending truck, and the hospitalization of two residents. The battle for the Whale House recommenced in 1984. The posts and screen this time got as far as Seattle before the Klukwan village council obtained a restraining order prohibiting further disposition pending judgment whether the sixteen vendors had legal ownership. The injunction halted sale to a New York party.

As long as there are collectors and museums, dealers and possible vendors, the process will continue in some way. Indeed, a few quite spectacular private collections are less than a decade old and one fine, small one has recently been assembled within a single year.[2] A contemporary development has been the conscious collecting of newly made pieces by museums, a major factor in the revival of Northwest Coast art that has been such a striking phenomenon of recent years. The revival has spread even to artists, native and white, with no biological affiliation to the Northwest Coast people.

The revival of Northwest Coast art was part of the twentieth-century reassessment of "primitive" art. In a process "justly celebrated as one of the most significant cultural achievements of our century," the artifacts of all periods and all cultures came to be admired as art.[3] Northwest Coast masks and rattles, bowls and halibut hooks, shared in this massive revaluation of taste.

The Northwest Coast pieces collected in the eighteenth century were viewed as "artificial curiosities," items of wonder made by human artifice, and, like "natural curiosities," were objects of study and enlightenment. The accounts of the eighteenth-century visitors commented upon them as they did upon the flora and fauna of the land. Artists drew and engraved them for publication and they were placed in museums. In the next century the artificial curiosities became "curios," an abbreviated and vulgarized term, or "relics," connoting a survival from the past. Later in the century "artifact," until then a rare word, came into usage for something made and left behind by man. These were survivals, testimony of an earlier, more primitive epoch in the evolutionary development of mankind.

To the museum curator, affected by the scientific spirit of his age and occupation, a mask or an arrow was increasingly a "specimen," an example or illustration of its kind, a term the more appropriate because of its relationship to the biological conceptualization that infected much of anthropology. In the twentieth century they began to be seen in yet another light, a process that eventually transformed these curios and relics, artifacts and specimens, into art.[4]

The leadership of this realization that relics were art has been credited to a small group of Parisian artists at the beginning of the century. Maurice Vlaminck bought several pieces of West African sculpture in 1905, and he, Henri Matisse, André Derain, and then Pablo Picasso began to be influenced in their own work by African sculpture whose conventions and forms were akin to their own artistic explorations. While Matisse sat in Collioure surrounded "by those sculptures in which the Negroes of Guinea, Senegal, and Gabon have represented, with a rare purity, their most passionate fears,"[5] primitive art was, through Ernst Ludwig Kirschner and other German artists, making an imprint upon expressionism.

At about the same time Indian art was attracting the interests of more conventional artists in the American and Canadian wests. These sought it out as subject matter, rather than as something to be formally incorporated into a new art. Theodore J. Richardson has been for years spending· his summers in Alaska, painting watercolor landscapes and then Indian villages, houses, and poles, finding in New York a reliable market. When Emily Carr, who had begun collecting Indian artifacts about 1906, took an Alaska cruise on the *Dolphin* the next year, she saw and admired Richardson's artistic preservation of the poles. She determined upon a similar mission. "I shall come up every summer among the villages of B. C.," she resolved, "and I shall do all the totem poles & villages I can before they are a thing of the past." For the next several summers, Carr painted poles and house fronts at Alert Bay, Campbell River, and elsewhere on the coast. Then, after study in France where she caught the color of the Fauves and even, perhaps, a glimpse of their interest in African art, she returned to paint at Alert Bay, up the Skeena, and across to the remote Skedans, Cumshewa, and Tanu of the Charlottes. Recognizing that the totems were "real art treasures of a passing race," she tried to interest Henry Esson Young in buying her pictures for the new legislative building wing. Newcombe was despatched to Vancouver to appraise her work, and though he bought three pictures for himself, thought them "too brilliant and vivid to be true to the actual conditions of the coast villages."[6] Carr was followed by a number of other artists, notably Langdon Kihn, Edwin Holgate, and A. Y. Jackson, taken to the Skeena by an enthusiastic Barbeau, and by W. J. Phillips, a strong interpreter of the Kwakiutl poles in woodcuts and wood engravings.

Ethnologists had long been studying the decorative and ceremonial artifices of primitive people and it was they, rather than art historians or connoisseurs, who attempted to make sense of primitive art and the basic principles of Northwest Coast sculpture and design. In the late nineteenth century, Putnam, Cushing, and Holmes in the United States, Balfour in Britain, and Stolpe and von den Steinen on the Continent had examined aspects of it. In the first decade of the twentieth century, Boas launched a "systematic study of decorative art" at the American Museum.[7] His own contribution was a long, analytic essay on "The Decorative Art of the Indians of the North Pacific Coast of America." In 1918 the young, Boas-trained anthropologist, Herman K. Haeberlin, published a "preliminary sketch" on the "principles of esthetic form in the art of the North Pacific Coast," in which he urged a culture-history study of the art that would examine its formal principles of composition and style, with an acceptance that the artist possessed both individuality and a "truly artistic imagination." He was convinced that such a study required a consciousness of "the essential identity of problems in primitive art and our own."[8]

Museum personnel were slower than artists and imaginative anthropologists to reflect upon the possibilities of Northwest Coast artifacts as art. The decorative carving and painting of non-literate people had long been classified, if only for want of other terms, as art, craft, or *kunst*. Ethnologists tended to concern themselves with technique and with arguments about whether abstract patterns were degenerations of representational forms or vice versa. Art museum directors, trained in the Great Tradition of European sculpture and easel painting, were uninterested.

*The "West Coast Art, Native and Modern" exhibition in Ottawa, 1927.
Courtesy of the National Gallery of Canada, Ottawa.*

Apparently the first commercial exhibition of primitive art was
held in 1919 in Paris. The next year London's Burlington Fine
Arts Club held a public exhibition of "Objects of Indigenous
American Art." C. H. Read of the British Museum prefaced the
catalogue with the thought that this was the first exhibition, at
least in Britain, of autochthonous American art "viewed as art,"
and put down those "delicately nurtured dilettanti, bred only in
the school of Scopas or Pisanello," who might say that, "while it
may be indigenous, it is not art." To this, Read replied that art
was universal and each art "the outcome of the inherent genius of
the country."[9] The exhibition was dominated by Mesoamerican
pieces, but twenty-one Northwest Coast items lent by museums
and private collectors (including Victoria and Albert Museum
print curator A. P. Oppé) filled three cases.

By the 1920s Shotridge was displaying his Tlingit helmets in
ways to highlight their artistry, commenting on how they were
"evidence of a well developed aesthetic sense in the mind of the
native artist." Meanwhile, Culin was turning the Brooklyn
Museum more and more in the direction of primitive art and the

Denver Art Museum was exhibiting Indian objects as art. Harlan Smith published a large album of "Prehistoric Canadian Art," which urged manufacturers to adopt native designs, and Sapir chided anthropologists for having "forgotten that primitive art is art as well as ethnological material."[10]

The first museum to exhibit Northwest Coast pieces as art objects seems to have been the Denver Art Museum in the mid-1920s. The first North American special exhibition along the same lines was the 1927 "Exhibition of Canadian West Coast Art, Native and Modern," a joint project of the Canadian National Gallery and National Museum. Barbeau was the principal initiator. Native objects were hung beside the work, usually on native themes, of a number of white artists, especially Emily Carr, who had worked in the region. Four years later the Exposition of Indian Tribal Art in New York considered itself "the first exhibition of American Indian Art selected entirely with consideration of esthetic value."[11]

The trend was well established by the time of the North American Indian art exhibitions at the 1939 Golden Gate Exposition and the 1941 Museum of Modern Art shows organized by Frederick Douglas and René d'Harnoncourt. These exhibitions gave native art a legitimacy and influenced the public in a major way. 'In less than a generation, the definition of . . . Northwest Coast pieces had changed from 'ethnographic specimen' to 'fine art.' '"[12] Instead of being handled by curio shops that doubled as pawnbrokers or fur traders, artifacts entered the art market through their own commercial and public galleries and, eventually, with all the subsidiary phenomenon of art-historical scholarship, coffee-table books, attributions, very high prices, and faking.

The ethnological museum has increasingly taken on the air of an art museum and special exhibitions of argillite, of masks, of group or solo shows, proliferate. The transformation has not been universally admired. It has met some resistance among anthropologists, angered at the "de-contextualization" of material away from its surrounding culture and significance. And some public art museums are reluctant to accord it a status equivalent to easel painting or European sculpture.[13] But, right or wrong, artifact has become art, usually appealing to a new type of collector and now often too expensive for museums to purchase.

Chapter Eleven

Themes and Patterns

THE HEYDAY OF ANTHROPOLOGICAL COLLECTING on the Northwest Coast occurred between 1875, when Swan received his commission for the Philadelphia exposition, and the Great Depression, when public and private funds largely collapsed. During the half-century or so after 1875, a staggering quantity of material, both secular and sacred — from spindle whorls to soul-catchers — left the hands of their native creators and users for the private and public collections of the European world. The scramble for skulls and skeletons, for poles and paddles, for baskets and bowls, for masks and mummies, was pursued sometimes with respect, occasionally with rapacity, often with avarice. By the time it ended there was more Kwakiutl material in Milwaukee than in Mamalillikulla, more Salish pieces in Cambridge than in Comox. The city of Washington contained more Northwest Coast material than the state of Washington and New York City probably housed more British Columbia material than British Columbia herself.

The major agent of demand in this transferral of cultural and physical patrimony was the museum. The period of most intense collecting on the coast coincided with the great growth of museums of all kinds. In the late nineteenth century national, civic, and academic pride had combined with governmental aid to science and culture, and more particularly with an enormous outpouring of capitalist philanthropy, to bring about the foundation or expansion of an incredible number of institutions devoted to the collecting and exhibiting of scientific and artistic objects. An amazing variety of museums dedicated to art and antiquities, to local history and folk-culture, to warfare and science, to natural history and medicine, to physical anthropology, archaeology, and ethnology, sprouted in every area of the westernized globe.

Anthropology museums were a significant part of this Museums Movement. In every capital, in most provincial and many university cities, anthropological museums were established or enlarged. Despite a "great burst of museum research" in the 1880s and 1890s,[1] museum collecting overran museum research: from every non-modern area of the globe, museum agents, friends, correspondents, commissioned collectors, and expeditions gathered the art and anthropological detritus of primitive and traditional peoples and sent it to the museum.

Anthropological collecting had special impetus behind it: the realization that time was essential, that civilization was everywhere pushing the primitive to the wall, destroying the material culture and even extinguishing the native stock itself. Once the culture of these people was gone, wrote Adolf Bastian, the most gloomy of museum sages, it could not be recalled to fill the gaps required by an inductive ethnological science. "What can be done must be done now. If it is not, the possibility of ethnology is forever annulled."[2] This sense of urgency, this notion of a scientific mission, was a constant theme of nineteenth- and early twentieth-century anthropology. "In a few years it will be impossible," wrote John Wesley Powell, "to study our North American Indians in their primitive history." Stewart Culin decided that his archaeology could wait; things could be left in the ground for later excavators, "but the Indian — as a savage — is soon to disappear" and "there will soon be nothing left upon the reservations."[3]

As archaeology could be left to those who came later, so, some thought, could synthesis and theorizing. "Those of us who are at work today should make it our business to save all that is possible before it is too late." That was the curator's principal task. "Those who come after us can work out the problems just as well as we if they have the data, but they cannot provide the data, because it will no longer exist." The salvage impulse was to an extent self-fulfilling. Much had disappeared from the field not because Indians and their culture were doomed, but because it had already been swept up by other museums. Gordon was half-conscious of the paradox when he wrote that the saving of all that was possible meant that "we will be in competition with the other great Museums of the country, a competition that grows close as the materials that all are anxious to get become more rare, but we must take an active part and be prepared to meet this competition."[4]

Working with such compelling urgency — and with an eye to the acquisition programs of other museums — vast amounts of money poured into collecting activities. Some was government money but most of the means for the large metropolitan museums was provided by the new wealth of Guilded Age capitalism, by the Bleichröders, Heckers, Rautenstrauchs, Morgans, Jesups, Heyes, Wellcomes, Harrimans, Hearsts, Fields, Wanamakers, and their less-known contemporaries. The great museum collections of Northwest Coast materials that reside in New York, Chicago, Washington, London, Berlin, and a dozen other cities are merely one epiphenomenon of the generosity and the competitive acquisitiveness of western capitalism and its Museum Age.

Competition was a prominent factor in the scramble for Northwest Coast museum collections. The race against time was also a race against museum rivals. Spencer Baird waged a battle with Congress so that he might fight one with the French and German interlopers on his continent. Bastian feared the imminent destruction of the tribes north of the Columbia, but he also feared that the Krauses might beat him there. Washington was mortified by the Emmons collection in New York. Chicago was intent upon rivalling New York, while Putnam was determined to go Chicago one better. "I might state frankly," Dorsey wrote, "that at the present time they have at least twenty-seven poles in New York and we have twenty-three in Chicago. I do not like to have the difference in number remain against us." The rivalry passed down the line and into the field. Nowell wanted $62 so he could buy Mrs. Klaklikla's feast dishes "before George Hunt knows that she want to sell them."[5]

While the intercontinental and intercity rivalries waxed and waned, Canadians occasionally lamented that so much of their heritage was being shipped to foreign museums or being bought up by private collectors. G. M. Dawson felt strongly that Boas's collections were "lost to us," a view which Boas rejected as narrow. "If this work were not done now it would never be done," Boas wrote, and with telling accuracy, added that "Canada has no means of carrying it on." Moreover, it was important to him that things were preserved "in a large and accessible museum" rather than "in a remote place like Victoria where, at best, few scientists will have a chance to see them" or worse, "to let them rot and be lost in private hands."[6]

After 1905 the major museums had turned their attention from the Northwest Coast and even from North America, but some collectors, particularly George Heye, went on omnivorously. His coastal collecting brought resentments that were more regional than national. "It riles me considerably," the director of the Washington State Museum wrote Newcombe, that Heye and others "come to our coast here and strip it of material which should be retained." But he, like the curator of the Vancouver city museum who complained that foreign relic hunters were constantly denuding the country, felt "helpless at present."[7]

The foreign transgressions did elicit sporadic local responses in the early years. Victoria's museum was a reaction, initially ineffectual, to the collections by Jacobsen and Powell. Dawson persuaded his minister that Aaronson's collection ought to be bought on the grounds that foreign collectors had "so completely cleared the British Columbian coast of ethnological specimens" that it was doubtful whether a comparable collection could again be obtained. He was able to get small appropriations for Newcombe to collect. The Geological Survey, looking forward to its new museum building, purchased Newcombe's own collection in 1906. He was probably pleased that it went to Ottawa rather than out of the country. His son certainly felt that "keeping it in Canada seems better than letting it get to the U. S."[8] He would have preferred it in the Provincial Museum but there seemed no chance of that at the time. After 1911, with a new building and a scientific staff headed by Sapir, the Canadian National Museum was in a better position and, with Smith, Jenness, McIlwraith, Barbeau, and Sapir himself variously in the field, it made up for much of its early neglect.

Toronto's Royal Ontario Museum of Archaeology had also tended to disregard the Northwest Coast. Its director, the flamboyant C. T. Currelly, had bought from J. E. Standley,

Landsberg, and Aaronson in 1912, the museum had inherited odd pieces from Victoria College and the normal school collection, but only in 1922 did Currelly decide that the institution deserved a large coastal collection. "As we are, and probably always will be, the big archaeological museum of Canada, I would like to have a much better representative collection of West Coast things than we have."[9] With the help of Newcombe, Barbeau, the potlatch confiscation, and later purchases from Emmons, the ROMA secured a respectable collection.

A wide field was open for those museum curators who were concerned with salvaging the material culture of primitive people before it was too late. The Northwest Coast was but one of hundreds of cultures alluring to the museum, but within North America the material culture of the north coast groups was at once attractive in nature and abundant in quantity. Nearly everything of ethnological interest on the coast, from large sculpture to small charms, from finely crafted masks to fishhooks and arrows, was ornamented in some way. This feature made Northwest Coast material showy and desirable.

Museum officials had various desiderata, but evidence of native artifice was a consistent feature over the years. Antiquity was another, though new pieces were acceptable if "genuine." Particularly in early years this led to an emphasis in instructions upon stone and bone, the presumption being that these would be older than fiber or wood. G. M. Dawson summed up the most common attitude: "almost anything of a manufactured kind and of some antiquity would be of service, particularly if ornamented by carving, painting or otherwise."[10] Such an attitude of universality became characteristic of the systematic field collector. Boas was concerned with the undistinguished everyday as much as with the striking and the remarkable.

The 1920s saw an increased emphasis upon aesthetic artifice and, with it, some shift away from the ordinary. Gordon and Shotridge were after "treasures" and the Royal Ontario Museum felt it must "concentrate largely on the best."[11] While thorough collecting was a characteristic of the systematic acquisitions of the Field and the American museums, every collector had always had an eye for the "good" and the "old." In a time when "a collector did not need tremendously discriminating tastes to gather a spectacular collec-

tion" (as a later curator noted),[12] there were, nevertheless, standards, some defined, most undefined, upon which the collector
operated. Quite intangible was the ambiguous "good."
Newcombe, Dorsey, Boas — probably everybody — used the
word but without definition. Sometimes it seems to have meant
old; certainly it meant genuine; probably it also contained a
strong, if vague, aesthetic sense. Boas felt that old masks were
"much finer than the new ones," presumably not simply because
they were older. Yet age was, of all the factors of Boas's selection
criteria, by far the most important.[13]

Age was also a test of "genuineness," of its reality as a piece of
traditional native culture. "I only wish good old material and
none of the commercial specimens the Indians are now making,"
Heye wrote. J. W. Powell advised against purchasing Emmons's
1893 collection because it contained too little "genuine aboriginal
art" and too much trade and acculturated material. McIlwraith
told Barbeau that, though he was personally interested "in any
modern survivals of Indian art," such things fell outside the Royal
Ontario Museum's interest. New pieces were acceptable if the old
were no longer available, but they had to be authentic. Even
Swan, who unguardedly wrote of making a collection entirely
new, insisted on authenticity. Boas, seeking "a real good arrow
and bow," suggested that, if unfindable, they be made. This
would be all right "as long as they were made correctly."[14]
Newcombe commissioned, among other things, nets, mats, a
cradle, and a loom; Swan found new harpoons as good as old and
certainly much cheaper.

The Northwest Coast societies had never been static and they
had been in contact with European culture for a century by the time
Swan made his Centennial collection. Collectors gave priority to
the uncontaminated, but were never absolute purists. Even Boas
equipped his Chicago Kwakiutl with material for button blankets
and ordered some from Hunt during the Jesup Expedition.

All collectors included some measure of what J. W. Powell
termed "articles of acculturated arts," those "showing the method
by which the Indians have adapted European ideas to their own
stage of culture." Powell admitted having collected, in his twenty-
three years with the U. S. Geological Survey and Bureau of Ethnology "a few things" of the acculturated class, but he claimed
never to have spent a dollar on pieces made solely for sale to the

white man.[15] While this exaggerates the purity of Powell's collections, the bias for totally indigenous material is clear.

On the coast there were many things that fell into Powell's acculturated arts category and several, especially silver, argillite carving, and some masks, model poles, and canoes, which were made for the trade. Even these might be ambiguous since silver bracelets and carvings were used by the Indians, notably for distribution at potlatches, and some models undoubtedly had a position in native society as childrens' toys.

The attitude of museum collectors to such pieces varied. Most collected, even commissioned, models because whole houses, poles, and canoes were very difficult to ship. Canoe models were collected as early as the Vancouver expedition. John Swanton had Charles Edenshaw and John Robson make a set of model poles for the American Museum, and the British Museum in 1898 received a model pole from Rev. Keen only to find that the full-size Kayang pole which it represented was exactly the one Newcombe, quite coincidentally, sent them four years later.[16]

Silver and gold bracelets were only partly made for the curio and tourist trade. Swan collected a lot for the Smithsonian and many came into museum collections as later gifts and donations. The professionals, Boas, Newcombe, Emmons, and Barrett, avoided silver, though Newcombe bought it on rare occasions. Many — Barbeau, Jenness, and McIlwraith, as well as Swan and Jackson — collected it for themselves or for family and friends.

Argillite carvings were similarly treated. Many came to museums as donations, some as purchases. Swan had a great weakness for argillite in native patterns illustrating totems and myths. Powell and Dawson collected argillite for Ottawa. Emmons collected it rarely and then usually as a gift. He got some, of course, as portions of entire collections that came his way. Heye acquired a number of argillite pieces in the same way, especially in the Crosby collection, though he deliberately bought some from Landsberg and Standley.[17]

Powell's bias against argillite was stronger. Argillite carvings were articles of trade, and since they were "designed for sale to the higher race, they chiefly embody the ideas of the white race and in no proper sense represent Indian arts." Newcombe also did "not particularly care for those carvings unless they illustrate some story or feature otherwise inaccessible in works of art."

Queen Charlotte Island Agent Thomas Deasy made a collection which he tried to sell to several museums. Newcombe recommended against either the Provincial or the National museum making the purchase unless it could select according to his stated principle; in any case, he felt there was nothing remarkable about Deasy's collection and "you could do just about as well at Mrs. Aaronson's at a far more reasonable figure." Moreover, several carvers, including Charles Edenshaw — "the best of them" — were still working.[18]

Deasy resorted to selling to a private Vancouver collector, then made a new collection which he sold to the avid American argillite collector, Col. Leigh Morgan Pearsall. The New Jersey man had already acquired a sizable collection, made through purchases from a Seattle dealer and by cleaning out Mrs. Aaronson's eighty-five or so carvings, but he wanted more. Having a good thing going, Deasy made yet another collection (largely through Haida Alfred Adams of Masset) and bought back his first collection (for double the price), to send to Pearsall. At last Pearsall, with almost six hundred carvings, perhaps the largest single collection in the world, called an end to the process. Emmons, who lived close by, thought him "a rather ignorant man with money who proposes a private museum with little knowledge." His argillite was sold to the University of Florida in 1963.[19]

Argillite, because of its lack of indigenous authenticity, was more a passion of private collectors than of ethnological collectors. Mary Lipsett, wife of a Vancouver ship chandler, made a large collection that was eventually donated to the Vancouver City Museum. In recent years, curatorial attitudes have changed and argillite has become a coveted, researched, and exhibited artifact.

Every knowledgeable collector knew that argillite and silver were adaptations. Most new pieces were readily recognizable, though commercial paints had come into native use very early. As prices rose, there were instances of deliberate deception, the documentable ones being almost invariably the work of dealers. Stadthagen's frog pole might fool a Cambridge don — though even he knew it was not a good piece — but not Newcombe. A. C. Haddon was a professional, but his inability to spot the fraudulence of a mask he bought from Standley is excusable. It was probably copied from a published illustration and went undetected for years.[20]

In 1905 Emmons discovered a Skagway "manufactury" of Tlingit objects, done principally in copper, shell, and bone, which "through a simple process can be aged." Organized by an Alaska-California dealer (probably B. A. Whalen of Alaska Indian Curios), masks, rattles, knives, pipes, and spoons were made into "very beautiful and interesting pieces . . . wholly of native design, conception & work." The "growing tendency to make *new* old things" was, Emmons wrote, "fooling even those who should know better." Emmons himself was accused by Heye of planting "reconstructed sheep horn rattles pretty much all over Europe."[21] Restoration was a different matter. Swan had his "big canoe" painted and Newcombe sometimes arranged for a pole to be repainted and restored. Charlie Nowell frequently repaired imperfect pieces for him. One knows of these things when there are papers extant, but much restoration and almost all "reconstruction" is unrecorded.

The documentation which collectors gathered with their pieces varied enormously and fairly predictably. Amateurs and casual collectors were not thoughtful about these things. Emmons was punctilious from the first. Boas insisted on high standards, though his own collections are not particularly well catalogued. He was concerned that each specimen carry not only name, locale, and, if applicable, lineage and secret society, but also that it should bear its associated "story" and song. His critical attitude was developed early while he tried to increase the ethnological value of Jacobsen's sparsely labeled Berlin pieces. The professional curator and collector by the 1890s was conscientious about documentation; George Heye was not.

Even if the collector's lament of scarcity began very early, the amount of collectible material on the coast was enormous. Seasoned field collectors were surprised to return to old haunts and find respectable amounts of articles available where they thought they had been picked clean. In considering this abundance, evident in museums around the world, several things need be noted. First, the Northwest Coast was one of the few North American areas of rich and striking material cultures which remained relatively unshattered at the advent of the Museum Age. Only in the far western and northern portions of the continent could fairly complete collections still be made.

Secondly, on the coast the impact of western culture was simultaneous with the collector's work and in great measure assisted it. The calamitous decline of the native population from contact until the later decades of the nineteenth century, for example, must have created a surplus of many objects at precisely the period of most intense organized collecting. Helen Codere long ago pointed out that there were among the Kwakiutl in the historical period more named ranks of status than men to fill them.[22] Similarly, there may have been more Hamatsa masks than there were society members to wear them. While population declined, creating a surplus of ceremonial items, the introduction of European manufactured goods rendered many utilitarian objects obsolete and therefore disposable. Thirdly, the introduction of European tools and the changes in native society from post-contact wealth led to a florescence of artistic production in the nineteenth century.

Even after the climax of this process, ethnological objects were a renewable resource. The extent of skill retention varied from group to group but never quite died out. The external demand for objects to some extent encouraged the continuity of production and even the growth of new lines of production especially for the trade.

In the process of transferring this abundance from the coast to the museum gallery or storeroom, several factors confronted the collector of Northwest Coast artifacts. The most obvious was mere accessibility. The area was (and remained in many of its parts) a pioneer country in which the infrastructure of transportation was rude and undeveloped. The simple rule was that the more remote the Indians from European transportation, the more likely they were to have desirable objects at reasonable prices. Getting there, of course, presented problems. Skidegate and Masset were remote, yet even they were relatively accessible. Steamers called regularly, there was a commercial oil-works at Skidegate and a trading post at Masset.

The Haida had traditionally been involved in regional trade and increased this commercial travel in the nineteenth century. The Queen Charlottes had already been partially depleted of their traditional goods by collectors and tourists. G. M. Dawson collected there in 1878 and I. W. Powell for the Canadian Indian Affairs department in 1879 and for the American Museum in

1881. The accessibility of transportation had brought not only collectors but tourists on their way north to Alaska. "Skidegate Inlet," Jacobsen wrote, "is one of those steamer landings where tourists usually buy 'curiosities' or commission the making of such objects and pay well."[23]

The Indians were, of course, astute enough not simply to wait for collectors to come to them. Newcombe noted that the recently converted Kaigani villagers took their dance properties and sold them at high prices at Ketchikan and Wrangell. George Hunt was baffled by the high prices demanded by the Friendly Cove Nootka. "I never see any Body like these People for asking so a High Price for there things as this People, for they say that they can go to seatle and tacoma and get High Price for What Ever they Bring there." Despite the ability of the sellers to seek metropolitan prices, a significant discrepancy remained. In 1886 Boas estimated that his $70 Nuwitti collection was worth $200 at Victoria prices and Swanton in 1900 found Skidegate prices half those of Victoria.[24]

The most obvious way to overcome these problems was to seek more out-of-the-way villages. Swan judged that among the more remote groups north and inland from Sitka "twenty five cents worth of tobacco will buy as much as twenty dollars will, either at Sitka or any place south of that point." Jacobsen, after his experience at Skidegate and Masset, avoided tourist stops and commercial centers. Prices at Quatsino he found were not as high as those he had experienced earlier. Remote villages were both richer in objects and these were priced lower, yet transportation was difficult (often the only means was by rented canoe) and this put the collector at the mercy of high demands for services. In early years this might also represent a risk to property, even to life.[25] Newcombe could overcome the problem by taking his *Pelican,* but that was a rare solution. Only in the 1910s were motor launches available.

Remoteness also brought its own special obstacle to collecting: the Indians tended to be more traditional, ceremonial objects remained more meaningful and thus more difficult to buy or even to see. At Nuwitti the natives in 1882 were still almost untouched by white influences; they were not inclined to sell Jacobsen their masks, rattles, and other ceremonial pieces. Only through the efforts of the highly respected George Hunt was the chief persuaded to sell a number of excellent pieces and, of course, only at a good price. A second Nuwitti visit met with even less success and for the same reason: the people held so firmly to their old customs and dances that they were unwilling to sell masks. Again, Jacobsen had to pay dearly for the few things offered. Swan encountered similar resistance at Klue. The Haida there were not anxious to sell "as they have not yet come under missionary influence but keep up their tamawas ceremony in ancient style."[26]

The reverse situation occurred at Port Essington where the majority of Indians had converted to Christianity and moved to a new village; they no longer had many original or interesting ethnological items. The most unpromising areas, therefore, were those like Port Essington or Metlakatla where the Indians had most lost their traditional culture and, at least in the earlier years, those like Nuwitti where they strongly retained it.

The white economy had another influence besides accessibility: the integration of Indian labor into the wage structure. Indians who had access to wages, usually in salmon, sealing, or oil industries, could afford to hold out for high prices. Jacobsen found the coastal Indians avaricious, overcharging for canoe transportation and always demanding what he considered to be exorbitant prices for their goods. They had been, he felt, corrupted by the earlier gold miners and now they could earn good wages at the canneries. Newcombe noted in 1908 that the Haida were even more independent and less likely to be moderate in their charges. They were, he wrote Culin, so flushed with money from new mining and forestry developments as well as from the customary fishery, that it made little sense even to try to negotiate for totem poles. The marked effect of native prosperity upon availability and price was noticeable even to the tourist. "Owing to the good salmon season and the steady employment given them at the cannery," wrote Miss Scidmore in her account of a trip to Alaska, the Indians of Tongass "held their things so high that even the most insatiate and abandoned curio-buyer made no purchases."[27]

The experienced field collector took measure both of the seasonal employment and of the years when the salmon fishery failed. There was a strong *schadenfreude,* the pleasure at someone else's misfortune, inherent in the collector's craft. A poor fishing summer meant a good collecting winter. As a Skagway trader reported to the Field Museum in 1903: "owing to the partial failure of the salmon catch on the Pacific Coast this year, and consequently owing to the impoverished conditions in which the Indians find themselves," some of the prominent clan members talked of selling their carvings.[28]

Even in good fishing years, the seasonal nature of Indian fishing income meant that late winter was the best time to collect since money would be running short before the beginning of the new season. The element of *schadenfreude* appears again in Hunt's 1893 report to Boas: "if I had some money now I can Get things Very cheap, for the Indians have no money . . . so we can get things at our ohn Price for if we let it alon till June then there Will all go and Work for the cannerys and get cash." Winter had additional advantages. Most of the Indians were in their home villages where they kept their best goods. Summer found most villages virtually abandoned for the fishing boats or canneries. Summer collecting was a common mistake of the neophyte. Even coast residents like Swan (in 1875) and Newcombe (in 1897) discovered to their cost that summer collecting could be a waste of time. While winter, especially late winter, was far the best time to collect, it too had disadvantages. Winter travel could be most difficult on the stormy waters, especially on the open west coast, and many desirable pieces would be in use during the winter ceremonials and hence obtainable, if at all, only at high prices. In such a situation, the best solution, where possible, was to wait. "I can't get any cedar Bark yet," Hunt wrote to Boas in 1895, "for the Indians would not sell them yet for they are using them yet in there Winter Dance, as soon as there Done with the Dance . . . then there will sell it for Half the Price."[29]

The want occasioned by a poor fishing season or even the late winter after a good one was predictable, but individual poverty need not be seasonal or cyclical. The collector and his museum were beneficiaries of distress and also its potential alleviators. Lucy Roberts, an old and indigent woman of Skidegate, had no resources except two poles standing at Cumshewa. "I would like to sell," she wrote Newcombe through the Methodist missionary, "as I am very much in need of money. I will leave it with you to say what the poles are worth." Jack Curley, a Clayoquot who had gone with Newcombe to the St. Louis World's Fair, was another destitute vendor whose simple appeal, "Now I want you to dry

[sic] to sell my totem pole, because I am very poor and have no money," was followed within a year by Mrs. Curley's "Jack Curley is dead . . . , but Newcomb I wish you to help me to take care of my babys to I am very poor." Less dire circumstances also brought offers of sale. Henry Moody's purchase, at a cost of $295, of a headstone for his uncle prompted him to offer three coppers for sale. "I kind of hard up after spent my money on the grave stone," he wrote. The headstone theme became a familiar one. John Robertson of Skidegate offered a pole to Newcombe because he wanted a gravestone to commemorate his wife. When Annie Showett-Kock died at Klukwan her last wish was to have a marble headstone representing the two crests belonging to her son Charlie Klaydoo. Klaydoo asked the collector and governor, James G. Brady, to provide a marble stone, carved with a crest on each side, in exchange for four carved boards he owned.[30]

Accessibility and season, prosperity and poverty, were important variables in the collecting process. So too was the purely fortuitous factor of Christian conversion. Jacobsen was able to buy a fifty-foot pole in the Charlottes at a very low price because its owner "had been converted to Christianity and had adopted many ways of the white man." George Dorsey had "a bit of good fortune" at Hazelton in 1897 when he came across the complete paraphernalia of a shaman who had just converted to Christianity. When Newcombe heard in June 1901 that two Alaska villages had recently abandoned their pagan ways and were selling off their ceremonial property, he sailed north only to find that easy accessibility to the Ketchikan and Wrangell markets in large part defeated his hopes. Barrett was able to make his "real killing" at Fort Rupert partly because some of the Kwakiutl were taking up "some new-fangled religion." Too, Barrett's unusual success in 1915 was attributable to another extraneous factor: the federal government's efforts to eradicate the potlatch. Seven years later Agent Halliday and Sargeant Angerman gathered their four-hundred-plus pieces of "voluntarily surrendered" potlatch gear for the museums of Ottawa, Toronto, and George Heye.[31]

Collectors developed various "tricks of the trade" in dealing with Indian vendors. Few Indians after the 1870s were impervious to the cash economy and, with the close relationship between wealth and status within their social system, the demand for money, whether as cash, blankets, or other media of exchange, was always very strong.

Jacobsen found two coastal villages so enthusiastic at the prospects of sales that they interrupted the winter dances to bring out their merchandise. Often the natives would cagily hold off until the collector was about to leave before bringing out their material. At Skedans, only when Swan was leaving did the villagers begin to bring their material for sale. More interesting was George Dawson's experience near the same place five years earlier. Surveying in his small boat off Skedans, he was met by several canoes, led by Chief Skedans, which brought "a quantity of wooden bowls etc. to trade as curiosities." More items were brought the next day. On his fifth day in the inlet Dawson found himself "besieged by Indians with various things to sell" and then, soon after dark, Captain Klue and three of his people arrived, "disgusted that they had not been knowing enough to offer ictus for Sale when we were in their country, and having heard that Skedans was making a big thing of us." The Klue group, smarting from having missed a good thing the week before, "had evidently brought their best things to cut out Skedan and his friends." This was a traditional trade tactic and Dawson, for two dollars, took a remarkable mask with a nose six-feet long, but left behind a dance wand and cedar bark headring studded with arrows.[32] Here, quite clearly, the natives were more eager to sell than Dawson was to buy.

The propensity of the Indians to sell varied greatly according to the kinds of objects concerned. Household utensils, implements, weapons, and tools became in various degrees obsolescent once substitutes were available or were easily replaced by new native manufacture. These were readily sold, and so bowls, baskets, spoons, knives, and fish hooks are abundant items in every collection. Objects that still possessed cultural meaning were much more difficult to obtain from the Indian. It should not be thought, Jacobsen observed, that the natives merely wait for a collector to come to buy up their revered relics. On the contrary, there was a certain art to taking an Indian's dearest possessions. A high-ranking woman at Howkan, a Kaigani village in Alaska, showed Swan a large quantity of dancing masks and costumes, "but she asked such exhorbitant prices for some and refused to part with others, so I can't make no trade."[33]

Some items were replaceable: Kwakiutl masks, for example, might be sold and new ones made, since the prerogatives they represented were retained. Many objects were not owned privately but were the joint and communal possessions of societies, families, or lineages. Moreover, some pieces were secret, known only to society initiates. These might be sold but only against the grain of social pressure and group convention and thus secretly. Even when ceremonial items had lost much of their meaning, many held on to them dearly, putting them at "the bottom of the family chest" or elsewhere. Near Terrace on the Skeena River, a chief showed Louis Shotridge a magnificent carved stone eagle that he kept buried in bushes behind his cabin. Shotridge tried his customary pitch about putting it in a museum where people from all parts of the world might see and study it. The man "hesitated for a moment and then said: 'I like to do that, if only I have something besides this piece by which to keep in mind the memories of my uncles and grandfathers, but this is the only thing I have left from all the fine things my family used to have, and I feel as if I might die first before this piece of rock leaves this last place.'" Shotridge encountered the "everlasting esteem" of the Tlingit for their hereditary pieces and Newcombe found a similar potency of family heirlooms too strong to overcome among the Kaigani. As late as 1929 Marius Barbeau knew of fine pieces "not looking for buyers." Even with their limited knowledge of the past, "the present generation hold on to the old things," wrote Shotridge, "each man with a fear that another man might laugh if he let go what he has in exchange for the needed cash."[34]

Stealthy selling was a characteristic noted as early as 1778 by Cook's men at Nootka, and later collectors learned quickly that privacy was a most important part of the craft. Jacobsen obtained objects at night or by arranged meetings outside the villages. To obtain ceremonial whistles, for example, he bargained in secret away from the village." Very early in his coastal travels he learned the wisdom of providing himself with a large sack into which he could stuff confidential acquisitions. In such secret dealings he was often very successful, but they might also hinder later purchases. He had in this way bought a good deal of Fort Rupert ceremonial material, including Nutlematla and Hamatsa masks and rattles in October 1881. When he returned the following March, he found it impossible to buy: "the Indians here will now sell me nothing more because they have had strife because of it. It is not permitted that they sell me their holy relics." By now an experienced collector, he was not depressed. In the end he got the masks he wanted, but only by giving a feast and buying at very high prices a great many things he did not want.[35] The Kwakiutl had their tricks of the trade.

His younger brother Fillip quickly learned the art of nocturnal privacy and most of his significant purchasing in the summer of 1884 was done at night. "You see," he wrote in his peculiar English, "no Indian will sel any of his wolluabele Dans mask and let any of his neabor know any thing obout it." "Any ordinary haus article I of couce could buy in the Day time but when it cam Wooden masks Dans Ratels and wissels wich was all uset in the secret Danses I had to be soo careful."[36]

Some ceremonial pieces, at least among the Bella Coola, were supposed to be destroyed after use or when their owner died. When Jimmy Kimquish, one of Jacobsen's Bella Coola troupe, died in 1899, his masks, instead of being destroyed, were brought to the Indian agent's house and dropped through an open window in the dark of night. They were paid for in a similar way, for "I was not to know which of the tribe brought them."[37]

A much more complicated situation was related by T. F. McIlwraith while working among the Bella Coola in the early 1920s. In 1921 a government official (probably Harlan Smith) bought a ceremonial representation of a merganser duck.

> Although this should have been destroyed after use, no difficulty would have been raised if the transaction had remained secret. Unfortunately, the buyer allowed the object to be seen by several Bella Coola and by some Carriers. This caused indignation throughout the community and news of it reached the Bella Bella, who concluded that the vendor would suffer disaster for allowing a secret object to be seen by the despised Indians of the interior. Within a year, his wife died. The Bella Bella believed that his sin had brought its own punishment, but the Bella Coola, who knew the details of the sale and did not consider the exposure of the article to have been the fault of the seller, attributed it to the power of the thoughts of the Bella Bella. They all expected that he would be punished; therefore he was punished; the expectation was sufficient to effect its own fulfillment. This incident was too fresh

in the minds of several men to allow them to sell ceremonial objects to the writer.[38]

A number of instances illustrate resistance and controversy when a private sale became known. Kitkune sold Swan "a few rare and curious masks," but then, under pressure from his mother and an old man, unsuccessfully tried to get them back. C. E. S. Wood also retained a finely carved shaman's rattle he bought from Asonques in Alaska in 1877. "A skinny hag snatched it from my hand," he wrote, "just as I had concluded the bargain and compelled the 'Doctor' to return my tobacco." She said that the rattle had been a favorite one of her dead husband, a shaman who had left his rattles to his nephew, "who certainly did not seem too happy" about the controversy. Wood, "by judicious coaxing and tobacco," succeeded in pacifying her and keeping the rattle.[39]

In 1897 Fillip Jacobsen sent a rare rattle from the Nootka shaman, Dr. Atlieu, to the American Museum. The rattle was quite old and had been used for years to call the salmon into the rivers. "I am not allowed to show it to any one here or tell about it," Jacobsen wrote, "or Dr. Atleo would get himself into a great trouble." "He has not used it this year as he sold it some time ago to me, and now he begins to regret it as they get very little fish at present and he blames himself for it."[40]

Private transactions were a major way to secure meaningful ceremonial material. In quite a different way Adrian Jacobsen was able to secure secreted possessions at a Nootka village. The Catholic priest simply accompanied him from door to door asking after dance masks. To the natives' reply that they no longer had such things, the priest — privy to household secrets pried from school children — merely smiled and said, "But you have an idol in a box in your bedrooms; these thing can bring a high price." Masks and other pieces came out of hiding and went into Jacobsen's bag.[41]

Most of the resistance related to dance, ceremonial, or ritual objects and yet something as open and practical as whaling harpoons could be invested with a magic through success. Swan was disappointed in his quest for Makah harpoons by the Indians' "superstituous idea that if they let me have their whale gear they would kill no more whales." Such material was hard to pry from the Makahs and then at so high a cost that the collector thereafter commissioned new, unused, and thus unritualized gear.[42]

Resistance to the sale of totem poles altered with acculturation. Lord Dufferin, the Canadian governor-general, tried in 1876 to buy a Haida pole but "the answer was a decided 'no.' "[43] Jacobsen, who had more time and arrived five years later, was able to buy one from the recently converted Stilta, and by the turn of the century Newcombe, though plagued by disputed ownership, by vendors who changed their "tum-tum," and by transportation difficulties, could buy Haida poles with relative ease.

The Kaigani were a different case. Though Governor Brady was able without difficulty to obtain a number of poles as gifts to the government, Newcombe could buy none. Similarly, he could buy no poles from the traditional Nishga of the Nass or the Gitksan of the Skeena. Their asking prices were prohibitive — calculations of the costs of the feast and potlatch associated with their erection were regarded as integral — and Newcombe was both conservative and mindful of his own interests, refusing to set a high standard of price. The first Gitksan pole was sold only in 1923 and its vendor then forced to yield to his relatives more than he had received. By the late 1920s and early 1930s, the resistance of the Nishga eroded and Barbeau was able to buy fourteen poles for museums from Toronto to Edinburgh.

A successful technique in overcoming sellers' resistance was the kind of patient ingratiation that Boas employed at Nuwitti on his first coastal visit. He spent a full eleven days at the remote Kwakiutl village, broaching the subject of buying only on the seventh day, by which time he had secured the confidence of the chief and villagers. He bought all the best masks, except two he was not allowed even to see, and many other good pieces. Newcombe, Emmons, and Barbeau, by their frequent presence among their specialty groups, were able to operate similarly. A near-substitute was the use of a local intermediary. These men and women on the spot were often missionaries, traders, or Indian agents. The most useful were natives or half-bloods. There were several types of native middleman, from mere guide, canoeist, and interpreter to full-fledged collector.

Captain Edward Fast, serving as an officer with the U. S. Army in Sitka, amassed an important collection both through ingratiation and the use of a middleman. From the moment of his arrival in the small capital he made it his business to become on good terms with the Indians and this he accomplished by gifts of tobacco and other presents. Emil Teichmann, who visited him in 1868, was impressed with the respect Fast received in the village and with Fast as "a master in the art of gaining the goodwill of the natives." The German-born officer collected much in this way but also depended upon a shaman as guide, interpreter, and collector. "In collecting his curiosities the Captain made use of the wily old medicine man as a medium" and "with great success." In one of the most detailed preserved accounts of a transaction, Teichmann related the negotiations between Fast and his native middleman.

Every morning at a fixed time, the tall, thin, blanket-wrapped figure appeared at Fast's rooms. He would take a chair, remarking in Tlingit that "the chief is very thirsty." Fast then produced a glass of whisky. A requested second glass was refused. The ritual would proceed with Fast asking "What do you want?" followed by the set reply, 'I don't want anything." A period of silence was followed by the Indian taking out a pipe and asking for tobacco. Then another pause ensued while he smoked. At last, "as if by accident," he produced an old object of slight value. The captain took no notice. The Indian laid it on the table. Fast shook his head as if it was worthless. The Indian revealed a much better piece. The captain concealed his pleasure. Then a long haggling process began, the Indian asking ten dollars but being finally beaten down to a quarter. Such a ceremony, Teichmann noted, was repeated daily. The young Teichmann, a visiting agent for a New York fur merchant, thought it scarcely excusable for an Indian of such influence "to enter the service of a white man whose object it was to exploit the Indians for his own purposes," but did not conceal his admiration for Fast and his wonderment at the weapons, axes, knives, spears, costumes, armour, helmets, and chests filled with amulets, utensils, baskets, headdresses, and other artifacts that filled the captain's rooms.[44]

In the early period, native intermediaries, although not entrusted with actual collecting, were very useful assistants. Swan found that the young Haida, Johnny Kit Elswa, "as an interpreter and buyer of curiosities, proved himself exceedingly capable." Emmons, perhaps the greatest collector of Northwest Coast material, used local Indians wherever possible. Jacobsen's Kwakiutl collecting was measurably assisted by his use of George and William Hunt, the half-blood sons of the Fort Rupert trader. George Hunt, who spoke Kwakwala like a native and was "acquainted with the customs and usage of the local Indians as if he were himself as Indian," was especially useful.[45]

At a later stage a few natives or half-bloods became actual collectors, notably Shotridge, Charlie Nowell, George Hunt, and William Beynon for Henry Wellcome. Hunt, it has been estimated, may have collected the majority of extant Kwakiutl specimens from the period in the world's museums.[46] To be entrusted with collecting, the native or near-native had to be reliable in a European sense and, for communicating and recording, he had to be literate. While Hunt, Nowell, Beynon, and the young Shotridge were not paragons of grammatical or spelling perfection, their hands were legible and their sentences conveyed their meanings plainly. Neither Hunt nor Nowell was a comfortable writer, but they did not avoid a necessary letter. Shotridge even became something of a stylist.

The great advantage of the native or near-native was the ability to act as insider, a position which even patient ingratiation could only approximate. Hunt is the outstanding example. He lived his entire life among the Kwakiutl and had a broad circle of relatives and acquaintances. Others might collect in the region: Rev. A. J. Hall for people in London, and Newcombe for Chicago, but Boas could be assured of Hunt's superiority. "You see," Hunt wrote New York, "I have lots of friend and that is Where we get the Best of all."[47] As an insider, he could raid the old caves with comparative impunity; an outsider would have caused great resentment to more than merely Rev. Hall's people. As a member of Kwakiutl society he could give a feast to scotch rumors circulating against Boas and himself.

Hunt, though not born a Kwakiutl, was raised as one. (His English father even potlatched.) Shotridge, on the other hand, was born a Tlingit but was raised in large part among mission whites. Although he stretched the advantages of his rank and relationships beyond their limits, even his tactless vanity did not keep him from utilizing his favorable position as an insider to collect things others could not. "It was only through a claim to some distant relationship that I was, at last, permitted to open the old chests and to take out and carry away from their sanctuaries the fine old pieces that had not seen daylight since the white man's religion and laws had supplanted those of the native."[48]

A few things did not need to be bought. Some were just given away. Atlieu's gift to Newcombe of a harpoon, which no money could buy, the masks given to McIlwraith, and the house and poles donated to Governor Brady have been mentioned. A Kaigani chief willed his pole to Stephen Lounsbury, passenger agent for the Great Northern, because "the old man thought that his name sounded like that of his own clan and because the railway man had told him he did not have a totem outside his home." Lounsbury erected it in front of the railway's New York passenger office.[49]

More frequent was the final trick of the collector's craft: some things were obtained simply by theft. Few collectors were above a little stealing and skulls and skeletons, highly regarded by museums in the nineteenth century, could scarcely be obtained in any other way. John Lord, a boundary survey naturalist who visited Fort Rupert, told a grisly tale of his fascination for the sugarloaf-shaped head of a Koskimo shot and decapitated by the Fort Ruperts on a recent raid. Hung as a trophy by a rope from a pole, it was "fresh, bloody, and ghastly," but Lord "determined at any risk to have the skull." At night he upset the pole and "*bagged* the head" in his game-sack. Packed in a pork-barrel, the next morning it went on board the *Otter,* as yet unmissed by the chief who owned it and whose canoe took Lord to the steamer. "Imagine what I felt when he seated himself upon the cask wherein I had hid his property." Lord gave it to the British Museum where he regarded it as "well worth investigation" by any who might be curious to compare it with a flathead skull.[50]

Jacobsen did not do much osteological collecting, but he, too, thought that the cranial deformity of the Koskimo "longheads" made their skulls "especially valuable" and he was intent on securing examples. With the assistance of half-blood guides he secured five for his handy sacks. At Comox he was unsuccessful in his attempts to climb to tree-hung burial boxes, but had more success in a night excursion to a burial site. Circumstances did not allow digging, but he appropriated from the graves whatever wood figures and masks he thought valuable. "I had already seen that I could buy none of these from the Indians, so I thought the rule here is: 'Help yourself.' "[51]

Graves were a constant temptation to those who were prone to "help themselves"; Malaspina had surrendered to it in 1792 and the precedent then established continued. The practice of disposing of the dead varied among the Northwest Coast groups, but burial boxes and shaman grave houses, common among the Tlingits and used by the Tsimshian and Haida as well, were a rich and inexpensive source for very excellent artifacts — staffs, shaman rattles, soul-catchers, charms, headdresses, and masks. They were easy marks for anyone with the necessary boat or canoe. American revenue and naval vessel crews were "the great riflers" of these graves in the early years. The Tlingits, who often hung Chilkat blankets on their grave houses soon learned better; "now that the white man does not hesitate to steal what is valuable in Indian graves, decoration is ceasing," wrote Kate Field in 1888. Emmons accumulated an enormous amount of material from gravehouses. Non-marine personnel had more difficulty, needing to hire a boat and, if close to native habitation, incurring some risk of discovery. Captain Fast and his native helper were almost caught in the act of raiding graves. John J. McLean secured skulls and a large drum from three gravesites, but the cost of a boat and two assistants made the acquisitions expensive — "and as there was a great deal of risk in robbing the graves, the money had to be paid."[52]   Boas collected hundreds of skulls and skeletons. Stealing bones from a grave was "repulsive work" but "someone had to do it," he wrote in 1888 during his major osteological field season.[53] Discretion was required, though the rule seems to have been that all was permitted so long as one did not fall afoul of the Indians or the law. Indian Superintendent Vowel gave Hunt permission to raid cave burials that were beyond the memory of living Indians. Dorsey's rip-and-run plunder c Skungo's cave and other sites earned him public and privat rebuke. Boas's collectors, the Sutton brothers, ran into troub but avoided prosecution. Newcombe engaged in a great deal commissioned bone robbery and had the advantage of his ov boat in which to hide the goods. He was discreet, though he, tc was caught at Chemanius and had to pay to keep things qui Emmons seems to have limited his gravehouse plunder to ethi logical items.

Excepting the contents of grave sites, ethnological pieces w less often stolen, if only because they were kept inside inhab villages. In the great population movements, spurred by disease and the introduction of canneries and missions to the north coast, many villages were abandoned, occasionally almost intact. The grand Edward H. Harriman Alaskan Expedition happened upon a deserted Tlingit village and its members felt quite free to take whatever was portable, including several large poles and posts. Harriman, the great railway and shipping magnate, had chartered the *George W. Elder* for a combined family holiday and expedition with a cast of leading American scientific supernumeraries made up of geologists, botanists, zoologists, and mining experts. The old Alaska hand Dall was along, so was wilderness enthusiast John Muir and the future ethnologist and Indian photographer, Edward S. Curtis.

In July, after having touched at the major southeastern cities, at Yakutat Bay, Cook Inlet, the Shumagin and Aleutian islands, and even Siberia, the steamer stopped at Cape Fox, a village abandoned as a permanent residence by the Sanyakwan Tlingit in 1893 in order to move to Saxman. Not only had they left some nineteen poles but many of their other possessions — masks, baskets, and carvings. Harriman's party found ransacked boxes and scattered pieces that indicated a previous pillage. With a feeling that what was unguarded was unowned, screens, boxes, crests, inside houseposts, and memorial poles went from shore to ship. The California Academy of Science, the Chicago Field Museum, the state universities of Michigan and Washington, and the Peabody Museum of Harvard all received examples of monumental sculpture.[54]

About a month later a Seattle Chamber of Commerce touring party came ashore at the village of Tongass, temporarily empty during the summer fishing and cannery season. Seattle's prominent citizens thought the village had been permanently abandoned, "that its relics were therefore the property of all the world," and helped themselves to a pole. Tongass, however, was not completely forsaken. The removal was observed and three Tongass natives went to William Duncan to complain. "They are greatly distressed," he wrote Governor Brady, "to think that white men should be so inconsiderate as to take away such costly property which they had erected over the remains of two of their head chiefs — the person being alive who bore all the expense & labor in honor of their dead." The Indians asked for return or restitution. The *Alaskan* newspaper had a stern editorial condemning "people who have had the benefit of centuries of the refining influences of Christian civilization, and who . . . actually steal from a people who less than a half century ago were savages."[55] After lengthy negotiations the Indians were compensated; the pole stood in Pioneer Square until it was destroyed by fire and rot in 1938. As a goodwill gesture, Civilian Conservation Corps-employed Tlingits carved another. One of the owners of the pole was Mary Ebbetts, mother of George Hunt. The Hunt family owned a duplicate pole, carved by a Kwakiutl, at Fort Rupert.

Other artifacts and poles walked off without leaving records. D. F. Tozier reputedly stole much of his collection, but museum collectors generally did not. They may have bought from some who did not have full rights to sell, but they normally paid for what they took and many were scrupulous about settling disputed claims to ownership. While theft was not uncommon, it should not be exaggerated. Most of the ethnological material which left the coast was purchased at prices mutually agreed upon between vendor and vendee. The collecting process was a trading relationship affected by normal economic factors of supply and demand, competition, accessibility, costs of transportation, by wars and trade cycles, by ethnological fashion and museum budgets.

Some tourists and visitors were cheated, some natives had to make sales under forced conditions, but the great majority of items changed hands at prices defined by normal market factors. The Northwest Coast Indians were not naive. They were experienced traders who refused offers as often as they accepted them and who were seldom prepared to part with anything cheaply. They sometimes responded to the demand quickly and adroitly, seeking higher prices in cities when field collectors offered too little and adjusting production to collecting fashion. The variation in argillite design between native and European iconography, sometimes seen as the result of internal processes, can more plausibly be attributed to the carvers' perception of the most marketable patterns. The same is true for silver work.

While it is indubitable that most material was bought and sold according to usual commercial practices, it is not the whole picture. In retrospect it is clear that the goods flowed irreversibly from native hands to Euro-American ones until little was left in possession of the descendants of the people who had invented, made, and used them. This situation, often regretted and sometimes deplored, in which the natives are divorced from the products of their heritage, has created some demands for repatriation, demands like those of the Greeks for the return of the Elgin Marbles.

If most exchanges were normal commercial transactions, the entire process can also be viewed as an unequal trading relationship, the product of a colonial encounter in which, in the long run, the terms of trade were stacked in favor of those who were part of the dominant economic system, tilted toward those whose economic system generated a surplus of the cash upon which all had come to depend. The Indian economy's own surplus, not inconsequential, was most often expended upon conspicuous status consumption, upon blankets, pans, flour, sewing machines, and other trade goods. The Indians may have retained heirlooms; they did not collect Indian artifacts. The Whale House of the Chilkats might be seen as a kind of *schatzkammer,* but there were no indigenous museums.[56] The museum, as an institution dedicated to acquisition, exhibition, and preservation, was a European phenomenon.

To the museum and its collectors is owed the preservation of most of the surviving art and cultural objects of the Northwest Coast peoples. "Only blind passion," Adolf Michaelis wrote of the Parthenon frieze, "could doubt that Lord Elgin's act was an act of preservation."[57] Elgin, of course, also had other motives and even museums are imperfect instruments of preservation. While always concerned with their own interests, they nevertheless saved and conserved artifacts that otherwise would have been lost, dispersed, or decayed. By making these available for scholarly, popular, and artistic study and publication, even museums geographically far removed from the Northwest Coast became repositories of native culture. While only Sheldon Jackson's Sitka museum conceived as one of its purposes the preservation of material for later generations of natives, all museum collections developed into more than showcases of alien and dead cultures. Like the cameras which have caught and captured images of the historical past, museums captured the material heritage of the Northwest Coast. They are now partial legatees of that great culture.

Notes

NOTES

PRESCRIPT

*Boas to children, 14 December 1930, Boas Family Papers, American
Philosophical Society.

Chapter 1
PRELUDE

1. Donald C. Cutter, ed. and trans., "Diary of Tomás de la Pena y
Saravia," in *The California Coast: A Bilingual Edition of Documents
from the Sutro Collection* (Norman: University of Oklahoma Press,
1969), 156–61; "Diary of Juan Crespi," in *ibid.*, 232–41; Warren L.

Cook, *Flood Tide of Empire: Spain and the Pacific Northwest, 1543–1819* (New Haven: Yale University Press, 1973), 59–63.

2. Pérez diary, 19 July 1774, in Cook, *Flood Tide,* 60. For treatments of the Indians and the fur trade period, see Joyce A. Wike, "The Effect of the Maritime Fur Trade on Northwest Coast Indian Society," Ph.D. dissertation, Columbia University, 1951, and Robin Fisher, *Contact and Conflict: Indian-European Relations in British Columbia, 1774–1890* (Vancouver: University of British Columbia Press, 1977), chs. 1 and 2. Erna Gunther, *Indian Life on the Northwest Coast of North America* (Chicago: University of Chicago Press, 1972) must be used with great caution.

3. Rioux quoted in J. C. Beaglehole, ed., *The Journals of Captain James Cook on His Voyages of Discovery: The Voyage of the "Resolution" and "Discovery," 1776–1780* (Cambridge: Hakluyt Society, 1967), I, 295–96 n5. Alejandro Malaspina, *Viaje político-científico alrededor del Mundo . . . 1789 á 1794* (2nd ed.; Madrid, 1885), cited in Frederica de Laguna, *Under Mount Saint Elias: The History and Culture of the Yakutat Tlingit* (Washington, D. C.: Smithsonian Institution Press, 1972), Part I: *Through Alien Eyes: A History of Yakutat,* 143.

4. Beaglehole, ed., *Journals,* I, 296; II, 1091; Robin Fisher and J. M. Bumsted, eds., *An Account of a Voyage to the North West Coast of America in 1785 & 1786 by Alexander Walker* (Vancouver: Douglas & McIntyre; Seattle: University of Washington Press, 1982), 120.

5. Fisher and Bumsted, eds., *Walker,* 43.

6. Beaglehole, ed., *Journals,* I, 319–20; *James Strange's Journal and Narrative of the Commercial Expedition from Bombay to the North-West Coast of America . . .* (Madras: Government Press, 1929), 25.

7. Rioux, in Beaglehole, ed., *Journals,* I, 322 n2; Fisher and Bumsted, eds., *Walker,* 113.

8. James Burney, *A Chronological History of North-Eastern Voyages of Discovery . . .* (London: Payne & Foss, 1819), 218; King quoted in Beaglehole, ed., *Voyages,* II, 1414.

9. Fisher and Bumsted, eds., *Walker,* 119–20. On good evidence Fisher and Bumsted think this a wolf mask, but its description as a human face with two flaps projecting from the ears like Mercury does not fit and Walker had shown himself sensitive to the differing representation of masks resembling a "fox" and those with a human face. Two which may have approximated it are Museo de América, 1308, illustrated as no.7, p. 13, of Museum of New Mexico, *The Malaspina Expedition: "In the Pursuit of Knowledge"* (Santa Fe: Museum of New Mexico Press, 1977) and Edward Malin, *A World of Faces* (Portland: Timber Press, 1978), p. 177.

10. King, in Beaglehole, ed., *Voyages,* II, 1414. See J. C. H. King,

Artificial Curiosities from the Northwest Coast of America: Native American Artefacts in the British Museum Collected on the Third Voyage of Captain James Cook and Acquired through Sir Joseph Banks (London: British Museum Publications, 1981), 77–78.

11. Urey Lisiansky [Iurii Lisianskii], *A Voyage Round the World . . . in the Ship Neva* (London: John Booth [et al.], 1814), 149–50, 240–41.

12. Henry R. Wagner, ed. and trans., "Journal of Tomás de Suría of His Voyage with Malaspina to the Northwest Coast of America in 1791," *Pacific Historical Review*, 5 (September 1936), 259; Pedro de Novo y Colson, *Political-Scientific Voyage . . . under the Command of the Naval Captain Don Alexandro Malaspina and Don José de Bustamente y Guerra from 1789–1794* (Madrid, 1885), trans. Carl Robinson (typescript, University of British Columbia, 1934), 334.

13. John White to Miss Blackburne, 18 October 1780, in Beaglehole, ed., *Voyages*, II, 1560.

14. The literature on Cook material is now both rich and available; see especially J. C. H. King, *Artificial Curiosities*; Adrienne L. Kaeppler's several publications, especially *"Artificial Curiosities": An Exhibition of Native Manufactures Collected on the Three Voyages of Captain James Cook, RN* (Honolulu: Bishop Museum Press, 1978); Roland W. Force and Maryanne Force, *Art and Artifacts of the 18th Century: Objects from the Leverian Museum as Painted by Sarah Stone* (Honolulu: Bishop Museum Press, 1968). For Menzies, see Richard H. Dillon, "Archibald Menzies' Trophies," *British Columbia Historical Quarterly*, 15 (1951), 151–59. For the Spanish voyage, see Anna Rustow, "Die Objekte der Malaspina-Expedition im archaölogischen Museum zu Madrid," *Baessler-Archiv*, 22 (1939), 172–204; Norman Feder, "The Malaspina Collection" *American Indian Art*, 2 (Summer 1977), 40–48ff; Museum of New Mexico, *Malaspina Expedition*.

15. See Susan Stewart, "Sir George Simpson: Collector," *The Beaver*, 313 (Summer 1982), 4–12. *Physician and Fur Trader: Journals of William Fraser Tolmie* (Vancouver: Mitchell Press, 1963), 327–28, 313; see "Collection Scouler," *Revue d'Anthropologie*, (1872), 355; E.-T. Hamy, "John Scouler, ses traveaux et sa collection" in "Décades Americanae: Mémoires d'archéologie et d'ethnographie américaines," 3rd Decade, 9–13.

16. For the Russian collections, see I. A. Zolotarevskaja et al., "Ethnographical Material from the Americas in Russian Collections," *Proceedings of the Thirty-second International Congress of Americanists, Copenhagen, 1956* (Nendeln: Kraus Reprint, 1976), 221–31; Erna Siebert and Werner Forman, *North American Indian Art* (London: Paul Hamlyn, 1967); and a series of articles, "Muzei Materialy po Tlingitan," which appeared in *Akademiia Nauk SSR: Muzei Antropologii i Etnografii: Sbornik,* v. 6, 79–114; v. 8, 270–301; v. 9, 167–86.

17. Henry N. Michael, ed., *Lieutenant Zogoskin's Travels in Russian America, 1842–1844: The First Ethnographic and Geographic Investigations in the Yukon and Kuskokwim Valleys of Alaska* ("Arctic Institute of North America Anthropology of the North: Translations from Russian Sources," no. 7; Toronto: Arctic Institute of North America by University of Toronto Press, 1967). Professor R. A. Pierce of Queen's University, Kingston, was helpful on this point.

18. E. E. Bloomkvist, "A Russian Scientific Expedition to California and Alaska, 1839–1849," trans. Basil Dmytryshyn and E. A. P. Crownhart-Vaughan, *Oregon Historical Quarterly,* 73 (June 1972), 100–170.

19. See William Stanton, *The Great United States Exploring Expedition of 1838–1842* (Berkeley: University of California Press, 1975), esp. ch. 18; Charles Coleman Sellers, *Mr. Peale's Museum: Charles Willson Peale and the First Popular Museum of Natural Science and Art* (New York: W. W. Norton, 1980). Some of Peale's material is now in the Peabody Museum, Harvard.

Chapter 2
BAIRD AND SWAN BUILD A COLLECTION

1. Dall, *Spencer Fullerton Baird: A Biography* (Philadelphia: J. P. Lippincott, 1915), 293; Smithsonian Institution, *Annual Report* (hereafter SIAR), 1853, 55; Baird to George P. Marsh, 2 July 1853, in Dall, *Baird,* 305; SIAR, 1854, 25.

2. Quoted in Curtis M. Hinsley, Jr., *Savages and Scientists: The Smithsonian Institution and the Development of American Anthropology, 1846–1910* (Washington, D. C.: Smithsonian Institution, 1981), 67. I am greatly indebted to Professor Hinsley's fine work on this period of the Institution and American anthropology.

3. SIAR, 1860, 39; Smithsonian Institution, "Smithsonian Miscellaneous Collections," v. 7, no. 160 (Washington, D. C., 1863), 1, 2, 4.

4. Henry, "Circular Relating to Collections in Archaeology and Ethnology," vol. 8, no. 205 of "Smithsonian Miscellaneous Collections" (1869), 1.

5. SIAR, 1868, 33.

6. Henry to Ring, 14 December 1868, Record Unit (RU) 33, v. 12; 10 November 1869, RU 33, v. 16, Smithsonian Institution Archives (hereafter SIA).

7. Henry to Colyer, 22 December 1870, RU 33, v. 22, SIA.

8. Purchased from Leavitt, Strebeigh & Co., New York, who had charge of the collection at Clinton Hall Art Galleries. "Catalogue of Antiquities and Curiosities Collected in the Territory of Alaska by Edward G. Fast" (np, nd [New York, 1869?]); Gibbs to Jeffries Wyman, 19 October 1869, Letterbook I, no. 188, Peabody Museum.

9. Quoted in Lucile McDonald, *Swan among the Indians: Life of James G. Swan, 1818–1900* (Portland: Binfords & Mort, 1972), 108. A more imaginative treatment of Swan may be found in Ivan Doig, *Winter Brothers: A Season at the Edge of America* (New York: Harcourt Brace Jovanovich, 1980).

10. *The Northwest Coast, or Three Years' Residence in Washington Territory* (New York: Harper & Brothers, 1857), republished by the University of Washington Press in 1957, and in facsimile by Ye Galleon Press, Fairfield, Washington, 1966.

11. Norman H. Clark, "Introduction" to Swan, *Northwest Coast,* Seattle: University of Washington Press, 1957), xx.

12. Swan to Baird, 9 June 1863, Acc. 244; 6 July 1863, Acc. 269, USNM.

13. Swan to Baird, 13 October 1863, Acc. 295; 22 March 1864, 9 June 1864, Acc. 418; 19 July 1864, Acc. 494, USNM; Baird to Swan, 9 December 1863, RU 53, v. 29, SIA.

14. Swan, "The Indians of Cape Flattery, at the Entrance to the Strait of Fuca, Washington Territory," *Smithsonian Contributions to Knowledge,* v. 16 (Washington, D. C.: Government Printing Office, 1869). Two later papers dealt with the Haida.

15. Swan to Baird, 22 January 1867, Acc. 928, USNM; 9 March 1869, RU 26, SIA.

16. Swan to Baird, 9 March 1869, 24 May 1870, RU 26; 20 March 1873, RU 52, v. 10, SIA.

17. Swan to Baird, 12 May, 3 June 1873, RU 26; Baird to Swan, 22 February 1873, RU 53, v. 47; Swan to Baird, 3 June, 12 May 1873, RU 26, SIA.

18. Baird to Swan, 14 May, 7 April 1873, RU 53, v. 47; Swan to Baird, 28 April 1873, RU 26, SIA.

19. Swan to Baird, 24 November, 22 December 1873, RU 26; Baird to Swan, 10 December 1873, RU 53, v. 48, SIA.

20. Swan to Baird, 12 February, 1 January 1874, RU 26, SIA.

21. Swan to Baird, 10 March 1874, RU 26, SIA. The Museum für Völkerkunde, Vienna, records show a limited purchase by Steindachner; Swan Diary, 21 and 22 November 1873, University of Washington Archives. See also [Christian F. Feest], *Indianer Nordamerikas* (Vienna: Museum für Völkerkunde, 1968), 27, 107–27.

22. Baird to Swan, 22 July 1874, RU 53, v. 50; Swan to Baird, 19 and 26 June 1874, RU 26, SIA.

23. Swan to Baird, 1 September, 16 October 1874; Swan to Henry, 30 October 1874, RU 26, SIA.

24. SIAR, 1875, 67.

25. E. C. Chirouse, agent at the Duwamish-Tulalip Reserve, complied with the Department of the Interior's request by shipping 53 specimens, collected without cost, all well labeled and catalogued. These

seem not to have reached Philadelphia and were transferred to the National Museum only in October 1889, Acc. 22,496, USNM. Swan, who was in touch with Chirouse, may have been responsible for the collection.

26. Baird to E. P. Smith, 14 and 16 December 1875, Record Group (RG) 75, Office of Indian Affairs, Records of Bureau of Indian Affairs, quoted in Robert A. Trennert, Jr., "A Grand Failure: The Centennial Indian Exhibition of 1876," *Prologue,* 6 (Summer 1974), 122–23.

27. Baird to Swan, 13 March 1875, RU 53, SIA.

28. Swan to Baird, 25 March 1875, RU 53; Swan Diary, 27 May 1875.

29. Swan, *San Francisco Evening Bulletin,* 22 May 1860, in Swan, *Almost Out of the World: Scenes from Washington Territory: The Strait of Juan de Fuca, 1859–61,* William A. Katz, ed. (Tacoma: Washington State Historical Society, 1971), 79.

30. Swan, "Official Report," in United States Treasury Department, Special Agents Division, *Report upon the Customs District, Public Service and Resources of Alaska Territory,* 45th Cong., 3rd Sess., Senate Executive Document 59, 143–45.

31. Swan to Baird, 17 June 1875, RU 70, SIA.

32. Swan, Acc. 4,730, USNM; Swan to Commissioner of Indian Affairs, 11 October 1875, "Report on His Cruise on the Coast . . . ," National Anthropological Archives, 1207-a; Swan, "Official Report," 147–48.

33. Swan to Baird, 23 July 1875, RU 70, SIA.

34. Swan to Baird, 29 July, 3 August, 14 September 1875, RU 70, SIA.

35. Swan to Baird, 30 September 1875 (Victoria), 11 and 18 November 1875, 25 and 28 March 1876, RU 70, SIA.

36. SIAR, 1876, 69; Baird to Swan, 16 December 1875, RU 53, v. 60, SIA; Trennert, *Prologue,* 6 (Summer 1974), 124–26; Swan to Baird, 30 December 1875, RU 70, SIA.

37. Swan to Baird, 30 December 1875, RU 70; 2 May 1876, RU 26, SIA. The "Indian Ring" was a clandestine group of contractors, Indian agents, and politicians who allegedly made illegal profits from government transactions with Indians.

38. Swan to Baird, 10 April 1876, RU 70; 2 May 1876, RU 26; Baird to Swan, 8 June 1876, RU 53, v. 69; Swan to Baird, 7 July 1876, RU 70, SIA.

39. See Trennert, *Prologue,* 6 (Summer 1974), 127; Judith Elise Braun, "The North American Indian Exhibits at the 1876 and 1893 World Expositions: The Influence of Scientific Thought on Popular Attitudes" (Master's thesis, George Washington University, 1975.)

40. Swan to Baird, 30 September (Victoria), 3 August, 9 November, 4 October 1875, RU 70, SIA.

41. Swan to Baird, 17 June, 29 July, 6 December 1875; 24 January, 27

March 1876, RU 70; 9 April 1876, RU 26, SIA; *Daily British Colonist* (Victoria), 5 April 1876, 3.

42. Swan to Baird, 24 September 1875, 15 May 1876, RU 70, SIA. The Tsimshian pole from Fort Simpson is illustrated in Marius Barbeau, *Totem Poles* (Ottawa: National Museum of Canada, 1950), I, nos. 163, 164; the Kaigani pole in II, no. 307.

43. Thomas Crosby to Swan, 2 November 1875, quoted in Swan to Baird, 15 November 1875; Swan to Baird, 10 April 1876, RU 70, SIRA.

44. H. Craig Miner, "The United States Government Building at the Centennial Exhibition, 1874–77," *Prologue,'* 4 (Winter 1972), 211; Trennert, *ibid.,* 6 (Summer 1974), 129; Frank H. Norton, ed., *Frank Leslie's Historical Register of the United States Centennial Exposition, 1876* (New York: Frank Leslie's, 1877), 106; *Evening Star* (Chicago), 5 July 1876, Centennial Scrapbooks, vol. 17, Philadelphia City Archives.

45. "Characteristics of the International Fair," *The Atlantic Monthly,* 38 (1876), 497; Howells, "Sennight of the Centennial," *ibid.,* 103. For treatment of the Centennial Exhibition within the context of racial thought, see Robert William Rydell II, "All the World's a Fair: America's International Expositions, 1876–1916" (Ph.D. dissertation, UCLA, 1980), I.

46. Swan to Baird, 16 June 1873, RU 26; 25 January 1876, RU 70, SIA.

47. Swan to Baird, 20 August 1876, RU 26, SIA.

48. SIAR, 1877, 37.

49. Swan to Baird, 6 February 1881, RU 26, SIA.

50. McLean to Baird, 27 July 1881, Acc. 10,803, USNM.

51. McLean to Baird, 7 and 8 September 1881, Acc. 11,616, USNM.

52. Baird to Jackson, 31 October 1881, typescript, Sheldon Jackson Papers, Presbyterian Historical Society, Philadelphia; Baird to McLean, 20 March, 8 August 1882, RU 33, vols. 119, 127, Acc. 11,616, USNM.

53. McLean to Baird, 11 May 1882, Acc. 12,009, USNM.

54. SIAR, 1879, 39.

55. Baird to Samuel Randall, 15 April 1880, in William Jones Rhees, ed., *The Smithsonian Institution: Documents Relative to Its Origin and History, 1836–1899* ("Smithsonian Miscellaneous Collections," vol. XLII), 2 vols. (1901), I, 858; SIAR, 1879, 39; Baird to Swan, 5 May 1882, Baird to McLean, 5 May 1882, RU 33, v. 122, SIA.

56. Baird to Swan, 2 June, 31 October, 1882, RU 33, vols. 124, 131, SIA.

57. Powell to S. B. Massa, n.d., cited in Virginia H. McK. Noelke, "The Origin and Early History of the Bureau of American Ethnology, 1879–1910" (Ph.D. dissertation, University of Texas at Aus-

tin, 1974), 187; Baird to Powell, 10 August 1882, 7 July 1883, RU 31, box 23, SIA. In the end Baird was persuaded to keep only $3,000 in 1883, but thereafter reverted to the $5,000 reserve. This funding as well as other aspects of the Bureau and its relationship to the Institution are well treated by Noelke.

58. Swan to Baird, 2 October 1882, Acc. 12,054, USNM.
59. Baird to Swan, 21 November 1882, RU 33, v. 131, SIA.
60. Baird to Swan, 30 January, 29 May 1883, RU 33, vols. 137, 142, SIA.
61. Swan to Baird, 7 February, 20 March 1883, RU 26, SIA.
62. "Extract from Diary of Cruise to Queen Charlotte Islands, B. C. by James G. Swan," 1883, 22, University of Washington Archives; *Daily British Colonist,* 28 September 1883, 2; Swan to Baird, 3 August 1883, Acc. 13,780, USNM.
63. Swan Diary, 1883, 38; Swan, "Report on Explorations and Collections in the Queen Charlotte Islands, British Columbia," SIAR, 1884, 143.
64. Swan Diary, 1883, 38, 55; *Daily British Colonist,* 28 and 29 September 1883, each p. 2.
65. Swan Diary, 1883, 57. See George F. MacDonald, *Haida Monumental Art: Villages of the Queen Charlotte Islands* (Vancouver: University of British Columbia Press, 1983), 93, where it is House 5.
66. Swan Diary, 1883, 57, notes that it cost him six dollars. It is illustrated in Robert Bruce Inverarity, *Art of the Northwest Coast Indians* (Berkeley: University of California Press, 1950), no. 104.
67. Swan Diary, 1883, 59–60.
68. Swan to Baird, 12 December, 17 November 1883, RU 26, SIA.
69. Swan to Baird, 3 August 1883, Acc. 13,780, USNM; Swan Diary, 1883, 31–32; Swan to Baird, 15 April 1884, RU 26; Baird to Swan, 14 December 1883, RU 33, v. 154, SIA. Swan's total bill, as rendered on December 4, 1884, was $3,694.07; his total income from January 1883 to February 1884, $3,150. He paid off the HBC at the end of April 1884 and the Skidegate Oil Company on November 18, 1885. Swan accounts, 11, University of Washington Archives.
70. Swan to Baird, 4 September 1884, RU 70, SIA.
71. Did Swan fiddle? Did he hold back 1883 collections? It appears so from his accounts, yet he made no effort to disguise the sources of these 1884 shipments. Acc. 15,152 and 15,690, USNM.
72. Swan to Baird, 21 July 1884, RU 26, SIA.
73. U. S. National Museum, *Annual Report,* 1888, 225–386.
74. Swan to G. B. Goode, 27 July 1889, RU 189, SIA.
75. ("The Works of Hubert Howe Bancroft," v. 39; San Francisco: The History Co., 1890), 540.
76. Baird was a consummate diplomat in dealing with his collectors and

his treatment of Swan fits the pattern described by William A. Deiss in his "Spencer F. Baird and His Collectors," *Journal of the Society for the Bibliography of Natural History*, 9 (1980), 635–45.

Chapter 3
THE FRENCH AND GERMAN COMPETITORS

1. SIAR, 22.
2. Kriston Bahnson, "Ueber ethnographische Museen," *Mitteilungen der anthropologischen Cesellschaft in Wien* 18 (1888), 112. For a brief overview of anthropological museum history, see William C. Sturtevant, "Does Anthropology Need Museums?," Biological Society of Washington, *Proceedings,* 82 (1969–70), 619–25.
3. Bahnson, *Mitteilungen . . . Wien,* 18 (1888), 113; Brinton, "The Aims of Anthropology," *Science,* n.s. 2 (30 August 1895), 244; Bahnson, *Mitteilungen . . . Wien,* 18 (1888), 113.
4. Bahnson, *Mitteilungen . . . Wien,* 18 (1888), 115.
5. The most complete and accessible treatment of Pinart is Ross Parmenter, *Explorer, Linguist and Ethnologist: A Descriptive Bibliography of the Published Works of Alphonse Louis Pinart, with Notes on His Life* (Los Angeles: Southwest Museum, 1966).
6. File DT84.91 and catalogue, Musée de l'Homme. Along with its unsighted twin, collected by I. W. Powell in the same area in 1879, the mask is featured in Wilson Duff, *Images Stone B. C.: Thirty Centuries of Northwest Coast Indian Sculpture* (Toronto: Oxford University Press; Seattle: University of Washington Press, 1975), 160–67, 188.
7. Pinart struggled along, after his family fortune collapsed. He worked for the de Lesepps company at Panama for a time, and returned to France where he remained, save for an 1896 trip to Central America. The hard times may have contributed to marital problems. In 1880 he had married Zelia Nuttall, an American accustomed to wealth. Although they shared anthropological interests (she was to establish a much sounder reputation than he), she divorced him eight years later and bitterness characterized their later relations. Pinart continued to publish, not very significantly, married again, and died just short of his sixtieth birthday in 1911.
8. The expedition's original leader was forced by ill health to resign. The preparations are recorded in "Correspondenz &c betreffend die Expedition Mtgl. Dr. Krause n. der Tschuktschen-Halbinsel," Acta Verein für Polarforschung, Stadtarchiv Bremen.
9. "Die wissenschaftliche Expedition der Bremer geographischen Gesellschaft nach den Küstengebieten an der Beringstrasse (Reisebriefe der Gebr. Dr. Krause)," *Deutsche geographische Blätter* 4 (1881),

245–47. See Aurel Krause, *The Tlingit Indians: Results of a Trip to the Northwest Coast of America and the Bering Straits,* trans. Erna Gunther (original 1885; Seattle: University of Washington Press, 1956), 1–10, which includes a list of reports and accounts.

10. This account depends upon the just-cited publications as well as on a typescript of letters and reports compiled by Ella Krause and in possession of Dr. Werner A. Krause, Ratzeburg. The most relevant portion of this was published as Aurel Krause, *Journey to the Tlingits by Aurel and Arthur Krause, 1881/82,* trans. Margot Krause McCaffrey (Haines: Haines Centennial Commission, 1981).

11. See Krause, *Tlingit Indians,* 145–46; "Katalog ethnologischer Gegenstände aus den Tchuktschenlande und dem südöstlichen Alaska," *Deutsche geographische Blätter,* supplement to vol. 5, no. 4 (Bremen: Carl Schünemann, 1882). Aurel Krause, *Die Tlingit-Indianer* (Jena: Hermann Constenoble, 1885), 420; *Sechster Jahresbericht des Vorstandes der Geographischen Gesellschaft in Bremen* (Bremen, 1883), 4.

12. The most recent treatments of Bastian are Annamarie Fiedermutz-Laun, *Der kulturhistorische Gedanke bei Adolf Bastian: Systematisierung und Darstellung der Theorie und Methode mit dem Versuch einer Bewertung der kulturhistorischen Gehaltes auf drei Grundlage* (Wiesbaden: Franz Sterner Verlag, 1970); Klaus Peter Koepping, *Adolf Bastian and the Psychic Unity of Mankind: The Foundations of Anthropology in Nineteenth-Century Germany* (St. Lucia, Qld.: University of Queensland Press, 1983).

13. "Die Einweihung des neuen Museums für Völkerkunde in Berlin," *Correspondenz-Blatt der deutschen Gesellschaft für Archäologie, Ethnologie und Urgeschichte* 18 (January 1887), 3; Franz Hager, 'Die Einweihung des neuen Museums für Völkerkunde in Berlin," *Mitteilungen der anthropologischen Gesellschaft in Wien* 17 (1887), [15–20].

14. George A. Dorsey, "Notes on the Anthropological Museums of Central Europe," *American Anthropologist,* n.s. 1 (1899), 468.

15. A. Bastian, "Erwerbungen der Ethnologischen Abteilung des Berliner kgl. Museums von der Nordwestküste Nordamerikas" (Berlin [1882], 3; "Hr. Bastian spricht, unter Vorlage zahlreicher Gegenstände, über die Haida's," *Verhandlungen der Berliner anthropologischen Gesellschaft,* 12 (1882), 278–89, 297.

16. Horst Hartmann, "Abteilung Amerikanische Naturvölker," in K. Krieger and G. Koch, *Hundert Jahre Museum für Völkerkunde Berlin, Baessler-Archiv,* n.f. 21 (1973), 219–20. This anniversary volume presents an excellent history of the museum.

17. Bastian, "Erwerbungen," 3; Bastian, *Verhandlungen der Berliner anthropologischen Gesellschaft,* 12 (1882), 284.

18. Bastian to Dall, 8 July 1881, box 6, Dall Papers, RU 7073, SIA.

19. See Sigrid Westphal-Hellbusch, "Zur Geschichte des Museums," in Krieger and Kock, *Hundert Jahre, Baessler-Archiv,* n.f. 21 (1973), 65–68.

20. Biographical details of Jacobsen's early life may be found in the autobiographical appendix to A. Woldt, ed., *Captain Jacobsen's Reise an der Nordwestküste Amerikas, 1881–1883* . . . (Leipzig: Max Spohr, 1884), available in English as Johan Adrian Jacobsen, *Alaskan Voyage, 1881–1883: An Expedition to the Northwest Coast of America,* trans. Erna Gunther (Chicago: University of Chicago Press, 1977), 215–23.

21. Carl Hagenbeck, *Von Tieren und Menschen: Erlebnisse und Erfahrungen* (Berlin: Vita Deutsches Verlagschau, 1908), 96.

22. Tagebuch I (May 1877–December 1881), 139, insert, and 24 July 1881, Jacobsen Papers, Hamburgisches Museum für Völkerkunde.

23. *Ibid.,* marginalia (c. 1931) at 30 July 1881.

24. Woldt, ed., *Jacobsen's Reise,* 66 (Gunther, 40).

25. Jacobsen to Hagenbeck, 3 November 1881, Jacobsen Papers; Hagenbeck to Jacobsen, 4 February 1882, Acta Jacobsen, Museum für Völkerkunde, Berlin (hereafer BMfV).

26. Tagebuch II, 4–8 April 1882, Jacobsen Papers; Hagenbeck to Jacobsen, 17 March 1882, telegram, Acta Jacobsen, BMfV; Woldt, ed., *Jacobsen's Reise,* 137. The Gunther translation omits a key paragraph which tells of the telegram. It should be at the bottom of her page 77. The next paragraph's first sentence is hopelessly mangled.

27. Hagenbeck to Jacobsen, 17 March 1882, Jacobsen Papers. One died in Paris in 1881, one in February en route to Zurich, four died there, and another was to die on the way back to South America — in all, seven of eleven. Prof. Dr. Bollinger, "Ueber die Feuerländer, *Correspondenz-Blatt der deutsche Gesellschaft für Anthropologie, Ethnologie und Urgeschichte,* 15 (April 1884), 25–27.

28. *Daily British Colonist* (Victoria), 19 April 1882.

29. Tagebuch I, 24 September 1881, Jacobsen Papers; also Woldt, ed., *Jacobsen's Reise,* 27 (Gunther, 17); Jacobsen to [Bastian], 4 October 1881, Acta Jacobsen, BMfV.

30. Tagebuch I, 3 October 1881, Jacobsen Papers; for Dufferin, see Molyneux St. John, *The Sea of Mountains: An Account of Lord Dufferin's Tour through British Columbia in 1876* (2 vols.; London: Hurst and Blackett, 1877), II, 34; Jacobsen to Hagenbeck, 3 November 1881, Jacobsen Papers; Krause, *Journey to the Tlingits,* 55.

31. A. Bastian, *The Northwest Coast of America: Being Results of Recent Ethnological Researches from the Collection of the Royal Museums of Berlin* (New York: Dodd, Mead [1883], n.p.); A. Krause, "A. Bastian: Amerikas Nordwestküste," *Zeitschrift für Ethnologie,* 15 (1883), 220.

32. *Neueste Ergebnisse ethnologischer Reisen aus den Sammlungen der Königlichen Museen zu Berlin* (Berlin: A. Asher, 1883). Bastian wrote the introduction, Albert Grünwedel and Edward Krause the descriptions, and Wilhelm Reiss did the illustrations. A pirated English edition, condemned by Bastian, is cited above.

33. Jacobsen's written German was, as might be expected, quite awful and had to be made "literary and human." Albert Grünwedel to Franz Boas, 6 May 1887, Boas Professional Papers, American Philosophical Society; "Reise in Alaska/Eskimos, 1882–83," 379, Jacobsen Papers.

34. This figure does not include the northern Indian and Eskimo collection he made after leaving the coast.

35. "Autobiographische Aufzeichnungen: Fortsetzung and Lebenbeschreibung," 5, Jacobsen Papers. A diary of the journey to Japan is in the Jacobsen Papers, but it does not continue for the Northwest Coast.

36. "Reminiscences of B. F. Jacobsen," 19–20, Provincial Archives of British Columbia (hereafter PABC).

37. F. von Schirp, *Bella-Coola Indianer* (Berlin: Verlag Jacobsen und von Schirp, n.d.), a program to accompany the Bella Coola troupe, a copy of which is in PABC; "Die Bella-Coola-Indianer in Zoologischen Garten," *Leipziger Tageblatt,* 20 September 1885, newspaper cuttings, I, Jabobsen Papers.

38. *Daily British Colonist* (Victoria), 21 July 1885; "Autobiographische Aufzeichnung," n.p., Jacobsen Papers.

39. "Agreement made between nine Indians of the Bella Coola Tribe of British Columbia and J. A. Jacobsen," 25 July 1885, Urkunde und Dokumente, Jacobsen Papers.

40. *Daily British Colonist* 28 July 1885.

41. The following account is dependent upon the newspaper cuttings in the Jacobsen Papers.

42. These are Kwakiutl names, not Bella Coola, which would be variants of Elaxo'LEla and OlEx.

43. *Leipziger Zeitung,* 1885, newspaper cuttings, I; *Leipziger Nachrichter,* 29 September 1885, II (quoted). For some comparable features, see T. F. McIlwraith, *The Bella Coola Indians* (2 vols.; Toronto: University of Toronto Press, 1948), II, 158–59, and Charlie Nowell's account of a "Towidi" (Toogwede) dance in which a girl is burned in a box. Using a tunnel, she escapes, substituting for herself a blanket-wrapped seal. The voice is provided by a kelp tube. Clellan S. Ford, *Smoke from Their Fires: The Life of a Kwakiutl Chief* (New Haven: Yale University Press, 1941), 120.

44. *Breslauer Zeitung,* 12 February 1886, newpaper cuttings, II, Jacobsen Papers. The meaning of the eight skulls is probably erroneous: see

Franz Boas, "The Social Organization and the Secret Societies of the Kwakiutl Indians," U. S. National Museum, *Annual Report,* 1895 (Washington, D. C.: Government Printing Office, 1897), 447.

45. *Berliner Tageblatt,* 27 January 1886, newspaper cuttings, II, Jacobsen Papers.

46. *Staatsbürger Zeitung,* 26 January 1886, newspaper cuttings, I, Jacobsen Papers.

47. Boas, "Social Organization" 433–35, and "The Winter Ceremonial," *Kwakiutl Ethnography,* Helen Codere, ed. (Chicago: University of Chicago Press, 1966), 280–85. The later career of Pooh-Pooh is unknown, though Boas refers to him in "Social Organization," 649, based on information probably gathered after 1886.

48. "Autobiographische Aufzeichnungen: Fortsetzung und Lebensbeschreibung," 5; *Cöln Sonntags Anzeiger,* 6 June 1886; *Breslauer Gerichtszeitung,* February 1886, newspaper cuttings, II, Jacobsen Papers; *Daily British Colonist* (Victoria), 18 August 1886, 2.

49. Stumpf, "Lieder der Bellakula-Indianer," *Vierteljahrshefte für Musikwissenschaft,* 2 (1886), 405–26.

50. See Boas, "The Language of the Bilhoola in British Columbia," *Science,* 7 (5 March 1886), 218; "Sprache der Bella-Coola-Indianer," *Verhandlung der Berliner Gesellschaft für Anthropologie, Ethnologie und Urgeschichte,* 18 (1886), 202–6; "Mitteilungen über die Vilxula-Indianer," *Originalmitteilungen aus den Kaiserlichen Museum für Völkerkunde* (1885–86), 177–81; "Kapitän Jacobsen's Bella-Coola-Indianer," *Berliner Tageblatt,* 25 January 1886, newpaper cuttings, I, Jacobsen Papers.

51. Virchow, Die anthropologische Untersuchung der Bella-Coola," *Verhandlung der Berliner Gesellschaft für Anthropologie, Ethnologie und Urgeschichte,* 18 (1886), 214–15.

52. *Leipziger Tages Anzeiger,* 11 October 1885, newspaper cuttings, I, Jacobsen Papers; see Cliff Kopas, *Bella Coola* (Vancouver: Mitchell Press, 1970), 236. A photo of one Bella Coola, seated with a German girl, is in the Jacobsen Papers.

53. *Daily British Colonist,* 18 August 1886. Adrian Jacobsen enjoyed a long life. After collecting in Indonesia, he settled into the restaurant business, ending as manager of the large restaurant at Hagenbeck's zoo. He travelled to South Dakota in 1910 to bring back a group of Teton Sioux for a show and led game expeditions to the Arctic when he was past seventy. He died in Hamburg in 1947, age ninety-three. His collection at Berlin suffered severe losses during the war. About 1,675 of 2,036 catalogued entries survive, but most of the larger pieces, including his pole, were destroyed by fire after the liberation of Berlin. The Krauses' Hamburg collection was almost totally lost

after being evacuated from the museum building (which survived almost intact).

Chapter 4
The North American Rivals

1. See Ted C. Hinckley, "Sheldon Jackson as Preserver of Alaska's Native Culture," *Pacific Historical Review*, 33 (November 1964), 411–24; "Sheldon Jackson, Presbyterian Lobbyist for the Great Land of Alaska," *Journal of Presbyterian History*, 40 (March 1962), 3–23; Harrison A. Brann, "Bibliography of the Sheldon Jackson Collection in the Presbyterian Historical Society," *Journal of the Presbyterian Historical Society*, 30 (September 1952), 139–64.

2. W. Henry Green to Sheldon Jackson, 13 May 1881; William C. Roberts to Jackson, 14 July 1881; Green to Jackson, 10 August 1882, Jackson Papers, Presbyterian Historical Society, Philadelphia.

3. Jackson to John G. Brady, 8 July 1882, John G. Brady Papers, Yale Collection of Western Americana, the Beinecke Rare Book and Manuscript Library, Yale University.

4. See Donald Baird, "Tlingit Treasures: How an Important Collection Came to Princeton," *Princeton Alumni Quarterly*, 16 (February 1965), 6–11, 17; Frederica de Laguna, *Under Mount Saint Elias: The History and Culture of the Yakutat Tlingit* ("Smithsonian Contributions to Anthropology," vol. 7; Washington, D. C.: Smithsonian Institution Press, 1972), I, 192–94).

5. Erna Gunther, "Sheldon Jackson Collection at Museum of Paleontology, Princeton University" (typescript, Guyot Hall Museum, Princeton, 1961). A visiting primitive art specialist advised selling them, but both Gunther and Frederica de Laguna judged the collection valuable as a record of the kind of things made for sale in Alaska at that time. See de Laguna to Glenn L. Jesup, 21 February 1964, Guyot Hall Museum.

6. See Dawson, "On the Haida Indians of the Queen Charlotte Islands," Geological Survey of Canada, *Report of Progress*, Appendix A (Ottawa: Queen's Printer, 1880), 103–239. The collection is now in the McCord Museum of McGill University. There is yet no good study focusing on Dawson, but Morris Zaslow, *Reading the Rocks: The Story of the Geological Survey of Canada, 1842–1972* (Toronto: Macmillan of Canada, 1975) offers a very good treatment of the Survey and Dawson's role in it. It contains the best history of the present National Museum of Man, an account of whose ethnological collections can be found in Judy Hall, "Canadian Ethnology Service, National Museum of Man, National Museums of Canada," *American Indian Art Magazine*, 9 (Winter 1983), 50–59.

7. Selwyn to deputy minister, 8 April 1879, copy, Canadian Ethnological Service, National Museum of Man, Ottawa. Robert Bell,
another Survey geologist, sold a large northern collection to the
American Museum in New York. Selwyn seems to have viewed this
and Dawson's McGill loan with an equanimity born of unconcern.

8. Powell to Superintendent-General of Indian Affairs, 26 August
1879, in Canada, *Sessional Papers,* 1880, no. 4, pp. 111, 122, 127. For
biographical treatments of Powell, see B. A. McKelvie, "Lieuten-
ant-Colonel Israel Wood Powell, M. D., C. M.," *British Columbia
Historical Quarterly,* 11 (1947), 33–54 and Norma Jean Mercer, "Dr.
Israel Wood Powell," (BA essay, University of British Columbia,
1959). A small notebook recording some of his 1879 purchases is in
the Powell Papers, PABC.

9. Swan to Baird, 27 November 1882, copy, Acc. 12,690, USNM; Daw-
son to Powell, 20 November 1894, letterbook 89, RG 45, Geological
Survey of Canada Papers, Public Archives of Canada (hereafter
PAC).

10. Selwyn to Powell, 3 June 1862, copy, vol. 3626, file 5646, RG 10,
Department of Indian Affairs Papers, PAC; Selwyn, "Summary
Reports of the Operations of the Geological Corps, 1881," in Can-
ada, *Sessional Papers,* 1882 (Ottawa: Queen's Printer, 1888), 2.

11. Dawson in *Internationales Archiv für Ethnologie,* 2 (1889), 231; Dawson to Franz Boas, 29 April 1887, Boas Professional Papers, American Philosophical Society (hereafter BPP); Selwyn, quoted in
Zaslow, *Reading the Rocks,* 127 n28; Horatio Hale to Dawson, 26
November 1888, BPP.

12. USNM, *Annual Report,* 1888 (Washington, D. C.: Government Printing Office, 1890), 9.

13. The best treatment of the American Museum's history, to which I
am greatly indebted, is John Michael Kennedy, "Philanthropy and
Science in New York City: The American Museum of Natural His-
tory, 1868–1968," (Ph.D. dissertation, Yale University, 1968).
Henry Fairfield Osborn, *The American Museum of Natural History: Its
Origin, Its History, the Growth of Its Departments* (2nd ed.; New York:
Irving Press, 1916) remains useful. For Jesup, see William Adams
Brown, *Morris Ketchem Jesup: A Character Sketch* (New York: Chas.
Scribner's Sons, 1911).

14. Brown, *Jesup,* 151; Jesup, "Report to trustees, September 1880,"
n.p., quoted in Kennedy, "Philanthropy and Science," 79.

15. Bickmore to Bishop, 28 May 1880; Bishop to Bickmore, 27
November 1880; Bickmore to Powell, 11 and 14 October 1880,
archives, American Museum of Natural History (hereafter AMNH).

16. Powell to Superintendent-General of Indian Affairs, 27 November

1881 in Canada, *Sessional Papers,* 1882, XV, no. 5, 139–54; Swan to Dr. Samuel Swan, 30 April 1884, copy; Powell to Bickmore, 5 [October] 1882, 29 January 1885, AMNH.

17. Powell accounts, Acc. 1869–90–94, AMNH. Allen Wardwell, *Objects of Bright Pride: Northwest Coast Indian Art from the American Museum of Natural History* (New York: Center for Inter-American Relations and the American Federation of Arts, 1978; distr. University of Washington Press), 23, puts the sum at $2,500; Invoice, J. Isaacs & Co., 11 September 1886, Acc. 1869–90–94, AMNH. Bishop added another collection in 1889 or 1890, mostly from the interior of British Columbia.

18. Powell, *Sessional Papers,* 1880, no. 4, 113; Powell to Bickmore, 21 March 1883; "The Haida Canoe," 27 March 1970, Acc. 1869–90–94, AMNH.

19. Powell to Bickmore, 21 March 1883, 5 [October] 1882, Acc. 1864–90–94, AMNH.

20. Bishop to Bickmore, 22 November 1887, 30 January 1888; Emmons to Bishop, 28 January 1888, copy; Bishop to Jesup, 14 February 1888, archives, AMNH; see also Wardwell, *Bright Pride,* 26.

21. For treatments of G. T. Emmons, see Jean Low, "George Thornton Emmons," *Alaska Journal,* 7 (Winter 1977), 2–11; David E. Conrad, "Emmons of Alaska," *Pacific Northwest Quarterly,* 69 (April 1978), 49–60.

22. H. W. Seton Karr, *Shore and Alps of Alaska* (London: Sampson, Low, Marston, Seale & Kingston, 1887), 59–60; Baird, *Princeton Alumni Quarterly,* 16 (February 1965), 6–11, 17; de Laguna, *Under Mount Saint Elias,* I, 192–94.

23. Bickmore to Jesup, 4 January 1888; Bishop to Jesup, 30 January 1888; Bickmore form letter, n.d.; Emmons to Bishop, 28 January 1888, copy; Bishop to Bickmore, 30 January 1888; Emmons to Bickmore, 12 February 1888, archives, AMNH.

24. Franz Boas, "American Museum of Natural History," *Internationales Archiv für Ethnologie,* 2 (1889), 171; Boas, "Gleanings from the Emmons Collection of Ethnological Specimens from Alaska," *Journal of American Folk-Lore,* 1 (October–December 1888), 218; Bishop to Jesup, 30 January 1888, archives, AMNH.

25. Niblack to Professor [Mason or Goode], 26 June 1889, National Anthropological Archives, Washington; Emmons to Bickmore, 12 February 1888, archives, AMNH; USNM, *Annual Report,* 1888 (Washington, D.C.: Government Printing Office, 1889), 9.

26. Bastian to Boas, 21 October 1887, BPP.

27. Swan to Baird, 2 and 24 April 1884, RU 26, SIA.

28. Petition of 14 January 1886, in Francis Kermode, "Inception and

History of the Provincial Museum" *Report of the Provincial Museum of Natural History,* 1928 (Victoria: Queen's printer, 1929), F7. The actual beginning of Fannin's appointment is confusing: the recommendation for him to begin "as from the first of August last," is dated October 23 and his salary began at least in July. *Ibid.;* Finance Department, *Public Accounts of British Columbia,* 1886.

29. "Papers Relating to the Museum at Sitka," file D, Sheldon Jackson Papers, Speer Library, Princeton Theological Seminary; "The Alaska Society of Sitka," *Science,* 10 (9 December 1887), 281; Esther Billman, "History of Sheldon Jackson Museum," in *A Catalogue of the Ethnological Collections in the Sheldon Jackson Museum, Sitka, Alaska* (Sitka: Sheldon Jackson Museum, 1967), 7–10.

30. Jackson to Mrs. Margaret V. Shephard, 29 April 1893, Jackson Papers, Speer Library, Princeton Theological Seminary; see also Jackson to Edwin Hale Abbot, 19 October 1887, Jackson Papers, Presbyterian Historical Society.

31. Abbot to Jackson, 3 December 1887, transcript, Jackson Papers, Presbyterian Historical Society; *Special Report of the Board of Education, Educational Exhibits at the World's Industrial and Cotton Exposition, New Orleans, 1884–85.* Part I, *Catalogue of Exhibits* (Washington, D.C.: Government Printing Office, 1886), 98; Jackson to Abbot, 19 October 1887, typescript, Jackson Papers, Presbyterian Historical Society; Alaskan Society of Natural History and Ethnology, minutes, 8 November 1887, copy, Sheldon Jackson Museum.

32. Hinckley, *Pacific Northwest Quarterly,* 33 (November 1964), 416–17; *The Alaskan* (Sitka), 23 May 1891, 1; Billman, in *Catalogue of the Ethnological Collection,* 7–10; *The Alaskan,* 8 June 1895, 3; 8 August 1895, 3. Marsden was an important figure in his own right; see William Gilbert Beattie, *Marsden of Alaska: A Modern Indian* (New York: Vantage Press, 1955).

33. Jackson to F. E. Frobese, 23 March 1897, Jackson Papers, Speer Library, Princeton Theological Seminary.

34. *The Alaskan* (Sitka), 29 October 1887, 4; April 1888, 2; Abby Johnson Woodman, *Picturesque Alaska* (Boston and New York: Houghton, Mifflin, 1889), 114.

35. See Ted C. Hinckley, "The Inside Passage: A Popular Guilded Age Tour," *Pacific Northwest Quarterly,* 56 (April 1965), 67–74.

36. Frances Knapp and Rheta Louise Childe, *The Thlinkets of Southeastern Alaska* (Chicago: Stone and Kimball, 1896), 9; Scidmore, *Alaska: Its Southern Coast and the Sitkan Archipelago* (Boston: D. Lothrop, 1885); Ernest Gruening, *The State of Alaska* (rev. ed.; New York: Random House, 1968), 568 n11.

37. John Muir, *Travels in Alaska* (Boston and New York: Houghton,

Mifflin, 1915), 276; Schwatka, *Along Alaska's Great River* (New York: Cassell, 1885), 27.

38. Knapp and Childe, *Thlinkets,* 11; "In an Old Russian Fort," *New York Times,* 14 October 1888, 10; Scidmore, *Alaska,* 38, 40, 89–90.

39. The most recent treatments of argillite are Carole Natalie Kaufmann, "Changes in Haida Indian Argillite Carvings, 1820–1910" (Ph.D. dissertation, UCLA, 1969); Leslie Drew and Douglas Wilson, *Argillite: Art of the Haida* (North Vancouver: Hancock House, 1980); Carol Sheehan, *Pipes That Won't Smoke; Coal That Won't Burn: Haida Sculpture in Argillite* (Calgary: Glenbow Museum, 1981); Peter L. Macnair and Alan L. Hoover, *The Magic Leaves: A History of Haida Carving* (Victoria: British Columbia Provincial Museum, 1984); and a number of particularly good articles by Robin K. Wright, e.g., "Haida Argillite: Carved for Sale," *American Indian Art Magazine,* 8 (Winter 1982), 48–55.

40. Swan to Baird, 16 June 1873, RU 26, SIA; W. H. Dall, "The Native Tribes of Alaska," American Association for the Advancement of Science, *Proceedings,* 34 (1885), 368; Scidmore, *Alaska,* 39, 49–50; Knapp and Childe, *Thlinkets,* 169; Isabel S. Shephard, *The Cruise of the U. S. Steamer "Rush" in Behring Sea: Summer of 1889* (San Francisco: Bancroft, 1889), 235. Miss Scidmore was at least partially in error: the very earliest silver seems to have followed European motifs, with Indian designs appearing alongside European ones later.

41. Jackson to Frances P. Gifford, 19 November 1885, Jackson Papers, Speer Library, Princeton Theological Seminary; Dall, AAAS, *Proceedings,* 34 (1885), 368; see also Scidmore, *Alaska,* 106, who says a trader, "who has received and filled large orders for eastern museums and societies, threatens to bring up a skilled stonecutter to supply the increasing demands of scientists, now that the Indians have parted with most of their heirloom specimens."

42. Scidmore, *Alaska,* 49; Jackson to Duncan, 18 October 1887, bill of 6 July 1887; Duncan to Jackson, 24 December 1888; Jackson to Duncan, 16 August 1888, typescripts, Jackson Papers, Presbyterian Historical Society.

43. Swan to Baird, 30 September 1882, Acc. 12,054, USNM; Swan to Baird, 25 February 1883, RU 26, SIA; *The Alaskan* (Sitka), 18 May 1889, 3.

44. Boas to parents, 18 September 1886, in Ronald P. Rohner, ed., *The Ethnography of Franz Boas,* trans. Helena Boas Yampolsky and Hedy Parker (Chicago: University of Chicago Press, 1969), 20. For the readers convenience, I cite the Rohner edition page number even if I have on occasion used my own translation where I thought a better reading possible.

Chapter 5
MUSEUMS AND EXPOSITIONS

1. See George W. Stocking, Jr., "From Physics to Ethnology," in Stocking, *Race, Culture, and Evolution* (Chicago: University of Chicago Press, 1968), 133–60. There is a large literature on Boas, but no good biography. The writings of Stocking, some collected in *Race, Culture, and Evolution,* and in his edition of Boas's writings, *The Shaping of American Anthropology, 1883–1911: A Franz Boas Reader* (New York: Basic Books, 1974) are fine studies. See also Alexander Lesser, "Franz Boas," in *International Encyclopedia of Social Sciences* (New York: Macmillan and Free Press, 1968), II, 99–110, and Lesser, "Franz Boas," in *Totems and Teachers: Perspectives on the History of Anthropology* (New York: Columbia University Press, 1981), 1–31.

2. Boas to Sophie Boas, 13 January 1883, Boas Family Papers (hereafter BFP), American Philosophical Society. For the Baffin Island experience, see Stocking, *Race, Culture, and Evolution,* 133–60, and Douglas Cole, ed., " 'The Value of a Person Lies in His *Herzensbildung' :* Franz Boas's Baffin Island Letter-Diary, 1883–84," in *Observers Observed: Essays on Ethnographic Fieldwork* ("History of Anthropology," George W. Stocking, Jr., gen. ed.; vol. 1; Madison: University of Wisconsin Press, 1983,), 13–52.

3. These paragraphs are based on a series of family letters in the BFP.

4. Boas to M. Krackowizer, 21 January 1886; Boas to parents, 25 January 1886; Boas to M. Krackowizer, 28 February 1886, BFP; "The Language of the Bilhoola in British Columbia," *Science,* 7 (5 March 1886), 218.

5. Boas, *The Kwakiutl of Vancouver Island* (*The Jesup North Pacific Expedition,* Franz Boas, ed.; "Memoir of the Museum of Natural History"; New York: American Museum of Natural History, 1909), 307.

6. Boas to Vorsitzender, 17 November 1886, *Verhandlungen der Berliner Gesellschaft für Anthropologie, Ethnologie, und Urgeschichte,* 19 (1887), 65; Boas, "The Use of Masks and Head Ornaments on the North-West Coast of America," *Internationales Archiv für Ethnologie,* 3 (1890), 7.

7. Boas to parents, 19 September 1886, 7 October 1886, BFP.

8. Quotations in this and subsequent paragraphs are from Boas to parents, letter diary, 9–15 October in Ronald P. Rohner, ed., *The Ethnography of Franz Boas,* trans. Hedy Parker (Chicago: University of Chicago Press, 1969), 37–40. Again, I quote from this invaluable translation except where I think a better reading of the original is possible.

9. Boas, "Some Principles of Museum Administration," *Science,* 25 (14 June 1907), 928.

10. Boas to Carl Schurz, 27 October 1886 (draft), Boas Professional Papers (hereafter BPP); Boas to parents, 23(?) November 1886, BFP; Boas to parents, letter diary, 9 November 1886, 15 November 1886, in Rohner, ed., *Ethnography of Boas,* 57, 60.

11. Boas to parents, 23(?) November 1886, BFP.

12. Boas to parents, 28 January 1887, BFP; Bickmore to Bishop, 1 February 1887, archives, AMNH; Boas to Bastian, n.d. [received 30 March 1887], Acta Boas, BMfV; Bastian to Boas, 20 March 1887, telegram, BPP.

13. Ph.-Fr. de Siebold, *Lettre sur l'utilité des musées ethnographique et sur l'importance de leur creation dans les états éuropeen qui possèsent des colonies . . . à M. Edmé-François Jomard* (Paris: Benjamin Duiprat, 1843); Jomard, *Lettre à monsieur Ph.-Fr. de Siebold, sur les collections ethnographiques* (Paris: Bourgogne et Martinet, 1845).

14. Kristian Bahnson, "Ueber ethnographische Museen," *Mitteilungen der anthropologischen Gesellschaft in Wien,* 18 (1888), 164; Klemm, "Fantasie über ein Museum für die Culturgeschichte," *Allgemeine Cultur-Geschichte der Menschheit* (10 vols.; Leipzig, B. G. Teubner, 1843–52), I, 352–62; A. Jacobi, *1875–1925: Fünfzig Jahre Museum für Völkerkunde zur Dresden* (Dresden, 1925), 66. The third edition (1896) of the museum's guide shows only a geographical order.

15. Beatrice Blackwood, *The Classification of Artefacts in the Pitt-Rivers Museum, Oxford* ("Occasional Papers on Technology," no. 2, Pitt Rivers Museum; Oxford: Oxford University Press, 1970), 7; Pitt Rivers, "Presidential Address," Section H, *British Association for the Advancement of Science,* 1888 (London: John Murray, 1889), 824.

16. A. Lane Fox, "On the Principles of Classification Adopted in the Arrangement of His Anthropological Collection, Now Exhibited in the Bethnal Green Museum," (1874), in Pitt Rivers, *The Evolution of Cultures and Other Essays,* J. L. Myres, ed. (Oxford: Clarendon Press, 1906), 3, 2, plate III, 13.

17. Balfour, *Report of Museum Association,* 1897, 51, quoted in A. B. Meyer, "Studies of the Museums and Kindred Institutions of New York City, Albany, Buffalo, and Chicago, with Some Notes on Some European Antiquities," USNM, *Annual Report,* 1903 (Washington, D. C.: Government Printing Office, 1904), 534; Haddon, "Report on Some of the Educational Advantages and Efficiencies of London Museums," 27 June 1904, env. 3067, Haddon Collection, Cambridge University Library; London County Council, *Guide for the Use of Visitors to the Horniman Museum* (2nd ed.; London, 1912), 11, 13.

18. For an excellent treatment of the National Museum and the assumptions behind its work, see Curtis M. Hinsley, Jr., *Savages and Scientists: The Smithsonian Institution and the Development of American Anthropology, 1846–1910* (Washington, D. C.: Smithsonian Insitution Press, 1981), especially ch. IV. I am greatly indebted to this and to the dissertation which proceeded it. Mason, "The Leipsic Museum of Ethnology," SIAR, 1873 (Washington, 1874), 390.

19. Frederic A. Lucas, *Fifty Years of Museum Work* (New York: American Museum of Natural History, 1933), 16; Goode, in SIAR, 1882, 128, 129.

20. Goode, SIAR, 1882, 130.

21. Mason, SIAR, 1885, 63; 1886, 87, 89.

22. Boas, "The Occurrence of Similar Inventions in Areas Widely Apart," *Science,* 9 (20 May 1887), 485–86; "Museums of Ethnology and Their Classification," *Science,* 9 (17 June 1887), 587–88; *Science,* 9 (24 June 1887), 614. The arguments of Boas's three letters in the controversy are diffuse, touching on various points, the coherence of which was no doubt clear to him, but do puzzle the reader. This provided much of the reason for John Beuttner-Janusch's attack upon them in "Boas and Mason: Particularism versus Generalization," *American Anthropologist,* 59 (April 1957), 318–24. I hope that my summary is clearer, without distorting Boas's intention. See also Stocking, "The Basic Assumptions of Boasian Anthropology," in Stocking, ed., *Shaping,* 1–20, Hinsley, *Savages and Scientists,* 98–99, and Thomas M. Brown, "Cultural Evolutionists, Boasians, and Anthropological Exhibits " (M. A. thesis, Johns Hopkins University, 1980), which came to my attention after this book was written. Brown emphasizes similarities among the disputants and how even Boas retained some typological features in his own exhibition ideas. Boas was much clearer in his 1896 "The Limitations of the Comparative Method of Anthropology," reprinted in Boas, *Race, Language and Culture* (New York: Free Press, 1940), 270–80.

23. Mason, "The Occurrence of Similar Inventions in Areas Widely Apart," *Science,* 9 (3 June 1887), 534–35.

24. Powell, "Museums of Ethnology and Their Classification," *Science,* 9 (24 June 1887), 612–14; Dall, "Museums of Ethnology and Their Classification," *ibid.,* 9 (17 June 1887), 577; Putnam in *18th and 19th Annual Reports of the Trustees of the Peabody Museum of American Archaeology and Ethnology,* 3 (1886), 481–82.

25. Boas, *Science,* 9 (17 June 1887), 589; Mason, SIAR, 1887, 65.

26. SIAR, 1888, 30.

27. SIAR, 1888, 87, 129–36, USNM, *Annual Report,* 1893, 127; SIA, 1890,

125; Mason to Goode, "Letter from Europe," 17 July to 7 October 1889, quoted in Hinsley, "The Development of a Profession," 315; USNM, *Annual Report,* 1893, 127.

28. USNM, *Annual Report,* 1893, 128–29. See also Mason "Ethnological Exhibit of the Smithsonian Institution at the World's Columbia Exposition," in C. Staniland Wake, ed., *International Congress of Anthropology: Memoirs* (Chicago, 1893), 208–16; John C. Ewers, "A Century of American Indian Exhibits in the Smithsonian Institution," SIAR, 1958, 520–21. A minor footnote to the controversy was the conversion of the Soviet Academy of Science's Leningrad Museum of Anthropology and Ethnology from a geographical to an evolutionary and typological display in the 1920s, revised in the 1930s to a three-stage evolutionary system. This was modified after 1945 to reflect ethnological areas, but "the main stages of the development of primitive-communal society" remained one of the basic displays. T. V. Stanyukovich, *The Museum of Anthropology and Ethnology Named after Peter the Great* (Leningrad: Nauka, 1970), 35–40.

29. Boas, "The Indians of British Columbia," Royal Society of Canada, *Transactions and Proceedings,* 1888, Section II, 47. See also Stocking, *Race, Culture, and Evolution,* 151–53.

30. Boas, diary, 6 and 12 June 1888, in Rohner, ed., *Ethnography of Boas,* 88, 90; William J. Sutton to Boas, 15 November 1888, BPP.

31. *Ibid.*

32. *Ibid.,* 23 January 1889, 22 February 1889; Boas to Horatio Hale, 2 April 1889, draft, BPP.

33. Acc. 1869–90–105A, nos. 769–826, AMNH; Dawson to Boas, 29 May 1889 and 4 August 1889, BPP; "Purchases," I, 39, Pitt Rivers Museum; Tylor to Boas, 16 October 1889, 9 December 1889, BPP; Boas to Tylor, 16 January 1890, Tylor Papers, Balfour Library, Oxford. The Pitt Rivers Museum already had a fine soul-catcher from Frederick Dally.

34. For Putnam, see "Frederic Ward Putnam," in Joan Mark, *Four Anthropologists: An American Science in Its Early Years* (New York: Science History Publications, 1980), 14–61; *The Selected Archaeological Papers of Frederic Ward Putnam,* intro. by Stephen Williams (New York: AMS Press, 1973); and articles by Ralph W. Dexter, especially "Frederick Ward Putnam and the Development of Museums of Natural History and Anthropology in the United States," *Curator,* 9 (1966), 150–55; "Putnam's Problems Popularizing Anthropology," *American Scientist,* 54 (1966), 315–32; "The Role of F. W. Putnam in Founding the Field Museum" *Curator,* 13 (1970), 21–26; "The Role of F. W. Putnam in Developing Anthropology at the American

Museum of Natural History," *ibid.,* 19 (1976), 303–10; and "F. W. Putnam's Role in Developing the Peabody Museum of American Archaeology and Ethnology," *ibid.,* (1980), 183–94.

35. Putnam, monthly report for October 1891, box 35; Boas, "The Exhibits from the North Pacific Coast," box 36, Putnam Papers, by permission of the Harvard University Archives.

36. "Collections from North Pacific Coast, Department of Ethnology, World's Columbian Exposition, Haida Indians, Collection James Deans," Archives, FMNH, which lists the Skidegate models; Acc. 21, FMNH; *Daily Colonist* (Victoria), 25 May 1892, 2. See also Rossiter Johnson, ed., *A History of the World's Columbian Exposition* (4 vols.; New York: D. Appleton, 1897), I, 344ff.

37. Boas, "The Exhibitions from the North Pacific Coast," box 36, Putnam Papers; Putnam, monthly reports, November 1892, box 35, Putnam Papers.

38. Frank C. Lockwood, *The Life of Edward E. Ayer* (Chicago: A. C. McLurg, 1929), 75, 80.

39. Johnson, ed., I, 316; "Prof. Putnam's Hard Luck," *New York Times,* 22 May 1893, 9; Dexter, *American Scientist,* 54 (1966), 315–32.

40. T. J. Morgan to Haytor Reid, 12 September 1892, vol. 3865, file 85,529, DIA.

41. Agreement between Putnam and Hunt, 29 September 1892 (signed by Hunt, 19 January 1893), monthly reports, box 36, Putnam Papers; Johnson, ed., *History of World's Columbian Exposition,* II, 355; Putnam, monthly report, April 1893, box 35, Putnam Papers; Boas to parents, 8 May 1893, BFP; Putnam to George R. Davis, 29 April 1893, box 34, Putnam Papers.

42. Johnson, ed., *History,* I, 503; III, 433.

43. *New York Times,* 25 May 1893, 2.

44. "A Brutal Exhibition," *New York Times,* 19 August 1893, 5; "Horrible Scene at the Fair," *The Sunday Times* (London), 20 August 1893, 3.

45. Hall to L. Vankoughnet, 24 August 1893, vol. 3865, file 85,529, DIA. There was, as Vankoughnet pointed out to Hall, also a Canadian Indian school — from the Northwest Territories — displayed at the fair.

46. Vankoughnet to J. S. Larke, 6 September 1893; Vankoughnet to Vowell, 6 September 1893; Pidcock to Vowell, 18 October 1893; Larke to Vankoughnet, 3 September 1893, vol. 3865, file 85,529, DIA.

47. Boas, "The Social Organization and the Secret Societies of the Kwakiutl Indians," *Report of the USNM, 1895,* 495–97; Clellan S. Ford, *Smoke from Their Fires: The Life of a Kwakiutl Chief* (New

Haven: Yale University Press, 1941), 115–17; see also W. M. Halliday, *Potlatch and Totem and the Recollections of an Indian Agent* (London and Toronto: J. M. Dent & Sons, 1935), 230; Dexter, *American Scientist*, 54 (1966), 237.

48. *Daily Colonist* (Victoria), 21 July 1897, 6; *World's Columbian Exposition, 1893, Official Catalogue, part XII, Department M. Ethnology* (Chicago: W. B. Conkey, 1893), in *Selected Archaeological Papers of F. W. Putnam*, 180–81.

49. Vowell to Vankoughnet, 19 October 1892, Vankoughnet to Vowell, 7 November 1892, vol. 3865, file 85,529, DIA; British Columbia, Department of the Provincial Secretary, *Report of the Executive Commissioner for British Columbia at the World's Columbian Exposition, 1893* (Chicago, 1893), 1152.

50. *The Alaskan* (Sitka), 9 January 1892, 13; 17 September 1892, 3; 26 August 1893, 3.

51. Otis T. Mason, "Report on the Department of Ethnology," USNM, *Annual Report*, 1892; Mason, "Ethnological Exhibition of the Smithsonian Institution at the World's Columbian Exposition," in Wake, ed., *International Congress*, 208–16; Paul Topinard, "L'Anthropologie aux Etats-unis," *L'Anthropologie*, 4 (1893), 334. For a larger treatment of anthropology at Chicago, see Robert William Rydell II, "All the World's a Fair: America's International Expositions, 1876–1916" (Ph.D. dissertation, UCLA, 1980), II.

52. Putnam to J. F. Lee, 18 November 1893, box 34, Putnam Papers; Boas to parents, 21 October 1893, BFP; Hunt to Boas, 15 January 1894, 7 February 1894, BPP; Deans to Boas, 20 January 1894, BPP. The agreement was for $20 per month for 7½ months, commencing 1 April, or a total of $150 each, plus expenses from Alert Bay. Hunt was paid $90 a month for 8 months, plus expenses.

53. *Vancouver Daily World*, 15 May 1891, 6; *Daily Colonist*, 24 July 1894, 5; draft to Larke, [18?] April 1894, vol. 3865, file 85,529, DIA.

54. Putnam to Ayer, 21 December 1893, Boas file, Registrar's Office, FMNH.

55. Boas to W J McGee, 17 February 1894, Bureau of American Ethnology, "Letters Received," quoted in Curtis M. Hinsley, Jr. and Bill Holm, "A Cannibal in the National Museum: The Early Career of Franz Boas in America," *American Anthropologist*, 78 (June 1976), 311.

56. For the development of figure groups, see Hinsley, *Savages and Scientists*, 108–9; USNM, *Annual Report*, 1893, 23–58; Ed. Sayous, "Les musées ethnographiques du Copenhague et de Moscow," *Bulletin de la Société de Geographie*, 6th ser., 7 (1874), 171–72; Edward P. Alexander, "Artistic and Historical Period Rooms," *Curator*, 7 (1964),

270; Thomas Wilson, "Anthropology at the Paris Exposition of 1899," USNM, *Annual Report,* 1890, 653–57; Mason, "Anthropology in Paris during the Exposition of 1889," *American Anthropologist,* 3 (1890), 32.

57. G. B. Goode, "Recent Advances in Museum Method," USNM, *Annual Report,* 1893, 54.

58. *Ibid.,* 55; *ibid., Annual Report,* 1894, 79.

59. Boas to Mason, 20 May 1894, Goode to Boas, 5 February 1895, BPP; Putnam to Jesup, 8 November 1894, archives, AMNH; Putnam to Boas, 16 July 1894, Boas to Putnam, 25 July 1894, BPP.

60. See Ira Jacknis, "Franz Boas and Photography," *Studies in Visual Communication,* 10 (Winter 1984), 2–60, and his "Franz Boas and Museum Exhibits," forthcoming in *History of Anthropology,* vol. 3.

61. Published in Hinsley and Holm, *American Anthropologist,* 78 (June 1876), 306–16.

62. John H. Winser to Putnam, 27 December 1895, letterbooks, archives, AMNH.

63. Putnam to Boas, 14 May 1894, 16 July 1894, 9 August 1895, BPP.

64. Putnam to Alice Putnam, 9 September 1895, Putnam Papers, quoted in Dexter, *Curator,* 19 (1976), 305.

65. Putnam to Jesup, 16 October 1894, 17 November 1894, 5 December 1895, quoted in Michael Kennedy, "Philanthropy and Science in New York City: The American Museum of Natural History, 1868–1968," (Ph.D. dissertation, Yale University, 1968), 137.

Chapter 6
THE AMERICAN MUSEUM AND DR. BOAS

1. Michael Kennedy, "Philanthropy and Science in New York City: The American Museum of Natural History, 1868–1968," (Ph.D. dissertation, Yale University, 1968), 132–34; Ralph W. Dexter, "The Role of F. W. Putnam in Developing Anthropology at the American Museum of Natural History," *Curator,* 19 (1976), 303–10.

2. Emmons to Bickmore, 12 February 1888, archives, AMNH; Emmons to Boas, 15 December 1888, BPP.

3. George R. Davis to Putnam, 22 May 1891, Putnam to Davis, 26 May 1891, box 34, Putnam Papers, Harvard University Archives; "Alaskan Curios at the Fair," in "Kate Field's Washington," *The Alaskan* (Sitka), 21 October 1893, 1, 3–4; John H. Winser to Perry R. Pyne, 23 October 1894, archives, AMNH.

4. Kennedy, "Philanthropy and Science," 3; Putnam to Alice Putnam, 25 December 1895, quoted in Dexter, *Curator,* 19 (1976), 306.

5. Winser to Putnam, 7 January 1896, archives, AMNH.

6. Boas to Putnam, 7 November 1896, copy, file 13, archives, AMNH.

7. Acc. 1896–42, AMNH; Boas to Jesup, n.d. [ca. 10 December 1896], archives, AMNH; Kennedy, "Philanthropy and Science," 137; Boas to Villard, 23 December 1896, Acc. 1897–30, AMNH.

8. J. Hampton Robb to Jesup, 18 March 1896, quoted in Kennedy, "Philanthropy and Science," 122; F. W. Putnam, "Synopsis of Peabody and American Museum of Natural History Anthropology Departments," *Proceedings of the XIII International Congress of Americanists* (New York, 1902), xliii; William Adams Brown, *Morris Ketchum Jesup: A Character Sketch* (New York: Chas. Scribners' Sons, 1910), 169. Boas's private correspondence shows that his initial plans were restricted to the Siberian coast. Boas to parents, 19 and 25 January 1897, BFP.

9. *New York Times,* 13 March 1897, 2.

10. Boas, "Operations of the Expedition in 1897," *The Jesup North Pacific Expedition* ("Memoirs of the American Museum of Natural History"), II, folio, 7.

11. Emmons to Jesup, 13 January 1898; Emmons to Winser, 21 April 1898, 12 June 1898, archives, AMNH. A manuscript *was* finished much later, with versions now in the American Museum and in the Provincial Archives of British Columbia. Frederica de Laguna has completed an edition of the two typescripts which, with a biographical introduction by Jean Low, should soon be published.

12. Boas to Hermon C. Bumpus, 11 November 1903, AMNH. Ira Jacknis kindly provided this memorandum.

13. Emmons to C. F. Newcombe, 21 November 1899, Newcombe Papers, PABC; Emmons to Holmes, 26 April 1900, 9 October 1900; Mason to Holmes, 5 April 1900, Acc. 37,889, USNM.

14. Dorsey to F. Skiff, 26 November 1901, Acc. 807; Dorsey to Skiff, 9 April 1903, registrar's office, Acc. 843, FMNH.

15. Boas to Dorsey, 19 June 1902; Boas to L. Farrand, 20 June 1903, AMNH. I am indebted to Ira Jacknis for these citations.

16. Boas to Swanton, 5 November 1900, Acc. 1901–31, AMNH.

17. [Boas], "Recent Ethnological Work of the Museum" *American Museum Journal,* 2 (October 1902), 66; *New York Times,* 13 March 1897, 2; Boas to Jesup, 1 October 1900, archives, AMNH.

18. Boas to Hunt, 14 April 1897, Acc. 1897–43; Boas to Jacobsen, 6 May 1897, Acc. 1897–44; Boas to Swanton, 5 June 1900, Acc. 1901–31; Boas to Hunt, 14 April 1897, Acc. 1897–43, AMNH; Boas to Hunt, 30 April 1897, BPP; Boas to Hunt, 13 January 1899, Acc. 1899–50, AMNH.

19. Boas to Hunt, 30 April 1897, BPP; Smith to Boas, 17 May 1898, 1 August 1898, Acc. 1898–41, AMNH.

20. *New York Times,* 2 January 1899, 12; Boas to Jesup, "Memorandum on Acquisition of Specimens from the North Pacific Coast," 27 October 1900, archives, AMNH.

21. Boas to Newcombe, 11 October 1897, Newcombe Papers, PABC.

22. Hunt to Boas, 31 December 1902 [1901], 8 April 1902, Acc. 1902–46, AMNH; Hunt to Boas, 22 February 1901; Boas to Vowell, 7 October 1901; Hunt to Boas, 12 August 1901; Boas to Hunt, 29 November 1901, BPP; Hunt to Boas, 4 July 1902, Acc. 1902–46, AMNH.

23. Boas to Marie Boas, 22 November 1894, in Ronald P. Rohner, ed., *The Ethnography of Franz Boas: Letters and Diaries of Franz Boas Written on the Northwest Coast from 1886 to 1931,* trans. Hedy Parker (Chicago: University of Chicago Press, 1969), 183; Boas to M. Boas, 21 July 1897, 20 July 1897, 1 September 1897, in *ibid.,* 214, 211, 236. The best work on Hunt is Ira Jacknis's unpublished " 'George Hunt, Collector of Indian Specimens,' " presented at the 1981 B. C. Studies Conference, Simon Fraser University. See also Jeanne Cannizzo, "George Hunt and the Invention of Kwakiutl Culture," *Canadian Review of Sociology and Anthropology,* 20 (1983), 44–58.

24. Boas to friends, 14 April 1897. The first half of this letter is in Acc. 1897–43; the second half is in Jesup Expedition file H. I owe Ira Jacknis for this second half.

25. Hunt to Boas, 4 March 1898, 10 January 1899, BPP. I have been unable to find the Smiths' newspaper interview.

26. Boas to Hunt, 3 February 1899; Boas to Hamasaka, 3 February 1899, BPP. These letters are printed in George W. Stocking, Jr., ed. *The Shaping of American Anthropology, 1883–1911: A Franz Boas Reader* (New York: Basic Books, 1974), 125–27.

27. Boas to Hunt, 7 January 1901, 4 April 1901, 1 May 1901; Hunt to Boas, 1 June 1901, BPP.

28. Boas to Hunt, 3 January 1900, BPP; Hunt to Boas, 5 February 1900, 31 [c], American Indian Linguistics, American Philosophical Society.

29. Hunt to Boas, 14 March 1898, 26 September 1899, BPP.

30. Philip Drucker, *The Northern and Central Nootkan Tribes* (Smithsonian Institution Bureau of American Ethnology, Bulletin 144; Washington, D. C.: Government Printing Office, 1951), 171–72, describes it as a shrine. See "A Nootka Ceremonial House," in Boas, *The Religion of the Kwakiutl Indians* (Columbia University Contributions to Anthropology, vol. X, part 2; New York: Columbia University Press, 1930), 261–69 with plates.

31. Hunt to Boas, 9 June 1904, Acc. 1904–38, AMNH.

32. Hunt to Boas, 9 and 22 June 1904, 27 July 1904, 1 August 1904; Lewis to Hunt, 5 July 1904, Acc. 1904–38, AMNH.

33. Jesup to Putnam, 22 September 1898, Jesup to Boas, 10 February 1903, cited in Kennedy, "Philanthropy and Science," 142; Boas, "The Jesup North Pacific Expedition, *Proceedings of the XIIIth International Congress of Americanists, 1903* (New York, 1905), 98, 99; Boas to Jesup, 20 February 1903, archives, AMNH.

34. Emmons to Newcombe, 14 January 1906, Newcombe Papers, PABC.

35. Dorsey, "The Anthropological Exhibits at the American Museum of Natural History," *Science,* ns 25 (12 April 1907), 584.

Chapter 7
THE FIELD MUSEUM AND DR. NEWCOMBE

1. For the origin and early years of the museum, see J. Christian Bay, "History" (typescript, FMNH, 1929); Donald Collier, "Chicago Comes of Age: The World's Columbian Exposition and the Birth of the Field Museum," *Field Museum Bulletin,* 40 (May 1969), 3–7; Collier, "Men and Their Work," *ibid.,* 43 (September 1972), 7–9; Ralph W. Dexter, "The Role of F. W. Putnam in Founding the Field Museum," *Curator,* 8 (1970), 21–26; Frank C. Lockwood, *The Life of Edward E. Ayer* (Chicago: A. C. McClurg, 1929), ch. XI; George A. Dorsey, "The Department of Anthropology of the Field Columbian Museum — A Review of Six Years," *American Anthropologist,* n.s. 2 (1900), 247–65, quoting Annual Report of 1895–96.

2. Putnam in *Chicago Tribune,* 31 May 1890, quoted in Bay, "History," 7; *Chicago Republican,* 5 July 1894, in Clipping Book, Registrar's Office, FMNH; Bay, "History," 25.

3. Dorsey, *American Anthropologist,* n.s. 2 (1900), 251, 253.

4. A. L. Kroeber, "The Place of Boas in Anthropology," *American Anthropologist,* 58 (1956), 156.

5. Stewart Culin, "Report on a Collecting Expedition among the Indians of New Mexico and Arizona, April–September 1903," (typescript, Brooklyn Museum), 147.

6. Putnam to Boas, 7 March 1894, BPP.

7. *"meine Liebfeinde,"* Boas to parents, 29 May 1897, BFP.

8. Skiff to Boas, 7 and 23 June 1894, BPP; Boas to Dorsey, 14 September 1896, Acc. 68, Registrar, FMNH. It may never have existed: I have been unable to find any trace of it among the Boas Papers.

9. W. H. Holmes to Dorsey, 12 May 1897, FMNH; Dorsey, "A Cruise among Haida and Tlingit Villages about Dixon's Entrance," *Popular Science Monthly,* 53 (June 1898), 160–74; Field Museum, *Annual Report,* 1896–97, 186–87.

10. Dorsey, *Popular Science Monthly,* 53 (June 1898), 168–69; Acc. 528, FMNH.

11. *Ibid.,* 170; James Deans, "How the Haida Dispose of Their Dead," written for Boas, a copy of which is in vol. 36, env. 49, Newcombe

Papers; Dawson to Newcombe, 24 March 1897, letterbook 94, RG 45, Geological Survey of Canada, PAC. See also George F. Mac-Donald, "Haida Burial Practices: Three Archaeological Examples" (Mercury Series, Archaeological Survey of Canada, Paper 9; Ottawa: National Museum of Canada, 1973), esp. 43–50, for a description of a recent research visit.

12. Acc. 551, FMNH; Field Museum, *Annual Report,* 1896–97, 187; Newcombe, "Visit to Queen Charlotte Islands, 1897," vol. 35, env. 3a, Newcombe Papers.

13. Dorsey, *Popular Science Monthly,* 53 (June 1898), 171, 173.

14. Acc. 537, FMNH; Dorsey, "Up the Skeena River to the Home of the Tsimshian," *Popular Science Monthly,* 54 (December 1898), 181, 186, 187; Acc. 540, 541, FMNH.

15. Boas to M. Boas, 9 August 1897, in Ronald P. Rohner, ed., *The Ethnography of Franz Boas: Letters and Diaries of Franz Boas Written on the Northwest Coast from 1886 to 1931,* trans. Hedy Parker (Chicago: University of Chicago Press, 1969), 221–22.

16. Presumably the *Times* of 11 August 1897, *Daily Colonist* (Victoria), 12 August 1897, 2. The unfortunate scholars were on a marine sciences expedition from Columbia University. Boas to M. Boas, 7 August 1897, in Rohner, ed., *Ethnography of Boas,* 242.

17. Berthold Laufer to Boas, 13 April 1908, copy, BPP. "According to the Dorsey method," continued Laufer, "it is possible for every ethnologist to work in any territory; he photographs a little bit, buys indiscriminately everything he can get his hands on, has a good time with the people, and that settles the matter." *Daily Colonist,* 12 August 1897, 2; Keen to Newcombe, 23 September 1897, Newcombe Papers.

18. J. C. Keen, letter dated Masset, 19 October 1897; *Daily Colonist,* 31 October 1897, 8.

19. Deans to Dorsey, 19 November 1897, 13 February 1898, FMNH; Boas to Newcombe, 8 November 1897, Newcombe Papers; Dawson to Boyle, 17 November 1897, letterbook 96, RG 45, Geological Survey of Canada; Boyle to Dorsey, 10 December 1897, 24 January 1898, FMNH.

20. Newcombe to Dorsey, 18 October 1897; Deans to Dorsey, 5 October [1897], FMNH.

21. Dorsey, "The Duwamish Indian Spirit Boat and Its Use," *Bulletin of the Free Museum of Science and Art of the University of Pennsylvania,* 3 (May 1902), 227–38; *Daily Colonist,* 27 September 1899, 5.

22. The best treatment of Newcombe is Jean Low, "Dr. Charles Frederick Newcombe," *Beaver,* 312 (Spring 1892), 32–39. My account is based also on various material in the Newcombe Papers.

23. J. Wissenborn, "Der Totempfahl der Haida in Städtischen Museum für Natur-, Völker- und Handelskunde," *Jahrbuch der bremischen Sammlungen,* 1 (January 1908), 24; Dawson to Newcombe, 24 March 1897, Boas to Newcombe, 12 June 1897, Newcombe Papers; Dawson to D. P. Penhallow, 8 January 1900, letterbook 102, RG 45, Geological Survey of Canada, PAC; Dawson to Newcombe, 1 June 1897, Newcombe Papers.

24. Newcombe, "Visit to Queen Charlotte Islands, 1897," vol. 35, env. 3a, Newcombe Papers; Newcombe to Stewart Culin, 4 August 1900, The University Museum, University of Pennsylvania.

25. Dawson to Newcombe, 9 November 1897, letterbook 96, RG 45, Geological Survey of Canada, PAC.

26. Newcombe, "Visit to Queen Charlotte Islands, 1897," vol. 35, env. 3a; Newcombe to Dorsey, 18 October 1897, FMNH; Dorsey to Newcombe, 26 October 1897, Newcombe Papers; Newcombe to Dorsey, 14 November 1899, FMNH.

27. Dawson to Newcombe, 17 April, 23 March 1899, letterbook 100, 99, RG 45, Geological Survey of Canada, PAC.

28. Newcombe, "Notebook, 1899, Kwakiutl," vol. 35, env. 4, 28 October 1899, Newcombe Papers; Newcombe to Dorsey, 14 November 1899, FMNH.

29. Newcombe to Dorsey, 2 January 1900, FMNH; Dawson to Newcombe, 4 December 1899, 13 January 1900, letterbook 101, 102, RG 45, Geological Survey of Canada, PAC. The two pieces are National Museum of Man VII-E-390 (bowl) and VII-E-406 (figure). The organs were not obliterated. Dorsey to Newcombe, 4 December 1899; Read to Newcombe, 2 December 1901, Newcombe Papers.

30. Stewart A. Culin, "A Summer Trip among the Western Indians," *Bulletin of the Free Museum of Science and Art of the University of Pennsylvania,* 3 (May 1901), 153; Newcombe to Culin, 4 August 1899, The University Museum, University of Pennsylvania; Culin to Newcombe, 23 July 1900, Newcombe Papers.

31. Newcombe to Culin, 20 September, 5 November, 14 December 1900, University Museum, University of Pennsylvania.

32. Newcombe to Culin, 20 September 1900, The University Museum, University of Pennsylvania; Swanton to Boas, 30 September 1900; Boas to Swanton, 5 November 1900, Acc. 1901–31, AMNH; Boas to Newcombe, 9 September 1900, Newcombe Papers.

33. Boas to Newcombe, 7 December 1900, Acc. 1901–36, AMNH; Dorsey to Newcombe, 7 December 1900, Newcombe Papers; Newcombe to Boas, 14 December 1901, 25 January 1902, 8 and 16 January 1901, Acc. 1901–36, AMNH.

34. Newcombe to Boas, 14 December 1900, Acc. 1901–36, AMNH.

35. Newcombe to Culin, 25 July 1900, The University Museum, University of Pennsylvania; Newcombe to Dorsey, 12 March 1901, FMNH; Hunt to Boas, 4 July 1902, Acc. 1902–46, AMNH; Hunt to Boas, 26 September 1899, BPP; Newcombe to Dorsey, 8 February 1901, FMNH.

36. Newcombe to Dorsey, 15 January, 8 February 1901, FMNH; Newcombe to Dorsey, 2 April 1901, Newcombe Papers.

37. Newcombe to Dorsey, 8 February, 7 March 1901, FMNH; Dorsey to Newcombe, 10 and 22 October 1901, Newcombe Papers.

38. For his life, see the autobiography he dictated to Clellan S. Ford, *Smoke from Their Fires: The Life of a Kwakiutl Chief* (New Haven: Yale University Press, 1949).

39. Newcombe to W. A. Newcombe, 1 November 1905, 26 June 1906; Nowell to Newcombe, 7 June 1912, Newcombe Papers.

40. Newcombe to Dorsey, 2 April 1901, Newcombe Papers.

41. Newcombe to Boas, 9 May 1901, Acc. 1901–36, AMNH; Newcombe, diary, 7 May 1901, vol. 33, Newcombe Papers; Newcombe to Dorsey, 8 May 1901, FMNH.

42. Newcombe, diary, 18 May 1901, vol. 33, Newcombe Papers; Newcombe to, Boas, 27 May 1901, Acc. 1901–36, AMNH. Todd decided according to Canadian law.

43. The New York pieces are illustrated in John R. Swanton, *Contributions to the Ethnology of the Haida* ("The Jesup North Pacific Expedition," Franz Boas, ed.; Memoir of the American Museum of Natural History, New York; Leiden: E. J. Brill; New York: G. E. Stechert, 1905), 128, 131, 132, 133, 146. The coffin box is also in color in Allen Wardwell, *Objects of Bright Pride: Northwest Coast Indian Art from the American Museum of Natural History* (New York: Center for Inter-American Relations and the American Federation of Arts, 1978), no. 70.
44. Newcombe to Swanton, 5 October 1901, copy; Newcombe to Boas, 15 January 1902, Acc. 1901–36, AMNH.

45. Boas to Newcombe, 23 March 1899, Newcombe Papers; Newcombe to Boas, 27 May 1901, Acc. 1901–36, AMNH; Newcombe to Dorsey, 8 May, 20 June 1901, FMNH.

46. Newcombe to Dorsey, 20 June, 8 August, 5 October 1901, FMNH; Newcombe to Boas, 29 December 1901.

47. Boas to Newcombe 15 January 1902, BPP; Newcombe to Boas, 5 February, 25 January, 1902, Acc. 1901–36, AMNH.

48. Dorsey to Skiff, 8 January 1900, director's file, "Expeditions, 1897–1915," FMNH, cited in Victoria Wyatt, "A Study of C. F. Newcombe's Haida Collection for the Field Columbian Museum, 1900–1906," (typescript, FMNH, 1978), 4. I am much indebted to this

intensive study of a portion of Newcombe's collecting; Dorsey to Newcombe, 14 November 1901, Newcombe Papers; 29 January 1902, FMNH, 14 November 1901, Newcombe Papers.

49. Newcombe to Dorsey, 21 November 1901, Newcombe Papers.

50. Newcombe to Dorsey, 15 February, 2 March, 14 April 1902, FMNH.

51. Newcombe to Dorsey, 7 and 8 May 1902, FMNH.

52. Dorsey to Newcombe, 23 May 1902, Newcombe Papers.

53. Newcombe to Dorsey, 24 May 1902, FMNH.

54. Newcombe to Dorsey, 5 July 1902, FMNH; Newcombe, diary, 1902, vol. 33, Newcombe Papers; Newcombe to Dorsey, 20 October 1902, FMNH.

55. Newcombe to Dorsey, 23 and 12 April 1903, FMNH.

56. Newcombe to Dorsey, 26 June 1903, FMNH; Newcombe, 23 June 1903, accounts, vol. 31, env. 3a.

57. Dorsey to Newcombe, 7 July, 2 and 16 October 1903, Newcombe Papers.

58. Newcombe to Dorsey, 1 November 1903, FMNH.

59. Newcombe to Dorsey, 30 March 1903, FMNH; Newcombe to Dorsey, 22 November 1903, Newcombe Papers.

60. McGee to F. W. Lehmann, 19 August 1901, McGee Papers, Library of Congress.

61. Newcombe to Dorsey, 13 April, 31 March 1904, vol 54, env. 9, Newcombe Papers.

62. Atlieu to Newcombe, 4 April 1904, vol. 45, env. 56a, Newcombe Papers. Mungo Martin and other Kwakiutl have insisted that it was not Bob Harris, but a brother who went to St. Louis (Bill Holm, personal communication).

63. McGee, "Anthropology at the Louisiana Purchase Exposition," *Science,* n.s. 22 (22 December 1905), 826, 823, 822, 824.

64. *Ibid.,* 826; Ford, ed., *Smoke,* 186–90; Newcombe, diary, 2 August 1904, vol. 34, Newcombe Papers.

65. See Ted C. Hinckley, *Alaskan John G. Brady: Missionary, Businessman, Judge, and Governor, 1878–1918* (Columbus: Ohio State University Press for Miami University, 1982). Brady's personal collection was purchased in 1912 by Mrs. W. H. Harriman and shared by the American Museum and the U. S. National Museum. See folder 908, archives, AMNH; Acc. 54,171, USNM.

66. Son-i-hat to Brady, 29 October 1901, box 3, Brady Papers, Beinecke Library, Yale University; *The Alaskan* (Sitka), 2 November 1901, 1; Brady to Son-i-hat, 29 August 1901; Brady to Bunard, 14 March 1902, box 4, Brady Papers.

67. Brady to Emmons, 21 November 1901, box 5, Brady Papers; *The Alaskan* (Sitka), 8 March 1902, 3; Brady to B. F. Milard, 22 October

1903, box 4; Brady to Elizabeth Brady, 23 September, 4 November 1903, box 1; Brady to Thomas Ryan, 19 November, box 4; Brady to Elizabeth Brady, 2 and 4 November 1903, box 1, Brady Papers.

68. Brady to Thomas Ryan, 6 September 1905, box 5, Brady Papers. See *Carved History: The Totem Poles & House Posts of Sitka National Historical Park* (Sitka: Alaska Natural History Association, 1980).

69. Newcombe to Dorsey, 30 June 1904, FMNH; Newcombe to Teit, 25 April 1905, Newcombe Papers; Dorsey to Newcombe, 24 October 1904, FMNH. For a larger treatment of anthropology at St. Louis, see Robert William Rydell II, "All the World's a Fair: America's International Expositions, 1876–1916" (Ph.D. dissertation, UCLA, 1980), VI.

70. Newcombe to Dorsey, 30 July 1904, FMNH; Dorsey to McGee, 5 October 1904, copy, vol. 45, env. 56, Newcombe Papers.

71. Ford, ed., *Smoke,* 190. Nowell reported that he did well on tips, "besides what I was paid which was $7.50 a day." His actual salary was a quite respectable $2 a day plus expenses. Harris received $1.50 plus expenses. *Ibid.,* 191; Newcombe, accounts, vol. 31, env. 4, Newcombe Papers.

72. Newcombe to Dorsey, 24 October 1904, FMNH; Newcombe to McGee, 2 November 1904, vol. 45, env. 57; Newcombe, diary, 1 November 1904, vol. 34; Newcombe to McGee, 2 November 1904, vol. 45, env. 57; Turner to Newcombe, 3 December 1904, 25 January 1905; W. J. Stone to Newcombe, 14 November 1905, Newcombe Papers.

73. Records of Minutes of the Executive Committee, 13 November 1901, FMNH.

74. Dorsey to Skiff, 6 January 1904, Director's file; Minutes of Executive Committee, 15 January 1904; Dorsey to Skiff, 14 March, 3 April 1905, Acc. 959, Registrar.

75. Minutes of Executive Committee, 24 July 1905; Dorsey memorandum, n.d. [1904], Acc. 846; Dorsey to Skiff, 26 January 1906, Acc. 959, Registrar, FMNH.

76. Minutes of Executive Committee, 8 November, 25 November, 9 August 1905, FMNH.

77. Dorsey to Skiff, 6 January 1904, Director's files, FMNH.

78. [Dorsey], "Recent Progress in Anthropology," *American Anthropologist,* n.s. 8 (July–September 1902), 474; Dorsey to Emmons, 9 February 1909, FMNH.

79. Emmons to Newcombe, 11 February 1917, Newcombe Papers; Laufer to Emmons, 3 March 1920, 23 December 1921, 4 March 1922.

80. Memo 598, 599, a list of poles and posts for sale, FMNH.

Chapter 8
A DECLINING MARKET

1. Emmons to George Dorsey, 9 December 1902, FMNH; Emmons to Newcombe, 7 October 1907, 30 December 1906, Newcombe Papers.

2. William C. Sturtevant, "Does Anthropology Need Museums?" Biological Society of Washington, *Proceedings,* 82 (1969), 624; Donald Collier and Harry Tschopik, Jr., "The Role of Museums in American Anthropology," *American Anthropologist,* 56 (October 1954), 772.

3. Franz Heger, "Der Zukunft der ethnographischen Museen," in *Festschrift Adolf Bastian zu seiner 70. Geburtstag* (Berlin: Dietrich Reimer, 1896), 590–91.

4. Dorsey to Emmons, 18 February 1909, FMNH.

5. Boas, letter to editor, *New York Times,* 7 January 1916, 8, reprinted in George W. Stocking, Jr., *The Shaping of American Anthropology, 1883–1911: A Franz Boas Reader* (New York: Basic Books, 1974), 331. See also Stocking, "Anthropology as Kulturkampf: Science and Politics in the Career of Franz Boas," *The Uses of American Anthropology* (American Anthropological Association, Special Publication 11, 1979), 33–37.

6. Boas to Jesup, 7 January 1902, quoted in Boas to George A. Plimpton, 7 April 1902, BPP; Boas to Jesup, "Plan of Operation for Making a Collection Illustrating the Industrial and Social Life of the Philippines," 12 March 1901, file 13, archives, AMNH; Boas to Zelia Nuttall, 16 May 1901, BPP; Boas to Jesup, 12 March, 9 April 1901, file 13, archives, AMNH.

7. Boas to Nuttall, 16 May 1901, BPP; Boas to Bumpus, 22 December 1902, file 293; 28 March 1904, file 13, archives AMNH; Emmons to Newcombe, 14 January 1906, Newcombe Papers; Wissler to Bumpus, 24 November 1905, curator's reports, 1905–1930, AMNH; Osborn to William Berryman Scott, 22 May 1908, quoted in Michael Kennedy, "Philanthropy and Science," 163.

8. J. Alden Mason, "George Gustav Heye, 1874–1956" (Leaflet no. 6; New York; Museum of the American Indian, Heye Foundation, 1958), 11. For Heye and his museum, see also U. Vincent Wilcox, "The Museum of the American Indian, Heye Foundation," *American Indian Art,* 3 (Spring 1978), 40ff; Kevin Wallace, "Slim-Shin's Monument," *The New Yorker,* 19 November 1960, 104ff; *The History of the Museum* ("Indian Notes and Monographs," Misc. Series, no. 55; New York: Museum of the American Indian, Heye Foundation, 1956).

9. Pepper, "The Museum of the American Indian, Heye Foundation,"

The Geographical Review, 2 (December 1916), 403; Wallace, *New Yorker* (1960), 118; S. K. Lothrop, "George Gustav Heye, 1874–1956," *American Antiquarian,* 23 (July 1957), 66.

10. Saville to Putnam, 5 May 1915, Peabody Museum Papers, Harvard University Archives.

11. Heye to Boas, 18 December 1907, Boas to Heye, 25 April 1910, BPP. See also Ira S. Jacknis, " 'George Hunt, Collector of Indian Specimens' " (unpublished paper, 1981), 30–33.

12. See Wilson Duff, "Stone Clubs from the Skeena River Area," British Columbia Provincial Museum, *Annual Report,* 1962, 2–12, and illustrated again in his *Images Stone B. C.: Thirty Centuries of Northwest Coast Indian Sculpture* (Toronto: Oxford University Press; Seattle: University of Washington Press, 1975).

13. Stewart Culin, "Report on a Collecting Expedition among the Indians of Arizona and California, June 18–October 6, 1905," 51, Brooklyn Museum.

14. Superintendent's Letterbook, 3–10 February 1902, 663–69, vol. 17, GR 61, B. C. Provincial Police Records, PABC. I am indebted to Terry Eastwood for calling this document to my attention. The justice of the peace who took the sworn testimony was the same James Sutton who had evaded charges while collecting bones for Boas in 1888–89. Culin, "Report," 1905, 53; Emmons to Newcombe, 26 January 1902, Newcombe Papers.

15. Culin, "Report," 1905, 53, 51; W. H. Gilstrap to Dorsey, 9 March 1901, FMNH; W. M. Smith to curator, 13 January 1904, RU 189, SIA.

16. G. L. Berg to Heye, 16 April 1917; Pepper to Heye, 9 May 1917 and wire, archives, Museum of the American Indian, Heye Foundation. The price cited is $25,000, but Pepper had been instructed to use doubled figures. A collection of baskets, formerly in the Tozier collection, was acquired by the Thomas Burke Memorial Washington State Museum in 1952 from the Alaska Fur Company.

17. Emmons to Newcombe, 12 April 1908, Newcombe Papers.

18. See M. C. D., "Herculean Task in Museum Administration," *The American Museum Journal,* 10 (December 1910), 226–28, 235–37; Sigurd Neandross, "The Work on the Ceremonial Canoe," *ibid.,* 238–43.

19. Emmons to Newcombe, 4 February, 17 October 1912; 5 September 1915, Newcombe Papers.

20. Newcombe to Dorsey, 5 November 1906; Newcombe to Kroeber, 4 April 1907, Newcombe Papers.

21. Culin, "Report," 1905, 44, Brooklyn Museum.

22. Newcombe to Kroeber, 7 November 1903; Newcombe to H. M. Ami, 29 December 1905; Newcombe to Dorsey, 24 July 1906, Newcombe Papers.

23. Culin, "Report on a Collecting Expedition among the Indians of California and Vancouver Island, May–August 1908," 79–81, 92, Brooklyn Museum.

24. Culin, "Report on a Collecting Trip among the Indians of Oklahoma, New Mexico, California and Vancouver by Stewart Culin. May 3–July 28, 1911," II, 114, Brooklyn Museum.

25. The following is based upon Culin's account in *ibid.,* 117–32.

26. Newcombe to Culin, 8 March 1911, Brooklyn Museum.

27. *Daily British Colonist* (Victoria), 15 April 1893, 6. Deans was paid $298.65 for his Haida collection, Jacobsen received $766, plus $231 expenses and $100 for services. Another small collection was also purchased. British Columbia, *Public Accounts,* 1892–93, 1893–94.

28. *Ibid.,* 1897–98, 1898–99; *A Preliminary Catalogue of the Collection of Natural History and Ethnology in the Provincial Museum, Victoria, British Columbia* (Victoria: Richard Wolfenden, 1898).

29. Culin, "A Summer Trip among the Western Indians," The University Museum, *Bulletin of the Free Museum of Science and Art,* 3 (January 1901), 153; Culin, "Report," 1905, 48; 1908, 88; Jacobsen to W. A. Newcombe, 14 September 1932, Newcombe Papers.

30. *Daily British Colonist,* 16 September 1900, 5; 5 April 1903, 10.

31. *Ibid.,* 1 November 1903, 7.

32. *Ibid.,* 7 August 1903, Landsberg file, PABC; Landsberg to A. von Hügel, 14 March 1903, Cambridge Museum of Archaeology and Ethnology; Minute Books, 5 April 1904; Executive Committee to Premier McBride, 13 January 1904 (copy), Natural History Society of Victoria, PABC.

33. *Victoria Daily Colonist,* 18 April 1902, 3.

34. Hill-Tout to Newcombe, 4 March 1901, Newcombe Papers.

35. British Columbia, *Provincial Museum of Natural History and Ethnology, Victoria, British Columbia* (Victoria: R. Wolfenden, 1909), 7; *Guide* (Victoria: R. Wolfenden, 1909); British Columbia, "Report of the Provincial Archivist," 1911, N10.

36. See Terry Eastwood, "R. E. Gosnell, E. O. S. Scholefield and the Founding of the Provincial Archives of British Columbia, 1894–1919," *B. C. Studies,* 54 (Summer 1982), 51–57; Culin, "Report," 1908, 93–94, Brooklyn Museum; Natural History Society of Victoria, minutes, 7 August 1911, PABC; Peter Neive Cotton, *Vice Regal Mansions of British Columbia* (Victoria: Elgin Publications, 1981), 103–104.

37. Scholefield to Newcombe, 10 May 1911, Newcombe Papers. The words are W. A. Newcombe's in W. A. to C. F. Newcombe, Newcombe Papers. See also Culin, "Report," 1911, 111.

38. Newcombe accounts, vol. 31, env. 3, Newcombe Papers; British Columbia, *Public Accounts*, 1911–12, 1912–13, 1913–14, 1914–15.

39. Emmons to Dorsey, 20 August 1913, FMNH; Emmons to F. S. Hall, 26 July 1913, Acc. 42, Thomas Burke Memorial Washington State Museum; Emmons to W. H. Holmes, 22 July 1913, RU 192, file 44522, box 121, folder 10, SIA.

40. Newcombe to Culin, 9 July 1914, Brooklyn Museum.

41. Newcombe to Culin, 10 April 1908; Newcombe to Kroeber, 20 April 1907, Newcombe Papers.

42. Kroeber to Newcombe, 21 June 1911, vol. 41, env. 33, Newcombe Papers. Despite Newcombe's indications that it came directly from Skidegate, the California pole seems to have been bought from T. S. Gore of Victoria. He paid $175 for it, but charged California $350. T. S. Gore to W. A. Newcombe, 22 August 1911; C. F. Newcombe to Kroeber, 18 August 1911, vol. 40, env. 33, Newcombe Papers.

43. Newcombe to Dorsey, 11 March, 28 September 1913, FMNH.

44. *Ibid.*; Barbeau, *Totem Poles of the Gitksan, Upper Skeena River, British Columbia* (National Museum of Canada, Bulletin no. 61, Anthropological Series, no. 12; Ottawa: F. A. Acland, 1929), 7n3.

45. Zantise per J. C. Spencer to Thomas Deasy, 11 September 1911, vol. 38, env. 50, Newcombe Papers; George Green to Newcombe, 27 September 1911; Deasy to Newcombe, 28 September 1911; Newcombe to Mrs. Oliver, 26 December 1911, vol. 38, env. 50, Newcombe Papers.

46. Gleisher to von Hügel, 29 November 1907; von Hügel to Gleisher, 26 December 1907; Stadthagen to Gleisher, 16 December 1907, Cambridge Museum of Archaeology and Ethnology; Culin, "Report," 1908, 79–80, Brooklyn Museum; Dorsey to von Hügel, 1 April 1913, FMNH.

47. Newcombe to Barrett, 8 and 18 August 1914, Newcombe Papers; Newcombe, "The Haida Totem Pole at the Milwaukee Public Museum," Milwaukee Public Museum, *Yearbook*, 2 (1922), 197.

48. *The Milwaukee Journal*, 20 September 1922, 15; 22 September 1922, 2; 1 October 1922, II, 1–2; 24 September 1922, II, 1; 12 October 1922, 19; 26 October 1922, 2; 12 October 1922, 19.

49. Some of this material is illustrated in *Soft Gold: The Fur Trade & Cultural Exchange on the Northwest Coast of America* (Portland: Oregon Historical Society; distr. by University of Washington Press, 1982). The Cass mask is in J. C. H. King, *Portrait Masks from the Northwest Coast of America* (London: Thames and Hudson, 1979),

plate 51, and in Henry B. Collins, *et al.*, *The Far North: 2,000 Years of American Eskimo and Indian Art* (Bloomington: Indiana University Press for the National Gallery of Art, 1977), no. 294, pp. xxii and 236–37.

50. Farlow to Willoughby, 25 December 1903, box 21, 28 January 1908, box 23, Peabody Museum Papers, Harvard University Archives. See "Nicholson (Grace) Collection, Summary Report," typescript inventory, Huntington Library; Sally McLendon, "Preparing Museum Collections for Use as Primary Data in Ethnographic Research," in *The Research Potential of Anthropological Museum Collections,* eds. Anne-Marie E. Cantwell, et al. ("Annals of the New York Academy of Sciences," vol. 376; New York, 1981), 201–27.

51. Willoughby to Newcombe, 28 February 1917; Newcombe to Willoughby, 12 March, 22 May 1917, Acc. 17–17, Peabody Museum; Newcombe accounts, vol. 31, env. 3, Newcombe Papers.

52. Willoughby to Newcombe, 19 October, 1 February 1919, vol. 41, env. 30, Newcombe Papers.

53. See the above-cited envelopes, Newcombe Papers; Acc. 17–17, Peabody Museum; Peabody Museum, *55th Annual Report,* 1920–21, 4–5; *56th Annual Report,* 1921–22, 5.

54. McIlwraith to A. C. Haddon, 22 August 1922, Haddon Collection, Cambridge University Library; P. E. Goddard, "Charles Frederick Newcombe," *American Anthropologist,* 27 (April 1925), 252.

55. Newcombe to Currelly, n.d. [1923], vol. 42, env. 87, Newcombe Papers.

56. Ridgeway to W. A. Newcombe, 17 June 1925, vol. 45, env. 58, Newcombe Papers; Ridgeway-Newcombe correspondence, Cambridge Museum.

57. Board of Archaeological and Anthropological Studies to W. A. Newcombe, n.d., vol. 45, env. 58, Newcombe Papers; accounts and correspondence, vol. 31, env. 3; vol. 37, env. 50; vol. 42, env. 87; vol. 43, env. 14; vol. 45, env. 58, 59, Newcombe Papers.

58. Edenshaw to Newcombe, 2 April 1906, Newcombe Papers.

59. Victoria Wyatt, "A Study of C. F. Newcombe's Haida Collection for the Field Columbian Museum, 1900–1906" (typescript, FMNH, 1978), 37; Bell to Newcombe, 25 May 1912, Newcombe Papers.

60. Emmons to W. H. Holmes, 27 April 1900, Acc. 37,889, USNM.

61. Emmons to Dorsey, 18 November 1902, FMNH; Emmons to Newcombe, 22 February 1903, Newcombe Papers; Emmons to Heye, June [1943?], 2 July 1943, archives, Museum of the American Indian, Heye Foundation.

62. Emmons to H. F. Osborn, 19 February 1909, archives, AMNH;

Dorsey to Newcombe, 19 July 1911; Emmons to Newcombe, 9 September [1906], Newcombe Papers.

63. Emmons to Newcombe, 28 July 1907, Newcombe Papers; Emmons basketry notes, no. 84003, FMNH.

64. Emmons to Dorsey, 10 January 1904, 8 August 1905; Emmons to Holmes, 14 May 1911, box 81, file 33418, RU 189, SIA; Emmons to B. Laufer, 3 December 1919, FMNH; Barbeau to Currelly, 21 June 1929, Royal Ontario Museum.

65. Emmons, in his letters to Newcombe, did not hide his contempt for these Jewish merchants. A strong anti-Semitic streak is an Emmons trait, emerging also against Boas and "the Jews . . . coming into Ethnology through Boas." Emmons to Newcombe, 14 October 1910, Newcombe Papers.

66. Brady to F. R. Falconer, 25 May 1903, box 2; Brady to Theodore Roosevelt, 19 February 1902, box 4, Brady Papers, Beinecke Library, Yale.

Chapter 9
COLLECTING IN THIN COUNTRY

1. L. F. Pourtoles to Jeffries Wyman, 20 October 1868, Letterbook I, 129; Gibbs to Wyman, 19 October 1869, Letterbook 1, 188, Peabody Museum, Harvard University; Bishop to Jesup, 30 January 1888; Emmons to Jesup, 25 July 1896, archives, AMNH; Emmons to Thomas Burke, 5 April 1911, Burke Museum; Newcombe to Stewart Culin, 27 March 1911, 2 September 1908, Brooklyn Museum.

2. Newcombe to Culin, 27 March 1911, Brooklyn Museum; Emmons to Holmes, 14 May 1911, box 81, RU 189, SIA; Emmons to Dorsey, 20 August 1913, FMNH.

3. Culin, "Report on a Collecting Expedition among the Indians of California and Vancouver Island, May–August 1908," 78–92, Brooklyn Museum.

4. Large to David Boyle, 23 November 1906, Normal School file, Royal Ontario Museum.

5. Shotridge to George B. Gordon, 7 January 1924, The University Museum, University of Pennsylvania.

6. Barrett to Sapir, 21 March 1914; Sapir to Barrett, 28 March 1914, Sapir Papers, Canadian Ethnology Service, National Museum of Man, Ottawa.

7. For a remarkable documentation of the creation of this film, which required the making of a number of Kwakiutl "artifacts," see Bill Holm and George Irving Quimby, *Edward S. Curtis in the Land of the War Canoes: A Pioneer Cinematographer in the Pacific Northwest* (The

Burke Memorial Washington State Museum, monograph 2; Seattle: University of Washington Press, 1980).

8. Barrett letters of 3 February and 4 March 1915, quoted in Board of Trustees minutes, 9 February and 10 March 1915, Milwaukee Public Museum; recorded interview with S. A. Barrett, August 1962, in Robert Ritzenthaler and Lee A. Parsons, eds., *Masks of the Northwest Coast: The Samuel A. Barrett Collection* ("Publications in Primitive Art," 2; Milwaukee: Milwaukee Public Museum, 1968), 21; Barrett to Henry L. Ward, 5 April 1915, Milwaukee Public Museum Papers, Milwaukee Public Library.

9. Barrett interview, 9 August 1962, transcript, n.p., Milwaukee Public Museum.

10. Barrett interview, in Ritzenthaler and Parsons, ed., *Masks,* 17.

11. Marius Barbeau, *Totem Poles* (Anthropological Series, no. 30; Ottawa: National Museum of Canada, 1950), II, 448.

12. Barrett to Newcombe, 3 February 1915; Newcombe to Culin, 9 June 1914, Newcombe Papers.

13. For the anti-potlatch policy, see F. E. La Violette, *The Struggle for Survival: Indian Culture and the Protestant Ethic in British Columbia* (Toronto: University of Toronto Press, 1961) and Daisy (My-yah-nelth) Sewid-Smith, *Prosecution or Persecution* (Cape Mudge?: Nu-Yum-Balees Society, 1979).

14. Newcombe memorandum, "Alert Bay, 16 May 1921," vol. 43, env. 14a, Newcombe Papers; Scott to agents, 21 October 1918, vol. 3630, file 6244-4, pt. 2, DIA.

15. His January 1921 potlatch earned him a three-month sentence at Oakalla penitentiary. Newcombe, according to Nowell, secured his parole after six weeks. Clellan S. Ford, ed., *Smoke from Their Fires: The Life of a Kwakiutl Chief* (New Haven: The Institute of Human Relations by Yale University Press, 1941), 224. H. S. Clements to Halliday, 16 May 1919, quoted in Sewid-Smith, *Prosecution,* 27.

16. Halliday to J. D. McLean, 24 January 1922, vol. 3630, file 6244-4, pt. 2 DIA. For details of the Cranmer potlatch, see Helen Codere, "Kwakiutl," in Edward H. Spicer, ed., *Prospectives in American Indian Cultural Change* (Chicago: University of Chicago Press, 1961), 470–71.

17. Halliday to Scott, 1 March 1922, gives the number as thirty-four; Halliday to Scott, 10 April 1922; Serg. Angerman, "Criminal Report," 1 March 1922, DIA. Halliday is a much maligned man — rather unfairly so. In an underpaid bureaucracy that did not recruit highly competent men (this was not the India Civil Service), Halliday ranked well above average in fairness and discretion. He acted in this instance under very clear orders from D. C. Scott.

18. Quoted in Sewid-Smith, *Prosecution,* 47.

19. Halliday to Scott, 19 April 1922, quoted in *ibid.,* 39.

20. Halliday to McLean, 6 September 1922; McLean to Halliday, 20 September 1922, DIA.

21. Sapir to Scott, 9 January 1923, DIA.

22. Bell in Sewid-Smith, *Prosecution,* 69; Halliday, *Potlatch and Totem and the Recollections of an Indian Agent* (Toronto: J. M. Dent & Sons, 1935), 192. Dan Cranmer, in a 1934 letter, makes it clear that "the dancing paraphernalia was all paid for." Cranmer to Boas, 14 February 1934, Rukeyser additions, BFP.

23. Wawrpigisawi, *et al.* to Scott, 6 April 1920; Halliday to Scott, 1 March 1922, DIA; Hunt, "History of 20 Coppers from Alert Bay," A127, American Indian Linguistics Collection, American Philosophical Society.

24. Emmons to Newcombe, 22 February 1903, Newcombe Papers.

25. There is a difficulty with his age. The death certificate lists him as born on 15 April 1886, but he listed himself as age thirty, not twenty-six, when, in September 1912, he enrolled at the University of Pennsylvania. I have accepted the official record.

26. Gordon to Shotridge, 9 January 1906, The University Museum, University of Pennsylvania.

27. Emmons to Heye, 2 December 1911, copy, The University Museum.

28. Gordon to Shotridge, 8 February 1907, The University Museum; Gawasa Wanneh, "Situwaka, Chief of the Chilcats," *American Indian Magazine,* 11 (1914), 282.

29. Mary Elizabeth Ruwell, archivist at The University Museum, informs me that the village is again on display.

30. Shotridge file, University of Pennsylvania Archives; minute book, Board of Managers, 16 April 1915, The University Museum.

31. Illustrated in Mason, *"Expedition",* 2 (Winter 1960), 13–14.

32. Shotridge to Gordon, 22 August 1922, The University Museum. For the significance of crest hats and helmets, see John R. Swanton, "Social Conditions, Beliefs, and Linguistic Relationship of the Tlingit Indians," Bureau of American Ethnology, *Annual Report,* 1904, 416; Kalervo Oberg, *The Social Economy of the Tlingit Indians* (Seattle: University of Washington Press, 1973), 124–26. Many of Shotridge's collected pieces are illustrated in Shotridge, "War Helmets and Clan Hats of the Tlingit Indians," *The Museum Journal,* 10 (March–June 1919), 44–48.

33. Shotridge to Gordon, 22 August 1922, 28 June 1918, The University Museum.

34. Shotridge to Gordon, 14 June 1923; George T. Emmons, "The

Whale House of the Chilkat," *American Museum Journal,* 16 (1916), 454, 563, with illustrations.

35. Newcombe to Dorsey, 8 May 1902; Emmons to Dorsey, 1 June, 16 August 1902, FMNH.

36. Shotridge to Gordon, 12 March, 27 July 1906, The University Museum; Emmons to Heye, 2 December 1911, copy; Shotridge to Gordon, 14 June, 17 January 1923, The University Museum.

37. Shotridge to Gordon, 27 January 1927; [Shotridge?], "The Vanishing Nobility of Alaska," undated typescript, ca. 1930; Shotridge to Gordon, 15 February 1927, The University Museum.

38. R. L. Olson, *Social Structure and Social Life of the Tlingit in Alaska* (Anthropological Records, vol. 26; Berkeley and Los Angeles: University of California Press, 1967), 8, calls him Yetlkak, and Oberg, *Social Economy,* 82, Yehlgak, the *ankaua* or "rich man" of the Ganaxtedi.

39. Shotridge to Gordon, 24 March 1923, The University Museum.

40. Shotridge to Gordon, 23 April, 8 October 1923, The University Museum.

41. Shotridge to Gordon, 7 January 1924, The University Museum.

42. Shotridge to Gordon, 3 June 1924, The University Museum.

43. Shotridge to Gordon, 7 August 1924, The University Museum.

44. Shotridge to Gordon, 12 January 1925, The University Museum; Olson, *Social Structure,* 6, who adds, 8 n10, "The furor and indignation forced him to leave Klukwan."

45. Shotridge to Gordon, 29 September 1925.

46. Emmons to J. Alden Mason, 10 May 1942, Mason Papers, American Philosophical Society; Emmons to Newcombe, 10 April 1923, 17 October 1918, Newcombe Papers.

47. Edmund Carpenter, "Collecting Northwest Coast Art," introduction to Bill Holm and Bill Reid, *Indian Art of the Northwest Coast: A Dialogue on Craftsmanship and Aesthetics* (Institute of the Arts, Rice University; distr. by the University of Washington Press, 1975), 18; Gordon, "Brief Report of the Alaskan Expedition, 1922–1927," 18 November 1927, typescript, The University Museum; Shotridge, "The Kanguanton Shark Helmet," *The Museum Journal,* 20 (September–December 1929), 343.

48. *Ibid.,* 339–40; Shotridge to Gordon, 16 March 1931, The University Museum.

49. Olson, *Social Structure,* 6, 22; Jayne to Shotridge, 22 December 1931, Shotridge to Jayne, 23 July, 23 November 1932, Jayne to Shotridge, 30 January 1933; Shotridge to Jayne, 2 August, 20 December 1933; Shotridge to J. A. Mason, 29 September 1934, The University Museum; Olson, *Social Structure,* 6. "When a man of high rank

makes a speech to his clan it is good manners to say, 'We are all poor,' but Shotridge always said 'high caste there are and there are low people,' " *ibid.,* 13, 48.

50. Office of Vital Statistics, Territory of Alaska, Certificate of Death, 7 August 1937; Carpenter, in Holm and Reid, *Indian Art,* 22, who accepts the "Sitka version"; Polly Miller and Leon Gordon Miller, *Lost Heritage of Alaska: The Adventure and Art of the Alaska Coastal Indians* (New York: Bonanza Books, 1967), 252, which has the "Klukwan version"; Andrew Hope III, ed., *Raven's Bones* (Sitka: Sitka Community Association, 1982; distr. by the University of Washington Press), iv.

51. Shotridge to J. A. Mason, 29 September 1934, Mason to Shotridge, 9 November 1934, Mason Papers.

52. For Sapir, see David G. Mandelbaum, ed., *Selected Writings of Edward Sapir in Language, Culture and Personality* (Berkeley: University of California Press, 1963); Richard Preston, "Edward Sapir's Anthropology: Style, Structure and Method," *American Anthropologist,* 68 (1966), 1105–27; Preston, "Reflections on Sapir's Anthropology in Canada," *Canadian Review of Sociology and Anthropology,* 17 (1980), 367–75; Sapir, *Time Perspective* (Canada, Department of Mines, Geological Survey, Memoir 90, Anthropological Series, no. 13; Ottawa: Government Printing Bureau, 1916), reprinted in Mandelbaum, ed., *Selected Writings,* 389–462.

53. For Barbeau, see Richard J. Preston, "C. Marius Barbeau and the History of Canadian Anthropology," *The History of Canadian Anthropology,* Canadian Ethnological Society, *Proceedings,* 3 (1975), 123–35; Wilson Duff, "Contributions of Marius Barbeau to West Coast Ethnology," *Anthropologica,* 6 (1964), 63–96.

54. Barbeau to Sapir, 27 December 1914, Sapir Papers, Canadian Ethnological Service, National Museum of Man.

55. Barbeau to Sapir, 23 January, 6 and 25 March 1915, Sapir Papers.

56. Barbeau to Currelly, 25 May 1926; Jenness to Currelly, 31 May 1927, registrar's files, Royal Ontario Museum (hereafter ROM).

57. Barbeau to Currelly, 24 September 1927, "Some time," registrar's files, ROM; T. McIlwraith to Barbeau, 26 June 1929, 29 September 1929, McIlwraith Papers, box 1, University of Toronto Archives.

58. Emmons to F. S. Hall, 16 May 1914, Acc. 42, Burke Museum; Barbeau to Currelly, 24 September 1927, "Some time"; Barbeau to McIlwraith, 13 July 1929, box 1, McIlwraith Papers.

59. Barbeau to Currelly, 21 June 1929, registrar's files, ROM; Barbeau to McIlwraith, 13 July, 29 September 1929, box 1, McIlwraith Papers.

60. Alvin Thorne to Barbeau, 1 January 1930; Barbeau to Heye, 15 January 1930; Walter C. Walker to Barbeau, 31 August 1930;

Barbeau to Heye, 22 May 1930, Barbeau Papers, Canadian Centre for Folk Culture Studies, National Museum of Man.

61. Barbeau-Arthur Price correspondence, 1947, Price file, Barbeau Papers. Barbeau's agent and collaborator was plainly nervous about the rip-off, but no one in Vancouver caught on.

62. The following is drawn from David Darling and Douglas Cole, "Totem Pole Restoration on the Skeena, 125–30: An Early Exercise in Heritage Conservation," *B. C. Studies,* 47 (Autumn 1980), 29–48.

63. The purchaser was, it seems, J. E. Annable of Nelson, B. C., who had an agreement to buy the poles as early as September 1921. At least one of the poles seems to have gone to Vancouver's Stanley Park. See vol. 43, env. 9, Newcombe Papers.

64. Resolutions of May 1923, vol. 4088, file 507,787, RG 10, DIA. Indian Affairs material contained in files 507, 787 and 787-2 will be referred to merely as "DIA." Smith to Sapir, 10 June 1923; Sapir to Charles Camsell, 16 April 1923, Sapir Papers.

65. Jenness to Barbeau, 10 December 1923, Barbeau Papers; Barbeau to Charles Camsell, 24 August 1924, copy, DIA.

66. *Montreal Gazette,* 25 May 1925; Camsell to Barbeau, 5 September 1924, Barbeau Papers.

67. Barbeau, "Report on the Totem Poles of the Upper Skeena and Their Contemplated Conservation," 20 January 1925, 2–6, Barbeau Papers.

68. Internal memo, 17 February 1925; Sir Henry Thornton to Scott, 2 April 1925; Harkin to Arthur Gibson, 17 February 1925, DIA.

69. Williams, Manson and Gonzales to Scott, 16 May 1927, wire; E. Hyde to Scott, 25 June 1927, DIA.

70. Barbeau, "Report," 20 January 1920, 3, 4; Smith to Scott, 9 September 1926, DIA.

71. Canada, Department of Mines, National Museum of Canada, Bulletin no. 50, *Annual Report for 1926* (Ottawa, 1928), 81.

72. Kitsegukla Indian chiefs to Smith, 2 May 1927, copy; Hyde to Scott, 25 June 1927; Smith to Scott, 11 June 1927, copy; Barbeau to Scott, 21 June 1929; Hyde to Scott, 25 June 1927; see also Campbell to Scott, 21 June 1928, DIA.

73. Smith to Scott, 11 June 1927, copy; Barbeau to Scott, 8 July 1927, DIA; Jenness to Camsell, n.d., RG 45, Geological Survey of Canada, vol. 19, file 144A1.

74. Campbell to Scott, 20 October 1928; Hyde to Scott, 31 January 1929; Mortimer to Scott, 3 December 1930, DIA.

75. Village Committee to museum, 19 October 1931, copy. Barbeau's advice was not to answer one way or the other "and they will forget

their demands after a while." Barbeau to Scott, 23 November 1931, DIA.

76. Scott to Thomas Murphy, 31 January 1931; W. A. Newcombe to S. F. Tolmie, 25 January 1930; DIA; Carr to Mr. and Mrs. Eric Brown, 11 August 1928, National Gallery of Canada; Wilson Duff, *The Indian History of British Columbia: The Impact of the White Man* (Anthropology in British Columbia, memoir no 5; Provincial Museum of British Columbia, Victoria, 1964), 84.

77. Barbeau, "Report," 20 January 1925, 3; Campbell to Scott, 28 July 1928, DIA; Carr to Browns, 11 August 1928, National Gallery of Canada.

78. See vol. 324, I-6-G, GR 441, Premiers Papers, PABC, for Tolmie; Barbeau to Pattullo, 2 November 1934, box 97, file 1, GR 1222, Premiers Papers, PABC, for Pattullo.

79. McIlwraith to L. C. G. Clarke, 19 October 1923, Cambridge Museum of Archaeology and Ethnology; McIlwraith to family, 28 April 1922, McIlwraith Family Papers, in private possession; McIlwraith to A. C. Haddon, 29 August 1922, Haddon Collection, Cambridge University Library; McIlwraith to Sapir, 4 March 1924, Sapir Papers; McIlwraith to Clarke, 16 January 1924, Cambridge Museum. For yet another reason for his not collecting, see p. 302–3.

80. Boas to Toni Boas, 24 October 1930; Boas to R. Benedict, 13 November 1930; Boas to children, 14 December 1930, in Ronald P. Rohner, ed., *The Ethnography of Franz Boas: Letters and Diaries of Franz Boas Written from the Northwest Coast from 1886 to 1930,* trans. Helene Boas Yampolsky and Hedy Parker (Chicago: University of Chicago Press, 1969), 288, 291, 297.

81. Drucker to W. A. Newcombe, 25 October 1935, 8 April 1937, Newcombe Papers.

Chapter 10
EPILOGUE

1. Erna Gunther, *Art in the Life of the Northwest Coast Indians* (Portland: Portland Art Museum, 1966), 175–83.

2. Bill Holm, *The Box of Daylight: Northwest Coast Indian Art* (Seattle Art Museum; Seattle: University of Washington Press, 1983), 3.

3. Francis Haskell, *Rediscoveries in Art: Some Aspects of Taste, Fashion and Collecting in England and France* (Ithaca, N. Y.: Cornell University Press, 1976), 5. For the process, Robert Goldwater's *Primitivism in Modern Art* (rev. ed.; New York: Vintage Books, 1967) remains essential.

4. See Christian F. Feest, *Native Art of North America* (London: Thames & Hudson, 1980), ch. 1, for a brief overview.

5. Leroy C. Breuning, ed., *Apollinaire on Art: Essays and Reviews, 1902–1908, by Guillaume Apollinaire,* trans. Susan Suleiman (London: Thames and Hudson, 1972), 56.

6. Newcombe, "Miss Carr's Collection of Paintings of Indian Totem Poles," n.d. [December 1911], vol. 52, f. 19, Newcombe Papers; Maria Tippett, *Emily Carr: A Biography* (Toronto: Oxford University Press, 1979), 74–75; Carr to Young, n.d., Provincial Museum Papers, PABC, quoted in *ibid.,* 114; Newcombe to Kermode, 17 January 1913, Provincial Museum Papers, quoted in *ibid.,* 110.

7. Boas, "The Decorative Art of the North American Indian" [orig. 1903], in Boas, *Race, Language and Culture* (New York: Free Press, 1940), 547n3; *Bulletin,* AMNH, 9 (1897), 123–76, revised in Boas, *Primitive Art* (Oslo: H. Aschehoug, 1927; reprint, New York: Dover Publications, 1955), 183–298.

8. "Principles of Esthetic Form in the Art of the North Pacific Coast: A Preliminary Sketch," *American Anthropologist,* 20 (July–September 1918), 258–64.

9. Burlington Fine Arts Club, *Catalogue of an Exhibition of Objects of Indigenous American Art* (London: Burlington Fine Arts Club, 1920), vii.

10. Shotridge, "Emblems of the Tlingit Culture," *The Museum Journal,* 19 (December 1928), 350; Smith, *An Album of Prehistoric Canadian Art,* Canada, Department of Mines, Victoria Memorial Museum, Bulletin 37, Anthropological Series 8, June 1923; Sapir, intro. to Smith, *An Album,* iii.

11. Tippett, *Carr,* 139–51. See also Douglas Leechman, "Native Canadian Art of the West Coast," *Studio,* 96 (November 1928), 331–33; "West Coast Indian Art," *The Canadian Forum,* 8 (February 1928), 525; John Sloan, Oliver LaFarge, et al., *Introduction to American Indian Art* (2 vols; New York: The Exposition of Indian Tribal Arts, 1931), iii. The history of the San Francisco and New York exhibitions is told in Robert Faye Schrader, *The Indian Arts and Crafts Board: An Aspect of New Deal Indian Policy* (Albuquerque: University of New Mexico Press, 1983).

12. Aldona Jonaitis, "Creations of Mystics and Philosophers: White Man's Perceptions of Northwest Coast Indian Art from the 1930s to the Present," *American Indian Culture and Research Journal,* 5 (1981), 3.

13. Probably it should not be conceived of in such terms, except, of course, the work of contemporary artists. It is decorative art, which is not the same, though not inferior to, "fine art." This statement will not be acceptable to many. There is here, however, a subject for an interesting essay in the history of taste and of museums. The distinction, of argued validity, between applied and decorative art

and fine art is more appreciated in Britain and (especially) on the Continent than in North America. Germany, for example, has its Kunstmuseen and its Kunstgewerbemuseen.

Chapter 11
THEMES AND PATTERNS

1. William C. Sturtevant, "Does Anthropology Need Museums?" Biological Society of Washington, *Proceedings,* 82 (1969), 619–25; Donald Collier and Harry Tschopik, Jr., "The Role of Museums in American Anthropology," *American Anthropologist,* 56 (October 1954), 769.

2. Bastian, "Sechste Sitzung," *Correspondenz-Blatt der Gesellschaft für Anthropologie, Ethnologie und Urgeschichte,* 1880, 109.

3. Quoted in Jacob W. Gruber, "Ethnographic Salvage and the Shaping of Anthropology," *American Anthropologist,* 72 (December 1970), 1295. Gruber's article provides a good overview of the theme. Culin to Robert C. H. Brock, 3 April 1900, The University Museum, University of Pennsylvania.

4. G. P. Gordon to Eckley Brinton Cox, Jr., n.d. [1905], Gordon Expeditions file, Alaska trip, 1905, The University Museum; R. W. Brock, "Annual Report for 1910," in Canada, *Sessional Papers,* 1911, XLV, no. 26, 7; Gordon to Cox [1905], Gordon Expeditions file, Alaska trip, 1905, The University Museum.

5. Dorsey to Newcombe, 9 December 1903; Nowell to Newcombe, 24 February 1904, vol. 54, file 9, Newcombe Papers.

6. Powell to Bickmore, 5 October 1882, Acc. 1869–90–95, AMNH; Newcombe to Dorsey, 21 November 1901; Emmons to Newcombe, 7 August 1900; Dawson to Newcombe, 1 June 1897; Boas to Newcombe, 8 November 1897, Newcombe Papers.

7. F. S. Hall to Newcombe, 17 November 1922, Newcombe Papers; *Annual Report,* Art Historical and Scientific Society, Vancouver, 1904, 17.

8. Dawson to Sifton, 7 July 1899, RG 45, Geological Survey of Canada, D 15, reel C485, vol. 60, PAC; W. A. to C. F. Newcombe, 8 March 1906, vol. 53, file 2, Newcombe Papers.

9. Currelly to Newcombe, 6 September 1922, Newcombe Papers.

10. Baird to McLean, 12 February 1881, RU 33, vol. 106, p. 453; 3 June 1881, RU 33, vol. 112, p. 40, 10 August 1881, vol. 165, p. 484, SIA. See also J. G. Bourinot, "Circular to Officers of the Hudson's Bay Company in Regard to the Collection of Specimens . . . ," 5 March 1883, Royal Society of Canada, *Proceedings and Transactions,* 1882–83, I (1883), XXXI; Dawson to Newcombe, 24 March 1897, Newcombe Papers.

11. McIlwraith to Barbeau, 3 June 1927, box 1, McIlwraith Papers, University of Toronto Archives.

12. Peter Macnair, cited in Victoria Wyatt, "A Study of C. F. Newcombe's Haida Collection for the Field Columbian Museum, 1900–1906" (typescript, FMNH, 1978), 47.

13. Ira Jacknis, "'George Hunt, Collector of Indian Specimens'" (unpublished paper, 1981), 16.

14. Boas to Hunt, 18 May 1899, 3 January 1900, BPP; Powell to S. P. Langley, 15 August 1893, RU 31, box 23, SIA; McIlwraith to Barbeau, 26 June 1929, box 1, file 10, McIlwraith Papers.

15. Powell to Langley, 15 August 1893, RU 31, box 23, SIA. A recent exhibition focussed on "acculturated arts" of the Northwest Coast. See Victoria Wyatt, *Shapes of Their Thoughts: Reflections of Cultural Contact in Northwest Coast Indian Art* (Norman: University of Oklahoma Press for Peabody Museum of Natural History, Yale University, 1984).

16. T. A. Joyce, "A Totem Pole in the British Museum," *Journal of the Royal Anthropological Society of Great Britain and Ireland,* ns 33 (1903), 90–95.

17. Heye to W. A. Newcombe, 8 December 1937, vol. 12, Newcombe Papers.

18. Newcombe to Sapir, 11 April 1914, Sapir Papers.

19. Emmons to D. Jenness, 28 February 1928, Jenness Papers, Canadian Ethnological Service, National Museum of Man; Deasy Papers, PABC; Leslie Drew and Douglas Wilson, *Argillite: Art of the Haida* (North Vancouver: Hancock House, 1980), 169–75.

20. Haddon bought it in 1909 for the Horniman Museum. Bill Holm has identified it as an "artifake" and suggested it was copied from a line drawing in Boas's 1897 "Social Organization" publication.

21. Emmons to H. C. Bumpus, 21 July 1907, file 59, archives, AMNH; Emmons to C. C. Willoughby, 27 March 1905, Peabody Museum Papers; Emmons to Dorsey, 2 August 1906, FMNH; Heye to W. A. Newcombe, 5 November 1937, Newcombe Papers.

22. Helen Codere, *Fighting with Property: A Study of Kwakiutl Potlatching and Warfare, 1792–1930* (Seattle: University of Washington Press for the American Ethnological Society, 1950), passim.

23. A. Woldt, ed., *Captain Jacobsen's Reise an der Nordwestküste Amerikas, 1881–1883* (Leipzig: Max Spohr, 1884), 24. (Gunther, trans., 17.)

24. Hunt to Boas, 22 June 1904, Acc. 1904–38, AMNH; J. H. Keen to O. M. Dalton, 12 June 1897, archives, British Museum. The actual figures are 50/- and £3; Boas to parents, 28 October 1886, in Rohner, ed., *The Ethnography of Franz Boas,* 50; Swanton to Boas, 14 October 1900, Acc. 1901–31, AMNH.

25. Swan to Baird, 21 July 1884, RU 26, SIA; "Reminiscences of B. F. Jacobsen," 22–24, PABC.

26. Jacobsen to Bastian, 5 March 1882, Jacobsen Papers, Museum für Völkerkunde, Hamburg; Woldt, ed., *Jacobsen's Reise,* 128–29; Swan Diary, 1883, 59–60, University of Washington Archives.

27. Jacobsen, Tagebuch I, 21 September 1881, Jacobsen Papers; Newcombe to Culin, 3 September 1908, Newcombe Papers; E. Rhuamah Skidmore, *Alaska: Its Southern Coast and the Sitkan Archipelago* (Boston: D. Lothrop, 1885), 27.

28. Dorsey to Skiff, 15 September 1903, reporting conversation of B. A. Whalen, FMNH. Cf. "The misfortunes of others are always the good fortunes of art collectors." Joseph Alsop, *The Rare Art Traditions* ("Bollingen Series," xxxv; Princeton, N. J.: Princeton University Press, 1982), 147.

29. Hunt to Boas, 20 March 1895, BPP; Culin, "Report on a Collecting Expedition. . . . May–August 1908," 79, Brooklyn Museum; Newcombe to Culin, 4 August 1900, The University Museum; Hunt to Boas, 20 March 1895, Acc. 1895–4, AMNH.

30. Roberts to Newcombe via B. C. Freeman, 10 January 1902; Jack Curley to Newcombe, 11 April 1910; Ellen Curley to Newcombe, 3 April 1911; Moody to Newcombe, 4 January 1906, 6 May 1908, Newcombe Papers; Fred R. Falconer to Brady, 14 May 1903, box 2, Brady Papers; Brady judged that the boards would come "pretty high" in exchange for so elaborate and costly a slab. Brady to Falconer, 25 May 1903, box 4, Brady Papers.

31. Woldt, ed., *Jacobsen's Reise,* 40 (Gunther, trans., 25); Dorsey, "Up the Skeena River to the Home of the Tsimshians," *Popular Science Monthly,* 8 (1898), 187; Newcombe to Dorsey, 8 August 1901, FMNH; transcript of interview with Barrett, 9 August 1962, Milwaukee Public Museum.

32. Woldt, ed., *Jacobsen's Reise,* 84 (Gunther, trans., 51); Swan Diary, 1883, 60; Dawson Diary, 1878, 14–18 July, McGill University, Rare Book Room. The Chinook Jargon word *ictus* or *iktahs,* literally "thing," usually meant trade goods or provisions; collectors like Dawson, Newcombe, and Emmons employed it more narrowly to mean artifacts.

33. Jacobsen, "Erlebnisse beim Sammeln in den 3 Weltteilen" (lecture), Jacobsen Papers; Swan Diary, 1875, 2 July, University of Washington Archives.

34. Shotridge to Gordon, 7 January 1924, The University Museum; Shotridge, "A Visit to the Tsimshian Indians," *Museum Journal,* 10 (September 1919), 131 and photo, fig. 47; Barbeau to McIlwraith, 13 July 1929, McIlwraith Papers; Shotridge to Gordon, 22 August 1922, The University Museum.

35. Jacobsen to Hagenbeck, 3 November 1881, Jacobsen to Bastian, 5 March 1882, Jacobsen Papers; Woldt, ed., *Jacobsen's Reise,* 127–28 (Gunther, trans., 73).

36. "Reminiscences of B. F. Jacobsen," 19–20, PABC.

37. Mrs. C. R. Draney to W. A. Newcombe, 20 August [1937], Newcombe Papers.

38. McIlwraith, *The Bella Coola Indians* (Toronto: University of Toronto Press, 1948), I, 697.

39. Swan Diary, 1883, 57, 60, University of Washington Archives; C. E. S. Wood, "Among the Thlinkits in Alaska," *Century Magazine,* 24 (July 1882), 337.

40. B. F. Jacobsen, description accompanying no. 16–1966, Acc. 1897–44, AMNH.

41. Jacobsen, "Erlebnisse beim Sammeln in den 3 Weltteilen," Jacobsen Papers.

42. Swan to Baird, 30 January 1883, RU 26, SIA.

43. Molyneau St. John, *The Sea of Mountains: An Account of Lord Dufferin's Tour through British Columbia in 1876* (2 vols.; London: Hurst and Blackett, 1877), II, 34.

44. Otto Teichmann, ed., *A Journey to Alaska in the Year 1868: Being the Diary of the Late Emil Teichmann* (privately printed; Kensington: Cayne Press, 1925), 208–15.

45. Swan to Baird, 29 September 1883, RU 26, SIA; Woldt, ed., *Jacobsen's Reise,* 47 (Gunther, trans., 29).

46. For Beynon, see Marjorie Halpin, "William Beynon, Tsimshian, 1888–1958," in Margo Liberty, ed., *American Indian Intellectuals (Proceedings,* American Ethnological Society, 1977; Minneapolis: West Coast Publishing, 1978), 141–58. For Wellcome, see Helen Turner, *Henry Wellcome: The Man, His Collection and His Legacy* (London: The Wellcome Trust and Heinemann, 1980). For Hunt, see Jacknis, " 'George Hunt,' " 46.

47. Hunt to Boas, 26 September 1899, BPP.

48. Shotridge, "The Emblems of the Tlingit Culture," *Museum Journal,* 19 (December 1928), 351.

49. *The* (Seattle) *Post-Intelligencer,* Seattle Chamber of Commerce, Alaska Bureau, scrapbook, series I, vol. 3, 20, Northwest Collection, University of Washington Library.

50. John Keats Lord, *The Naturalist in Vancouver Island and British Columbia* (2 vols; London: Richard Bentley, 1866), I, 173 and illustrated, II, opp. 103.

51. Woldt, ed. *Jacobsen's Reise,* 62, 140 (Gunther, trans., 38, 79); Jacobsen, "Erlebnisse beim Sammeln in den 3 Weltteilen."

52. Alice C. Fletcher to Putnam, 19 November 1886, Harvard Museum Papers; Skidmore, *Alaska*, 255; Kate Field, "A Trip to Southeastern Alaska," *Harper's Weekly*, 32 (8 September 1888), 684; McLean to Baird, 14 September 1884, Acc. 15,504, USNM.

53. Boas diary, 6 June 1888, in Rohner, ed. *Ethnography of Boas*, 88.

54. See William H. Goetzmann and Kay Sloan, *Looking Far North: The Harriman Expedition to Alaska, 1899* (New York: Viking Press, 1982), ch. 12. Of an earlier expedition to Aegina, Russell Chamberlain writes, "all concerned seem to have regarded the marbles buried in Greek soil as a species of wild crop, to be harvested by whoever had the money," *Loot!: The Heritage of Plunder* (New York: Facts on File, 1983), 33. The Michigan pole was later exchanged to the Thomas Burke Memorial Washington State Museum to rejoin its twin. Two "Tongass" poles were given by expedition member W. R. Coe to the Peabody Museum, Yale.

55. Rev. J. P. D. Lloyd, *The Message of an Indian Relic* (Seattle: Lowman & Hanford, 1909), 5; Duran to Brady, 24 October 1899, box 2, Brady Papers; *The Alaskan* (Sitka), 9 December 1899, quoted in Ted C. Hinckley, "Sheldon Jackson as Preserver of Alaska's Native Culture," *Pacific Historical Review*, 33 (November 1964), 423–24.

56. The fee charged tourists to see the Whale House at Klukwan and a small, short-lived native-run museum at Kitwanga in the 1920s are interesting phenomena but do not invalidate the generalization.

57. Michaelis, *Ancient Marbles in England*, 1882, quoted in Chamberlain, *Loot!*, 38.

Index